CRITICAL INUIT STUDIES

D1601260

Critical Inuit Studies

An Anthology of Contemporary
Arctic Ethnography

Edited by
PAMELA STERN
and
LISA STEVENSON

UNIVERSITY OF NEBRASKA PRESS
LINCOLN AND LONDON

Chapter 4 originally appeared as
"Comment les Inuivialuit
parlent de leur passé,"
in *Anthropologie et Sociétés*
26, no. 2–3 (2002):193–13.

Library of Congress Cataloging-
in-Publication Data
Critical Inuit studies: an anthology of
contemporary Arctic ethnography /
edited by Pamela Stern and
Lisa Stevenson.
p.   cm.
Includes bibliographical references
and index.
ISBN-13: 978-0-8032-4303-3
(cloth: alk. paper)
ISBN-10: 0-8032-4303-0
(cloth: alk. paper)
ISBN-13: 978-0-8032-9348-9
(pbk.: alk. paper)
ISBN-10: 0-8032-9348-8
(pbk.: alk. paper)
1. Inuit—History.   2. Inuit—Politics
and government.   3. Inuit—Social
life and customs.   I. Stern, Pamela R.
II. Stevenson, Lisa.
E99.E7C764   2006
305.897'12—dc22
2005028939

for NHHG for asking questions that provoke *isuma*

CONTENTS

CRITICAL INUIT STUDIES

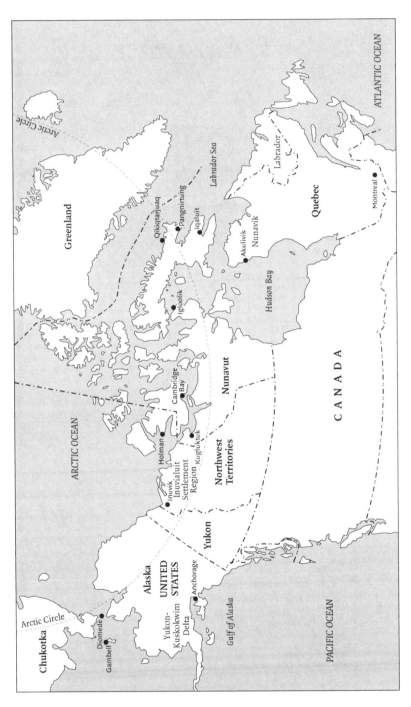

0.1. Communities mentioned in this volume.

INTRODUCTION

Lisa Stevenson

Starting Out

When I was just beginning to do fieldwork in the Arctic, a friend sent me the following quotation from Zora Neale Hurston's *Dust Tracks on a Road*: "Research is formalized curiosity. It is poking and prying with a purpose" (1995: 143). I like the quote because it moves beyond the debates over precisely how to write research notes, just what constitutes a scientific sample, and how data should be coded. Of course a researcher is constantly making such pragmatic decisions; it is simply that what unites all good research and researchers is an abiding sense of curiosity. It is the desire to *know* something that sustains the researcher, not the beautifully articulated grant proposals or innovative methodologies.[1]

The book in your hands is full of good research concerning the Inuit of the North American Arctic (northern Canada and Alaska).[2] And yet the merit of the book is due in no small part to the fact that not one of the contributors used precisely the same method as another. Some are accomplished archivists, while others have finely honed interviewing techniques. Still others have developed the anthropological art of "hanging out." The contributors are geographers, anthropologists, social workers, and social policy analysts. The result is a nuanced view of a people who have all too often been treated in a stereotypical fashion as the paragon of a hunter-gatherer society.

And while we might want to say that the contributors to this volume are generally curious people, it is also fair to say that we all suffer from an overweening interest in culture—culture as a constant in human life as well as the specificities of Inuit culture. But what do we mean by *culture?* Once the exclusive purview of the anthropologist, the term *culture* is used so frequently in the social sciences and the popular media that some claim it has been emptied of meaning. Anyone who uses the term *culture* today risks being misunderstood.

In this volume the contributors use *culture* as a term that artificially foregrounds the discontinuities between people, a term that is often more useful as a heuristic device (in the sense that Max Weber theorized the ideal-type) than a term with an empirically locatable referent. That is, although we may be convinced that "American culture" exists, its adherents do not all live in the same geographical space, nor do they share identical beliefs, values, or visions of what it means to be American. Thus while there are real people whose claims to particular cultural identities have life and death consequences (think of the Hutus and Tutsis in Rwanda), what binds a group together is often more of a "family resemblance" (Wittgenstein 1953) between dispositions and practices than a definable set of attributes that could ever be exhaustively defined or numerically tallied. Therefore, as Jean Briggs has pointed out, Inuit culture cannot be reduced to a list of iconic traits (1997). As a case in point, an Inuk policy analyst, who is also one of the most sensitive and creative scholars of Inuit culture I know, is allergic to caribou and hates eating seal meat—two seemingly quintessential Inuit cultural practices. Yet no one doubts that this man is an Inuk or that he understands Inuit culture.[3]

At a moment when scholars are struggling to understand the meaning and importance of globalization, the mere identification of certain practices or dispositions as culture-specific becomes politically charged. Is there, for instance, a core set of human values that we all share, as some civil servants in the new government of Nunavut claim, and is it possible that Inuit cultural values continue to differ in significant ways from the values of the western bureaucratic state? The current debates in Nunavut, with its majority Inuit population, over how to institutionalize Inuit *qaujimajatuqangit* (IQ, Inuit traditional knowledge) are addressed by Edmund (Ned) Searles, Nancy Wachowich, Nelson Graburn, and Lisa Stevenson in this volume.[4] The central node in this debate concerns whether Inuit traditional knowledge is commensurable with modern bureaucratic forms. In other words, can IQ be codified and operationalized within the Nunavut government? Since the inauguration of Nunavut in 1999, policy analysts have been attempting the difficult task of applying Inuit traditional knowledge and values to the day-to-day business of the government. These initiatives counter the implicit universalism of existing social welfare programs and education systems and the idea that difference will disappear in a globalized world. A close examination of the way specific cultural practices and beliefs confront the ideal of a universal humanity can teach us something essential about what it means to be human today.

The contributors to this volume believe that there is something valuable, invaluable perhaps, to be learned about the human condition by respectfully studying and experiencing a particular culture, even—and perhaps especially—if that culture is not one's own. In short, they all subscribe in one way or another to the ethnographic method. The word *ethnography*—composed of the Greek roots *ethnos*, meaning "nation," as in a "people or culture," and *graph*, meaning "that which writes, portrays or records"—might be loosely translated as "the writing of culture" (OED). One of the central tenets of early ethnographic research was that cultural difference could produce certain kinds of knowledge—knowledge that insiders might miss because it is too "obvious" or too sensitive to impart to, say, someone who is your grandfather's cousin's favorite nephew. A question I would like to pose to readers is: Does otherness (in whatever form it takes, and here we have to leave room for as yet unimaginable future configurations of otherness) still provide a useful research modality? I would contend that this question is central to rethinking the role of the contemporary social science researcher and is a particularly critical question to ask at a moment when there is a certain degree of skepticism regarding non-indigenous research and researchers among indigenous peoples and communities.

Another critical question raised by the present work is how to define the concept of "good" in Inuit research. Does "doing good" always involve direct action within the community, as Michael Kral and Lori Idlout's description of participatory action research would suggest? Or is influencing policy decisions at the local, national, or international level the most important good that may come of research? Ned Searles's chapter provides an interesting discussion of how certain arctic ethnographers in recent history have attempted to influence policy. What about knowledge as a good in itself, an idea close to academics but sometimes contested by Inuit communities (see Carol Jolles, this volume)? When considering Inuit attitudes toward knowledge as a good in itself, Ludger and Linna Weber Müller-Wille's work on the reincorporation of Franz Boas's place names into the Inuit community of Pangnirtung and Nelson Graburn's discussion of museums in Inuit communities are instructive. An implicit assumption in the debate over the role of research in Inuit communities is that it is possible to do good intentionally. But there are also numerous stories about researchers who, in trying hard to do the "right" thing, inadvertently offended or even hurt the people they were studying. Thus a two-pronged question any student of ethnography should ask is: What makes good research and what makes research good?

This book examining the state of Inuit studies had its origins in a session at the 2001 meetings of the American Anthropological Association. The theme of those meetings, honoring the hundredth anniversary of the association, seemed especially appropriate for a session about the first peoples studied by Franz Boas, "the father of North American anthropology." With history in mind, co-editor Pamela Stern and I organized a session entitled "Boas and Beyond: The State of the Art in Inuit Studies," in order to call attention to what we saw as the vibrancy in the current scholarship coming out of the circumpolar North. We wanted to reintroduce American anthropologists both to Inuit studies and to the Inuit—a group that had once been a standard of anthropology courses and textbooks but had become all but invisible there since the 1980s. We invited the panel participants, who included geographers, political scientists, and public policy specialists as well as anthropologists, to reflect on the complex relationships that arctic social scientists have with North American anthropology's forebears, especially Franz Boas, and with the discipline as a whole. And most important, we viewed the panelists' research as presenting some of the most promising directions for future social science research in the Inuit circumpolar North. Preliminary versions of several of the chapters in this volume were presented at that session.

The first section, "Figuring Method," deals explicitly with some of the *cultures* of research that make up Inuit studies today. Here authors examine the social and political changes in the academy and in Inuit communities that contribute to new and innovative ways of conducting research. They raise questions about the purpose of research and writing, the meaning of "objectivity," and the researcher's relationship to the communities in which he or she works. While an individual's responses to such questions may depend on a number of often contradictory influences (such as political views, personal history, or academic goals), what is clear is that there is no single way to approach these issues. Such differences, and the dialogue they produce, are a crucible for new ways of conducting the social sciences.

The next sections of the book take a fresh look at some of the categories that traditionally sustained the subdiscipline of Eskimology. Part II examines the way culture has been reworked for political and ethical ends by researchers and Inuit alike. In these works any sense of the naturalness of the concept of culture disappears. In much the same way, part III considers the paradigm of space and place and its role in Inuit lives and in the history of Inuit studies.

Figuring Method

A high-ranking Nunavut civil servant once confessed to me that while he greatly enjoyed the stories contained in a particular ethnographic research report, he felt that the validity of the work was seriously undermined by what he regarded as the weakness of the research methods. It was impossible, he felt, to extrapolate from a few dozen interviews in one community to the population of Nunavut as a whole. He spoke hopefully, as if through my status as "researcher" I would be able to make a compelling case for the truth claims of my colleague's research and, more important, for its general policy implications. The conversation made me feel tired. How could I begin to explain that even the most rigorous and seemingly empirical methods have hidden or unobserved biases that make generalizing dangerous? How could I explain my own belief that fiction can often be truer than fact or the possibility that the elucidation of ideal types (Weber 1949) or strategic exemplars (e.g., Foucault 1977; Rabinow 1989) can be more telling than a carefully tabulated chart?

Methods sections of any research report, article, or monograph are sometimes tedious and difficult to wade through. Tiring as they may be, they are crucial to the evaluation of the research. What many people fail to understand (and I failed to communicate to my interlocutor) is that what is really at stake is a *relationship*—the relationship between what the research claims to do or reveal and how it claims to do or reveal this. A relationship, that is, between research objectives or outcomes and research methods.

To illuminate this relationship it is necessary to adumbrate the primary methods used by the researchers who have contributed to this volume—in short: the interview, textual analysis and archival work, and variations of the old standby, participant-observation. In fact most of the contributors use methods that are participatory in the broadest sense. Yet not all have included a methods section, and many did not write explicitly about methods employed. Some, however, do provide beautiful explications of their methods, to which we now turn.

Peter Kulchyski, writing about Inuit gestures, describes his method as "going there" and "visiting, listening, talking, waiting, assisting: mimetically adopting to the extent possible the norms of community life." So far he has telegraphically conveyed the central elements of participant-observation—a method that has come to be seen as the cornerstone of anthropological field research. Pioneered by the anthropologist Bronislaw Malinowski among the Trobriand Islanders (1984 [1922]), participant-observation has of late become a catchphrase and an accepted field method in disciplines as diverse as education and linguistics. However Kulchyski, chair of a native studies department, prefers to characterize his method as "bush work" instead of fieldwork and to insist on an "ethics of reading" rather than participant-observation. The distinctions he makes are important. Participant-observation has often been the handmaiden of an entrenched belief in cultural relativism—the belief that cultures have a logic of their own within which even the most unpalatable practices are said to make sense; consider head-hunting among the Ilongot (Rosaldo 1980) or early sexual initiation of children (Mead 1961 [1928]; Shostak 1983).

Kulchyski refuses the epistemological security of the participant-observer—that cool and levelheaded belief that everything "makes sense," the bracketing of the natives' various truth-claims, and the search for a cultural logic that could "explain" or "explain away" the natives' strange beliefs (Rabinow 1983). Rather Kulchyski wants to be open to the "ethic of the other," allowing himself to be transformed by his experience in the bush. This means he does not bracket the truths he encounters but views them as possible sites of resistance to the hegemonic truths of western culture. The claim he makes about his research is *not* that it is representative of all Inuit or even that it is the final word on the Inuit of Pangnirtung, where he researches. Instead he claims that his writing and readings can "give a sense" of Inuit culture: "If a culture embodies values, if a gesture articulates these, then a reading of gestures can give a sense of a culture." More important, he is making a value judgment about the "sense of culture" he develops: "Pangnirtung is one of the markers for the possibility of something else"—indeed a site of resistance to the cultural logic of capitalism in western society. It is against these claims that Kulchyski's research methods must be measured; he is not out to recommend specific policy changes or to compare gestures across Inuit communities. Those are projects for other methods and other times.

The Interview

By far the most ubiquitous method used by contributors to this volume is the interview. The interview has many incarnations, from casual conversation to the verbal administration of a predetermined schedule of questions. What you want to know informs what type of interview you choose to do, whom you choose to interview, and whether you will do an interview at all. Contributors have worried about how, when, where, and why to do an interview. Searles makes the point that our implicit and often unconscious notions about which potential informants are really Inuk determine who is to be interviewed in the first place. Molly Lee points out that her primary informant and research colleague squelched her attempt to ask questions about income, categorizing them as "nosey" questions that could not be asked. Kulchyski describes the all too familiar experience of having someone agree to an interview but then disappear for weeks out on the land. Was there really an agreement or just a deferral? Béatrice Collignon describes the process of learning what to ask—after being surprised by one informant's assertion that place names are not for traveling, she inserts a question on the subject into her interview schedule. Nobuhiro Kishigami has perhaps the most formal interview design—he has a predetermined set of questions that he administers to as many Montreal Inuit as he can find. His choice of method can be attributed partly to the fact that he wants answers to very specific questions, which he then wishes to turn into quantifiable data.

Textual Analysis

Many of the contributors to *Critical Inuit Studies*, including Searles, Stern, Stevenson, and Wachowich, complement their participatory methods with textual analysis. In fact Searles's chapter begins with the analysis of a report cover produced by Inuit Tapiriit Kanatami. Wachowich examines the production of films about and by the Inuit in relation to the (re)production of Inuit culture, and Stern includes as data Inuit representations of themselves in news stories. Only Frank Tester, however, can be characterized as being primarily engaged in archival work, and the interviews he describes seem to be supplements to textual analysis rather than the other way around. In his investigation of the archival record on Inuit housing Tester deals with government publications, internal reports, and official and personal correspondence of government officials. The chapter is complex, and a number methodological subtleties might be missed in a quick reading. But understanding the concept of "text" as Tester uses it can offer insight into his methods. Significantly, Tester does not deal with written texts simply as a series of *representations* of the events that occurred from the mid-1950s to 1965. Instead he regards the texts as events in themselves—as actions in the world. In this way he disrupts the usual dichotomy between text as a passive, documentary entity and practice as an active engagement with the world. He writes: "In this chapter I argue the importance of paying attention to the *textual means by which relations of ruling were (and are) created*—as a source of information that nevertheless moves us in this direction—and as data essential to attempting an understanding of both cultural formation and emerging cultural practices. Ethnographic data, combined with a critical reading of text, move the project along" (italics added). Tester is pointing to the fact that just as mobilizing armies may consolidate particular power structures, so too can the writing and reading of text.

While every researcher must contend with the question of methods, the contributors to part I, "Figuring Method," foreground method as an object of analysis in and of itself. For instance, Molly Lee's chapter concerns the dialogical relationships that form the core of anthropological fieldwork. In a personal and compelling essay she describes the relationship she developed with her collaborator, Flora Mark, and the way that their friendship changed Lee's relationship to her own fieldwork and even her own life: "I had more to gain from preserving my friendship with Flora than from the addition of a few more facts to my study. . . . Recently, when I had a cancer scare and Flora was out fishing and beyond the range of her cell phone, I realized it was she more than others I missed."

Lee recognizes the way her research is really a "double project." Instead of simply collecting data for a taxonomy of Yup'ik basketry, she becomes involved in a cross-cultural friendship that transforms her initial research goals. Having Flora Mark as a collaborator increases the richness and validity of her data, but the intensity and loyalty of this friendship also means that certain anthropological "facts" will not appear in her research. For Lee, the deepening relationship with her informant (her method) has led to a change in her research objectives. Coming to understand the day-to-day concerns of the Yup'ik basket makers results in her research moving from a straightforward taxonomy of Yup'ik basketry to an investigation of the "relationship between market arts and politics . . . and the links between the arts of acculturation and traditional culture." In Lee's case, as her method changed, the nature of her data also changed, allowing her to put Yup'ik basketry in a wider context.

Carol Zane Jolles describes her early experience as an anthropologist in Gambell, Alaska, and the mistrust that she felt her scholarly research generated locally. The people she had gone north to study wanted to know precisely *how* her research would benefit their children and grandchildren. In response, she developed projects less driven by particular concerns of anthropological theory and more attentive to the knowledge needs of the communities in which she works. She advocates for research that is collaborative from the outset and seeks to find innovative ways in which the research agendas of university-trained scholars and native communities can mesh.

Lee and Jolles break one of the unspoken taboos of anthropological writing when they discuss the role of money in attracting collaborators and informants. Lee writes: "At the beginning of our work together, the main attraction of the project for [Flora Mark] was the travel. The cost of airplane travel in rural Alaska is prohibitive, so the research offered her the chance to renew her friendships around the Delta and to sample the subsistence foods available in different localities," and thus she marks the way monetary compensation, at least initially, can help to establish a relationship. Molly Lee also contests another tradition in anthropological methods. While she is at first concerned by the way her repeated short trips to the field defy the anthropological ideal of long-term field research, she quickly comes to recognize that the serial nature of her trips affords certain unexpected benefits and that informants actually anticipate her visits by storing away interesting material.

Keeping with the theme of participatory methods, Michael Kral and Lori Idlout advocate for a research methodology known as participatory action research (PAR). They argue that PAR, in which the communities themselves are in charge of both the design and implementation of research, is the most appropriate way to disrupt the colonial and colonizing mentalities associated with much traditional ethnographic research. Ideally, with PAR, Inuit communities are further empowered to control the uses to which the research findings are put. Yet Kral and Idlout note that PAR is not a panacea. Its demand for consensus between the researchers and the researched is difficult and occasionally impossible to achieve.

Murielle Nagy also contends with the methodological and theoretical challenges that cross-cultural research collaborations pose. Specifically, she asks how a nonlinguist can approach the question of translation. Her chapter can be seen as a sustained reflection on the difficulties of doing research through translators—an issue that almost all cross-cultural researchers face at some point in their careers.

Nagy reminds us that stumbling blocks in translation may provide fruitful areas of research. In her own work using oral history narratives she notices that Inuit temporal concepts, particularly first childhood memories, are not translated in a consistent way. She questions why certain concepts might be translated in a variety of ways: "Was it to get the closest equivalent in the language of the translation and thus make the translation more fluid? But more important, were words changed because the translator could not find similar concepts in the language of the translation?" The answers to such questions, Nagy contends, can help us understand the language and culture of the narrator. Nagy found that with the exception of first childhood memories, translators used the present tense in English to translate events that occurred in the past. She explains this by describing how space and time are synchronized in Inuit languages, so that going back in time is also going to a particular place. She then looks at the translations for first childhood memories and indicates that a likely explanation for the confusion over memory terms involves Inuit possessing such a sophisticated understanding of cognitive development that it was difficult for translators to find sufficiently precise words in English for the Inuit concepts.

Ned Searles is also explicitly concerned with the methodological implications of indigenous empowerment. Yet he is less sure than Jolles or Kral and Idlout that research agendas can be easily conjoined. Searles notes that researchers seeking to work with Inuit often work to promote the "cultural survival" of the Inuit, thus taking the concept of culture for granted, as if it were obvious what it was that was to be preserved. This flies in the face of a dominant theme in contemporary anthropological theory holding that our whole concept of culture has to be rethought to take into account highly mobile persons, highly flexible capital, highly porous boundaries, and highly politicized debates about ethnicity and cultural diversity.

Searles asks several difficult questions. How can social scientists balance their desire to be advocates in the process of empowerment with their presumed professional need for critical distance? What happens to academic research when the anthropologist's version of the story is no longer politically correct? Searles worries that the current emphasis on Inuit traditional knowledge may lead to discriminatory practices against those who lack opportunities to participate in traditional land-based activities. He raises the question of the political implications of creating a measure of "Inuitness," and the role played by arctic anthropologists in defining what it means to be a real Inuk. Indeed Searles calls the very construct of "being Inuit" into question. Finally, as earlier noted, Searles observes that like the salvage ethnographers of old, how we (ethnographers) define being Inuit can affect whom we consider good interview subjects, which in turn affects the outcome of our research.

Students beginning field research are often told that they must have well-defined research questions, carefully specified variables, and precise methods for obtaining data. These are essential, if only to make it possible to begin. One of the unspoken secrets of ethnographic research is that some of the most useful insights about what is going on come when the methods fall apart (see, for example, Briggs 1970), or from places where no one is looking for data, or even from topics researchers did not expect to investigate. Several of the chapters describe research that started out as something quite different. Pamela Stern's examination of Inuvialuit citizenship and hydrocarbon development in the Mackenzie River Delta is an example of this. She was investigating the social linkages between wage work and subsistence work in one tiny Inuit community when a news broadcast on CBC Radio challenged what she thought she knew about Inuit and Dene attitudes toward megaprojects like the long talked-about and presumably dead plan to construct a Mackenzie Valley pipeline. The pro-development attitude expressed on that broadcast led her to begin investigating how the mere possibility of development in the Mackenzie Valley had affected attitudes and practices surrounding employment in a community at the periphery of any likely development.

To recap, the chapters in this volume describe a variety of research practices—participant observation, structured interviews, participatory action research, extended fieldwork, and repeated short research trips. The authors report research on a variety of topics—indigenous knowledge, foodways, traditional subsistence, mental health, kinship, and art. They share the recognition that ethnographic research must be a collaborative effort between researcher and researched, and yet each struggles to define the nature and scope of that collaboration.

Reconfiguring Categories: Culture

As I have indicated, *culture* is a ubiquitous term in both the social sciences and the news media, and the definition of it should not be taken for granted. And even as countless debates in the academy hinge on how the term is defined, it is important to bear in mind that its widespread use is a relatively recent phenomenon.

This is not the place for an exhaustive genealogy of the term. However, a few signposts in the evolution of this plastic term may be in order. A. L. Kroeber and Talcott Parsons (1958), in an article that appeared in the *American Sociological Review* more than forty years ago, suggest that the terms *society* and *culture* came into common usage following the publication of Charles Darwin's *Origin of Species,* as social scientists attempted to delimit an area of study distinct from the biological sciences. The realm of culture is thus defined negatively—everything that is "not-nature."

Bronislaw Malinowski (1984 [1922]) believed that if culture were to be a reputable object of study it needed form and substance of its own. He went to great pains to demonstrate that tribal cultures were stable and organic wholes, forming proper objects for scientific study. But his insistence on the consistency of tribal cultures made it difficult to conceptualize how any culture could change over time—and yet it is abundantly clear that they do. It is partly through the zealous search for such discontinuities (between peoples and between humans and nature) and organic wholes that difference has been overemphasized in contemporary studies of culture, and boundaries between people have engendered more attention than the tenuous and sometimes ephemeral connections between individuals and cultural groups. Claude Lévi-Strauss, a founder of structuralism, described culture as "a fragment of humanity which, from the point of view of the research at hand and of the scale on which it is being carried out, presents, in relation to the rest of humanity, significant discontinuities" (1953: 536). Lévi-Strauss's inclusion of point of view in his definition of culture is indicative of the sea change that was about to occur. With the rise of cultural studies in the 1960s and 1970s, scholars became increasingly concerned with questions of difference, and at the same time the lines between cultures came to be seen not as natural objects but as human constructions.

One way to challenge the notion of a culture as static, timeless, and preferably pristine is to debunk the myth that culture "exists" as an object in the world and to see it instead as practice, as something that happens, that occurs day in and day out, wherever and whenever human beings interact. According to the sociologist Georg Simmel, "society is not a 'substance,' nothing concrete, but an *event*: it is the function of receiving and effecting the fate and development of one individual by the other" (1950: 9). Simmel's view of society as event highlighted the importance of human action and foreshadowed the rise of what has become known as "practice theory." As

Sherry Ortner states, modern practice theory seeks to explain the relationships that obtain between human action, on the one hand, and some global entity that we may call "the system," on the other (1984: 392). Contributors to this volume highlight just a few of the ways in which culture may be seen as a practice rather than as an organic whole. Organic wholes, after all, always seem somehow to be situated outside and beyond history.

Part II is devoted to writers who explore the links between contemporary Inuit culture and larger national and international social, economic, and political processes. Each author in this section refuses to reify Inuit culture as something located in a primordial past that can only be accessed through elders' narratives or reconstructions of pure cultural forms untainted by contact with outsiders. Thus Pamela Stern examines the more overt set of power relations that emerge in the debate over hydrocarbon development in the western Canadian Arctic. The discovery of gas and oil deposits on Inuit lands catapulted onto the national and international stage questions of Inuit rights to ancestral land, to national citizenship, and to direct economic development. Stern documents the way that seemingly contradictory claims about "cultural difference" and "equal citizenship" become political strategies for indigenous leaders attempting to secure equitable social, political, and economic development for their constituents. She describes the inherent contradiction between the two claims as follows: "The very acceptance of aboriginal land claims constitutes an acknowledgement that aboriginal peoples are culturally, historically, and socially distinct from the settler communities in Canada," yet a primary goal of these agreements is to incorporate aboriginal peoples into the national culture and society.

The way that the Inuvialuit (the modern ethnonym used by the Inuit of the Mackenzie Delta region of Canada) negotiate the tension between the two claims influences how they see themselves as a people and as a political force within Canada. Are Inuit just like other Canadians or are they fundamentally different? Can they simultaneously be ethnically and culturally different and have equal rights to citizenship as in the rest of Canada? What can "self-government" mean for indigenous peoples within modern nation states?

Just as Stern notes that debates over resource development can no longer be separated from questions of Inuvialuit citizenship and its attendant rights, Nancy Wachowich recognizes that cultural continuity and the marketplace can be separated only artificially. Wachowich's key metaphor is that of "showing" Inuit traditional culture. She reveals the way icons of traditional Inuit culture, such as sled dogs, can signify different things to different people depending on the context in which they are shown. For a recent widow a pair of sled dogs may no longer have any use-value, but for Parks Canada the same dogs, stuffed by a taxidermist, can be used to represent the presumed core of Inuit culture. The visual demonstration of what are considered to be traditional Inuit practices (through museum exhibits, photographs, and films) allows for a commodification of Inuit culture. Thus tradition itself becomes a good that can be exchanged in the marketplace and one that supplements the incomes of Igloolik residents and, ironically, enables them to continue to engage in culturally relevant practices. Wachowich is not, however, mourning the loss of an authentic culture. Rather, she notes how the income from this commodification enables Inuit to purchase the supplies necessary to make trips out on the land where they can hunt and camp in "traditional" ways. Her central claim, in fact, is that Iglulingmiut survival as a distinct and independent people in the modern world has become reliant on the production and circulation of Inuit identities through a variety of local and transnational networks. This points to one of the ironies of modern life because it makes clear that Inuit are *independent* only insofar as they are *dependent* on certain transnational networks.

Nelson Graburn, too, writes about Inuit cultural patrimony and the both ordinary and extraordinary means Inuit employ to preserve, reclaim, and transmit it to the next generation. Having done research in Inuit communities over a period of four decades, Graburn has the advantage of historical perspective. He describes the research and cultural preservation activities of several now famous Inuit—monolingual Inuktitut speakers—who individually appropriated the tools and methods of qallunaat (non-Inuit) to record Inuit culture. He makes analogies between the aims and practices of these "organic" ethnographers and current individual and institutional efforts at cultural preservation. In particular Graburn observes how, in the face of profound social change, Inuit have come to regard and defend their culture as something not ordinary and ephemeral but unique—a bundle of practices and ideas that can be described, recorded, and preserved.

Peter Kulchyski's analysis of six Inuit gestures (the facial yes and no, the gift of food, the handshake, unannounced entrance, kiss, and smile) demonstrates the dialogical space where the bonds of culture are made and remade. Such gestures may initially seem trivial, but as Sherry Ortner has remarked in her essay on practice theory, "it is precisely in those areas of life—especially in the so-called domestic domain where action proceeds with little reflection, that much of the conservatism of the system tends to be located" (1984: 394). However, Kulchyski is less interested in cultural "systems" than in communities as sites of resistance. We can see each gesture he describes as a call to form community, a way of binding a group of individuals through a series of meaningful practices. Kulchyski's use of the lowercase may also be seen as a gesture that speaks to the possibility of reconceptualizing boundaries:

> i find myself attempting to deploy modernist literary techniques (modestly) in my writing . . . in native studies, the issues of whether to capitalize native, aboriginal, indian, european, etc (not to mention elder, drum, spirituality . . .) in my view can all be displaced if everything is in lower case; in a sense it helps to "puncture" the aggrandizement that seems inherent in proper names.[5]

Ultimately Kulchyski is interested in how Inuit cultural practices, in the form of gestures, create a set of values that are different from the hegemonic cultural forms of mainstream Canada—and resist such mainstream, even globalizing forms. Implicit in this political stance is that Kulchyski treats Inuit culture as a "social value" rather than the "organic whole" of traditional ethnographic accounts. Thus one might say that "culture" for Kulchyski describes the possibility of an alternative to the dominant political forms of our day. Kulchyski raises the question of whether the face-to-face culture he identifies in Pangnirtung is dependent on small-scale societies or whether it is a political possibility that may be approached in any society.

Lisa Stevenson is interested in the way memory has become a self-conscious practice in contemporary Inuit life. She argues that the development of a kind of pan-Inuit cultural memory represents a shift or critical event in Inuit epistemology. This change has come about through the emergence of a collective politics defining Inuit difference through a set of traditions no longer practiced by the culture as a whole. However, the pervasive fear among social scientists and Inuit that cultural memory is being lost has led to what she calls "the ethical injunction to remember." In a twist on our usual understanding of the word *ethical*, she describes this injunction as ethical because it calls upon young people to transform themselves by engaging in certain practices that are considered to be foundational to Inuit identity. This Inuit orientation toward the *practice* of cultural activities rather than in the articulation of cultural norms in textual documents underlines the Inuit belief that one learns by doing.

The chapters in part II are centrally concerned with the intersecting contexts of human action. For Stern, the drama of hydrocarbon extraction in the

Northwest Territories exposes the dilemma of Inuit citizenship in a multicultural Canada. In the case of Wachowich the global consumer society supports and is supported by "traditional" Inuit activities. For Kulchyski, the simplest and most routine human action, such as the smile, can reveal a whole world of ideas, beliefs, and relationships. Stevenson wants to understand the critical event that created the conditions of possibility for a pan-Inuit cultural memory to emerge. These authors step outside traditional Inuit studies models to reveal Inuit culture as globally integrated and dynamic. They show Inuit as actors in the world, producing cultural narratives and building connections.

Reconfiguring Categories: Place

John Amagoalik (2000: 138), an Inuit politician from the Canadian territory of Nunavut, has observed: "In the 1950s and 60s, when journalists first discovered the Arctic, they would come up and interview a cop, a teacher, or the local government administrator. Having spent a few days in the Arctic and spoken to 'Arctic experts,' they would return to their homes in the south and write their stories. Somewhere in their article a familiar line usually appeared. They almost never failed to refer to the Arctic as a 'wasteland where nobody lives.'"

It is fair to say that the colonial inability to see the North through Inuit eyes and instead to "see through" Inuit bodies has resulted in a great deal of unnecessary suffering in the Canadian Arctic. During the 1950s and 1960s the Canadian government relocated Inuit from one part of the Arctic to another as a way of asserting Canadian sovereignty over all that white space on the map (cf. Tester and Kulchyski 1994, Marcus 1995). "Such were the differences in climate and environment from their old homeland that they used to ask each other: . . . are we still in the same world?" reports Alan Marcus (1995: 207). Relocation policies assumed that Inuit could make a place for themselves in any space, thus ignoring the political, ethical, and spiritual nature of place (see Collignon, this volume). Are all spaces not interchangeable?

Before becoming too smug about how dated and overtly colonial such plans sound to enlightened twenty-first-century ears, we must remember that a 1999 newspaper article had the following to say about the newly created territory of Nunavut:

> With little likelihood of solving Nunavut's problems any time soon, federal taxpayers could be forgiven for wondering if it might be wiser to ship

its entire population south. Housing and feeding an Inuit family of four in Orlando, Florida, where a decent two-bedroom apartment rents for under $1,000 per month, would be far cheaper than the $100,000-plus in transfers the same family requires in Nunavut. Even if the family opted for a two-bedroom, two-bathroom air-conditioned suite with full kitchen facilities at the Sea World Ramada, the annual room charge of $62,800 and a $2,500 monthly allowance would still save Canadians almost $10,000 a year. (McFeely 1999)

This kind of evaluation of the costs associated with maintaining Inuit communities and services has a long history in the folklore of northern civil servants. The various social architects of the latter half of the twentieth century failed to understand the difference between space and place, a distinction contemporary geographers take very seriously. In one geographer's words, "A centered and meaningful space involves specific sets of linkages between the physical space of the non-humanly created world, somatic states of the body, the mental space of cognition and representation and the space of movement, encounter and interaction between persons and between persons and the human and non-human environment" (Tilley 1994: 10). Suggestions to move Inuit to Florida, serious or not, begin from an understanding of space as abstract and interchangeable, devoid of the layers of associations and meanings that transform space into a place with names, memories, and history. The repercussions of such misrecognition continue to be tragic.

The chapters in part III attempt to rectify such misconceptions by bringing to the fore Inuit ideas of place; what Collignon calls "geosophy" or geographical wisdom. The discussions range from traditional Inuit place names to social housing and a description of the way urban Inuit navigate their lives in Montreal. Collignon contests the assumption pervasive in human geography that indigenous place names have enabled nomadic peoples to find their way in hostile and often monotonous environments. "When I started my research it seemed obvious to everyone I could talk to in academia that place names were a very useful knowledge on which Inuit relied when traveling to stay on the trail and to avoid getting lost." Collignon attributes this commonplace attitude to a tendency among scholars of Inuit cultures to emphasize the importance of material culture over the intellectual one. She describes her initial surprise at meeting an Inuit elder who was an excellent hunter but knew few of the local place names.

Instead Collignon makes the claim that place names, rather than being good for travel, are good to think with. That is, place names exist in the universe of memories, associations, and beliefs that make up a community's collective knowledge. In particular Collignon argues that place names and their associated stories describe specific human relationships to the physical environment and among the people who share those spaces, and the names are thus "founded on a very high sense of context and relations, where space and networks are indeed more important than places."

Like Murielle Nagy, Collignon describes the challenges involved in doing research through translation and also the richness that the second language can reveal. She describes the translator giving two seemingly distinct translations for the same place name. "Whenever I expressed my perplexity I would be told that, yes, the name means 'where the ice piles up' but its *real* meaning is 'hard to cross' because this is what people think about immediately when they hear the toponym Nilak." The multiple layers of meaning in Inuktitut are revealed through confusion over an apparently simple translation. Invoking place names in stories about the past is one way that multilayered cultural knowledge is passed from one generation to another and that cultural meanings are both contested and reinforced.

The transformation of Inuit social organization is the subject tackled by Nobuhiro Kishigami in his chapter about Inuit living in Montreal. Kishigami begins by noting that virtually every arctic anthropologist since Boas agrees that kinship provides the overriding organizing principle for social relations in Inuit communities. He argues, however, that for the 17 percent or so of Canadian Inuit who today live in southern Canadian cities, those ties are difficult to maintain and have been replaced by social networks based on friendship. This is especially the case, says Kishigami, for urban Inuit without jobs or access to secure incomes.

Through the examination of a series of the practices of urban Inuit, including the sharing of traditional Inuit foods, telephone calls from Montreal to the North, and the organization of community feasts, Kishigami examines the way urban Inuit social organization is constructed and maintained. He suggests that for Inuit in Montreal, social relations and the practices that create them more closely resemble those of other urbanites than of northern villagers. Kishigami's findings are provocative; they run counter to narratives that place Canadian indigenous peoples outside the unifying discourse of Canadian multiculturalism and ethnic inclusiveness (cf. Paine 1999) as well as to narratives asserting the importance of kinship for economically disadvantaged urban and rural minorities and for recent urban migrants (Kearney 1986; Stack 1974; Stack and Burton 1998).

The repatriation of indigenous cultural patrimony is a public acknowl-edgment of the ways indigenous histories are connected to histories of colo-nialism. Usually when we think of the repatriation of indigenous cultural patrimony we think of the return of actual objects—such as the millions of items recently repatriated in the United States under the Native Amer-ican Graves Protection and Repatriation Act (NAGPRA). However, in the case that Ludger and Linna Weber Müller-Wille describe, it was not physical artifacts or human remains that were taken from the community but Inuit geographic knowledge, translated into textual form and removed for use in academic journals and scholarly geographies. They report on the return to the community of Pangnirtung of the geographic place names Franz Boas collected on his research trip to Baffin Island in 1883–84. They report that "in no case did they discard or disregard 'forgotten' Inuit place names; rather they were accepted as Inuit knowledge that had been lost but had now been rediscovered and recovered for reintegration as part of the overall cultural heritage." In part this chapter is an exploration into the persistence of Inuit place names in contemporary Pangnirtung, much as Collingnon is interested in the same question among the Inuinnait (see later discussion). But the chapter really concerns the way that Inuit regain some of their own history, partly through the use of western documents. This use of western documents to maintain what the Müller-Willes call "cultural integrity" un-derlines the folly in searching for pure, unmediated cultural forms. Cultures are always already hybrid forms.

Frank Tester describes the way that Canadian Inuit housing policy emerged in the 1950s and '60s. Tester treats "the move from igloo to rigid-frame housing as a window through which we may debate theoretical and methodological considerations relevant to understanding social transfor-mations in an age dominated by State and now by global institutions, in which rule is by fiat, text, and often by force." As in all of his writing, Tester is committed to documenting the relationship between the State (to be understood here as the Canadian nation-state) and a particular ethnic or cultural group, in this case the Canadian Inuit. One noteworthy aspect of Tester's writing is his attention to the complexity of the colonial impulse. He acknowledges the universality of certain colonial sensibilities, including "the logic of the welfare state," "the idea of progress," and "the discourse of dependency relations," yet he insists on portraying the individual agents of colonialism (and the State itself) as internally fractured. He describes their desire to do good, their ambivalence about how to go about doing it, and the contradictory results of their actions on the lives of the Inuit.

Tester also documents the ambivalent Inuit response to Canadian housing policy—while a house makes life easier, and makes it possible to participate in the wage economy, it sets in motion changes that irrevocably alter Inuit ways of life.

Conclusion

The title of this volume is *Critical Inuit Studies*. But what is it that makes the articles collected here particularly *critical*? It may be helpful initially to think of "critique" in terms of distance. By this I mean a distance from received wisdom, familiar categories of thought, and our usual ways of doing things. Recall that to gain perspective on a work of art or a difficult situation we must stand back from it, literally or figuratively, and that we refer to what we have gained as "critical distance."

This sense of critique as distance is related to the modernist practice of "defamiliarization," in which the aim is to reveal the strangeness, even absurdity, of that which is most familiar. It can also mean describing familiar objects (or gestures, as in the case of Kulchyski) in unfamiliar ways to reproduce the effect of seeing them for the first time. Critique often has value as shock—the sense that the ground under our feet has shifted and that our ways of doing things will never be the same.

Thus, in part, the term *critical* in the title marks our position of a certain distance vis-à-vis the tradition of Eskimology, while at the same time recognizing its richness and scientific importance both to scholars and to modern Inuit seeking their roots. And indeed early ethnography (including Eskimology) sought to distance Europeans critically from their fervently held beliefs in the superiority of particular races or in the universality of particular moral standards. Yet it also inadvertently reified other categories as natural and ahistorical. A critical Inuit studies therefore marks a distance from the presumed naturalness of the categories and power relations that sustained early Inuit ethnography. This entails the recognition that knowledge is always situated within a particular historical moment that can never fully reveal its own blind spots. Nonetheless the work of bringing the politics of truth to the foreground, of contesting the naturalness of our thought and practice, is precisely what a critical approach to Inuit studies entails. In this volume concepts such as Inuit, history, culture, time, and place are all brought into question, examined, and reassembled. For example, instead of attempting to describe traditional Inuit culture, Nancy Wachowich describes the way traditional Inuit culture is reproduced through international circuits of exchange. Peter Kulchyski points out that Boas "discovered" culture, in the sense in which we use it today, among the Inuit of the Cumberland Sound—thus highlighting the contingency and historicity of the very term. Nelson Graburn then demonstrates the ways in which the efforts by Inuit to reconstitute their own culture are embedded in the political project of Nunavut.

One of the persistent ironies of ethnographic research is that any distance it achieves from our usual, everyday mode of perceiving the world is gained precisely from the ethnographer's intimacy, or closeness, with the people he or she studies. This opens up a series of ethical questions about the power relations that invest all research. But *such questions are also "critical."* This second use of the term to mean a critique of ideology and power has a complicated history that runs through the Frankfurt School of critical theory to the post-Marxist accounts of power in critical medical anthropology. Its central node is an analysis and critique of existing power relations and the concepts that sustain them. And in fact, as philosopher Michel Foucault pointed out, these two uses of the term are historically related. Foucault argued that the modern critical attitude has its roots in the Enlightenment question of how best to govern and be governed. He suggests that a first definition of critique might be "the art of not being governed quite so much" (1997: 27). Thus we can see that critique and the critical attitude are always tied up with degrees of human freedom.

The question of critique in Inuit studies is therefore a question not only of what we know but of how, by what means, we know what we know. Answering this question requires a reflexivity toward the power relations that make a volume such as *Critical Inuit Studies* possible. How is it that Inuit let outsiders into their homes and their private lives? What do they have to gain from such relationships, and what do they have to lose? What kinds of power does the ethnographer accrue from publishing articles based on the lives of Inuit? These are some of the questions that Lee, Kral and Idlout, and Jolles address.

In general our use of the word *critical* indicates that we are conscious that what we write about other cultures and how we write is a choice that has consequences within and beyond the academy (see e.g., Marcus and Fischer 1986; O'Neil et al. 1998; Searles, this volume). As scholars of Inuit culture, we are just beginning to foreground the collusion between paternalistic descriptions of Inuit and ill-conceived (although often well-meaning) government policies that have been foisted on the Inuit (see Tester, this volume).

As social scientists we can no longer afford to study the local and the global independently, nor can we presume that it is possible to separate the two completely. George Marcus's suggestion that the contemporary anthropologist needs to be "sensitive to both the inner lives of subjects and the nature of world historical political economy" (Marcus 1986: 188) seems particularly apt. Today the ethnographer in a remote northern community must take into account the high-speed traffic in goods, ideas, policies, and legal norms that traverses the continent and even the world. It is to this challenge that the authors in the following chapters respond.

Notes

1. I want to thank Lucinda Ramberg for introducing me to Zora Neale Hurston's anthropological writings. I would also like to thank Pam Stern, Nelson Graburn, and Eduardo Kohn for their helpful editorial comments.

2. Inuit are indigenous to Greenland, arctic Canada, Alaska, and Chukotka. The Inuit Circumpolar Conference, the nongovernmental organization representing Inuit on the world stage, estimates that there are 150,000 Inuit worldwide (http://www.inuit.org/). The research described in this volume concerns Inuit communities in Canada and Alaska, which are home to as many as two-thirds of Inuit.

3. Inuk is the singular of Inuit.

4. In the words of Louis Tapardjuk, "The term Inuit Qaujimajatuqangit (IQ) encompasses all aspects of traditional Inuit Culture including values, world-view, language, social organization, knowledge, life skills, perceptions and expectations. Inuit Qaujimajatuqangit is as much a way of life as it is sets of information" (Nunavut Social Development Council 1998). The term is commonly used in Nunavut government circles as an equivalent for the English "Inuit traditional knowledge."

5. Personal communication with author.

PART 1

Figuring Method

ONE

Flora and Me

Molly Lee

NOTES FROM THE FIELD, SALLUIT, NOUVEAU QUÉBEC, MARCH, 1986: *No matter how often we enter an Inuit household for the first time, it never loses its terror for me. This morning, NHHG [Nelson Graburn, my dissertation adviser at UC Berkeley] and I ducked into the arctic entryway of yet another matchbox house, the kind provided to the Inuit in the 1960s when they came in off the land. We beat the snow off our boots with our gloves and reshouldered our backpacks. With his knuckles halfway to the doorframe, Nelson looked over at me and, shaking his head in disbelief, said: "In the South, if you barged into a house like this, you'd probably be run off the property!"*

Many times during my subsequent fieldwork in southwestern Alaska, as I have stood on the threshold of other Eskimo houses thousands of miles to the West, this scene has flashed before my eyes. In broad general outline, the circumstances are identical: I am poised to insert myself uninvited into an Inuit household for purposes other than social. The particulars, however, contrast markedly. In the Canadian Arctic I was unknown; in the Yukon-Kuskokwim Delta region of Alaska the occupants of the house will probably recognize me. Chances are I have visited the village or one nearby before. More important though, Flora Mark (a pseudonym), my Yup'ik Eskimo collaborator, is there beside me.

During our six years' work together, Flora's role in my long-term field research has grown from translator and facilitator to fully participating collaborator. At the same time, our relationship has developed from one based on professional need into a close personal friendship. Recently, when I had a cancer scare and Flora was out fishing and beyond the range of her cell phone, I realized it was she more than others I missed.

Weaving Culture

I have been studying beach-grass basketry among the Yup'ik Eskimo women of the Yukon-Kuskokwim Delta (known familiarly as the Y-K Delta or simply the Delta) in southwest Alaska since 1995. In the early 1990s during a two-year postdoctoral research fellowship at the American Museum of Natural History focused on a related topic, I realized that almost nothing had been written about modern Yup'ik baskets despite their prominence in the Alaska Native art market. Because I was returning to Alaska to start a job at the University of Alaska Museum in Fairbanks, I wrote a proposal to the National Science Foundation asking them to fund such a study. I envisioned the research as a straightforward documentation of the art form focused on history and taxonomy. My proposed field sites would include basket-making villages of the Delta, arts and crafts shows in Alaska's regional and urban centers, and museums and private collections in Alaska and the Pacific Northwest. I estimated that the research would require two to three years at most. How wrong I was!

The project was funded in 1994, and I began the research for "Weaving Culture" shortly after my arrival in Alaska in autumn, 1995. As I thought through the specifics, I was immediately confronted by several problems. I had envisioned carrying out the research in the Yup'ik villages during the two following autumns when the grass was harvested and many women were making baskets for the pre-Christmas craft shows. It was soon clear, however, that my curatorial and teaching duties at the university would not permit such extended absences. This meant I would have to design the project as a series of shorter trips, which would take longer, would be more expensive, and would challenge the anthropological convention of intensive and extended ethnographic field research. The Yup'ik area too, presented logistical complexities. For one thing, compared to an earlier study I had done on Alaska's North Slope involving just two villages (Lee 1998, 1999), there were some fifty-two villages in the Y-K Delta with appreciable numbers of baskets made in about half of them. Also unlike the North Slope, where most Iñupiaq Eskimos speak English, many of the artists in the Y-K Delta spoke only Yup'ik, which I did not know. I had budgeted for a modest amount of technical and logistical assistance, and further along in the project, for consultations with a committee of Yup'ik basket makers, but for all these reasons, I saw that it would be necessary to work closely with a Yup'ik-speaking collaborator from the outset. My first chore was to find one.

Finding a Collaborator

Given that I was unknown in the Y-K Delta—and the Yup'iks were unknown to me—I began my search by going to craft fairs. Among the first I attended was the Camai Festival, the annual Yup'ik dance and craft fair held in Bethel, the regional hub of southwest Alaska. Like so many events in rural areas, Camai takes place in the high school, and for three days each spring, the building teems with Yup'iks from all over the Delta—mothers with babies peering out of their parka hoods, swarms of children running full-tilt every which way, men shaking hands all around in the standard-issue rural Alaska uniform of blue nylon varsity jacket and baseball cap. And then there are the older women in *qaspeqs*, the ubiquitous Mother Hubbard–style cloth parka worn throughout the Delta, lined up at long cafeteria tables packed with baskets, beadwork, beaverskin hats, and other crafts to sell, greeting friends with one hand and making change with the other. Josie Sam, a Nunivak Island artist, was in town to sell her small, tightly coiled baskets and to compete in the Smile Contest, held every year at Camai to promote healthy teeth (she won). Warm and friendly—and, I learned later, sensing my shyness—Josie welcomed me, politely answering my questions. I left Camai that first year feeling that at last I had made a Yup'ik friend.

Josie and I kept in touch, and the next fall we traveled together to Platinum, a community on Goodnews Bay, a two-hour bush-plane ride south of Bethel, where Yup'ik women from all over the Delta converge to harvest basket grass. It was at Platinum that I first caught sight of Josie's sister-in-law, Flora Mark. An accomplished basket maker in her fifties, Flora was there like the rest of us to cut grass for winter basket making. I was immediately drawn to her infectious laugh and take-charge attitude. When she saw me struggling with bundling my cut grass, she quickly took me in hand, showing me how to whack my bundle against my knee to rid it of stems that were too short. When we broke for lunch at the home of one of her friends, Flora gave me my first lesson in Yup'ik etiquette, silencing my query about the relationship between two people in the house with a look that I have since come to recognize as the "Nosey Question" rebuke.

I soon realized that Flora, on the basis of her people skills alone, was the ideal collaborator for the Weaving Culture project. Furthermore, unlike Josie, whose home village was an expensive plane ride from any of my field sites, Flora lived part-time in Anchorage and traveled home to the Delta several times a year to participate in subsistence activities. Flora's dual residency would mean she would be more easily available to travel to my various field settings. But I said nothing for the time being, and when we left Platinum, bearing our black plastic lawn-and-leaf bags overflowing with grass, we hugged and exchanged phone numbers. Several weeks later I ran into Flora at a craft sale in Anchorage and invited her to come along on my next field trip to several basket-making villages in the Delta. It was the best decision I have made for the project, bar none.

Fieldwork with Flora

On our maiden voyage, as we changed from the Alaska Airlines jet to a smaller bush plane in Bethel, I discovered that Flora had another talent that would prove an asset to our project. She knew everybody. As we dragged our duffel bags across the Bethel airport lobby, our route was impeded every few feet by a stop to greet this aunt or that cousin. Flora's family is widely distributed across the Delta: she was born and raised in a one of the Yup'ik villages on Kuskokwim Bay, but her mother was a Nelson Islander and her husband came from Nunivak Island, where Flora lived for many years and raised three children before moving to Anchorage in 1994. That took care of half the people who crossed our path. The rest were friends from various places, including childhood chums, craft-show contacts, or chance encounters on the Anchorage bus system. When Flora recognized but could not place one of the innumerable schoolboys milling around the airport on a basketball trip, she planted herself directly in his path and without further preliminaries delivered her standard opening line: "Who's your mom?" Apparently such direct questions were permissible if you were Yup'ik but not for outsiders such as I.

With funding from my grant for airfare, per diem, and Flora's time, we have worked in several kinds of settings. In the rural areas we have interviewed basket makers in their homes and participated in the annual autumn beach-grass harvest. In the early days we made two to three trips each year, covering villages from Dillingham in the south to Scammon Bay in the north, a distance of several hundred miles. At the time of writing we have visited eighteen of twenty-two basket-making villages, some more than once. Generally we go to two or three villages per trip and spend three to five days in each. The trips are short, but the intensity of the work and the stresses and strains of bush travel make more time than that too exhausting.

When we get off the plane in a village we follow a more or less set routine: we nail down a place to stay, check in with the village council office (I request permission via fax, followed up by a phone call, before leaving home), and set to work. Finding a place to stay in rural Alaska, where there are usually no public accommodations, is stressful. Almost always we have to scramble, but thanks to Flora's social network and the general courtesy extended to visitors in Yup'ik communities, we have managed remarkably well. Her normal modus operandi is to stop dead in her tracks after she has collected her luggage from the plane, put two fingers on her lips, and ponder: "Let's see, who lives here? I know, let's try my sister's husband's family (or my mother's cousins, or some other familial variant)," and off we go, perched precariously on the fender of the airline agent's snow machine, our bags bumping along behind on a sled, to burst in unannounced on the designated household, Yup'ik collaborator in the advance guard, non-native anthropologist bringing up the rear. Sometimes the hosts are dismayed by an uninvited kassaq (non-native) houseguest, for kassaqs are notoriously picky about native food. But Flora quickly reassures them. "Don't worry," I understood her to say once after I had picked up a little Yup'ik, "she eats anything but dog."

Flora and I also attend several annual art and craft fairs held in Alaska's urban and regional centers. The largest is the Alaska Federation of Natives craft sale in October with one hundred to two hundred vendors, the smallest the Festival of Native Arts at the University of Alaska, Fairbanks, with forty to fifty. At the fairs Flora is both observer and observed. Sharing the rent for a table with a friend, she sells baskets, sealskin dolls, and other small ornaments. I help her set up her table and watch her interact with customers, skillfully parrying variants of the same three questions ("That's the price; I don't bargain," "I'm Yup'ik Eskimo," "No, I don't live in an igloo"). I keep her company when business is slow, run out for coffee, check out and report on the competition, and fill in for her when she takes breaks.

In return she answers my by now carefully edited questions: "How come you didn't mind if that lady had copied your baskets?"—(but never, fearing the Nosey Question rebuke, "How come so-and-so charges so much for hers?"). If internalizing the Yup'ik prohibition against questions has cut down on the accumulation of certain kinds of data, it has also made me more observant. Once I asked Flora if it was possible to tell a Chevak and a Togiak qaspeq apart—would the cloth parkas from two villages located three hundred miles apart be identifiably different? "You ask too many questions," she replied. Several weeks later, when we were in the grocery store in Bethel, I spotted Flora's friend from Chevak. "There's Mary," I said. "She has big sleeves on her qaspeq." Flora looked at me hard: "Pretty smart, aren't you?"

It was this incident and our verbal exchange that afforded me valuable insight into the difference between the Yup'ik and the kassaq attitudes toward questions. I had figured out something for myself, and Flora was praising me more directly than usual for displaying independence of thought and action. I remembered something Barbara Bodenhorn had written about Iñupiaq Eskimo learning styles on Alaska's North Slope and how in a culture in which people were living on the margins of the habitable world, survival could depend on the ability to put observational skills into practice (Bodenhorn 1997: 127; see also Stern 1999: 508, 510). Could this have been what Flora in her own way had been trying to teach me by deflecting my questions? As I thought back I realized she had often admonished me for not being able to find my way to another house in a village where they all looked the same. "You've got to notice and remember," she would chide.

In 2002–2003 Flora and I wound up our visits to museums to study their collections of Yup'ik baskets. In stored museum collections we recorded measurements, took digital photos, and researched accession files. I had been apprehensive about how Flora would take to this work since it is technical and tiring. As it turned out, though, I need not have worried. Intensely interested as she is in Yup'ik history in general and the history of Yup'ik basketry in particular, her decades as a basket maker have given her a sharp eye for technique. "Lookee here," she would say. "This lady was left-handed. See? These stitches slant the wrong way."

The chance to handle hundred-year-old baskets from "her area" was also thrilling. Yup'ik baskets are made for sale, and almost all of them soon leave the Y-K Delta. This means that today's artists rarely get to see, let alone handle, old ones. Flora's mother sold baskets all during her childhood, and Flora often talked about wishing she had kept one. One day, when we were working with the collection at the Alaska State Museum in Juneau, Flora spotted one that she instantly recognized as her mother's work. She was delighted and returned home with photos of it to share with her sisters.

From Coordinator to Collaborator

The expansion of Flora's role from translator and logistical coordinator to full-fledged collaborator came about through her own volition. At the beginning of our work together, the main attraction of the project for her was undoubtedly the travel. Airplane travel in rural Alaska is prohibitively expensive, so the research offered her the chance to renew her friendships around the Delta and to sample subsistence foods available in different localities. "Let's go to Nightmute this time," she would say when we were planning a trip—"there's black fish there this month." Soon, however, Flora's strict Yup'ik upbringing, which emphasized the work ethic, got the upper hand. Part of her job was to administer questionnaires to Yup'ik-speaking basket makers, but before long she began to count the number she completed each day, often commenting on the information they contained. When I could not attend a craft fair, she took photos for me and would report on the different artists who had been there and describe the baskets they had brought to sell.

I often reflect on the differences that carrying out the research for Weaving Culture in many short rather than in one or two extended field trips has made. Like most anthropologists working in the North, I have Franz Boas's year-long sojourn among the Baffin Island Inuit a century ago as a model (Boas 1964 [1888]). Certainly a community study would be ill served by my method, but for a project carried out in many villages and one focused on a specific aspect of a culture, as mine is, the method has some advantages. For one thing, it has forced me to plan the trips and carry them out with a few very focused objectives in mind. For another, it has allowed time for reflection between trips and the chance on later visits to recheck information or to get additional information that I overlooked initially. Then too, when we return to a place for the second visit, people are usually glad to see us and, because they have not tired of us over a longer stay, are probably more receptive to intensive research. Once when Flora and I returned to stay with her Auntie Rita, an outstanding basket maker in her community, Auntie Rita announced that she had been saving something to show us when we came back. She pulled out a children's coloring book about Canadian Inuit life. It included a simple illustration of a Baffin Island–style kayak, which she had further simplified on graph paper for use as a basket design. Had I been paying a single visit I would have missed this remarkable detail, and I often wonder at the confusion finding a Baffin Island kayak on a Yup'ik basket must have caused a kayak aficionado. Thus, idealized though Boas's single protracted visit may have been, short, intense bursts of fieldwork, which the anthropologist Margaret Blackman (pers. comm.) has christened "hit-and-run ethnography," are sometimes advantageous. With the advent of universal air travel, furthermore, my approach is fast becoming the rule.

During the second or third year of our fieldwork together, Flora and I found our friendship gradually strengthening. The adversities of bush travel often threw us into bizarre situations, and surmounting them brought us the shared experience that is the raw stuff of friendship. Twice, marooned on Nelson Island because of weather, we had to move between villages by sled rather than bush plane. In Tooksook Bay one January, faced with the third in a series of impending snowstorms and running out of knitting yarn, Flora got on the CB (citizens band radio, the main form of communication in rural Alaska) and found a hunter leaving by snow machine for Nightmute, a nearby village where we might get a plane out if the weather cleared. For the cost of his gas the man agreed to hitch up his sled and take us along.

Riding a sled behind a snow machine is a harrowing way to travel. Most of today's Yup'ik sleds are inverted, shallow-sided boxes pounded together out of heavy discarded lumber. They are attached to the snow machine by a rope, which with luck is drawn through a metal loop so that it does not fray en route. Flora and I, a pair of respectable middle-aged women, were tied down like a couple of dead caribou in the sled and wrapped in a tarp for warmth. Careening wildly behind the snow machine at the end of four or five feet of rope, the sled whipped back and forth, flinging its cargo—us—into the air with every bone-jarring bump. Five minutes out, we were rigid with terror; fifteen minutes out, as we picked up speed and rounded a corner on one edge of the sled, there was nothing to do but laugh, and laugh we did, all the way to Nightmute, where we were unceremoniously dumped with our bags at the door of another of Flora's relatives. Now, whenever one of us has to face something unpleasant, the other will say: "Don't be scared, remember the sled!" and we dissolve into peals of laughter.

Our working relationship has not been without stresses and strains, how-ever. There have been days when moving around a village with an anthro-pologist trudging in her wake—someone who is culturally the equivalent of a Yup'ik five-year old—has proven too much for her. *The more Flora bosses me [around], the clumsier and more helpless I become. . . . 'Don't sit at the table if you're not eating,' 'Finish everything on your plate,' 'Don't use somebody else's coffee cup,'* I wrote, dispirited, at the end of one long day when I could do nothing right. Having me along when she wanted to socialize was also frustrating for Flora, especially in the steam bath. "Steaming," as it is known, is the gold-standard social event in the daily life in any Yup'ik village, and as I was to learn, it is an occasion attended by a protocol as intricate as that of a Zen tea ceremony. At first I was left alone to knit while Flora went off with her friends to steam. Gradually though, I began to be included, and eventually, with enough prompting from Flora, I learned the rituals well enough not to embarrass her.

The questionnaire I devised for us to administer was an early cause of contention between Flora and me. I had included in it some questions about basket economics: *What percentage of your income comes from selling baskets?* was one. *How much do you charge for 6-in (or 8- or 12-in) baskets?* was another. Looking back, I marvel at my naïveté. "I'm not asking that," Flora said flatly, tapping her pen on the offending questions. "It's nosey." I capitulated. In a more hierarchical relationship it might have been possible to insist, but having internalized Flora's Yup'ik norms, I opted in favor of reticence, reasoning first that objective social science had long since proven an chimera, and second that I had more to gain from preserving our friendship than from the addition of a few extra facts to my study.

At some point during the research I realized that I have been engaged all along in a double project. My study of Yup'ik basketry is inextricably tied to the growth of a cross-cultural friendship, and the friendship has molded the form this study has assumed. While not unique among anthropologists and those with whom they work, such friendships are still unusual. Today most granting agencies require the participation of indigenous people in the research of those who study them, but in my experience this participation is more apt to take the form of oversight committees than of day-to-day collaboration on a one-to-one basis over an extended period.

As the study has shaped my friendship with Flora, Flora has likewise shaped my research, both positively and negatively. On the downside this friendship, like any other, requires self-censorship, and this in turn means that when the time comes to write things up, I am prevented by loyalty from discussing topics such as social interactions in the depth that I otherwise might. And knowing this, I experience pangs of conscience. On the positive side my friendship with Flora has benefited my research in more than the incidentals of travel. I set out to do a straightforward project that would reconstruct the history and generate a taxonomy of Yup'ik basketry. But experiences such as harvesting basket grass each fall have given me an appreciation of the importance of subsistence activities in the lives of Yup'ik women—and the hardship that denial of these activities would bring to them. This in turn has led me in the direction of the relationship between market arts and politics; the social interactions suggested by activities at craft fairs; the symbolic resonance of contemporary Native art forms in the political sphere; and the links between the arts of acculturation and traditional culture, even as the time gap between them widens (Lee: 2002).

Rewarding as the study has become, however, the pleasure I take in Flora's company is more rewarding still. For it is this friendship that now propels me across alien thresholds without the clutch of fear I felt on that snowy March morning in Salluit so many years ago.

Acknowledgments

I am grateful to Margaret B. Blackman and Aldona Jonaitis for their helpful comments on earlier drafts of this paper. It has also profited immeasurably from Pamela Stern's judicious editing. My Yup'ik collaborator, known here as Flora Mark, deserves special thanks for granting me permission to write about our work together.

TWO

Listening to Elders, Working with Youth

Carol Zane Jolles

> The methodologies and methods of research, the theories that inform them, the questions which they generate and the writing styles they employ . . . need to be "decolonized." . . . Research has not been neutral in its objectification of the Other. Objectification is a process of dehumanization. In its clear links to Western knowledge research has generated a particular relationship to indigenous peoples which continues to be problematic. (L. T. Smith 1999: 39)

Native scholars have long viewed the conduct of research in and about indigenous American communities by non-natives as problematic. Donald Fixico, director of the Center for Indigenous Studies at the University of Kansas, locates the problem in what he sees as a lack of respect for native communities writ large. Fixico notes that "whether racially prejudiced or guilt-ridden, patronizing, paternalistic or romantic Indian history mainly has been perceived from a white perspective, based on the idea that 'the conquerors write the history' " (Fixico 1998: 86). He is especially concerned that "non-Indian scholars have sought to define the parameters of the field [and] . . . have attempted to determine its forms of evidence only as written accounts, professed limited theories, and devised methodologies from a non-Indian tradition" (Fixico 1998: 86).

Fixico's immediate dissatisfaction, and that of other indigenous scholars, is with the seemingly monofaceted view and presentation of indigenous history and culture by non-native scholars (see for example Deloria 2001; Deloria and Wildcat 2001; Fixico 1998; L. T. Smith 1999). While Fixico addresses only a single aspect of a single academic discipline, his concern has widespread application and his arguments can be applied to a broad spectrum of other social scientific disciplines. And importantly, his arguments are directly relevant to the conduct of research among native peoples in arctic and subarctic regions. ~~As he points out, research focused on the indigenous peoples of North America, as well as on native peoples worldwide, has been primarily a non-native, scholar-driven enterprise in which native peoples are likely to be the subjects of research.~~ Not only is this true of my own field, anthropology; it is also true of other social science disciplines. In addition, until very recently social science research in targeted populations was seldom posed beforehand to the subject communities. At the same time their home communities were often unaware of the scope, protocols, methodologies, and other particulars that had been "approved" through individually acquired oral consent, since the details had not been disclosed to the consultant's community.

While most scientific research, almost by definition, generates products such as reports and publications of results, product audiences have frequently been a researcher's peers from the scientific community to the exclusion of the residents of the communities where research is conducted. When reports are sent to constituent communities such as Alaska Native villages, these reports are often written in scientific language that is hardly understandable to the layman. Furthermore, not all reports actually find their way back to local communities even when the research contains information that has implications for a community's health and well-being.

A growing appreciation of this situation, precipitated largely by the demands of native communities, has led a growing number of non-native scholars working with native communities to review the histories of research in their disciplines and to rethink their relationships with and responsibilities and obligations to the native peoples and communities who are the subjects of their research. In this chapter, I address the ways in which my own research in Alaska Native communities has changed in response to these concerns.

Research in Alaska Native Communities

In the late nineteenth century many Alaska Native communities experienced an influx of outsider or non-native institutions. ~~The church, mission school, and supply store came to dominate landscapes once thought to be the province and domain of northern indigenous peoples.~~ In the northern reaches of the Alaska Territory, the arrival of nineteenth-century outsiders coincided with the purchase of that territory by the United States from Russia in 1867.[1] Roughly fifteen years after the purchase transaction, the U.S. government sought to solidify its presence in the newly acquired territory and to shoulder its presumed obligations to its newest citizens. To do so, the government introduced its version of the triumvirate into the Alaskan North. Schooling in particular was central to the nation's understanding of its imagined responsibilities to educate and thereby "civilize" supposedly "wild and savage" Alaska Natives. Through schooling, natives could achieve literacy, read the Bible, accept Christianity, embrace principles of individual property ownership, and learn the rudiments of an essentially agrarian lifestyle. Schoolteacher–missionaries recruited after 1885 by Sheldon Jackson, general agent for education in the territory, were to be the instruments of these changes. Jackson, himself a Presbyterian minister, interviewed teacher candidates to determine their Christian commitment before hiring them.

While explorers, teachers, missionaries, and storekeepers are among the best known non-natives to enter the Alaskan North in the late 1800s and early 1900s, federal agents, such as the captains of the revenue cutters that patrolled northern waters for rum runners, were also common. Not the least among these government-sponsored and privately supported interlopers were the researchers who entered Alaska during the same period and whose research help solidify American intellectual knowledge about Alaska Native peoples and cultures. Among the best known was Edward Nelson, a naturalist who collected objects for what would become the Smithsonian Institution. Between 1877 and 1881 Nelson obtained over ten thousand artifacts, took more than a hundred photographs, acquired skeletal remains from native graves and piled them three deep into containers, shipped the accumulated objects and skeletal remains to the nation's capital, and wrote extensively of his observations in Eskimo settlements and whaling camps along the Siberian and American Bering Sea coasts (Nelson 1983 [1899]).

By 1897 anthropological research had also commenced under the watchful eye of Franz Boas of Columbia University, who was instrumental in implementing the Jesup North Pacific Expedition on the Russian and American shores. A major objective was to document the culture history of the North Pacific region and to determine the place of its hunter-gatherer residents in the evolutionary framework of human societies. Following patterns of research already established among Native American tribal peoples in the United States proper, Boas initiated research that reiterated a form of data collection seldom acknowledging native community concerns (see Freed et al. 1988).

The biases that shaped much of the early anthropological research in the North (and elsewhere) have long since been exposed (see Fardon 1990; Fox 1991; Stocking 1992). Many theories prominent at the beginning of the twentieth century were quietly retired, but the colonialist tendencies that fostered them persisted, and the burden of a colonialist-imperialist legacy still lies heavy on the shoulders of contemporary sociocultural anthropologists and other researchers with northern interests.

The Other in the North

More than a century after Nelson and Boas, postmodernist preoccupations with researcher interactions with and responses to an objectified Other reflect the ongoing discourse that flows from this heritage and continues to influence the theoretical landscape of anthropologists and others engaged in social scientific research. In anthropology preoccupations with the Other, however that is construed, first surfaced almost two decades ago in discussions generated by James Clifford, Michael Fischer, George Marcus, and others (see Clifford and Marcus 1986; Marcus and Fischer 1986) and challenged the validity and authority of a meta-discipline that for almost seventy-five years had sent its acolytes as self-proclaimed omnipotent, omnipresent, professional observers into communities singularly beyond and outside each observer's own native homeland. Michel Rolph Trouillot (1991: 23–26) has observed that such authority probably grew from attitudes commonly found in earlier observations recorded by eighteenth- and nineteenth-century missionaries and travelers to foreign regions and sold as popular travelogues. Such observations promoted and eventually reified categories that persist in the popular imagination and to a certain extent continue to inform anthropological research methodologies and the resulting literature.

Ethics and Northern Research

Several professional scientific organizations have recently taken steps to redress the wrongs of the past. Among those representing anthropologists, the American Anthropological Association (AAA) and the National Association of Practicing Anthropologists (NAPA) have endorsed principles of ethical research designed to protect study "subjects." The wording of these principles suggests that, in general, anthropological research is and will continue to be commonly carried out by outsiders, either non-natives or native scholars whose circumstances give them outsider status. Given this assumption, the principles stress that those designated as study subjects—that is, the Other or the Natives—should be protected to ensure personal privacy and should receive just compensation for work, although what that work might be is not defined. Thus the principles are based on the likelihood that most anthropological research will focus on individuals within a society whose personal privacy should be protected in conjunction with the researcher-client relationship. Nevertheless the AAA principles also note:

> Every effort should be exerted to cooperate with members of the host society in the planning and execution of research projects. . . .
>
> In accordance with the Association's general position on clandestine and secret research, no reports should be provided to sponsors that are not also available to the general public and, *where practicable,* to the population studied (emphasis added). (http://www.aaanet.org/stmts/ ethstmnt.htm)

These statements suggesting broader community or society involvement create a circumstance that may make protection of personal privacy and/or the researcher-client relationship difficult if not impossible and illustrate some of the tensions generated by the somewhat conflicting objectives facing the profession.

The AAA's statements can be compared with ethics principles adopted by the International Arctic Social Science Association (IASSA) and adhered to, at least in theory, by most social scientists working in the North. Researchers funded by the Arctic Social Science Program of the National Science Foundation (NSF) are required to agree to a similar set of principles regarding the ethical conduct of research. Both stress the researcher's responsibility to include native peoples in *all* levels of research as well as to encourage and promote local educational endeavors, to respect sacred sites, to gain written permission or consent (rather than oral consent) to conduct research, to give fair compensation for work performed, to protect anonymity where required, and to provide

> research results . . . to local communities in non-technical terms and where possible translated into local languages. Copies of research reports and other relevant materials should be made available to local communities. (http://arcticcircle.uconn.edu/SEEJ/ethics.html)

The principles adopted by IASSA and the Arctic Social Sciences Program at NSF were a formal response to a changing research climate. Northern indigenous communities were making demands for more inclusive, more socially relevant research in their communities. At the same time reflexive evaluation within the social sciences generally, and within anthropology particularly, created a climate that favored cooperative and multidisciplinary research.

Indigenous communities in the North, whose intellectual, social, and political concerns range across disciplinary and methodological boundaries, have been especially critical in this shift. Multidisciplinary research projects remove some of the narrowly defined boundaries that have characterized past research projects, while cooperative research opens up the possibility that researchers not only seek permission from local communities to engage in scientific research but also take specific concerns of indigenous communities into consideration before proceeding with research. Significantly, involving indigenous communities in cooperative research opens up new methodological and theoretical territory.[2] To illustrate, let me turn to my personal experiences as a non-native anthropologist in the North.

A Personal Account

In 1982 after spending sixteen years as a schoolteacher in the American lower forty-eight states, I handed in my resignation. Like many other women caught up in the social changes of the 1980s, I changed careers, and in the autumn of 1981 I applied to graduate school in a field in which I had not taken a single undergraduate or teacher certification class. Thus, in my early forties, I found myself a member of the 1982 entering cohort of graduate students in sociocultural anthropology at the University of Washington in Seattle. I was a late entrant to be sure; only one student in the cohort of sixteen was older than I, and I was several years older than many of my professors. I entered the anthropology program a bit jaded and worn with almost two decades of teaching English to high school students in the inner city public schools of west Philadelphia, the south side of Chicago, and Minneapolis.

Inspired by my experiences working with Native American high school students in Minnesota, I ventured into graduate studies in anthropology, a discipline familiar to me only because I had once, in the 1950s, attended a lecture by Margaret Mead. Immediately I was infused with the kind of excitement that only comes with being reborn. I, who had been a teacher for so long, loved returning to the classroom as a graduate student and embraced wholeheartedly the new ideas (new to me, at any rate) that marked the beginning of my anthropology career. The ideas and theories of French sociologists Emile Durkheim, Marcel Mauss, Pierre Bourdieu, and Claude

Lévi-Strauss and American anthropologists Clifford Geertz, Victor Turner, George Marcus, and James Clifford especially excited me. As I struggled to master the unfamiliar theories and methodologies, I took particular comfort in the knowledge that both Geertz and Turner had been English literature students before becoming anthropologists. As my studies progressed, I became more and more wedded to the ideologies and paradigms of this newly chosen field. By the time I had passed my Ph.D. general exams in 1986 and had begun to prepare for the field experience that usually distinguishes anthropological research from its sister disciplines in the social sciences, the new ideas were very much a part of my thinking.

Under direction from my Ph.D. thesis committee, ~~I narrowed my intellectual focus to a concentration on the nature of ethnicity and identity and the impact of colonialism and imperialism on identity formation in northern Native North American societies.~~ Gradually this focus had led me to the small Siberian Yupik village of Gambell on St. Lawrence Island, Alaska, where I hoped to demonstrate that Christianity could be considered a major component of contemporary identity in this Eskimo community. My traveling equipment included ideas informed especially by theoretical arguments drawn from ~~Harold Isaacs, Clifford Geertz, and others with what anthropology refers to as a primordialist slant. For these men, identity contained many of the same qualities as blood or skin color: it was something so ingrained, so deeply embedded, that it could not be separated from the person. From Lévi-Strauss I carried the classical notions of the primacy of exchange of persons, places, and ideas in all cultures. And from Bourdieu I carried a developing understanding of a theory of practice.~~

With the enthusiasm of the newly converted, I arrived in Gambell in the fall of 1987. I had just spent a hot July in the archives of the Presbyterian Church in Philadelphia and the Seventh-Day Adventist Church in Tacoma, Maryland, where records of Alaskan missionaries were housed. The unairconditioned circumstances of the Presbyterian archives had led the archive staff to note that I had turned somewhat green with the oppressive late summer heat, but my enthusiasm transported me to the imagined snowy North as I turned the pages of the journals and diaries of the first schoolteacher-missionary evangelists who had encountered Gambell residents and whose lives gave substance to the narratives I read in the sweltering heat of the Philadelphia summer.

As I learned more and more about the people who had inhabited St. Lawrence Island between 1878 and 1955, I felt reassured that I had done everything necessary to acquaint myself with the community's population and its history. I had perused almost every written record produced by outsiders who had journeyed to the island in the 125 years that had passed since explorer Henry Elliott had stood on the island's southern shores in 1875 and had remarked on the robust health and well-being of the local residents he met. And I had spoken to retired missionaries and researchers who had been there. I had also spent a number of hours on the telephone with the president of the local tribal council and looked forward to being her guest on my first, unofficial visit to the community (my presence would become "official" only after I received some type of endorsement from a local Gambell agency).

All of this "contact" with voices from the past and the present culminated in my highly anticipated journey to Gambell in the spring of 1987. I found it not at all strange to make that initial trip, and upon my arrival I used my time to negotiate with Gambell Presbyterian Church Session elders, the church's governing body, and its supervising minister for permission to conduct research the following year. I came away from that first visit to Gambell believing that I was fully prepared to spend the next year or more away from husband and family in a small arctic community in northwest Alaska engaged in something called participant-observation. I thought I was ready.

Like others who have attempted extensive research among strangers, my research agenda reflected years of academic training but lacked information about current community needs and interests. The work in Gambell was sponsored jointly by the local Presbyterian Church and a village leader. In October 1987 I moved into a new Yupik friend's household, having agreed to live with and care for the friend's mother, a community elder, while my friend was absent for professional reasons. When I arrived I already had a well-developed research agenda and methodology approved by my doctoral committee and a clearly defined vision of ways in which the results of the research would benefit the community. I had much to learn.

Shortly after my arrival in Gambell, I attended the first of many church services in the Gambell Presbyterian Church. A woman about my own age, or perhaps a few years younger, approached me at the end of the service, introduced herself, and began to question me. Why exactly had I come, she asked, and what did I expect to offer the community? Was I coming to spy on the community? Would I steal the community's history and then attempt to sell it back to them? How would my proposed project benefit the community, especially the children?

I made my recitation on the presumed benefits of my presence and my research, and the woman politely moved away—thoroughly unconvinced, if body language was any indicator. Her concerns, quietly expressed and unaggressively displayed, were undoubtedly echoed in the minds of many others I met that year as I went about the business of listening to, learning from, observing, and finally working with members of the community. For the most part during that first year, I interviewed elders. I hired one or two older women to work with me as interpreters, transcribers, and translators. I learned to eat Yupik food—what locals call *neqepik* (real food)—and I traipsed across the village in all kinds of weather. By the end of the first year I had become a well-known form, easily identified by my Eddie Bauer men's parka, a type worn by at least fifteen men in the village that year. Mine alone had red and yellow embroidery on the hand-warmer pockets.

What does this have to do with the changing face of arctic research and the necessity for new research models? Let me backtrack. To prepare for my first field trip north, I garnered my own notions of what fieldwork should entail based on information provided in mandatory classes on the conduct of fieldwork and from anecdotal accounts by anthropology faculty. From them I learned to focus on theoretical questions, to remain "objective," and to avoid too thorough an integration into the community, since that would disturb scientific distance. From my professors I learned that I should keep detailed notes and carefully guard my information. When conducting interviews, I should obtain some kind of permission, either oral or written. Oral permission was quite acceptable. Knowing that my research would explore the extent to which a new religious system had been absorbed by the community, one of my professors even suggested audiotaping the sounds of people entering a spiritual state and speaking in tongues during church services. If necessary, this faculty member remarked, I could "just tuck my tape recorder into a pocket out of sight." I still shudder inwardly at the recollection of this piece of advice.

My obligation to the community was to conduct myself in an "ethical manner," whatever that meant. I now believe that to have been a code phrase for "not overtly offensive." Consultation with the community to learn what would be meaningful to them was not required and might compromise the project's integrity. Instead I believed (at least at some level) that the research had value for the community because of the attention I planned to give to its history. Throughout, the theoretical dimensions of the research along with the community's unique island location and position in the path of northern migrations across Bering Strait were of far greater interest than were my interactions with and responsibilities to the Alaska Native community where I would live and work for a year. Only one of my professors, a Native American, suggested that the scope of the work should be informed by intention and purpose that went beyond an academic research agenda.

The Gambell community accepted at face value my initial statement that the research objective was to document the "history of Christianity in Gambell." The objective seemed harmless, vaguely promising, and much easier to explain than identity concepts. Once I was established in Gambell, interviews with elders and other prominent community members commenced. Interview subjects (consultants) were paid for their time, an unusual practice in 1988. I considered the interviews intellectual labor. The money itself was appreciated because Gambell residents are poor. Elders used the money to buy tea and other needed commodities. Bolstered by an academic perception of the value of the research and the undoubted good that I must be doing, I assumed my worth in the community. Now I believe I was mistaken.

At the end of the spring in 1988 I returned home to write my dissertation. Later, with a growing sense of unease, I sent copies of my thesis to Gambell and told myself that I had fulfilled my obligations. I know now that my discomfort stemmed from the inadequacy of the research process.

In 1990, IASSA members who hammered out documents outlining the Conduct of Ethical Research in the Arctic gave substance to what had seemed problematic to me. The anthropological task starts with the notion of basic research, but research itself and the right to conduct it are embedded in a history formulated on what Trouillot (1991: 34–35) and others have referred to as the West and the Rest. On the one hand there is the observer, armed with "culture" writ large and history, known and recorded. On the other hand is the Other, living somehow within "Nature" writ large and holding onto the past through stories. Obviously this is a simplification of processes that affect human societies at population centers and in multiple peripheries. Nevertheless this perceived dichotomy has been at work on anyone who embraces a western academic tradition, assumes the role of researcher, and arms herself theoretically for a journey to the field.

Following adoption of the IASSA principles, arctic social scientists became some of the first to embrace more openly cooperative research models. Many of these researchers already lived in the North and were aware of the range of social scientific questions coming from native communities concerned with documenting community-based knowledge and knowledge systems and with incorporating native epistemologies into both research and public policy. Arctic social scientists accepted with little controversy the demands of northern indigenous communities to be included in all phases of research, and a decade and a half later, there are numerous examples of cooperative and multidisciplinary research in the North. The models employed are various. Some are similar to those employed by Richard Lee, Marjorie Shostak, and Richard Katz as part of the original study to document Ju/'hoansi society in the Kalahari desert region of Namibia, Botswana, and South Africa (Katz 1982; Lee 1979; Shostak 1983). They integrate across subdisciplines and disciplines alike to create a more informed, holistic scientific view.

One such multidisciplinary example from Alaska is a project (hereafter identified as the Whaling Project) first begun under the combined efforts of Roger Harritt, Mary Ann Larson, Allen McCartney, Barbara Bodenhorn, Herbert Anungazuk, and others, including myself. Harritt, who increasingly took on overall responsibility for the project, noted that its objective "was to combine archaeology and sociocultural anthropology with whale biometrics and geomorphology, with the primary goal of studying the prehistoric development of whale hunting and historic patterns of whaling societies" (Harritt 2001: 5).

At its height in 1997–98 the Whaling Project included four distinct areas of study, was sponsored by the Alaska Eskimo Whaling Commission (AEWC), and was endorsed by six separate Alaska Native communities. One element was a commitment to include more than the research community proper in the planning and execution of the project as well as in the dissemination of results. In academic circles the Whaling Project traveled under an umbrella of scientific and social scientific theories, but generally it was understood by the Alaska Native communities that signed on to it and to the AEWC that supported it as contributing to the development of a traditional ecological knowledge database and as source material to be employed by each participating community as part of the larger search for a meaningful, contemporary Alaska Native identity. The project was one of the first northern examples of multidisciplinary research and involved modest cooperation with participating native communities.

The Whaling Project involved university-trained scientists from several disciplines and indigenous community members with significant training in traditional ecological knowledge (TEK) and/or varying levels of local experiential knowledge to produce research that had explicit value to both the academic and native communities. This type of explicitly cooperative and collaborative research is still in its infancy. There is, however, a great desire in northern communities to become actively involved in research, especially to document community histories and local knowledge systems such as those labeled TEK. It should be acknowledged that in some cases a concern that traditions be recorded before they disappear has lent a Boasian flavor to much of the cooperative research conducted in the North.

Determined to be both more relevant and more open about my research, I returned to Gambell in 1992 to begin a comprehensive study of community traditions and values. In order to be more inclusive I hired a multiclan team: a project director chosen from among several highly qualified elders, five adult research assistants selected from a cross section of interested adults, a translator, and a small group of high school interns.[3] The inclusion of more community members in the project was thus one characteristic of the research. If employed successfully, this model would meet scientific standards and would include both occupational and educational components. As principal investigator I set the research agenda, but execution of that agenda depended significantly on the performance of a locally constituted research team.

At first, the business of working "with" the community rather than "in" or "on behalf of" the community was cumbersome. As an ethnographer I was accustomed to performing all research tasks including all data collection. Now local research team members were responsible for portions of the data collection process. Inevitably it was more work to run a cooperative enterprise than proceeding alone. Team members had to be trained, and delegating tasks meant giving up control. Data collected by trainees were not always complete. Sometimes the data collected failed to meet my research objectives. On the other hand, team members contributed new perspectives on the research process. They suggested questions that were important to the community. At times the overall workload increased, not only because of the time devoted to training and attempting to keep the project on task but also because arriving at the ultimate product was difficult. Questions asked of each consultant were often subtly structured to avoid imposition upon local ideas and values. Yet the questions had to allow the research to go forward in a scientifically meaningful direction. This concept of the structuring of questions was particularly difficult for me to convey to local team members.

Most research projects are characterized by the theoretical questions they ask, the points they seek to prove or disprove, and by the theoretical foundation or context of the research. Nonacademic communities are generally less concerned with abstract theoretical questions than they are with the practical applications of the information that has been gathered. The research objective for the aforementioned project was to determine the val-

2.1. Elder Oscar Ahkinga (left) and Herbert Anungazuk
(right), Diomede, 1998. Photo by Carol Zane Jolles.

ues and underlying philosophies that supported a contemporary marine
mammal hunting society, whose members now rely on a mixed market-
subsistence economy. To do so, questions had to allow each consultant
to articulate the philosophy and beliefs that sustained him or her. At the
same time the local research team, with its mix of adults and teenagers with
little prior experience at such questioning, had to learn the rudiments of
this demanding interviewing procedure. One concern I had was that the au-
diotaped interviews would lack depth and substance. This concern was un-
founded. When the project was completed the interviews were satisfactory,
and I had developed several new research relationships, including writing
partnerships with two local women (Jolles and Kaningok 1991; Jolles and
Oozeva 2002). It was clear that employing a local research team had not
only assuaged my conscience but had unanticipated and highly rewarding
results.

While the second Gambell study and the Whaling Project each experi-
mented with cooperative research on an extremely modest scale, they paved
the way for more experimentation with cooperative community research.
Work on Harritt's Whaling Project had made it possible for me to work
with Herbert Anungazuk, an Iñupiaq man originally from Wales, Alaska,
employed as a native heritage specialist for the National Park Service. While
Anungazuk's background included no formal postsecondary education, it
did include "almost a decade and a half, acquiring very special skills and
knowledge from the elders of Northwest Alaska" (Anungazuk, pers.
comm., 2001). Anungazuk and I traveled to Gambell and to Little Diomede
Island as part of Harritt's project, and I was able to note firsthand com-

2.2. Elder Oscar Ahkinga with two student interns,
Diomede, 1999. Photo by Carol Zane Jolles.

munity appreciation of this pairing of native and non-native researchers.
Anungazuk and I developed a strong working relationship and became both
friends and research partners.

Thus when the opportunity arose in 2000 to prepare a project that would
reflect a cooperative philosophy and research model, I turned to him and to a
second native scholar, Deanna Kingston, to form a research team whose diversity and experience would be appreciated not only by the scientific community but by the communities where the research would be carried out.
The project design also drew on my experience as a consultant working
with the Diomede community in 1999 under the direction of principal investigator Robert Jarvenpa of the State University of New York at Albany.
The tribal community had agreed to that research, but the real support for
the research derived from our willingness to seek tribal council guidance
regarding persons to interview, community members to hire, methods of
recruitment to use when forming a community research team, and tribal
council recommendations of high school students to include in the project
as interns.

The response was immediate and positive. The project had much local visibility. It was advertised on the village scanner, a televised bulletin
board of weekly community events. Student interns described their work
to their friends and family members, and more students asked to work on
the project. The presence of teenagers as an audience at interviews encouraged elders. Team members took photographs, made drawings, and asked
questions. The level of community participation and enthusiasm exceeded
that of the second Gambell project. Working with a cross section of age

48

groups took some adjustment. The interns were inevitably hungry and usually demanded to be fed, but after the necessary soda and chip refueling, they settled into the task of research. In fact on at least one occasion, the interns provided local food for the refueling, raiding family food barrels to bring a combination of walrus and seal meat and "Eskimo" potatoes for the daily snack.[4]

Community members visited the research team at work in the community hall. Photography sessions and examination of traditional food storage areas brought community observers out to comment on our progress. By summer's end, the tribal council had requested that copies of interviews, photographs, and drawings be made available to the entire community. Unfortunately the Jarvenpa project had not been designed to accommodate such a request. Nevertheless the Jarvenpa project proved pivotal for me because it suggested the kinds of research products that might interest a local community as well as the levels of multigenerational participation by community members that were possible.

Consequently in August 2000 Anungazuk, Kingston, and I submitted to the National Science Foundation a proposal that reflected our prior experiences with cooperative research.[5] Rather than describe that project, which is still under way at the time of writing, let me outline instead how the proposal operates.

> *Research Team:* The senior project team consists of two Alaska Natives and one non-native. To the extent possible, the research team is meant to reflect the community populations where the proposed research will take place.
>
> *Project Design:* The project was designed primarily by me as principal investigator but received substantial contributions and critique from all team members. The project also reflects community concerns, indicated later under community benefits.
>
> *Tribal Permissions:* Once the project draft had been completed, formal written permission was sought from the three tribal councils in Wales, Nome, and Little Diomede, where the proposed research would be carried out.
>
> *Community Benefits:* Benefits to the local communities include local hire of and training of research assistants, translators, and student interns; payment for participation in the project as consultants (both adult consultants and teen consultants); and *the return of all data to the tribes, to the local schools, and to the individual participants.* Data return would be in the form

of bound notebooks containing verbatim translations and transcriptions of interviews conducted plus a selection of drawings and photographs produced during the project. One notebook goes to each household in each of the three participating tribal communities, to the tribal council and the mayor's office, one to the superintendent of the Bering Strait School District for use by curriculum specialists, and ten volumes to each school library. At least one set of notebooks is generated for each year of the study as well as work from 1997 and 1998 on the whaling and Jarvenpa projects. Individual participants would also receive copies of their own audiotapes and full-sized reproductions of any maps, drawings, and/or photographs.

The notebooks, which are spiral bound and contain upward of 250 pages each, have been enthusiastically received. Students and adults read their individual interviews with great interest as soon as the notebooks arrived. People are especially interested in the interviews with community members who have since passed away. The community has also made reference to some of the interviews that detail older hunting practices. In addition, the Bering Strait School District is making use of the volumes for curriculum development.

As a caveat, I should note that each of the research projects described above was generated outside the study sites and then brought to community attention for review, comment, and ultimately written endorsement. This suggests some of the inherent limits to full cooperation, since scientific projects are more often generated outside a local community than within it. However, if researchers commit to spending a number of years working with a single community or a collective of communities, it is also possible to generate projects with those local communities that arise directly or indirectly from community concerns and then are structured to reflect scientific concerns as well. The possibilities for fully cooperative research, once commitment to and interest in local communities are well established, are numerous.

Summing Up

For Native scholar Vine Deloria Jr., "Social science in the Western context describes human behavior in such restrictive terminology that it really describes very little except the methodology acceptable to the present generation of academics and researchers" (Deloria 2001: 126). His concern is with the focus or direction of research as much as it is with the researchers themselves. He and co-author Daniel Wildcat note that American Indian and, by extension, northern indigenous communities generally are most appropriately characterized as having a concern with whole systems. Both men advocate research that seeks information having "direct bearing on human individual and communal experience" (Deloria 2001: 126) and that acknowledges and incorporates "tribal views in which humans understand themselves to be but one small part of an immense complex living system" (Wildcat 2001: 12). In Alaska, native people, including Yupiaq educator Oscar Kawagley and Alaska Native Science Commission director Patricia Cochran, have expressed similar views and have sought to redress the lopsided western perspective that permeates most research programs. The Alaska Native Science Commission's website statement on the subject of traditional knowledge, the joining together of native and non-native knowledge perspectives, and the import of that process brings this home most eloquently:

> While it is not appropriate to compare scientific and traditional knowledge as equivalents, the use of traditional knowledge in scientific knowledge in science means that the two knowledge bases will be in contact with each other as practitioners attempt to weave the two together. . . . Together, these two sources of knowledge, traditional and nontraditional, articulate to produce a frame of understanding and validation that give meaning to the world around them. (http://www.nativescience.org/index .html)

The point is also made by non-native researchers. Susanne Dybbroe, speaking about the plight of northern indigenous peoples, picks up this theme and comments that "not the perceived loss of 'culture,' but the loss of self-determination in its widest sense, resulting from the process of foreign hegemony, is what threatens Inuit identity today" (1996: 50). Research aimed at returning community history through contemporary documentation of so-called "traditional" or "storied" pasts, using a mix of disciplines and the incorporation of native peoples into research projects at the local level, continues to deal with what Dybbroe refers to as "cultural loss." At the same time it is an attempt to narrow the gap between the West and the Rest and to downplay anthropology's tendency to maintain an objectified Other. This will change as native peoples of the North become full partners in social science research and in the other disciplines that regularly send researchers into the Arctic (marine biologists, botanists and ethnobotanists, ethnomusicologists, oceanographers, etc.). A quick scan of projects funded by the National Science Foundation's Office of Polar Program, Arctic Social Sciences Program division in the 1990s and early 2000s reveals only a handful of native principal investigators and co-principal investigators. Still the strength of arctic research is its ongoing concern with research models that incorporate native knowledge, commitment to community, multidisciplinary and cooperative approaches to research, and last and perhaps most politically charged, placement of research responsibility in the hands of native communities.

That northern researchers have embraced principles demanding cooperation across cultures and have actively and concretely acknowledged responsibility to local communities seems, in retrospect, a commonsense approach to meaningful and productive science. Yet this model is still not commonly employed across the social science disciplines. The gap epitomized in concepts of otherness remains. For Linda Tuhiwai Smith and perhaps for many indigenous peoples, the need to respond to western research through an active decolonization process "does not mean and has not meant a total rejection of all theory or research or Western knowledge. Rather, it is about [centering indigenous peoples'] concerns and world views and then coming to know and understand theory and research from our own perspectives and for our own purposes" (L. T. Smith 1999: 39).

Projects that depend on cooperative working relationships with native communities or that shift perspective and primary responsibility from western scholars to indigenous scholars are hardly ubiquitous in the Arctic and are rarely adopted elsewhere. Smith's cautionary words remind us that there is much work to be done if these models, much discussed and increasingly implemented in the Arctic, are to be considered more than the practices of a marginalized northern pole of the social science community conducting research in a rarefied periphery of the discipline.

Notes

1. Russian domination in Alaska in the 1800s also took its toll, beginning with the decimation and virtual enslavement of Aleutian Islanders and continuing with the imposition of Russian Orthodoxy and Russian-mandated schooling. However, the intent here is to focus particularly on American rather than Russian intervention in the Alaskan Territory.

2. While cooperative research attempts to take community concerns into consideration, it is distinguished somewhat from its near relative, participatory action research (PAR), which has a substantially applied character. Ideally, those who commit to cooperative research and/or multidisciplinary research now solicit written permission from local communities to conduct research and agree to include those communities in all aspects of the research process and to return research results in utilizable and easily accessible form.

3. A few elders are distinguished not only by their long, productive lives but also by their extensive memories of the past, their deep interest in the changes that have occurred in their communities, and their special abilities as storytellers and community historians. I have had the privilege of working with several men and women who have had these qualities.

4. Eskimo potatoes are roots that resemble Jerusalem artichokes, only much smaller. They are dug at the end of summer on the slopes of Diomede and possibly elsewhere in the Alaskan Arctic. On the Alaskan mainland these roots, known as *masru*, are identified as *Hedysarum alpinum*; however, the roots dug on Diomede do not appear to be the same as H. *alpinum*.

5. To date, two unpublished reports to the Native Village of Diomede document research in that community between 1997 and 1999, plus numerous presentations to the academic community that resulted from the Whaling Project. Three more volumes documenting research in Diomede and Wales in 2002 and 2003 were distributed in 2005. A partial list of reports and presentations includes Carol Jolles, comp., *Our Stories: Whaling and Subsistence in Ingaliq, Little Diomede Island, Alaska*, vol.2, pt. A: 1999, report to the Native Village of Diomede, Seattle WA, 2002; Carol Jolles and Herbert Anungazuk, comps., *Our Stories: Whaling and Subsistence in Ingaliq, Little Diomede Island, Alaska, 1997–1998*, vol. 1, report to the Native Village of Diomede, Seattle WA, 2001; "Hunting and Channel Surfing: Competing Visions of Time, Place and Identity in Northwest Alaska," American Anthropological Association Annual Meeting (Session Title: Consumption of Food and in Song), Chicago IL, 1999.

THREE

Participatory Anthropology in Nunavut

Michael J. Kral and Lori Idlout

This is the story of a research alliance between Inuit and non-native social scientists. Although collaboration between researchers and their informants is not new to anthropology (see Berman 1996 regarding Franz Boas's collaborations with "informants"), the extent and mechanisms of such collaboration have rarely been made explicit. Indeed, while the ideal of intellectual collaboration (across disciplines and theoretical camps and even between academics and their public) has become a stated ideal of many funding agencies and university review boards, we know little about either the challenges or the benefits of such engagements.

As co-authors of this chapter and players in the Unikkaartuit participatory action research (PAR) project described here, we have each been engaged in the minutiae of such collaboration in a project that has spanned almost ten years. Yet our professional worlds are very different. Michael Kral, with a Ph.D. in psychology, is currently pursuing a degree in medical anthropology at McGill University. Recently he taught a class on Inuit culture and political history at Yale University. He was the principal investigator for the Unikkaartuit research project. Lori Idlout, a longtime resident of Iqaluit and originally from Igloolik, Nunavut, has been centrally involved in the movement to incorporate *Inuit qaujimajatuqangit* (IQ, or Inuit traditional knowledge over time) into the structures of the Nunavut government (Wilman 2002). Many Inuit see the conscious incorporation of IQ as a tool for decision making as critical to the success or failure of Nunavut in aboriginal self-government. Lori has a degree in psychology from Lakehead University in Ontario.

Participatory ethnography is located in an intellectual and methodological space between traditional participant-observation and native or auto-ethnography, between researchers and informants. But this space also necessarily incorporates a new kind of dialogue, one that is informed by recognition of, and a desire to change, existing power relations. An emphasis is thus placed upon the *relational motif* between the researchers and those being researched, which includes trust, rapport, and respect (Kral et al. 2002). The relationship between natives and academics is a conjunctive moment between two worlds, the boundaries of which have already been mutually crossed (see Evers and Toelken 2001). It is what Julie Cruikshank (1993) referred to as the blurring of lines between researchers and those being researched. This transformative crossing is one of both opportunity and contestation. It is no longer anthropology meeting the Other, or two Others meeting as foreigners, but a global crossing into a new ethnography. A significant and sustaining strength of such research is the shared belief that the benefits of working collectively will outweigh the drawbacks. It is a philosophy reminiscent of the words of J. S. Mill (1955 [1859]: 52), here slightly paraphrased: Those who know only their own side of the case know little of that.

Ethnography and Participation

The notion of "participation" in anthropology is as old as the discipline. Participant observation has been anthropology's praxis of the in-out game of ethnography. It has been that of one foot living in, with, among, and through a few close Others in an unfamiliar culture for an extended period of time, and the other foot remaining "home," with observation taking place from some remove, theorizing from another place, and writing about all of it for the people of a western locale. Implicitly, this home has operated with its own host of beliefs, customs, and rituals. J. D. Brewer provides one common definition of ethnography as "the study of people in naturally occurring settings or 'fields' by means or methods which capture their social meanings and ordinary activities, involving the researcher participating directly in the setting, if not also the activities, in order to collect data in a systematic manner but without meaning being imposed on them externally" (2000: 6). Anthropologists have been aware of these features of participant observation for a long time and are familiar with the notion that ethnography begins, ends, and starts all over again with the act of translation between worlds. Or at least that is the way it has been.

Ethnography has been changing. The reflexive turn of the 1980s, at the very least, reminded ethnographers that they too can be subjective and that their actions have effects on the peoples and the places they study. Additionally informants can be objective (certainly about ethnographers), as well as agentic and political (Clifford and Marcus 1986; Harding 1987; Okely 1996 [1975]; Parkin 1982). Whereas ethnographers have historically learned the languages of the cultures they study, the people in those cultures have more recently learned the languages of anthropology. Critiques of ethnography have come from the academy, certainly, but an equally important critique has come from the field. A growing number of aboriginal and nonaboriginal scholars and nonacademics have argued for widening anthropology's methodological circle to include as researchers the people in the communities being studied. Caroline Brettell's edited volume *When They Read What We Write* examines some of the possible responses to the question of what to do "when the natives talk back" (1993: 9).

Anthropologists who work in North American aboriginal communities have frequently heard the complaint: "We are being researched to death!" A few communities reportedly have closed their doors to outside researchers (Darou et al. 1993; Oakes and Riewe 1996). It is not an antiresearch attitude per se, as there is great interest within many aboriginal communities to document traditions and histories and to use the tools of social science to promote the good life. The problem, rather, is one in which nonaboriginal researchers are perceived as (and may in fact be) intellectually distant from the people whom they study; they do not do enough to involve communities in the design and planning of the research and too often fail to provide results in forms that are useful to the people studied.

Many aboriginal peoples, like other nonacademics, sometimes find the problems and approaches of academic scholars too specialized or narrowly focused to have relevance outside the academy. While nonspecialists might be willing to accept such an approach in the physical or biological sciences, it is not acceptable where real peoples and communities are the focus of inquiry, as they are in anthropology. In Lori's experience Inuit recognize the complex and multilayered aspects of social phenomena and thus insist that cultures and communities be regarded in context. A broader perspective is important in research on cultures and societies that attempt to interpret states of people's lives.

The Empowered Participant

Participatory research, so labeled, has been around for about thirty years and takes a number of forms. Orlando Fals Borda described his own role in the founding of participatory action research (PAR) in the 1970s, when he and like-minded others were determined that the goal of science "should be to obtain knowledge useful for what we judged to be worthy causes . . . especially by and for the underprivileged classes which were in need of scientific support" (2001: 28). Participatory action research was born of dissatisfaction and disillusionment with received social science of the late 1960s and early 1970s. Suggestions for change included the addition of community participation to the research method. In the academy this was further supported by increased attention to critical theory emphasizing social action (Calhoun and Karaganis 2001), theory that necessarily included collaboration between researchers and those being researched (Susman and Evered 1978). Anthropology participated in this movement, thereby gaining the prefixes of applied, development, action, and advocacy (see van Willigen 1993).

Although participatory research has some meaningful overlap with the method of ethnographic participant observation, there is a fundamental difference. Where the participant observer as outside researcher participates in the everyday life of the culture or community being studied, the participants in participatory research include those being studied in the role of co-researchers. They are now also observing from beyond their traditional roles as research subjects. Participation here can include involvement in the planning, conduct, analysis, interpretation, and dissemination or knowledge transfer of research. According to Whyte (1991: 20), participatory action research "thus contrasts sharply with the conventional model of pure research, in which members of organizations and communities are treated as passive subjects, with some of them participating only to the extent of authorizing the project, being its subjects, and receiving the results. . . . In PAR, some of the members of the organization we study are actively engaged in the quest for information and ideas to guide their future actions." The participation of community members as research collaborators adds an unfamiliar dimension to the usual state of western knowledge production, but it opens a door to new theory, methodology, and knowledge.

Participatory Projects in Nunavut

The political territory of Nunavut was established in the Canadian Arctic in 1999. The creation of the Nunavut Territory signaled a new phase in the struggle for Inuit self-determination (see Dahl et al. 2000). Social science research, including anthropology, has a central place in formation of the programs and policies of the new Nunavut government. The mandate of the Nunavut Social Development Council—now the Department of Social and Cultural Development of Nunavut Tunngavik Inc., the agency behind the land claim agreement—and of the current Nunavut government (Government of Nunavut 1999b) includes support for research relevant to the documentation and implementation of IQ.

The need for research partnerships has become apparent to many Inuit as well as *qallunaat* (non-Inuit) researchers. Such partnerships are not only between researchers and governments but also between different Inuit organizations and community groups and between Inuit and professional researchers. At the same time, there are many different groups in Nunavut who wish to be heard before any research takes place (see O'Neil et al. 1998 for a description of an effort to reconcile the many conflicting demands of community research participants). Inuit communities differ from one another in numerous ways, and such heterogeneity must be taken into account. The requirement to have knowledge from and understanding by these various parties is important if the research results are to be accepted as valid by the researched. Many organizations feel that there is an obligation owed to them to ensure that they participate not only as informants but also as research planners, providing guidance as well as participation in the collection and interpretation of the data.

The term *participatory* has many meanings, and collecting signatures on a consent form or a broad grant of permission for a study to take place no longer constitutes an acceptable definition. Former Pauktuutit (Inuit Women's Association) president Martha Flaherty argued that for a study to be truly participatory among Inuit, it must recognize Inuit as equal partners and respect Inuit control. "It is time for Inuit to set our own terms [by which researchers] who want to come to our land and study us, our culture, traditions, and lives, must abide by" (1995: 182). Her paper was addressed to students, and she invited them to join Inuit in the discovery of practical knowledge through this new lens.

Many of the newer participatory research projects in Nunavut are aimed primarily at documenting IQ (Workshop on Inuit Qaujimanituqangit 2001) and/or local history (Gagnon and Iqaluit Elders 2002; Laugrand et al. 2001; Saladin d'Anglure 2001; Thorpe et al. 2003; Wachowich et al. 1999). John O'Neil, together with First Nations, Inuit, and qallunaat co-investigators, has conducted participatory action health research in northern Canada (O'Neil and Gilbert 1990; O'Neil et al. 1993).

The Unikkaartuit Project

The Unikkaartuit Project moved between the North and the South a number of times. Initiated in Nunavut, it went south for academic development toward grant funding, yet with significant involvement of Inuit. It returned to the North for local adaptation and implementation in two Inuit communities, and where translations and transcriptions from Inuktitut to English were done; then it was taken south for the writing of a final report for Health Canada; and at the time of this writing, the project has returned North for the revision, translation, and distribution of a Nunavut Unikkaartuit report.

Design and Preparation

Suicide rates for Canadian aboriginal people far exceed the average Canadian rate, and in Nunavut the prevalence of suicide is even higher. The suicide rate for the years 1993–97 in Nunavut was 88 per 100,000, compared with 15:100,000 for the western Canadian Arctic and 13:100,000 for Canada as a whole (Kral 2003). Suicide, which is almost exclusive to Inuit youth, is an issue of major concern in Nunavut.

The Unikkaartuit Project was designed to help understand the context for the high incidence of suicide in Nunavut. The project grew out of discussions between Inuit and qallunaat, including northerners, frontline mental health workers in the North and South, and academics, at the Canadian Association for Suicide Prevention conference held in 1994 in Iqaluit, Nunavut. During a session at the conference on the discussion of ideas for research to address the problem of suicide in Nunavut, one older Inuk spoke. She said that while there were many suicides in her community, she had relatives in another community with almost no history of suicide. She suggested going to a community with few suicides to learn how suicides might be prevented. Even within Nunavut, the prevalence of suicide differs between communities, and it was suggested that research of an ethnographic kind—the gathering of stories—might also allow high suicide communities to learn from the practices and experiences of lower suicide communities.

It was proposed that the research be conducted by a team and that both elders and youth be represented. Inuit participants in the discussion suggested that the research be done by Inuit and qallunaat working together but conducting the research in "the Inuit way" by involving communities, collecting narratives, and working together collaboratively. Questions, they stated, should not only be about suicide but should include an attempt to understand what makes people happy and sad. There was much support for these ideas. Discussions continued in Inuktitut and English with simultaneous translation. After a significant number of ideas had been generated at that session, and subsequently about how a study on the understanding of Inuit suicide could be done from both Inuit and qallunaat (as well as lay and academic) perspectives and aimed toward prevention, a few of us, qallunaat and Inuit, decided to pursue the impulse and plan a study. For the Inuit involved in the project, a primary goal has been to communicate Inuit voices concerning suicide, sadness, happiness, and wellness. Hence the project's title, Unikkaartuit: the people's stories.

I (Michael) had never heard of participatory action research at that point. It was something I learned about soon after, and I realized that this was the best approximation of what I had heard discussed as "research the Inuit way" during our meetings at the conference in Iqaluit. Nobody there had used the term PAR. Instead we had discussed working together toward a practical goal of suicide prevention founded on Inuit knowledge as the most sensible way to do this research. In a real sense I learned about PAR from Inuit before I learned about it from the books.

The next step was to develop a fundable research proposal. Following the Iqaluit conference, an Inuit steering committee was organized by Eva Adams, an Inuk from Iqaluit. A multidisciplinary academic research team from several universities was put together by Michael. Eva played a major role in the development of the steering committee and the project, gathering for the steering committee a group of Inuit who included youth, elders, and others involved in community health and wellness. Her death to cancer during the project was felt as a great loss. Eva's friend and fellow steering committee member Simona Arnatsiaq took over her role of leading that group.

The planning of the study took some time. Initially the research design called for a comparison between a high suicide and a low suicide community. The Inuit steering committee recommended inviting Qikiqtarjuaq (then called Broughton Island, population about 480) and Igloolik (population about 1,200) to represent these high and low suicide communities, respectively. Both communities agreed to join the project. A check of the suicide statistics provided by the then government of the Northwest Territories confirmed the committee's recommendations.

Members of the research team and steering committee met to plan the study, in person and via conference calls, over a two-week period in 1995 at an International Summer Institute funded by the Social Sciences and Humanities Research Council and titled "Social Science Perspectives on Health Service Delivery Issues in Rural and Remote Areas." This institute at Lakehead University was co-organized by one of the academic team members, Bruce Minore, for research teams to meet and plan their proposed studies. Most of the eight southern academic members of the Unikkaartuit Project participated in the institute, and phone conferences were held with the other academics and with the Inuit steering committee in Iqaluit. At the institute we were primarily in touch with Eva Adams, who represented the steering committee meeting in Iqaluit at the same time. We worked together through long days and nights during those two weeks.

After the first week of the institute, the academic research team members were split between wanting to understand Inuit suicide from a clinical epidemiological and social science perspective and wanting to develop a practical, useful project for Nunavut. Understanding versus action, curiosity versus advocacy; it has been a well-known and often debated conflict in academia between basic and applied research (see Wenzel 1997). Some of us felt that we must first study and understand Inuit suicide rather than propose prevention strategies, and others saw this project as primarily an effort toward the development and evaluation of an Inuit-based suicide prevention program.

We mended this split after an academic team member who arrived during the second week helped us see that both sides were critical and that the two positions were not really in opposition. By the end of the institute, we had developed research questions about well-being, unhappiness, and suicide and had elaborated our methodology of working with two communities in this project. It was an intensely productive time, and we realized how lucky we were to have been able to participate in such collaboration prior to the research grant proposal. I (Michael) then returned home and prepared a draft of the proposal that circulated and edited collaboratively for another month before submission. The project was funded by the National Health and Research Development Programs, Health Canada.

The research design called for the elicitation of life history narratives that would reveal Inuit meanings and experiences of wellness, happiness, health, unhappiness, and healing as well as for the collection of stories that would explicate local understanding of causes and consequences of suicide. It was expected that these might vary by generation, sex, or by other sorts of life experiences. The stories were to be elicited via semistructured and open-ended interviews.

The metaphor of the *umiaq* or large skin boat can be used to represent the project. The Inuit steering committee literally steered the study over several years as it progressed from ideas to grant writing to implementation. Youth and elders remained engaged in the project development and execution, and the youth committees in both communities as well as the Baffin Regional Youth Committee were particularly involved in developing appropriate questions and methods. Frequent communications between Michael and Inuit researcher-participants in each of the two communities took place during the six months before fieldwork began, mostly via individual or conference calls. This communication and partnership continued when Michael and the fieldworkers began the data collection in Nunavut.

Implementation

Two Inuit and two qallunaat fieldworkers (one was Michael) conducted the interviews over the course of a month in each community. One of the two Inuit fieldworkers was from Igloolik, but none of the other fieldworkers came from either community. Suggestions for making the study more appropriate to the local context were made by residents of the two communities. The interview schedule was reviewed by a number of Inuit in Igloolik, the first community visited, including members of the youth committee and elders, before any interviews began, and it was discussed and revised slightly. When we were ready with the general questions, we discussed them with two elders working in the community as traditional counselors. One, Anthony Qrunnut, asked that he be interviewed to "test" it out when we were finished. After completing the interview, he paused in thought for what seemed a very long moment. Then the elder broke out in a smile and said that he would ask the same questions in the same way if he were the interviewer. We all smiled together.

In both communities, it was primarily the local youth committees who worked to tailor the study to each community. For example, the Igloolik Youth Committee suggested that rather than rely exclusively on face-to-face interviews, we add an anonymous, open-ended questionnaire for youth in the high schools. This they felt would help ensure privacy and offered young people anonymity as a choice. The suggestion contradicted the belief of some qallunaat researchers from the south who believed that face-to-face methods, including open-ended interviewing, were the only way to go in aboriginal communities. High school youth were invited to participate in the interview or to complete the questionnaire. In the end ninety Inuit between the ages of fourteen and ninety-four were interviewed in the two communities. Another sixty-six students completed the questionnaires administered primarily in classrooms. Our umiaq had many rowers, but the direction was ultimately set by Inuit.

As already noted, the initial plan was to compare two communities that have a high versus a low number of suicides. Qikiqtarjuaq and Igloolik were selected to represent these high and low suicide communities, respectively. By the time of the fieldwork in 1998, however, the suicide rates of these communities were moving in opposite directions. Suicides had decreased significantly in Qikiqtarjuaq, while they had begun to increase dramatically in Igloolik. Thus rather than compare these communities as originally planned, we decided to investigate Inuit experiences of recent social change, including the suicide incidence in each community.

Participants were recruited by multiple means: telephone, home visits, social settings, and word of mouth. Interviews were held either in people's homes or in the project office in each community. All participants were given the option to have the interview conducted in either English or Inuktitut. All elders were interviewed in Inuktitut, while most of the younger participants chose to be interviewed in English. The interviews lasted on average between twenty minutes and one hour, although several were considerably longer or were held over several meetings. Elders' interviews tended fall into this latter group.

All of the interviews were tape-recorded, and nearly all were transcribed and translated. The names of the interviewees were kept confidential, and in order to ensure their anonymity, we made no master list of the interviewees. The matter of anonymity was first raised by the Ethics Review Committee at the University of Windsor (which managed the research grant) rather than by the Inuit steering committee or any of the participants. In hindsight, it seems that the concern with anonymity may reflect qallunaat assumptions, possibly not shared by Inuit, about the supposedly shameful nature of suicide or even about identifying participants. While all the interviewees understood that they would not be identified or associated with their narratives, in retrospect, I (Michael) wish we had given them the option.

The tapes themselves are to be destroyed and have been heard only by the transcriber/translators. The hamlet council in Qikiqtarjuaq requested that someone from outside the small community do the transcribing. The hamlet council of much larger Igloolik had no such concerns, and all of the transcription and translation was done there.

The fieldworkers met each morning to review interviews from the previous day and evening. We would discuss how we came to interview the people we did and what they talked about. This was where sometimes we modified a question based on what we learned from the people we interviewed. There was occasional disagreement about the phrasing of a question or the question itself, resolved by prolonged discussion and checking with youth committee members and others from the community. During the fieldwork, contact *about* the project with representatives of community groups, particularly the youth committees, was frequent. Themes emerged in our daily meetings as the interviews progressed. Prior to leaving each community, the fieldworkers met with the youth committee and representatives of other local organizations to review the major themes that emerged from the interviews. The fieldworkers also went on the local call-in radio to provide feedback and discussion of these themes with community members. We were struck with the consistency of the themes across age and gender and between the two communities.

I (Lori) joined the project after the interviews were completed. Michael and I originally met while I was working for the government of the Northwest Territories as the manager for health promotion. However, my involvement in Unikkaartuit began while I was a policy analyst at the Nunavut Social Development Council (NSDC), an Inuit organization established under article 32 of the Nunavut Land Claims Agreement (see Canada 1993). Under this article, NSDC was responsible for the development of social and cultural policies and programs. Michael and I found that we shared many similar values, including our attitudes toward research in Inuit communities. My involvement with the project was that of an advisor. After the board of the NSDC had agreed to be involved in the project, my role was to provide advice to Michael and advice to the board about the project. I collaborated with Michael, advising him while he wrote the project report for Health Canada and when it was being revised for Nunavut. The board of the NSDC agreed at the time to use the project findings in their annual report on the state of Inuit society and culture.

Major Findings

The major theme across all stories, across age and sex, was the central importance of the family. This should be no surprise since kinship has long been recognized as central to the social lives of Inuit (Briggs 1995; Damas 1968; Guemple 1972). Narratives of wellness, happiness, and sadness were most closely tied to family and kinship. The next most common theme was that of the importance of talking, whether to family, friends, or others in the community. The third theme was IQ (traditional Inuit values and practices) and its importance as part of the foundation for the good life among Inuit. Well-being was linked to the presence of these three themes, and sadness was linked to their absence or change in them.

Many people were concerned about high-speed change in their communities, especially as it contributed to a growing sense of anonymity and social distance. Many people reported that families seemed to be growing apart, both personally and physically. There was significant concern about the increasing segregation of the generations. It seems the elders and youth were both feeling rejected by the other, and each group was waiting for the other to make the first move toward repairing the distance. There was also unease about a decrease or change in traditional cultural practices, including hunting and language. Although Inuit children in Nunavut continue to learn Inuktitut, it is not the Inuktitut spoken by elders (Dorais and Sammons 2002), and this too is a source of friction.

The impact of the suicide epidemic has been horrendous, and in many ways Nunavut has become a place of bereaved survivors. Problems in romantic relationships were found to be the most common precipitating factor in suicides; however, distress among youth is tied to a myriad of factors within the context of social and family change. It was also found that suicide prevention in Qikiqtarjuaq, and in Igloolik since the fieldwork, appears to be tied directly to the community coming together for the well-being of their youth. These activities were typically run by youth in these communities. When the two communities took charge and developed their own activities toward well-being, something very noticeable happened. Suicides stopped for a while, in one case for a few years.

A final project report was submitted to Health Canada (Kral 2003). A revision of that report was disseminated in Nunavut and translated into Inuktitut, co-edited by Michael Kral and Qajaaq Ellsworth, an Inuk from Iqaluit who was a member of the steering committee from the beginning. The Nunavut report would have two new sections, one on policy recommendations and another on positive community examples of activities and programs by and for Inuit youth. These sections will be written by Inuit from a number of different communities in Nunavut.

I (Lori) feel that the Unikkaartuit Project has not only identified the three main themes already noted; it also identified the Inuit holistic version of the person and the Inuk's relations to people and to the environment. The lessons of the Unikkaartuit Project, if understood properly, could be used to advance both social science research and policy decision making in government. For example, the project will be useful not only within the Department of Health and Social Services but could also be helpful in documenting and discussing IQ.

There is growing activity toward suicide prevention in Nunavut. A number of reports on Inuit suicide and its prevention were released in 2003. One was by the Nunavut government on best practices for Inuit suicide prevention (Government of Nunavut 2003). Another was produced by a partnership of Inuit and national organizations (Stevenson and Ellsworth 2003). A comprehensive study was released by the Inungi Sapujjiit Task Force on Suicide Prevention and Community Healing, established by the Legislative Assembly of Nunavut. This last report provides community perspectives on the meaning of suicide and on the well-being of individuals, families, and communities. A national effort parallels the same increase in attention to aboriginal suicide and mental health (Health Canada 2003; Kirmayer and Valaskakis, in press; McCormick 2003; White and Jodoin 2003).

The reception of social science research in Nunavut has been generally positive, calls for Inuit control and involvement notwithstanding. Much anthropological research in the North has been conducted in the spirit of advocacy. This has included work not only on mental and physical health but involving land use and occupancy (Freeman 1976), harvesting research and hunter support (Wenzel 1997, 2000), and archaeology (McCartney 1984). Oral history projects are on the rise in many communities, exemplified by the projects in Igloolik (e.g., MacDonald 1998) and the Interviewing Elders projects at Nunavut Arctic College (see Oosten and Laugrand 1999).

Waters Are Not Always Calm

Although we believe in and enjoy participatory research, and are involved in more of these projects since Unikkaartuit, collective endeavors are human ones that contain human predicaments. We experienced challenges ranging from low-level to threatening of the project's existence. Resolution was attained, but not always to the pleasure of all, through continuous discussion. We encountered individual differences in goals, methods, outlooks, attitudes, and styles of interaction. Stereotypes and biases existed in both the academic and the Inuit community and were sometimes based on negative past experiences. We were not entirely prepared for the fact that collaborative projects take a long time.

Participants changed along the way, as did community organizations. Individuals' levels of commitment also changed over time. Delays were common, often frustrating those who were waiting. The audiotapes and transcribing equipment, for example, moved across three translators in Nunavut when new jobs or family issues prevented the work from being done or completed by a given person. Thus the process of translation and transcription lasted about eighteen months, a great deal longer than planned. At that point, the realities of academic life in the South became the major challenge. Michael's optimal window for analyzing and completing the project had by then expired as he moved into a heavy period of administration and teaching, delaying the project a few years more. This caused some temporary discord with a few participants in the study and with others in the North waiting for the report. Financing was complex. The money ran out and grants expired before the project was finished. Fortunately most of the translations were completed by that time. Yet a few interviews remained untranslated.

The biggest challenge was understanding our different cultural and professional perspectives. We have found that when meeting to discuss research in a group of Inuit and qallunaat, we needed to explain our taken-for-granted concepts to each other. In another study on which we are both working, in one such meeting we found that the Inuit and the qallunaat participants each had to provide our respective cultural meanings of adoption in order to begin discussing research questions on this topic. Our views and experiences of adoption were extremely dissimilar. Our worldviews and perspectives are different, and it takes time and effort to understand each other.

Unikkaartuit research team member Bruce Minore, research director of the Centre for Northern and Rural Health Research at Lakehead University, has noted a number of issues of which students should be aware when considering PAR. One can construct a "dream team" and have incredibly rich input, yet responsibility for the project tends to devolve onto one person, sometimes two. It can be a tremendous responsibility costing much in time, resources, and even personal funds. Having done a large amount of health PAR, Bruce also points out that the participating agencies sometimes do not get the information they think they will receive, for which grant money might have been allocated, and which might make up a significant part of a project. He adds another item for consideration:

> [There is] the difficulty of sustaining relations with communities, simply because people tend to change jobs. So the individuals who are excited and

initially commit to a project move on. Their replacements don't share their enthusiasm (maybe because it wasn't their idea and they want to leave their 'stamp' on the job), and the project loses its support from within. We had one PAR project that was initially embraced by a health director, essentially discounted by her successor, only to be celebrated by that person's replacement. So it finally got done with success, but not without a lot of frustration in the interim. (pers. comm. to MK)

Representation of the Unikkaartuit Project to the public is now a topic of discussion among the participants. At the time of writing we are working carefully together on the Nunavut revision of the report; however, some of the media coverage that has taken place has not pleased everyone. One article in a national newspaper reported that I (Michael) said that Inuit suicide is "caused" by the collision of the Inuit tradition of arranged marriage (suppressed by missionaries and other outsiders more than forty years ago) and introduced western concepts about romance, when in fact I had said that I was going to follow up the finding of a link between suicide and romantic troubles by looking at Inuit models of affinal relationships (marital/common-law/sexual). I do not believe that such a simple linear relationship exists between any single event and suicide (Kral 1998), but more important, it was a lesson for me in how to talk to the press. Although the reporter phoned some of the Inuit experts I had suggested he call, he still emphasized the "academic says" as the voice of authority about people who can speak eloquently for themselves. This is where we hope participatory research can help change the way both non-natives and natives regard previously authoritative knowledge.

We even had some hesitation about including our experiences of the process of the study in this chapter. We checked with the academic and steering committee members to see if they had any objections, and received support. However, similar to what Molly Lee (this volume) has observed, many of our experiences, "anthropological facts," will never be written about. A significant and sustaining strength of such research, in spite of vicissitudes along the way, remains the belief that in working collaboratively, we can do good work.

Directions for a Participatory Anthropology

We have described what is, in part, an indigenization of ethnography. Reflecting on anthropology's place in our current time, Marshall Sahlins (1999) has referred to the indigenization of modernity: the project of cultural reclamation by indigenous peoples through western-global constructs. Yet the path of indigenization goes both ways, as we have indicated. Participatory ethnography in Unikkaartuit emerged from Inuit methods of knowledge production—for example, bridging western research methods with close listening, collective involvement, and significant input from elders. It is important to note that the participatory design of the project, and the primary research questions of examining well-being, sadness, and suicide, came originally from suggestions of Inuit from a number of Nunavut communities. Indigenization thus not only refers to the use of non-indigenous concepts and practices by native peoples but to employing indigenous ones in western thought.

In the Unikkaartuit Project the directions did indeed shift to the benefit of the project. The extended dialogue and rapport often achieved through ethnography were deepened because the central research questions and methods were developed together with those whose lives were being studied. The action component of the project assures that a goal was to make the results useful to Inuit. Collaboration on interpretation and knowledge transfer leaves fewer surprises at the end stage of the research.

A participatory anthropology emerges from a participatory ethnography. Much as ethnography was articulated through what anthropologists were already doing, it is a practice in need of further identification and clarification. In our view, participatory research fills gaps and allows for stronger interpretations and broader understandings of the societies studied. A participatory anthropology is not a too-many-cooks-in-the-kitchen, anything-goes anthropology but one that we believe rests on the foundation of inclusiveness and respect. There is a movement, to be sure, toward a new respect for indigenous peoples by the largely non-indigenous academy, including museums, and by previously colonizing governments. This shifting intersection will include knowing when to ask and also knowing when to remain silent. And it will include not knowing everything. When respect becomes a political ideal, however, we believe that it is change in a good direction; one that opens the new roads of dialogue and knowledge construction. Respect and intermediate views become topics of needed discourse in the globalizing and still indigenous world.

Acknowledgments

We would like to thank Pamela Stern and Lisa Stevenson for their critical editing and Bruce Minore for his memory of the early stages of the Unikkaartuit Project. We also acknowledge the work of research team mem-

bers, including fieldworkers Eva Adams, Leappi Akoomalik, Kristianne Al-
lan, Eemeelayou Arnaquq, Simona Arnatsiaq, Ronald Dyck, Christopher
Fletcher, Laurence Kirmayer, Henri Migala, Bruce Minore, John O'Neil, and
David Wallace; Inuit steering committee members Eva Adams, Louise
Akearok, Simona Arnatsiaq, Rosemary Cooper, Qajaaq Ellsworth, Rosi Ells-
worth, Geela Giroux, Okee Kunuk, Sheila Levy, Annie Nataq, and Udlu
Pishuktie; and the benevolent participation of Inuit in the communities of
Qikiqtarjuaq and Igloolik. The Unikkaartuit report was dedicated to the
memory of steering committee members Eva Adams and Geela Giroux. M.
Kral is grateful for support that went toward the writing of this chapter from
the Canadian Bicentennial Professorship endowment of the Yale Center for
International and Area Studies, the Yale Department of Anthropology, a
SSHRC doctoral fellowship, and the Canadian Polar Commission.

Note

The opinions expressed in this paper are those of the authors and not of the government of
Nunavut or any of its departments. An electronic copy of the *Unikkaartuit* Health Canada report
is available as a free download from the National Inuit Youth Council (www.niyc.ca).

FOUR

Time, Space, and Memory

Murielle Nagy

When the raven became aware of himself,
light came into the world,
and grass tussocks turned into men.
                    Creation. Anonymous Eastern Inuit

Anthropologists working in the Arctic do not always have the time and opportunity before undertaking fieldwork to learn the language(s) of the people with whom they will work. Hence they need to hire local research assistants who will act as interpreters during the interviews. Since oral narratives are often the major sources of information with which anthropologists will work, the recorded interviews need to be transcribed and translated. However, translations are not perfect duplicates of the original narratives; they are only equivalents (e.g., Hannoum 2002; Tihanyi 2002). Although translators do their best to transfer into another language what the narrators have said, there are times when the original meaning of words and expressions is distorted, if not lost, during the translation process. Furthermore, once anthropologists interpret translated narratives, there is another level of translation going on, and if the translations do not represent the intention of the narrator, elements of the narratives may be misinterpreted.

Yet when the researcher realizes that translations of specific words from the original are somewhat peculiar and the words are given in a variety of different ways by the translators, the translations themselves can become a source of information. Indeed one then wonders why the translator chose to translate the words in that way. Was it to get the closest equivalent in the language of the translation and thus make the translation more fluid? But more important, were words changed because the translator could not find similar concepts in the language of the translation? The answers to such questions can help us to understand better the language and the culture of the narrator. This chapter deals with the theoretical and methodological implications of undertaking anthropological research through translation. More specifically I discuss how Inuvialuit talk about events in the past and how translators choose to translate their words. I became interested in the representations of time, space, and memory in narratives while editing English translations of archival tapes and interviews done with Inuvialuit elders during oral history projects (see Nagy 1994, 1999).[1]

Context of Research

The Inuvialuit make up the Inuit population living in the Northwest Territories of Canada. The traditional territory of the indigenous Inuvialuit extended approximately from Barter Island in the west to Cape Lyon in the east. Before contacts with whalers, traders, and missionaries at the end of the nineteenth century, their population is estimated to have been two thousand (Franklin 1971 [1828]: 86–228; Petitot 1876: x). The Inuvialuit were thus one of the largest Inuit populations in the Arctic before drastic decimation due to epidemics in the first two decades of the twentieth century (McGhee 1974: xi; D. G. Smith 1984: 349). By that time trapping had become the major economic activity and it was to flourish until the 1970s. In the land-claim agreement of 1984, the Inuinnait of Holman (on Victoria Island) became part of the Inuvialuit. Today, the Inuvialuit number about five thousand (Inuit Tapiriit Kanatami 2002).

The Inuvialuit belong to three distinct linguistic groups. They are the Uummarmiut, who live in the Mackenzie Delta in the communities of Aklavik and Inuvik; the Siglit, who live in the coastal communities of Tuktoyaktuk, Paulatuk, and Sachs Harbour on Banks Island; and the Kangiryuarmiut, who live in the community of Holman on Victoria Island (see map 4.1). The dialects of each linguistic group (which are named by adding the suffix -tun to the ethnonym) are mainly spoken by elders over sixty years old.[2] *Uummarmiut* means "people of the evergreens and willows." They are the descendants of people from Alaska who moved to the Mackenzie Delta at the end of the nineteenth century, again in the 1920s as muskrat trapping developed in the Mackenzie Delta, and finally in the mid-1930s and 1940s as stores closed down near the Alaska/Yukon border (see Nagy 1994). Linguistic evidence indicates that the majority of these people came from the

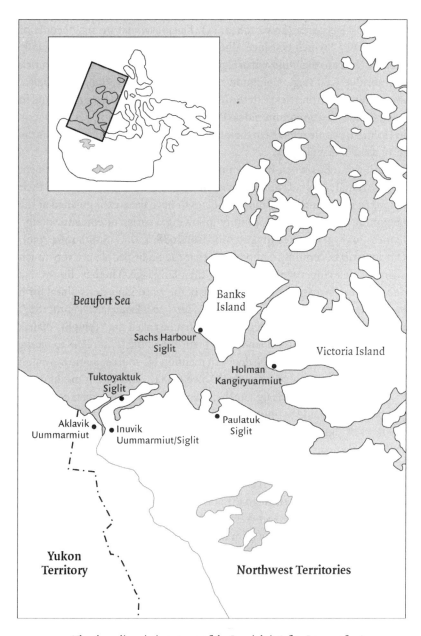

Beaufort Sea

Banks
Island

Victoria Island

Sachs Harbour
Siglit

Holman
Kangiryuarmiut

Tuktoyaktuk
Siglit

Aklavik
Uummarmiut

Inuvik
Uummarmiut/Siglit

Paulatuk
Siglit

Yukon
Territory

Northwest Territories

4.1. The three linguistic groups of the Inuvialuit (after Lowe 1985a).

Anaktuvuk Pass area (Lowe 1984a: xv). *Kangiryuarmiut* means "people of the large bay," which is Prince Albert Sound on Victoria Island. Culturally they are closer to the Inuinnait of Kugluktuk (Coppermine) and Ikaluktutiak (Cambridge Bay) (e.g., Collignon 1996; Condon 1996). Hence the dialect they speak has strong ties with the Inuinnaqtun spoken in Kugluktuk and in other Central Arctic communities (Dorais 1990: 194). During our interviews in Holman, people referred to their language as Inuinnaqtun, and this is the term used in this chapter.

Until the 1980s when the Committee for Original Peoples Entitlement (COPE) initiated a study of the Inuvialuit dialects, the Siglit people and their language were thought by most scholars to have been extinguished at the beginning of the twentieth century following a series of epidemics (e.g., Jenness 1928: 3; McGhee 1974: 5; Morrison 1988: 4; D. G. Smith 1984: 356). Our interviews certainly demonstrate that the Siglit people are very much alive and that elders are still speaking their language. There is, however, a debate as to the origin and the meaning of the word *Sigliq* or its plural form *Siglit*. The term appears in Émile Petitot's *Les Grands Esquimaux* (Petitot 1887) and in his French/Eskimo dictionary of what he called the "Tchiglit" dialect (Petitot 1876). D. G. Smith (1984: 357) writes that the term refers to paired labrets worn by males, but he does not mention his source. Some Inuvialuit elders suggested to linguist Ronald Lowe (1984b: viii) that it might come from an Indian word to designate them, but Athabaskan linguists consulted by Lowe were unable to find a possible source for the word. However, most speakers of Siglitun agree that the term *Siglit* is used by other people to refer to them (Nagy 1994: 2). The word *Inuvialuit* is used by speakers of the Siglit dialect to refer to themselves wherever they live. The suffix *-vialuk* (plural form *-vialuit*, as in *Inuvialuit*) is indeed unique to the Siglit dialect. However, for the last thirty years, through the political process of land claims, the term has been used to refer to all Western Arctic Inuit residing in the Inuvialuit territory. As a final note, the term *Inuvialuktun* refers to all three of the Inuvialuit dialects, as to say "the language of the Inuvialuit."

Initial Observations on the English Translations

Since the narratives I edited and analyzed came from projects aimed at collecting oral histories about the Yukon north slope and Banks Island, most of the interviews were about life experiences in these regions. The people interviewed spoke about where they used to live and what kind of activities took place there. There were some obvious differences in the ways men and women recalled specific events and details. The men interviewed focused mainly on subsistence activities and did not incorporate their stories into a chronological framework. Hence they could easily recall the number of animals they hunted and trapped, but they rarely mentioned during which years an event took place. In contrast, women were well aware of when events happened and often set their stories about specific places in relation to which of their children was born there. For example, Persis Gruben mentioned that "the first time we went to De Salis Bay, that year Sarah was born" (Aulavik-71A: 8 in Nagy 1999a). This way of using what has been called "family memory" has been noted by researchers interviewing women, particularly housewives (Baillargeon 1993: 62). In the case of the Inuvialuit women we interviewed, the birth of their children was used not only to give a temporal dimension to their stories but also to remember specific camps where people had lived.

One issue that particularly interested me in the English translations I worked with was the pervasive use of the present tense. Although these dialects all have a "present declarative" form that can be used in some contexts to refer to an event that is past (Lowe 1985a: 144), the English translators often chose to use the present tense in English. Why? It is possible that this is a reflection of the colloquial English spoken by the translators. However, it seems more likely that once the speaker makes it clear that he or she is going to talk about past events—by saying, for example, "when I was young" or "at that time"—then there is no need to emphasize that the story is happening in the past; hence the use of narrative present (see Lowe 1985c: 112). As remarked by Charles (2000: 38) about the Yup'ik language, "the narrative takes the listener . . . to the past and the past becomes present." The use of the narrative present also indicates that telling a story means to reenact particular experiences and to perform it (e.g., Hymes 1981). Traditional narratives in Inuinnaqtun like those collected by Métayer (1973) also show this lack of use of past tense, at least in their French translations.

However, there is another facet of Inuit worldview that helps to explain the pervasive use of the present tense. When narrators of both genders talked about the past, they did not seem to go back into time but rather into the places where events happened, and as previously mentioned, once they mentioned a specific place, Inuvialuit women would then add information about chronology through information related to the birth or the age of their children. The use of numerous locative suffixes (which were largely lost in the English translations) demonstrates how important space is in Inuvialuktun. Thus a "when" question was sometimes answered by a location rather than a time period. This linguistic merging of space and time was also mentioned by Mark Nuttall in his work with Greenlanders: "What is noticeable about the stories people told me about these areas . . . is how space and time become synchronized" (Nuttall 2001: 63).

This ethnographic observation is borne out linguistically. Although Uummarmiutun has a past declarative form, Siglitun and Inuinnaqtun do not have a past declarative form but do have suffixes and localizers (e.g., *taimani*, "at that time") to indicate past events. The prefix *ta-* is also used in other localizers and indicates a distance not only in space but also in time, as linguist Ronald Lowe explains: "In the particular case of the prefix ta-, the Eskimo language groups under the same sign, under the same representation in tongue, two sets of particular impressions: those related to space and those related to time. The two categories of space and time appear here indeterminate in tongue: they both belong to the general impression of distance" (Lowe 1985b: 220).

Lowe's observation certainly relates to my experience of asking a "when" question and getting a "where" answer. It should also be noted that in the three Inuvialuit dialects, the suffix *-vik* means both "a place or a time for X-ing" (Lowe 1983: 170, 1984a: 192, 2001: 360). Since here space and time are fused, only the context can tell which one is invoked.

Among the Inuvialuit, as in Inuit culture in general, narratives about places are numerous and history is intimately linked to toponymy. Place names themselves are part of what Nuttall (1992) has called memoryscape and are used as mnemonic devices (e.g., "the place where X happened"). As Béatrice Collignon (1996) demonstrated, toponyms are essential not for traveling or survival but to the integration of humans in their milieu, which then becomes humanized and allows cultures to flourish. Place names are used mainly as anchor points of history (Collignon 1996: 116). The traveler who knows the toponyms of an area will use them not to get oriented but to be connected to the land in a familiar way (117). This intimate link to the land and its temporal connotations was expressed beautifully by Mark Emerak: "I should send (that story) somewhere to the land where I first got my memory" (Aulavik-76B:1 in Nagy 1999b).

During our interviews with Inuvialuit who had lived on Banks Island, we were able to collect only a few toponyms, yet people interviewed had a definite knowledge of particular areas since they were able to show us on a map where they hunted and trapped. The majority of toponyms were those of camps, hence social places where families had lived. Although one might think that the people we interviewed simply did not have a good knowledge or memory of toponyms, this does not seem to be the proper explanation. A case in point is that of Edith Haogak, who was born in the 1930s and raised in the Kangiryuak (Prince Albert Sound) region on the western part of Victoria Island but who also traveled to Banks Island with her parents to hunt. In the late 1950s she moved to Sachs Harbour on Banks Island. Hence she had been living on Banks Island for almost forty years when we interviewed her. Having been a widow early in her adult life, she had to support her family by hunting and trapping on the island. Although she was one of the few people who knew most of the Inuinnaqtun toponyms for the east coast of Banks Island (the west and south coasts having mainly Siglitun and English names), these amounted to less than ten. Yet she had an extensive knowledge of more than 120 toponyms from the west coast of Victoria Island where she was raised. Hence Collignon's idea that toponyms are mainly landmarks of history rather than travel and survival aids seem to be well supported here. Indeed, as Cruikshank (1990: 354) remarked, toponyms do much more than identify places; they allow people to point in space to talk about time—they provide an entry to the past.

First Childhood Memories

An exception to the use of the narrative present is when narrators talk about their first childhood memories. Here past forms were used in the English translations of these narratives. While editing the English translations of interviews done during the Aulavik Oral History Project, I started to collect excerpts related to first childhood memories as I was intrigued by the manner in which these were expressed. Indeed Inuvialuit elders often started to tell about their lives by using words that can be translated in English by "when I became aware," "I came to my senses when," or "when I first started remembering" (see table 4.1, examples 1, 2, and 7), as if before that time, the child—who the narrator then was—could not remember anything since his or her consciousness had not been totally awakened. Furthermore, the use of "could" and "started" in the English translations ("when I first *could* remember," "when I first *started* remembering"; see table 4.1, examples 5, 6, and 7) made me think that in Inuvialuit dialects, the act of remembering first childhood memories might be expressed as starting in the past and not from present to the past, as in English (e.g., "I remember when X happened").

My earlier observations on first childhood memories being from English translations, I feared that my interpretation could be incorrect, since the meanings of Inuvialuktun words might have been lost or distorted through

Table 4.1. Examples of English translations from Inuvialuktun, with
original transcription and morphological analysis.

No.	Example	Dialect
1	[. . .] when I became aware [. . .] [. . .] *ilitchurigama* [. . .] ilitchuri = become aware, gama = causative (when), 1st sing.	Siglitun
2	I came to my senses when [. . .] *Ilitchurimmariksimmiyuami* [. . .] ilitchuri = become aware, mmarik = to X well, sima = having been X-ed, mmi = to also X, yuami = simple declarative, 1st sing.	Siglitun
3	I became aware when there was a sunshine. *Hiqinnarmi ilitchurinaqtuami.* hiqinnarmi = when there was sun, ilitchuri = become aware, naq = to cause a feeling of, tuami = simple declarative, 1st sing.	Siglitun
4	At the time I began to remember I was being packed by someone. *Taavyumani ilitchuriyuami aamaaqhiq&unga.* taavyumani = at the time, ilitchuri = become aware, yuami = simple declarative, 1st sing., aamaaq = packing a baby on back, hiq = to be X-ed, &unga = conjunctive (while), 1st sing.	Siglitun
5	[. . .] when I could remember [. . .] [. . .] *qauyiblunga* [. . .] qauyi = become aware, blunga = conjunctive (while), 1st sing.	Inuinnaqtun
6	[. . .] when I first could remember [. . .] [. . .] *tavJa ilitchurikkara* [. . .] tavJa = when, ilitchuri = become aware, kkara = past declarative, 1st sing.	Uummarmiutun
7	[. . .] when I first started remembering [. . .] [. . .] *qauyilirama* [. . .] qauyi = become aware, liq = to start doing X, rama = causative (when), 1st sing.	Inuinnaqtun
8	[. . .] when I could not forget anymore [. . .] [. . .] *puigulimaiq&unga* [. . .] puigu = forget, limaiq = cannot any longer, &unga = conjunctive (while), 1st sing.	Siglitun
9	That's when my memory was good. You know, when kids start remem- bering [. . .] *qauyimmariktunga. Nutaqalli* [. . .] *qauyimmarikpaliaqpaktun.* qauyi = become aware, mmarik = to X well, tunga = simple declarative, 1st sing. Nutaqalli = nutaqa = child, Ili = as for, qauyi = become aware, mmarik = to X well, paliaq = to X more and more, pak = habitual action, tun = simple declarative, 3rd pl.	Inuinnaqtun

Note: & is a voiceless lateral fricative sound. J is a retroflex fricative sound, halfway between the English r and
the French j.

Sources: For the English translations and Inuvialuit transcriptions, Nagy, ed. (1999a, 1999b, 1999c, 1999d).

the process of translation (e.g., Galley 1990; Swann 1992). Inuvialuit dialects being extremely different from English, it is inevitable that some distortion did occur. Indeed one word in Inuvialuktun can easily be translated as a full sentence in English since Inuvialuit dialects use wordbases and suffixes, and thus words "agglutinate" in one single word (e.g., table 4.1). Furthermore, I was intrigued by the fact that all translators had used past forms to translate words linked to first childhood memories. I wondered if past forms had been used in the original interviews. I was especially curious since in the majority of the translations not related to first memories, the narrative present was used. Hence I decided to analyze the original Inuvialuktun transcriptions and to isolate words that were linked to talking about first memories. In the next sections of this chapter, I discuss the results of my research.

Understanding Translations of First Childhood Memories

Since the focus of the Aulavik Oral History Project was on Banks Island, most of the interviews were done in Siglitun and Inuinnaqtun, which are the Inuvialuit dialects of the two main populations who have occupied the island. I first complied 245 examples of English translations related to early memories found in the interviews of thirty-seven Inuvialuit. I then selected the 219 examples for which Inuvialuktun transcriptions were available and, using the dictionaries and grammars written by linguist Ronald Lowe for the three dialects, I did morphological analyses, which I compared with the English translations done by the Inuvialuit translators. Not being a linguist, I followed Lowe's terminology, which is influenced by Gustave Guillaume's methodology. Although seven translators were involved in the translations, most interviews were translated by three translators: one Uummarmiutun speaker who did English translations from Uummarmiutun, Siglitun, and Inuinnaqtun; one Siglitun speaker who did mainly English translations from Siglitun, and one Inuinnaqtun speaker who did mainly English translations from Inuinnaqtun. Incidentally, 60 percent (N = 132) of the data selected is in Inuinnaqtun, 38 percent (N = 83) in Siglitun, and only 2 percent (N = 4) in Uummarmiutun (see table 4.2).

As mentioned earlier, only one of the three dialects, Uummarmiutun (which is very close to the Iñupiaq language of Alaska), has a past declarative form. Siglitun and Inuinnaqtun have a simple declarative form that can be used to refer to an event that is present or past. All dialects have suffixes and localizers that can be used to indicate past events. Furthermore, as noted

Table 4.2. Frequency of use by narrators and by translators of memory-related terms in Inuvialuit dialects.

Inuvialuit terms	Translation from dictionaries	Translations mainly used by translators*	Uummarmiutun (N = 4)	Siglitun (N = 83)	Inuinnaqtun (N = 132)
ihuma-	think	could remember	0	0	6
ilihima- / ilisima-	know	know, could remember, remember	1	12(14%)	13(10%)
ilitchari-	become aware, learn	remember, came to senses, became aware, started remembering	2	45(54%)	13(10%)
kangiqsi-	understand	can't understand	0	3	1
nalu-	unconscious, don't know	forgot, don't remember, don't know	0	2	7
nautchi-	watch what is going on	aware	1	2	0
puiguq-	forget	can't forget, could not forget, remember, had good memory	0	16(19%)	18(13%)
qauyi-	become aware, learn**	first started remembering, first could remember, became aware	0	0	41(31%)
qauyima-	be aware, know**	first started remembering	0	0	14(11%)
tupak-	wake up	like waking up, woke up first time	0	1	13(10%)
other terms	see table 4.3	see table 4.3	0	2	6

*Use of past tense indicated as in translations.

**Lowe (pers. comm., 2002) suggested different translations for qauyi- and qauyima- since the suffix -ma- means "having been X-ed."

by Lowe (1985a: 122), "a certain number of wordbases can refer to past or present depending on the situational or linguistic context." He also wrote that the distinction between past and present was of secondary importance in Siglitun (129). Although this seemed to be the case for most of our interviews, that statement puzzled me since the past was used in the English translations and Inuvialuktun transcriptions on first childhood memories. Indeed, 40 percent (N = 33) of the Siglitun data analyzed had event markers in the simple declarative form with suffixes (e.g., -ma-, "having been X-ed"; -maakiq-, "starting to X"; -lraaq-, "first"; -nraq-, "to X for the first time") and/or localizers (e.g., *taimani*, "at that time") that can suggest the past, and 17 percent (N = 14) were in the conjunctive form (i.e., "while" clause). For Inuinnaqtun, 30 percent (N = 39) of the data was in the simple declarative form with suffixes and/or localizers that can suggest the past; 27 percent (N = 36) in the causative form (i.e., "when" clause); and 16 percent (N = 21) in the conjunctive form (i.e., "while" clause).

This extensive use of the past when talking about first childhood memories has also been noted by Swift (2000: 101) for the Inuit of Nunavik (arctic Quebec), who then invariably used the suffix -lauqsima- ("long ago past"). Use of the past for similar translations to those encountered in the present study were found in the life stories of Inuit elders from the central and eastern Canadian Arctic (e.g., Briggs 2000; Mannik 1998; Oosten et al. 1999).

Working among the Nunamiut, Gubser (1965: 211) observed that "when a mature person speaks of his early youth, he refers to the time when he began to remember everything." This comment and Lowe's (1985a: 232) statement that "the past is a space of time from which bygone facts can only be recalled" influenced me to think that the use of the past by Inuvialuit narrators and translators was to set temporally the first childhood memories to be recalled and hence narrated. Contrary to what I first thought by interpreting only the English translations, the act of remembering was not the only subject discussed by the narrators; they also were qualifying and contextualizing their first memories. In fact, as we will see later, the narrators were indicating cognitive and chronological markers about themselves.

As reflected by their use of the wordbases *ilitchuri-* in Siglitun, and *qauyi-* and *qauyima-* in Inuinnaqtun, the narrators emphasized the time when their memories started. These wordbases are translated in dictionaries by "become aware, become conscious, come to senses" but also as "learn, know" (see Fortescue et al. 1994: 291). For Inuinnaqtun, Lowe (pers. comm., 2002) suggested a distinction between *qauyi-* ("become aware, learn") and *qauyima-* ("be aware, know") since the latter has the suffix -ma-, which indi-

Table 4.3. Translations of memory-related terms in Inuvialuit dialects.

English translations	Uummarmiutun	Siglitun	Innuinaqtun
become aware; become conscious; learn	qauJi-[1], ilitchuri-[4]		qauyi-[1]
come to senses		ilitchuriyuaq[4]	
be aware; be conscious; know	qauJima-[2]	ilitchuriyuaq[4]	qauyima-[2]
my memory			qauyimautiga[2]
is unconscious, is numb (is not aware)	qauJimaitchuq[2]		qauyimaittuq[2]
become unconscious		naluksituaq	nalukhi-[9]
be aware; watch X do something;			
took notice of X	nautchiu-	nautchiugaa	
recognized him	iliharigaa[3]	ilitariyaa[3]	ilitariyaa[3]
recognizes	ilihaqaJiJuq	qauyiyaa[1]	
knows	ilihimaJuq[5]	ilisimayuaq[5], qauyima-[1]	ilihimayuq[6]
doesn't know him/her/it	nalugaa[9]	naluyaq[9]	ilihimannigttuq
remembers	itqaqtuq[6]	itqaqtuaq[6]	itqariyaa[6]
tries to remember; recall	itqarniaqtuq[6]		itqakhaiyuq[6]

[1]Fortescue et al. (1994: 291): PE qa(C)un(əi)- "become conscious"; Naukan Siberian Yup'ik qaazi- "remember come to senses, become aware"; ECI qauyi- "notice, become aware of"; GRI qaaqqut(i)- "come to one's senses." For Iñupiaq, qaurl- "to become aware, of a growing child" in MacLean (1980: 48). For Inuinnaqtun, Lowe (pers. comm., 2002) suggested qauyi- "become aware, learn."

[2]Fortescue et al. (1994: 291): WCI qauyima- "know"; ECI qauyima- "know." For Inuinnaqtun, Lowe (pers. comm., 2002) suggested qauyima- "be aware, know."

[3]Fortescue et al. (1994: 105): PE əlit- "learn"; Sirenik (Chukotka) is(tə) "learn"; also siqəxt?R "recall, bring to awareness."

[4]Fortescue et al. (1994: 106): PI əlitcuRə- "become aware of"; WCI ilitsuri "know, become aware, learn"; GRI ilitsuRi- "become aware or conscious, remember something from earliest childhood."

[5]Fortescue et al. (1994: 105): PE əlicima- "know"; Naukan Siberian Yup'ik = "understand."

[6]Fortescue et al. (1994: 112): PE ənqaR- "remember"; WCI itqaq- "remember"; ECI iaaq(q)- "remember, be full of attention for."

cates a result and means "having been X-ed" (see also Briggs 1998: 236). In the Inuvialuktun narratives, ilitchuri-, qauyi-, and qauyima- were mostly translated by the verb "remember" in English (see table 4.1). However, the use of the word "remember" is somewhat misleading since the Inuvialuit narrators are not talking about remembering now about the past but telling when they began to become aware or conscious. In other words, they are remembering about beginning to remember, about being "able to remember" (see Mannik 1998: 209, 216). Once they made such statements, the narrators (and the translators) used the present form (as in "I remember when"), since they were now in the process of remembering about specific events. Similar patterns associated with the use of the past to talk about first childhood memories, and then the use of the present for introducing later memories, can be found in other Inuit narratives. Thus after being asked if

Table 4.3. Continued.

English translations	Uummarmiutun	Siglitun	Innuinaqtun
remember		ilitchuri-[4]	ilihima-[5],
		ilisima-[5]	qauyima-[2]
			ilitchuri-[4/7],
			ilituri-[4/8]
recalls	itqaraa[6]	itqagaa[6]	
recalled someone		itaqaiyuaq[6]	
distracted, lost, confused			ulapit-
understands	kangiqhiJuq	kangiqsiyuaq,	kangiqhiyuq,
		uingaigaa	uingaiqtuq
doesn't understand		uingayaq	kangihimaittuq,
			uingayuq
is difficult, impossible, to understand	kangiqhinaitchuq	uingaiqsiriittuq	nalunaqtuq[9]
wake up	itiqtuq	tupaktuaq	tupaktuq
forget	puiguq-	puiguq-	puiguq-
never forgets		puiguyuittuq	

[7]The base *ilitchuri-* was used by three Inuinnaqtun speakers living in Sachs Harbour where Siglitun is the main Inuvialuktun dialect.

[8]Two Inuinnaqtun speakers, who live in Sachs Harbour, used the base *ilitturi-* which seems equivalent to *ilitchuri-*.

[9]Fortescue et al. (1994: 212): PE na&u- "not know"; Sirenik (Chukotka) na&ikə(s)- "lose consciousness."

Note: Italics are used for English translations and terms that were not in Lowe's publications.

& is a voiceless lateral fricative sound. J is a retroflex fricative sound, halfway between the English r and the French j.

PE = Proto-Eskimo; PI = Proto-Inuit; WCI = Western Canadian Inuit; ECI = Eastern Canadian Inuit; GRI = Greenlandic Inuit.

Sources: Lowe (1983, 1984a, 1984b, 1985a, 1985b, 1985c, 2001) and Nagy, ed. (1999a, 1999b, 1999c, 1999d).

he recalled when he "started remembering," Hervé Paniaq explained that he recalled being on his mother's back, but "after that, I would have to reverse the events to talk about them" (Oosten and Laugrand 1999: 45). He seems to be indicating that for these later memories, he would need to remember events from his past rather than describing the moment when he actually started remembering.[3]

In the Siglitun data, *ilitchuri-* was used in 54 percent (N = 5), and in Inuinnaqtun, *qauyi-* was used in 31 percent (N = 41), *qauyima-* in 11 percent (N = 14), and *ilitchuri-* in 10 percent (N = 13) (see table 4.2). Hence in Inuinnaqtun 52 percent (N = 68) of the data referred to "becoming or being aware" (see table 4.2). One should note that the word *ilitchuri-*, which does not seem to be an Inuinnaqtun word, was used by Inuinnaqtun speakers who had learned Siglitun later in life. As for the word *itqaq-*, which is the closest equivalent to the verb "remember" in English, it was used in less than 1 percent in either Siglitun or Inuinnaqtun. Although this should be verified, *iqtaq-* was probably used more often when the narrators referred to their later memories. However, when introducing their first childhood memories, most narrators used the wordbases *ilitchuri-*, *qauyi-*, and *qauyima-*. This observation must be common to other Inuit cultures, since the Iñupiaq word *qauJi-* (spelled *qaurl-* in MacLean 1980: 48) is translated by "to become aware, of a growing child" (48), and the Greenlandic form of *ilitchuri-* by "became aware or conscious, remember something from earliest childhood" (Fortescue et al. 1994) (see also table 4.3).

To follow up on this last example, after presenting an earlier version of this paper I was told by a Greenlander colleague that "coming to one's senses" corresponds to a stage in child development equivalent to a two-year-old (Mariekatherine Poppel, pers. comm., 2001). In his interview, Lucassie Nutaraaluk was asked when he "became aware," and he answered "at two or three years old," as he was still breast fed at the time (Oosten et al. 1999: 105). This would explain translations such as "I came to my senses sucking a bottle," "I became aware when there was a sunshine," or "I became aware on the back of my mother" (see table 4.1, examples 3 and 4), where the narrators explained what they were feeling or doing at that precise moment. People also used the word *tupak-* ("wake up"), as in "when I woke up," which was likewise noted by Condon (1996: 63) during his own interviews in Holman. Incidentally, some Yupiit described conversion to Christianity as "waking up" (see Fienup-Riordan 2000: 94), which is similar to one Inuvialuk narrator who spoke of "becoming conscious" when converting (see N92–253-196A:1 in Nagy 1999b).

As Charles (2000: 44) remarked about the Yupiit, "the early years of memory are sometimes referred to as drifting between remembering bits and pieces of first realities, like going into a deep sleep." Indeed Yup'ik parents assumed that very young children lacked awareness or a lasting memory of their experiences (Fienup-Riordan 1994: 143). In the Central Yup'ik language of southwestern Alaska, the word *ellangelleq* means "awareness of existence, consciousness of a world process going on about one" and refers to a child's first conscious memories, between the ages of three and five (Orr et al., 1997: 614, footnote 4).[4] *Ellangellemni* means "when I became aware" and is "an expression Yup'ik people often use to refer to a significant moment of life, the point in one's childhood when permanent memories take shape and surroundings begin to make lasting impressions" (Orr et al.

1997: back cover). In the Eastern Arctic, the wordbase *suqqui-* is translated by "to become aware" (e.g., Oosten and Laugrand 2001: 96), while *qauyima-* is translated by "to be aware, to know, to understand (e.g., Briggs 1998: 236; see also footnote 2 in table 4.3).[5] Hence the awakening of consciousness is seen as a prerequisite to building a memory.

It thus seems that in Inuit languages when one talks about first childhood memories, these are introduced through terms that are linked to two stages of cognitive development among children. In the Inuvialuit narratives, this first stage was often introduced by terms translated by "when I came to my senses" or "when I became aware" (see table 4.1, examples 1 to 4) with a vivid description of feelings or actions during that precise moment (e.g.: "on my mother's back," "sucking a bottle," "when there was a sunshine," "alone in an igloo," "crying"). Narrators often insisted that there were still periods of unconsciousness ("I would forget").

Terms that were translated by "when I could not forget anymore, "when my memory was good," or even "when kids start remembering" (see table 4.1, example 9) correspond to a later stage, starting around five years old, when a child "gets a memory" (Mariekatherine Poppel, pers. comm., 2001). While referring to that stage, narrators insisted that at that time, they knew (i.e., they had gained permanent knowledge). Writing about the Nunamiut, Gubser (1965: 211) contrasted the child of two or three years old, who is always forgetting, with the child of four or five, who stops forgetting and begins to remember things when the child's *ishuma* (mind) has thus been formed.[6] Gubser added that the Nunamiut think of the ishuma as the seat of memory. Hence without a fully formed ishuma, one cannot store memories. Furthermore, in Nunavik (arctic Quebec), the term *isumanniq* means that a child has reached a state of consciousness at four or five years old (Schneider 1985: 102; Therrien 1987: 85–86). At the same age, Yup'ik children gained awareness and thus reached a stage of maturity in which memory was continuous rather than fragmented as in younger children (Fienup-Riordan 1994: 143, 145; 2000: 96). According to Eliza Orr, that later stage of development, a consciousness of one's self existing in an intelligible world of meanings and relationships, is called *usvinglleq* ("sense, understanding") in Yup'ik and corresponds to five years old or older (Orr et al. 1997: 614, footnote 4).[7]

The terms that were used by Inuvialuit elders when talking about their first childhood memories and those that can be found in other Inuit languages demonstrate a lexical sophistication that one finds in English only when reading literature specialized in cognitive development (e.g., Perner and Ruffman 1995; Tulving 1995). Hence it is possible that the Inuvialuit translators had difficulty finding equivalent English words for those used by the narrators, and they chose the word "remember" to convey the meaning of Inuvialuktun words that were very specific about two stages of awareness in children's development. The use of various past forms in the translations and in the original transcriptions was to set the event temporally and to give more precision regarding which stage of cognitive development the narrator had reached as a child. It would be interesting to verify if the same terms are used in non-autobiographical narratives of Inuit since in Yup'ik narrations, "a character's state of awareness is sometimes mentioned" (Orr et al. 1997: 614, footnote 4).

Conclusions

The theoretical and methodological implication of undertaking anthropological research through translations is a topic that warrants more attention from social scientists. My experience demonstrates that analyzing the inconsistencies and difficulties in translation helps us better understand Inuit language and culture. For example, the pervasive use of the present tense when describing past events may be explained by the Inuit synchronization of time and space. In contrast, the use of the past tense to describe first childhood memories led to the observation that a series of distinct wordbases in the Inuvialuit dialects were being translated by the single English word "remember."

Inuvialuit elders often started to tell about their lives by using wordbases like ilitchuri- andqauyi-, which can be translated by "when I became aware." Morphological analyses of excerpts from the Inuvialuktun interviews have shown that first childhood memories narrated in Inuvialuit dialects—and very likely in other Inuit languages—express when the consciousness of a child is awoken. However, in most cases wordbases like ilitchuri- and qauyi- were translated with the verb "remember," possibly to fit an English ear. The use of various past forms in the translations and the original transcriptions gave the temporal context and more precision regarding two stages of cognitive development. The first stage corresponds to about two to three years old, when a child "becomes aware" for the very first time; and the second to about four to five years old, when a child is fully aware and thus can store continuous memories. To verify these interpretations, I hope to consult the Inuvialuit translators to discuss the ways they translated Inuvialuktun words related to first childhood memories. Finally, the lesson from this research is that one should be careful when using translations, as they are often approximations of what was said by narrators.

Acknowledgments

Most sincere thanks to all the Inuvialuit elders who participated in the Yukon North Slope Inuvialuit Oral History Project and the Aulavik Oral History Project as well as to Inuvialuit research assistants Renie Arey, Elizabeth Banksland, Shirley Elias, Jean Harry, and Agnes White. Translations and transcriptions were done by Barbra Allen, Beverly Amos, Helen Kitekud-lak, Agnes Kuptana, and Agnes White. The projects were administered by the Inuvialuit Social Development Program in Inuvik. Funding and logistical support was provided by Parks Canada, the Yukon Heritage Branch, the Language Enhancement Program (GNWT), the Polar Continental Shelf Programme, and the Inuvik Research Center. Earlier versions of this paper were presented in November 2001 at the symposium on Memory and History in the North at the Lac Delage (Quebec), at the Annual Meeting of the American Anthropological Association in Washington, and in August 2002 at the Inuit Studies Conference in Anchorage. During the winter of 2002, I received financial support from the SSHRC project "Memory and History in Nunavut" to work on this paper. An extended version of this chapter was published in Nagy (2002). I also want to thank Jean Briggs, Louis-Jacques Dorais, Vivian Johnson, Lawrence Kaplan, Mick Mallon, Patricia Nagy, Mariekatherine Poppel, William Schneider, Michèle Therrien, and Deborah Kigjugalik Webster for their comments on issues related to first childhood memory. I am especially thankful to Ronald Lowe, Pamela Stern, and Lisa Stevenson for their suggestions on the structure of the text, their comments on its content, and their editorial help. Ronald Lowe also provided corrections for the spelling of the Inuvialuktun words and for the morphological analyses that can be found in my tables. Any misinterpretations are of course mine.

Notes

The original reference to Creation is in Houston (1972: 80), reprinted in Petrone (1988: 51). Thanks to Deborah Kigjugalik Webster for drawing my attention to it.

1. During these projects, we did a total of 140 interviews with 55 people and got about 100 archival tapes translated into English. Most interviews were done in the native language of the speakers.

2. Estimates made in 1981, based on the assumption that most Inuvialuit over forty spoke their dialect fluently, put their number at 215 for Siglitun; 175 for Uummarmiutun; and 125 for

Kangiryuarmiutun (i.e., Inuinnaqtun) (Lowe 1984a: viii). The loss of native language among the Inuvialuit was accelerated by the presence of residential schools in the 1930s where only English was used, and by 1950, after one generation, most Inuvialuit parents were exclusively teaching English to their children (Dorais 1989: 201). Thus as of 1981 only 16.8 percent of the Siglit spoke Siglitun, while 25.4 percent of the Uummarmiut spoke Uummarmiutun (Dorais 1990: 193). One should note, however, that some Inuvialuit under fifty have a passive knowledge of their language because of the presence of Inuvialuit elders who are still fluent in one of the three Inuvialuit dialects.

3. This said, the English translation from which I based my interpretation remains to be compared with its original Inuktitut transcription.

4. In Jacobson's (1984) Yup'ik dictionary, *ellange-* and *cellange-* are both translated as "to obtain awareness, to have one's first experience which leaves a lasting memory." Charles (2000: 12) notes that in Yup'ik, *ellangellemnek* means "from my first awareness, memory."

5. Thanks to Michèle Therrien and Louis-Jacques Dorais for their French translations of the original Inuktitut text of the English excerpts I had found in Oosten and Laugrand (2001: 96). Their translations and Michèle Therrien's note (pers. comm., 2002), helped me isolate the wordbase *suqqui-* from the other terms linked to memory in that text.

6. I am using Gubser's original orthography. That word is pronounced *isuma* in most Inuit languages.

7. In Jacobson (1984: 404), *usvi-* is translated by "intelligence, awareness."

FIVE

Anthropology in an Era of Inuit Empowerment

Edmund (Ned) Searles

"We are Inuit," proclaimed the cover of the 1999–2000 annual report of Inuit Tapiriit Kanatami (ITK). Formerly Inuit Tapirisat of Canada (ITC), ITK is an Ottawa-based organization representing the twenty-eight thousand Inuit of Canada. Okalik Egeesiak, ITC's president at the time, explained the title's meaning as "a source of our strength as individuals and as a people, and they continue to provide a sharp focus and vision for the work of ITC" (ITC 2000: 11). Egeesiak's vision signals the transformation of an abstract concept, Inuit identity, into a practical goal, thought to be achievable through the right policies, planning, and personnel. The title of ITK's annual report belongs to a growing concert of indigenous voices committed to linking cultural survival with political and economic empowerment.

But these words also underline a methodological and theoretical quandary for those who study indigenous peoples—how do we study and write about indigenous identity and culture in an era of indigenous political empowerment and heightened self-consciousness? (See Graburn, this volume.) What happens when the collective "we" becomes linked to a specific set of traits or emblems? (Briggs 1997; see Stevenson, this volume). Are anthropologists adequately attuned to the ways in which claims made about Inuit culture and identity by Inuit themselves can be divisive and disabling? (Strong and Van Winkle 1996; Sturm 2002).

Egeesiak, like many of her peers, believes that Inuit culture can and should be promoted and preserved. Supporting such views are those anthropologists and psychologists who identify the loss of culture with both acute and chronic episodes of psychological stress and other disorders, a condition that can be treated, it seems, by preventing the further erosion of culture (e.g., Berry 1999; O'Neil 1986). A vision of culture as panacea, however, has placed arctic anthropology in an awkward position within the discipline of anthropology. Just as arctic anthropologists are highlighting the need for cultural preservation, anthropologists working in other parts of the world claim that "culture," as a concept encompassing traits and enduring properties, has lost its relevance in a world characterized by mobility, flexibility, and fluidity (Gupta and Ferguson 1997; Jackson 1989; cf. Drummond 2001, Nash 2001).[1]

As an ethnographer of Inuit society and culture, I feel caught in a dilemma of how best to study and represent Inuit identity. Should I do what Okalik Egeesiak does and treat Inuit identity as a source of strength, vision, and focus? Or should I treat it as a resource for political power (and perhaps subgroup solidarity) that may in fact work against the interests and needs of some Inuit? (See Stern, this volume.) Ironically perhaps, today's anthropologists are not the first to confront such dilemmas, especially as they apply to the portrayal of Inuit as a cohesive group of people with a coherent culture. The history of Inuit studies is one in which scholars continue strategically to include and exclude different aspects of Inuit social and cultural life to create an image of the Inuit. To borrow from Stevenson's chapter (this volume), scholars actively discriminate from a myriad of data (e.g., experiences, field-notes, and other artifacts) to create a collective "cultural memory" that gradually becomes incorporated into the canon of Inuit studies. Today, Inuit organizations and the Nunavut government are engaged in similar acts of creation, and the effects are manifold: pride, political empowerment, and commercial success in some contexts (see Wachowich, this volume); anxiety, insecurity, and frustration in others. In this chapter I examine how arctic anthropology is implicated in the creation of an essentialized image of Inuit culture and consider its impact on Inuit society in general.

Research Background

The chapter is based on research conducted over a span of ten years in Nunavut, Canada (1990–2000). I first arrived in the Arctic as a research assistant for a team of archaeologists investigating the history of Inuit in Labrador and southern Baffin Island. After making friends with a number of the Inuit who acted as our navigators and guides, I applied for grants to work with young Inuit in Iqaluit (Nunavut's capital), specifically to study how they were adjusting to more urban lifestyles. My research took off in a new direction, however, when I was invited to live with a family in 1994, in one of the last remaining outpost camps on Baffin Island (see Searles 1998a; 1998b).

The outpost camp of Kuyait, where I lived for nine months, was established in 1977 by the Pisuktie family. It was abandoned in 1998 following the death of the camp leader, Aksujuleak Pisuktie. Inuit established outpost camps like Kuyait through loans and grants from the federal government and local hunters and trappers associations, which financed costs associated with construction (lumber, tools, etc.), transportation (fuel, boats, etc.), and the purchase of household supplies (heating stoves, cooking equipment, etc.). They call the camps nunaligalait, or "little towns," because they are occupied year-round. They are "outposts" because they are often located many miles from the nearest town. The Pisuktie family built their "camp" on ancestral land, a site renowned for its proximity to productive hunting, fishing, and/or trapping grounds, approximately 250 kilometers from Iqaluit. Many Inuit believe that outpost camps symbolize a more authentically Inuit existence, because they resemble, to some extent, how Inuit lived prior to their displacement to government-built and government-run towns and settlements.

Traveling back and forth between Kuyait and Iqaluit I learned how there is really no consensus among Inuit about what constitutes a more authentic lifestyle or who is really Inuit (see Graburn, this volume). For the Pisuktie family, the importance of being "on the land" and learning traditional hunting skills served as a marker of their Inuit identity—of their Inuitness. Living at Kuyait enabled them to be Inuit in a way that was impossible for them while living in Iqaluit. At the same time, however, my interviews with other Inuit revealed markedly different perspectives. For Susan Stoney, an Inuit resident of Iqaluit, outpost camps are more recreational than traditional. Working full-time as a garbage collector, Susan never doubted her Inuitness, even though she had little knowledge of hunting and no desire to live at an outpost camp.

I returned to Iqaluit in 1996, and again in 2000, and I have kept in contact with the friends who taught me about life in Nunavut. It is through my shared experiences with these families that I have come to understand some of the contested meanings associated with Inuit identity and the effects these meanings have on local attitudes about cultural preservation and self-determination (i.e., the idea that Inuit should have more control over their social, economic, and political development, a condition that until recently has been difficult given the power of non-Inuit government agencies).

My research experiences led me to the following understandings about

Inuit identity in particular and cultural identity in general. First, cultural identity originates in part through the experience of self-identity, or the recognition of oneself as belonging to a cultural group. Inuit cultural identity, I have argued elsewhere (Searles 1998a), is based not so much on the particular features of Inuit culture but on how Inuit culture is perceived as different from other cultures, particularly the culture of *qallunaat* (this word is used as both a noun ["white people"] and an adjective ["in the manner of white people"]). Negotiating a distinction between what is typically Inuit versus what is typically qallunaat is critical to creating an identity that is distinctive, historically continuous, and cohesive. Many Inuit believe that those who best remember how Inuit lived before the creation of towns in the Eastern Arctic in the 1950s and 1960s are those who are most qualified to identify the distinctiveness of Inuit culture and, by implication, Inuit identity. This is one reason why elders are the ones whom today's administrators consult when designing government programs and policies based on Inuit values and principles (see Wachowich, this volume).[2]

Second, Inuit identity is complicated by the fact that some Inuit are self-conscious about displaying their Inuitness while others are not. Briggs (1997) describes how one Inuk felt he should display his Inuitness (i.e., Inuit cultural identity) to others by learning how to build an igloo. Having grown up in town, he seemed to envy the hunting and land survival skills that some of his peers possessed. In the same article is a contrasting case study of another Inuk who felt no such need to display or prove his ethnicity even though he did not look like an Inuk (he had blonde hair and blue eyes). He was able to joke about his appearance, and the community accepted him as an Inuk. These examples lead to my third claim, that the dominant form of Inuit identity continues to be based on the memory of Inuit as "hunter-gatherers," a perspective that overlooks or understates the contributions of nonhunters to Inuit society (Nuttall 1998b; Searles 2001a; Stern 2001; see Stevenson, this volume, for a discussion of cultural memory). What I hope to show is how arctic anthropologists have contributed to this particular form of cultural memory.

Franz Boas and Salvage Ethnography

It is widely accepted that Franz Boas's year-long fieldwork project in the eastern Canadian Arctic moved him deeply (Cole and Müller-Wille 1984; Stocking 1968). His experiences with Baffin Island Inuit families in the 1880s made him sensitive to the extraordinary generosity and humility of

Inuit. The evolutionary theories of Edward Tylor and Lewis Henry Morgan, with their Eurocentric models of human progress, infuriated Boas so much that he went on to dedicate his professional career to challenging these theories and the idea that nonwestern groups were inferior morally and intellectually to western ones (Stocking 1968: 203). Boas's *The Central Eskimo* (1964 [1888]) provided a different portrait of a group known by many Europeans as exotic eaters of raw meat. Boas pushed cultural relativism and historical determinism to the forefront of his theoretical agenda by challenging Tylor's claim that culture exists only within the context of advanced, industrialized societies (e.g., Europe and North America). Boas's cultural relativism challenged the master narrative of a Eurocentric evolutionism because it extended culture to all groups, regardless of how "prehistoric" or "uncivilized" they appeared to a nineteenth-century European.

One of Boas's goals as an anthropologist was to document traditions, myths, and customs before they were lost or forgotten; that is, to salvage them. Boas believed that contact with Europeans and Americans, many of whom had hired Inuit to work on whaling crews, would lead to the loss of these traditions and customs. Boas's portrait of the Inuit of Baffin Island (1964 [1888]) is a collection of traditions, myths, and customs that predate contact with Europeans. He mentions only briefly that European (mostly Scottish) whalers and missionaries were living in Cumberland Sound while he was conducting research there in the late 1800s, and his ethnography focuses almost exclusively on Inuit knowledge of their traditions and land rather than their interactions with whalers, merchants, and missionaries (cf. Eber 1989).

Johnnie Mike brought Boas's biases and omissions to my attention. Mike is a descendant of both Inuit and American whalers in Cumberland Sound. "I have American blood in me," he explained proudly, "that is why I told the [Canadian] census that I am an American Eskimo." I met Johnnie Mike at his sister's home in Iqaluit in 1996. Born in Pangnirtung in the 1950s, Mike said his great grandfather used to trade skins with the American whalers and worked on whaling boats before getting a job with the Hudson's Bay Company. "I read *The Central Eskimo* but it is incorrect," Johnnie told me, "[because] capitalism was a lot stronger there [in Pangnirtung] at the time of Boas." Indeed, some Inuit had become relatively wealthy merchants during this era, owning their own whaleboats and acting as middlemen and brokers in their frequent exchanges with the whalers (M. G. Stevenson 1997). The non-Inuit whalers brought their own traditions to the Eastern Arctic, like tea, biscuits, and square dancing, traditions that Inuit of the Eastern

Arctic continue to value and enjoy but which never reached the pages of Boas's descriptions of Central Eskimo culture. Boas must have interpreted dancing to tunes from the British Isles and working for wages as examples of assimilation, not appropriation. Boas's description of Inuit culture is based on a way of life that existed prior to the presence of Europeans, one that he felt was threatened by the encroachment of European and Canadian values and traditions.

Unfortunately I was not savvy enough to ask Mike why he thought Boas excluded the activities of Inuit entrepreneurs from his scientific study of the Eskimo. Nor do I know why Boas excluded descriptions of Inuit tea drinking, biscuit eating, and square dancing, activities that he must have associated with Europe rather than the world of dog teams, skin clothing, and snow shelters. Boas clearly portrays Inuit as being technologically so-phisticated and intellectually advanced given their historical conditions.

The Colonial Era and Salvage Ethnography

Similar conventions of dividing Inuit into social categories began to take shape in Inuit communities once the number of permanent qallunaat res-idents began to increase. Instead of mixed blood and full blood, however, Inuit were labeled either *kabloonamiut* (a variation of *qallunaamiut*) or *nuna-miut*; classifications based largely on place of residency (Vallee 1962). Qallu-naamiut were those who lived in villages and hamlets built with government funding; they were literally "people of the qallunaat." These villages were effectively controlled and managed by a handful of qallunaat civil servants. Perhaps the most important, if not most problematic, figure in these vil-lages was the northern service officer (NSO). The NSO was responsible for administering all of the government programs, the ultimate goals of which were the integration of Inuit into contemporary Canadian society. Hugh Brody, a young researcher employed by the Canadian government in the late 1960s and early '70s, wrote a critical analysis of one NSO in an unidentified village (1975). Brody described how the NSO made decisions that affected the entire community without any consultation with the local population (i.e., Inuit), many of whom doubted the wisdom of the decisions of the NSO. Brody's understanding of the political situation echoed the sentiments of many of his academic colleagues, who criticized those government poli-cies that concentrated power and authority in the hands of a few qallunaat officials (e.g., Brody 1975; Dunning 1959; Paine 1977). Most of the NSOs and other civil servants who administered the programs and services had no prior experience in the Arctic and had no knowledge of Inuit other than what they had read by Boas or by one of the many scholars, adventurers, explorers, and missionaries who visited the Inuit in the 1800s and 1900s (e.g., Fleming 1956; Hall 1865; Rasmussen 1929).

In much the same way that Boas appeared to resent the intrusion of European culture in the Arctic, Brody resented the new bureaucratic culture of the government of the Northwest Territories. And like Boas, Brody focused much of his analysis on those Inuit who became adults prior to the arrival of qallunaat control. Brody used the term inummariit (literally, "purely Inuit") to refer to this group. According to Brody, inummariit were Inuit whose competence on the land and whose ability to endure hardship and duress were exceptional, even superhuman (Brody 1987). Individuals become inummarik only through a lifetime of regular participation in land-based subsistence activities, especially those activities that cultivate the development of a deep knowledge of the environment, the animals, and the landscape as well as a through a lifetime of perfecting one's ability to communicate in Inuktitut, the language of the Inuit. One effect of this description, however, was to make Brody unwilling and unable to identify those Inuit who grew up in town, or who lacked a detailed knowledge of the environment, as being inummarik.

Brody made Inuit elderhood an exalted category of personhood and inummarik the most persuasive reason to question negative stereotypes about Inuit. For Brody, qallunaat administrators were not only doing local Inuit populations an injustice with their paternalistic policies; they were missing an extraordinary opportunity to learn from those Inuit who possessed a wisdom and intelligence that comes from living a lifetime of hunting and fishing. Like Boas's decision to salvage Inuit culture in order to extract Inuit from the savage slot (Trouillot 1991), Brody invoked the concept of inummarik to rescue Inuit from the fate of dependent child in need of tutelage. Yet as with Boas, Brody's definition of inummarik seems to have been motivated as much by resentment of qallunaat culture as by respect for Inuit elders.

During an informal interview in Iqaluit in 1994, I recorded a different definition of inummarik. Jamasee Sataa described it as someone who is a unilingual Inuktitut speaker, referring to his father as an example. But rather than this being a condition to glorify, Jamasee thought of it more as a hindrance, for his father had always wanted to learn English but lacked the opportunity.

Other developments in anthropology in the 1960s and '70s served to re-

inforce the idea that real Inuit were not living in towns but were living on
the land. A revitalized interest in evolutionary theory and its application
to understanding hunter-gatherer groups like the Inuit became a popular
mode of anthropological investigation (e.g., Balikci 1970; Kemp 1971; E. A.
Smith 1991; cf. Nuttall 1998b). Building on the work of Julian Steward and
neo-Darwinian evolutionary theory, cultural ecology narrowed the anthropological gaze of arctic anthropologists to those families who hunted regularly. Because its objective was the study of human-environment relations
through the prism of natural selection and ecological adaptation, cultural
ecology focused almost exclusively on hunting and other foraging activities.
Uninterested in a growing population of Inuit who had limited ties to hunting (or who did not hunt at all), cultural ecology made active hunters and
fishers the de facto bearers of Inuit identity and the de jure experts on tradition and culture, a construction that reinforced the dichotomies produced
by Boas and reproduced by both Vallee and Brody.

For very different reasons, cultural ecologists enhanced Brody's political
agenda of localizing real, authentic personhood out on the land and away
from town, where many Inuit were working at wage labor jobs, attending
school, or collecting social assistance. Asen Balikci, a cultural ecologist
turned filmmaker, used the Netsilik Eskimo film series and an ethnography
to reconstruct precontact Inuit life and to resurrect Boas's salvage mode of
ethnography (Balikci 1970). Like Boas's, Balikci's intentions were to resurrect an image of how Inuit lived prior to contact with qallunaat. Balikci hired
Inuit to create costumes, build props, and act in ways that many Inuit themselves had learned about through films like *Nanook of the North* or accounts
written by explorers and authors of the early twentieth and late nineteenth
centuries.

Similar trends of representation were evident in the Inuit art market of the
1960s, when Inuit artists were actively discouraged from depicting scenes
that made any reference to qallunaat influences on Inuit society or from
drawing on symbols and themes from popular culture. Graburn (1987) describes how one young and successful artist was inspired by the comic book
hero Superman, a character who reminded him of the feats of Inuit he had
learned about in tales and myths told by his parents. His soapstone carving
of what Superman would have looked like if he were an Inuk was rejected by
Inuit art dealers and failed to reach the market, even though in Graburn's
opinion it was one of the artist's best pieces.

Inuit Cultural Politics and the Politics of Cultural Difference

If the traditions of cultural ecology and the critique of policies of assimilation served to narrow the scope of ethnographic inquiry in the Arctic, they also provided Inuit negotiators with the kind of evidence they needed to press claims to the title to their traditional lands. In fact a number of anthropologists worked with Inuit to map and document carefully the full range of Inuit occupancy in the Canadian Arctic. They did this by collecting place names and the locations of past and ongoing seasonal camps and seasonal migration patterns (Freeman 1976). This documentation provided Inuit and their lawyers with the evidence to prove they had justifiable claims to lands that were controlled by the federal government or that had been leased to developers. Thus the experience of growing up on the land, of being *inummarik* in Brody's sense of the term, became an indisputable source of Inuit power and authenticity.

The signing of land claims settlements and the increasing influence of Inuit organizations in the economic and political development of the Canadian Arctic signaled the arrival of a new era of Inuit empowerment and self-government. Inuit organizations fund a wide range of programs and services that actively promote Inuit culture and traditions; these programs have become the main sources of economic growth and job creation in many parts of the Canadian Arctic. One can find a similar transformation in the public sector, especially with respect to education, in which growing numbers of Inuit educators are actively involved in making greater use of traditional knowledge and Inuktitut in the classroom. Since the mid-1990s Nunavut's Arctic College has been offering an Inuit studies program that teaches Inuit culture and language. One instructor told me that Inuit who are unsure of their identity benefit greatly from this program, which is designed to be a bridge into more advanced education programs like translation and interpreting. One of the components of the Inuit studies program involves interviewing Inuit elders about their life histories and about various Inuit beliefs and practices, including those associated with child rearing, justice, and pre-Christian religious traditions (Briggs 2000; Oosten and Laugrand 1999; Rasing et al. 2000; Saladin d'Anglure 2001; Therrien and Laugrand 2001).

The spirit of reaching away from town and into the past to find more authentic sources of Inuit knowledge and wisdom is also evident in the implementation of a new Nunavut government policy called Inuit *qaujimajatuqangit* (or IQ, as it is known to most people in Nunavut). Qaujimajatuqangit refers to knowledge acquired a long time ago, prior to the arrival of qal-lunaat.[3] IQ has become the guiding ethical and intellectual template for building a new government and society, one that many Inuit believe is a formula for both cultural preservation and greater self-determination. Both Inuit and non-Inuit employees of the Nunavut government receive a packet of information about IQ and are expected to use IQ in the workplace and in the design and implementation of new programs and policies. A series of government-sponsored conferences and workshops in the late 1990s led to the creation of the basic IQ principles, and although implementation has been a challenge, many in Nunavut remain confident that it will take hold.

In the criminal justice system, Nunavut Inuit use the traditional knowl-edge concept to design and implement alternative sentencing programs, including "on-the-land" programs for both youth and adult offenders (Sear-les 1998b). These bear resemblance to Outward Bound and boot camp–style rehabilitation programs for convicted criminals, but for Inuit, the emphasis is on inspiring self-esteem through teaching Inuit survival skills—how to hunt seals, skin a walrus, or find one's way without a compass or map. Indeed, many Inuit have come to associate the experience of being out on the land or the sea, building shelters like igloos, learning place names in Inuktitut, and learning how to read the ice and changing weather patterns as resources that are necessary to heal those Inuit who suffer from addiction problems or those who cannot break the cycle of violence and abuse they experienced as children. If these programs signal a successful revitaliza-tion of Inuit culture and values, they also signify the continued vitality and saliency of Boas's salvage ethnography strategies. Carried on in different ways during different historical eras by different actors, including Inuit, anthropologists, and filmmakers, the image of a precontact Inuit life world continues to be a source of empowerment and authority, and even of public policy.

Inuit Cultural Politics and Its Malcontents

Promoting Inuit identity and tradition through metaphors of being on the land and learning how to survive in the natural environment raises many questions about the place of those who lack such knowledge, or who have little interest in developing it, within Inuit society (cf. Dorais 1997). Some of these questions include: Can Inuit who have grown up in town or who have dedicated their lives to town-based careers claim the same moral au-thority and social status as those who seem to exemplify better the concept of inummarik? Can an Inuk be a real, complete person without an intimate, firsthand knowledge of the precontact past or the arctic environment? Can a person be Inuit if he or she has never gone hunting or neither speaks nor understands Inuktitut? And finally, can Inuit identity ever be something that can be expressed and experienced in urban environments, in places like Iqaluit, Yellowknife, and Ottawa? (See Kishigami, this volume.) These are questions that have rarely been asked, much less answered.

In an article I wrote in 1998, I questioned the wisdom of placing young Inuit offenders in outpost camps, in large part because it seemed to me that the most important help for the youth was to help them handle their frustrations and heal the emotional scars caused by years of abuse and ne-glect (1998b). However, I also witnessed the healing effects of being on the land, away from town. The therapeutic effects of being out on the land are well-known to Inuit, and for this reason many treatment programs for criminals, alcoholics, and others often include an on-the-land component. And although today I am an advocate of land-based therapies for Inuit of all ages, I remain troubled by the precedent that policies like IQ establish for the construction of cultural identity. Such policies advantage Inuit who have hunting and survival skills and disadvantage those who do not, thus fragmenting Inuit society into castelike groups that typified Inuit-qallunaat relations in the 1960s and '70s (cf. Paine 1977). Policies based in IQ have the potential to marginalize and even alienate those Inuit who have chosen to pursue postsecondary education in Montreal or Toronto, in part because this type of education is often defined as antithetical to IQ. Furthermore, IQ as a system of knowledge and policy leaves little room for the adop-tion of hybrid forms of management and governance, policies that tran-scend dichotomies based on ethnicity or cultural knowledge. And finally, it is even possible that IQ policies will spill into other realms of Nunavut society in ways that discriminate against cultural mixing of other kinds, including against children with mixed ethnic backgrounds (i.e., Inuit and qallunaat).

Just as IQ treats Inuit and qallunaat knowledge systems as separate and better left that way, so might some Inuit decide to discourage interethnic marriages and civil unions in order to preserve "real" or "authentic" Inuit persons and create an apartheid system within Nunavut. John Amagoa-lik, one of the architects of the Nunavut government, vehemently opposed the creation of an ethnic-based government precisely because he feared Nunavut might become racially segregated much like the apartheid regime of South Africa. However, it is unclear if Amagoalik's fears are warranted, given the widespread acceptance of interethnic marriages and adoptions in

Nunavut society. Although I have interviewed some Inuit who felt discriminated against because they had a qallunaat father or mother, many Inuit with "qallunaat blood," to invoke Johnnie Mike's metaphor, are now political and economic leaders in Nunavut society. Perhaps an important new direction in Inuit studies is to reexamine local attitudes toward interethnic relations in Nunavut, especially in an era of IQ and the construction of a new Nunavut society.

Conclusion

Understanding indigenous peoples through the drama of cultural identity is more urgent than ever, I think, because identity is a key building block of ethnic resurgence. Although ethnic resurgence is often a powerful form of resistance to social injustice and inequality, it can also be used as a weapon of exclusion and even violence. Canadian political scientist Alan Cairns argues that Canada is ill prepared for the current era of ethnic resurgence on the part of its indigenous minorities (Cairns 2000). Cairns traces this ill preparedness to a legacy of injustice and inequality felt by many First Nations groups. This legacy is often translated into resentment of and contempt for the Canadian federal government and its inability to respond adequately to First Nation leaders' claims for greater cultural, economic, and political autonomy. Claims for autonomy are based on claims of cultural distinctiveness—of cultural identity. Having a better understanding of how Inuit construct their identity through the lens of cultural difference, political power, and everyday social relations will provide more than just a new theory to explain the complicated divide separating indigenous and nonindigenous Canadians. It will contribute to an ongoing dialogue about the place of "cultural survival" and indigenous identity in a world increasingly Balkanized by ethnicity and cultural difference.

One important role of ethnography is to situate how the boundaries I have discussed inform and influence not only the production of Inuit identity but also the experience of everyday life, a theme I have been wrestling with during the last several years (Searles 1998a; 2001b). The claims about Inuit identity that these boundaries authorize and legitimate now compartmentalize, in an ironic way, the contexts in which Inuit can be real Inuit or where real Inuit identity can be expressed (see also Adelson 2001; James 2001; Nuttall 1998b). Choosing a methodology that can contextualize the opportunities as well as the challenges that these boundaries create—especially with respect to social groups within Inuit society, including those who were raised in towns, those with mixed ethnic backgrounds, and those who lack

IQ—is critical, but it may not be popular with some Inuit (for a detailed discussion of research issues and trends in the Arctic, see Korsmo and Graham 2002). In short, I think it is essential that anthropologists begin to problematize and critique the intellectual legacy left by the Boasian project of salvage ethnography and to analyze how Inuit definitions of culture and tradition have become not just resources of political empowerment and self-enrichment but categories that are sometimes used to exclude and discriminate, especially against those Inuit whose personal interests and life choices have taken them beyond the boundaries of inummarik, or real authentic personhood.

Notes

1. Anthropologist Lila Abu-Lughod (1991) argues that the concept of culture has forced anthropologists to generalize about cultural and ethnic differences and to ignore the particularities of individual lives and social experience. Instead of enabling the recognition of a common humanity, the concept of culture is often used to reinforce dichotomies, including the divide between self and other, westerners and nonwesterners, anthropologist and subject.

2. Based on a series of conferences and workshops with Inuit elders in the late 1990s, the Nunavut government initiated a plan to implement Inuit qaujimajatuqangit, or traditional knowledge (literally that which was known prior to the arrival of qallunaat—Europeans and Canadians of European descent), at all levels of government.

3. Alexina Kublu of Arctic College in Iqaluit provided a detailed etymology of the term for me: *qauji* means to find out; *qaujima* means to know; *qaujimajaq* means what or that which is known; *qaujimajatuqaq* means something which has been known for a long time; and Inuit *qaujimajatuqangit* means something that Inuit have known for a long time.

PART 2

Reconfiguring Categories: Culture

SIX

Land Claims, Development, and the Pipeline to Citizenship

Pamela Stern

It is perhaps overly simplistic to describe Canada as a nation of immigrants. Since 1966, however, immigration has proven increasingly important to Canada's continued population growth. Immigration and the attendant issues of citizenship and identity provide the backdrop for a debate among Canadian intellectuals about multiculturalism, belonging, and the state of the Canadian nation (Bissoondath 1994; Kymlicka 1995; Paine 1999; Taylor 1994). Where are Inuit and other aboriginal peoples in a multicultural Canada? Are they citizens like any other? Or does aboriginality, by definition, distinguish indigenous peoples from other Canadians?

The various aboriginal land claims agreements Canada has negotiated with aboriginal peoples since the 1970s seek to erase difference while simultaneously requiring its continuation. The very acceptance of aboriginal land claims constituted an acknowledgement that aboriginal peoples were culturally, historically, and socially distinct from the immigrant settler communities in Canada. However, at the same time, the particular details of the land settlement arrangements did create an opening for substantive citizenship on the part of the aboriginal peoples. Although the negotiated agreements lay out how indigenous communities are to participate in governance, doing so as indigenous peoples perpetuates (some might say protects) difference. Thus land claims agreements expose some of the contradictions of indigeneity and liberal citizenship. In this chapter I examine some of these contradictions as the Inuvialuit in the Northwest Territories (NWT) experience them.

In the modern nation-state, citizenship encompasses a variety of meanings and practices, both formal and substantive. The formal, legal position of citizenship entails certain political rights such as the franchise, freedom of movement within and across borders, and residence within borders. More sociologically interesting than the legal criteria for citizenship, however, are the substantive aspects of citizenship. These are the civil, political, economic, and cultural benefits associated with societal membership. Citizenship, particularly in Canada, which projects itself as multicultural, often also entails the right to maintain cultural difference. Race, social class, gender, language, and ethnicity all impinge on an individual's real and imagined rights to participate in civic life and to partake of the social and economic benefits of society (Castles and Davidson 2000). Thus while being a citizen of a society implies full membership in that society, in any plural society not all legal citizens are able fully or equally to exercise their citizenship rights. In addition in some cases noncitizens have access to many of the substantive benefits of citizenship. The acquisition of the substantive benefits of citizenship is both social and dialogic, whereby people come to see themselves and are seen by others as members of a particular nation-state entitled to all the social and economic benefits of membership. With this in mind, I turn to a consideration of some of the micropractices that shape and reinforce Inuvialuit claims to and understandings of national citizenship.

Inuvialuit Canadians

In 1995 when Inuvialuit leader Nellie Cournoyea stepped down as premier of the Northwest Territories to take over the leadership of the Inuvialuit Regional Corporation (IRC), she gave several interviews with the press about her sixteen years in the territorial Legislative Assembly and about her vision for the political and economic future of the Inuvialuit. In one interview, printed in the national newsweekly *Maclean's*, Cournoyea was asked about her accomplishments as government leader. She mentioned improved communications, health care, and territorial support for the settlement of native land claims, and she noted that the government of the NWT now sits at the federal-provincial table. With respect to this latter issue, Cournoyea observed that while some other formal Canadian citizens (and she named the Quebequois) are "trying to get out" of Canada, "we're trying to get in" (cited in Nemeth 1995: 34). Importantly, the "we" Cournoyea referred to were not only the Inuvialuit, or even northern indigenous people, but northerners in general.

Cournoyea's statement in the widely circulated news magazine, as well as others she made after taking over as chief executive officer of IRC, suggest that this former land claims negotiator and articulate spokeswoman for aboriginal rights saw Inuvialuit goals as inseparable from those of other NWT residents. The state of affairs at the close of the twentieth century was markedly different from the one that existed two and a half decades earlier when the discourse about economic and political rights in the NWT was dominated by a politics that labeled all native peoples as having fundamentally different goals and orientations than non-natives. In other words, Inuvialuit and other northern indigenous people had been regarded, by themselves and others, as nonparticipants in the activities of the Canadian nation. Interestingly, the focal point of the discourse on indigenous citizenship at that time—hydrocarbon development and especially proposals for a gas pipeline through the Mackenzie River Valley—is at this writing once again at center stage.

The Original Mackenzie Valley Pipeline Proposals

Outsiders first became aware of the presence of oil in the NWT in the late eighteenth century. In 1798 on his exploratory trip down the river named for him, Alexander Mackenzie observed petroleum seeping from the ground near Fort Norman. In that preindustrial age, however, the oil was little more than a curiosity, and other resources—both renewable and nonrenewable—occupied the attention of newcomers and indigenous northerners. It was not until the early part of the twentieth century that arctic petroleum deposits drew more than passing notice. In 1923, U.S. President Warren Harding set aside an area of the North Slope of Alaska as a National Petroleum Reserve, but no attempts were made to extract the oil. In Canada a desire to exploit the Fort Norman petroleum led in 1920 to the signing of Treaty 11 between the government of Canada and Dene Indian bands living in that area. Nineteen years later only one well was producing oil—but it was enough to supply the petroleum needs of the then tiny communities in the Mackenzie River Valley. Moving the oil to southern markets was an entirely different matter.

With the entrance of the United States into World War II in late 1941, expanded production and a northern pipeline suddenly became cost-effective. The Canadian Oil (CANOL) pipeline from Norman Wells to Whitehorse, like the Alaska Highway and other militarily inspired development projects, was largely built by the U.S. Army. Completed only in 1944, the pipeline was abandoned at the end of the war, and northern petroleum production returned to prewar levels. Over the next two decades other nonrenewable resources, principally gold and uranium, attracted the attention of northern prospectors.

Arctic hydrocarbon exploration was not dead, however. In 1961 the Canadian federal government issued regulations that established royalty rates and liability rules intended to encourage northern petroleum development. In 1966 it took a 45 percent stake in Panarctic Oils, which was exploring in the High Arctic. Modest deposits of oil and gas were found in the High Arctic and in the Beaufort Sea–Mackenzie Delta region. The Prudhoe Bay oil strike in 1968 fueled the expectation that a Canadian Arctic oil field of similar dimensions merely awaited discovery. Stepped-up exploratory activity showed that natural gas, rather than oil, was abundant in the Beaufort-Mackenzie region, and by 1970 competing consortia of U.S. and Canadian companies were forming and reforming to build a pipeline to move the Prudhoe, Beaufort, and Mackenzie Valley gas to southern markets. That year Canadian Department of Indian Affairs and Northern Development Minister Jean Chrétien and Department of Energy Minister Joe Greene issued guidelines for the development of northern pipelines, describing them as "a potential major economic contribution to the country" (cited in Gray 1979: 46).

Within a short time there were essentially three distinct northern gas pipeline proposals: (1) the Foothills, southern, or Alaska Highway proposal, which would have carried gas along the route of the Alyeska Oil Pipeline to Fairbanks and then through the Yukon along the Alaska Highway; (2) a northern coastal pipeline, which would have carried gas from Prudhoe Bay to the Mackenzie River Delta and then south through the Mackenzie River Valley; and (3) the "Maple Leaf" all-Canadian route, which would have taken gas from the Beaufort-Mackenzie region through the Mackenzie River Valley.

The two Mackenzie Valley proposals were thought to be less costly and had the added benefit to Canada of including the Beaufort-Mackenzie gas deposits. Some reports indicate that backers of the competing pipelines spent in excess of U.S. $250 million (in 1977 dollars) for environmental, social impact, and logistical studies. [1] In 1977 Canada's National Energy Board and the U.S. Federal Power Commission approved the routing of a gas pipeline along the Alyeska Pipeline and Alaska Highway.

No gas pipeline was built. Although the reasons why are multiple and complex, the Mackenzie Valley Pipeline Inquiry led by Thomas Berger is frequently given the credit or the blame for scuttling any northern gas pipeline.

Mackenzie Valley Pipeline Inquiry

The Royal Commission known as the Mackenzie Valley Pipeline Inquiry was created by an order-in-council on March 21, 1974. Thomas R. Berger, then a justice on the Supreme Court of British Columbia, was chosen to head the inquiry. Dacks (1981: 136) suggests that the pipeline inquiry was created not as a true fact-finding body but rather to give Prime Minister Pierre Trudeau's Liberals the political cover they needed to develop resources they saw as being in the vital interests of the nation. [2] Nonetheless Berger was given complete discretion and an unlimited budget to investigate "the social, environmental and economic impact regionally, of the construction, operation and subsequent abandonment of the proposed pipeline in the Yukon and the Northwest Territories" (Privy Council 1974–641, in Berger 1977a).

The Berger hearings began in Yellowknife in March 1975 and were then convened in thirty-five Dene, Métis, and Inuit communities in the Beaufort-Mackenzie region before returning to Yellowknife in November of the following year. Berger took testimony from more than a thousand village residents (Hamilton 1994: 189). The village hearings, while unusual, were not unheard of—a decade earlier the Carrothers Commission on political development in the NWT had also visited communities—but the Berger hearings stretched the bounds of customary practice both by funding the testimony from indigenous organizations and by using CBC radio to democratize the flow of information within and between native communities and between native and non-native Canadians.

In the end Berger recommended in no uncertain terms against the immediate construction of a gas pipeline in the Mackenzie River Valley. In fact Berger made eight recommendations concerning resource and economic development in the Beaufort-Mackenzie region. Four directly concerned resource development. These were that: (1) there should be no pipeline connecting Prudhoe Bay gas fields with those in the Beaufort-Mackenzie region; (2) there should be a ten-year moratorium on pipeline development in the Mackenzie corridor; this was in order to allow for (3) the settlement of native land claims; and most interesting, (4) the development of a northern economy should be based on renewable resources—in this case, fur.

In writing his two-volume report Berger (1977a, 1977b) relied heavily on the testimony of "experts," weighing the testimony of pro-pipeline industry experts against that of anti-pipeline northern social scientists. The testimony of the mostly indigenous village residents, however, firmly tipped the scales against construction of a pipeline. Citing the native testimony,

Berger made repeated reference to the continued and important reliance on subsistence hunting and trapping by northern natives. The tone of the Dene testimony was far more strident than that from the Inuit witnesses (Usher 1993: 111), but both groups were unanimous in their statements regarding the immense social and emotional importance of subsistence as a way of life.[3] This should not be surprising. At the time the Berger hearings were conducted, many of the villages in the Beaufort-Mackenzie region had had local schools, medical services, and community councils for less than ten years. In the Inuit communities limited access to nonsubsistence protein foods meant that nearly all Inuit families depended upon hunting for large portions of their diets. Television was just beginning to arrive in the North. The fur market appeared secure, and with knowledge of and demand for manufactured goods low, Inuit communities heavily reliant on subsistence were, in relative terms, quite affluent (cf. Sahlins 1972). If Berger missed the signs that northern economies were changing, he correctly understood that northern natives were in no position at that time to reap the supposed financial or social rewards of nonrenewable resource extraction. Implicit in the native statements and Berger's application of them was the assumption that indigenous societies remained *apart from* the Canadian nation. Within a decade, the Inuvialuit signed a land claims agreement (Government of Canada 1984) setting the framework for a new understanding of an Inuvialuit citizenship based on rights.

Inuvialuit Land Claims and Citizenship

Canada committed to negotiating aboriginal land claims prior to the findings of the Berger Commission, but the two processes were not completely separate. Much of the research presented to the Berger Commission also found its way into land claims negotiations and vice versa, and many individual witnesses before the Berger Commission were intimately involved in the land claims negotiations. The Committee for Original Peoples Entitlement (COPE) representing the Inuvialuit was the first Beaufort-Mackenzie native group to settle its land claim with the government of Canada, which it did in 1984. As part of the agreement, the approximately thirty-five hundred Inuit from the six communities designated as the Inuvialuit Settlement Region relinquished their aboriginal title to 435,000 square kilometers of land they had occupied and used historically. In exchange for renouncing their claims to this land, the Inuvialuit Regional Corporation, the successor to COPE, received C$152 million paid over a fourteen-year period and title to approximately 91,000 square kilometers of land, which they were able to select on the basis of documented traditional use.

For a small portion of the land, which happens to be located closest to Inuvialuit communities, the Inuvialuit hold both surface and subsurface rights, but they have only surface rights on the remaining land. Equally important, I believe, IRC has some quasi-governmental functions and participates in regional management boards. It is not, however, a government. The language of the Inuvialuit Final Agreement (IFA) explicitly links the economic measures to Inuvialuit citizenship and indicates that the measures should lead to "full Inuvialuit participation in the northern Canadian economy; and Inuvialuit integration into Canadian society through development of an adequate level of economic self-reliance and a solid economic base" (Government of Canada 1984: 32).

It is my contention that the particular arrangements of the Inuvialuit Final Agreement have enabled the Inuvialuit (as represented by IRC) to embrace the substantive aspects of Canadian citizenship. There are no specific provisions for Inuvialuit self-government in the IFA.[4] Instead the Inuvialuit as individuals and as a group participate in the full range of civic institutions in the Beaufort-Mackenzie region. In addition it is significant that Inuvialuit leaders have held important positions in the government of the NWT. At this writing, IRC chair and CEO Nellie Cournoyea is the most prominent Inuvialuk to have served in government, but there have been others.

While it is possible than the Inuvialuit land claims would have been settled anyway, the Berger inquiry was important in swaying Canadian public opinion in favor of recognizing some measure of aboriginal land title—something that the Canadian courts had already done. Ironically perhaps, the political justification for aboriginal land claims agreements rests on claims of distinct indigenous rights derived from ethnic and cultural difference. This was the argument made by Berger inquiry witnesses for COPE, and as a result the inquiry served to "recast the issue of northern development and modernization of 'primitive' peoples to a more fundamental political question of the rights and interests of Native northerners vis-à-vis those of other Canadians and of corporate and bureaucratic interests" (Usher 1993: 99). The witnesses successfully advanced the point that land, and particularly the traditional uses of the land, constituted the material, cultural, and emotional security of northern natives and that hydrocarbon development would without doubt jeopardize that security. Furthermore, it was argued that while subsistence hunters did need a cash income in order to maintain a subsistence lifestyle, job training and wage employment were actually incompatible with the maintenance of a native way of life. The fundamental contradictions of this position were recognized, but aside from some hand wringing about the threat to traditional lifestyles (see for example Irwin 1989), modernization of northern communities continued at a pace largely determined by government bureaucrats. A decade earlier, the Inuvialuit residents of Sachs Harbour had begged the government of the Northwest Territories for a local school so that children would no longer be sent away to boarding schools, where they learned to scorn their parents' way of life. The petitioners wrote: "We want our children to get good educations, but at the same time wish that they be able to make a choice between trapping and going on to high school and getting wage work. They are no more able to make this choice by spending their childhood years [away from home] than they would be if they never went to school at all."[5]

The settlement of land claims produced the institutional basis for the Inuvialuit as a group to participate in regional decision making, including on economic development, but it was not until the mid-1990s with Cournoyea's assumption of the leadership position at IRC that both the rhetoric and activity reflected a shift in Inuvialuit citizenship claims. During the same period the price and demand for natural gas climbed on world markets, and once again there was serious interest in building a northern gas pipeline. The pipeline proposals from the 1970s were dusted off, modified only slightly, and at this writing are very much the subject of political gamesmanship and international diplomacy. The major difference between the pipeline proposals of the 1970s and the current ones is that the dominant rhetoric about development from indigenous leaders has changed from claims of ethnically based difference to claims for full participation in the presumed social and economic benefits of resource development. Yet Inuvialuit have not totally abandoned a claim to a distinct cultural identity. How is it that the change in rhetoric came about? I believe the answer lies not only in the political and economic powers entrenched in the land claims agreement but also in the determination of Inuvialuit leaders to exercise those powers in favor of integration.

During the 1990s the Inuvialuit Regional Corporation, through its investment practices, increasingly committed to successful development of a pipeline to move Beaufort-Mackenzie gas to southern markets. While IRC began expressing interest in northern hydrocarbon development soon after the signing of the Inuvialuit Final Agreement, its involvement increased markedly only after the loss of substantial sums of money in highly speculative foreign investments. Beginning in the mid-1990s IRC's development subsidiary, the Inuvialuit Development Corporation (IDC), began divesting from real estate and other ventures outside the region and reinvested in northern firms expected to provide logistical support to the northern hydrocarbon industry. The IDC also concluded joint venture agreements with gas producers, pipeline firms, and logistical support firms. Importantly, most if not all of the joint venture agreements included employment-training arrangements for Inuvialuit beneficiaries.

IRC's Inuvialuit Petroleum Corporation subsidiary became a major supplier of gas for heating and electricity generation in the town of Inuvik, where approximately half of Inuvialuit reside. Additionally in June 2000, IRC conducted its first lease-sale of gas rights on its lands near Inuvik and Tuktoyaktuk. The sale netted C$75.5 million to IRC as well as agreements for job training and potential future royalties and equity stakes.[6] Finally IRC led the formation of the Aboriginal Pipeline Group (APG), a consortium of entities representing the native peoples along the proposed Mackenzie Valley pipeline route. In June 2001, APG reached a memorandum of understanding with the consortium of multinational pipeline developers to acquire a one-third equity stake in a Mackenzie Valley gas pipeline.

Individual Inuvialuit, through IRC, have come to see hydrocarbon development as providing Inuvialuit with many of the substantive benefits of citizenship. In particular, IRC under Cournoyea's leadership has encouraged Inuvialuit to seek postsecondary education and then employment in northern industries and government. Inuvialuit interests in developing hydrocarbon resources are framed as the substantive citizenship rights to economic self-sufficiency. Hydrocarbon development is promoted as an important source of employment: "It's not good for communities not to be working. People here are used to working. They like work. . . . People desperately want to be independent" (Cournoyea, cited in Walker 2001). Furthermore in the current formulation, wage employment is no longer expressed as a threat to Inuvialuit culture; rather it is the absence of wage employment that threatens Inuvialuit culture and communities: "It's not like there were never any social problems before they started exploring for gas up here. With the jobs and wealth we'll get from these developments, we will be better able to deal with some of the problems" (Cournoyea, cited in Struzik 2001).

Much of the employment directly associated with hydrocarbon exploration and pipeline construction is targeted at young men, for whom any work, much less culturally suitable work, is seen as being in extremely short supply. Interestingly, the use of hunting metaphors is one way that hydrocarbon development is framed as culturally appropriate for Inuvialuit.

It should be noted that both Inuit and non-Inuit have attempted to equate modern economic institutions in the North with hunting. In the 1970s, Iñupiaq land claims negotiator and native rights advocate Charlie Edwardsen Jr. called the Alaska Native corporations "the new harpoon" (1974). A more recent and perhaps even more apt example comes from a news feature that ran in the *Christian Science Monitor* in May 2001. Accompanying a story about gas exploration in the Mackenzie Delta region was a photograph of a young Inuk standing next to a snowmobile. The young man was holding aloft and preparing to thrust an object that resembled a harpoon. The object was a seismic probe. The visual metaphor was completed by a caption reading: "Hunting for Hydrocarbons."

Discussion

Feminist discourses on citizenship provide one avenue to examine the approach of Inuvialuit and other northern indigenous groups to citizenship in the Canadian nation-state. The particular characteristic often identified with a woman-friendly citizenship—"an ethic of care" (Gilligan 1982)—is also a characteristic generally identified with northern indigenous cultures. In situations where citizenship practices are based on an ethic of care, often posed as the opposite of an ethic of justice, we should expect the formal institutions of government to reflect an ethic "where the daily caring of people for each other is a valued premise of human existence" (Tronto 1993: 178). In practice, citizenship based on an ethic of care is personalized and involves "noticing the need for care; taking care of or assuming responsibility for care; care-giving and care-receiving" (Lister 1997: 101). In Inuit society—where individuals are expected to be responsible for themselves and to place few demands on others but are also expected to anticipate the needs of others and are socially rewarded for this (Briggs 1970; Stern 2001: 90–91)—an ethic of care is the ideal.

One of the challenges for Inuvialuit is to retain this social characteristic in the creation of new institutions of governance in the Inuvialuit Settlement Region and in the face of economic and political change. An ethic of care functioned well in small, mostly kin-based communities in which the pressures to participate were personalized (cf. Kulchyski, this volume). It is a far more difficult proposition to accommodate traditional values of society in modern bureaucratized settings that so easily give way to an ethic of indifference (Herzfeld 1992).

Some may believe that Inuvialuit are supportive of hydrocarbon development for purely financial reasons, though the evidence is to the contrary. Nonetheless the settlement of land claims and the resulting involvement in land and resource management boards have given them confidence that they will be able to manage the development on their terms (H. Myers 2001: 38–39). According to one Inuvialuit business owner, in comparison to the 1970s when the Inuvialuit were barely consulted about hydrocarbon development and little money spent by the oil and gas companies stayed in the North, "now we are all partners and we are all involved in the development activities. That is really the big difference today compared to the last time the oil companies were here. We have opportunities now that were never available to us before" (Hansen, cited in Luhan 2001).

The Inuvialuit desire to participate as equals in resource development operates in parallel to the desire to establish governance that is not only sensitive to Inuvialuit culture but actually feels Inuvialuit in practice. The two are no longer separable, but they may be in tension. As Lister (1997: 97) notes, "there are certain political situations and political moments when it makes sense to emphasise [indigenous] citizenship claims with reference to arguments associated with 'difference' . . . there are others when arguments associated with 'equality' are likely to have more purchase." The Inuvialuit effort to participate in the building of a Mackenzie Valley pipeline is a situation in which it makes sense to emphasize equality. If and when a pipeline is built, or if it is abandoned entirely, the pendulum could swing in the other direction.

As was the case in the 1970s, discussion about and planning for a northern gas pipeline has occurred at an elite level. Inuvialuit political leaders clearly express interest in a pipeline, but it is not certain to what extent Inuvialuit living in villages support the construction of a pipeline or can expect to benefit directly from one. Those are not the Inuvialuit who are quoted in news stories. Still, when I asked a few Holman beneficiaries of the Inuvialuit Final Agreement if they thought it would be better if Holman had become part of the new overwhelmingly Inuit Territory of Nunavut, they uniformly responded that they were satisfied with the dividends they received as shareholders of the Inuvialuit Regional Corporation. Perhaps Nunavut Tunngavik Inc., the Nunavut equivalent of IRC, will pay consistent dividends, but Holman residents have no way to tell.

Only one man, a former member of the Holman Hamlet Council, had an opinion when I followed up with a question about whether it would make a difference to have an Inuit-controlled government as in Nunavut. He pointed to the joint Inuvialuit-Gwich'n self-government negotiations, meant to allow aboriginal control of some facets of governance, and told me that soon the hamlet council form of government would disappear to be replaced by an Inuit community council. In a very casual way I remarked, "No more qallunaat on Council."[7] "Oh no," he said. "They are citizens, too." A few years earlier this same man had told me that now that the Inuvialuit land claims had been settled, he no longer objected to paying income tax. To his thinking, there was a direct connection between the taxes he paid to the Canadian government and his annual dividend from IRC's investments. Somehow the rhetoric of modern citizenship has seeped into what are presumed to be aboriginal institutions.

Whether a gas pipeline will be built in the Mackenzie Valley corridor is anybody's guess. There are political, environmental, and financial barriers to each of the pipeline proposals, and where the North is concerned the development of oil and gas reserves is unpredictable and hinges upon processes and decision making independent of northern stakeholders. Dacks's observation about earlier efforts to build a pipeline still holds: "It is not at all safe to venture a prediction on when [Beaufort-Mackenzie gas] reserves will actually find their way to market. Any decision to transport northern gas and oil to market involves a complex of factors to challenge any decision-making process. The factors are numerous, in many cases are only partially understood, and frequently cannot be compared with one another to strike some kind of cost-benefit balance" (1981: 134).

IRC, however, has staked quite lot on the hope that not only will a pipeline be built but *their* pipeline will be built. Until recently the financial rewards to the Inuvialuit from oil and gas extraction have been minimal, but the post–land claims environment has created a constituency of native leaders who feel empowered to capture the presumed citizenship benefits of resource development. A vision of participating as full partners in the economic growth that is presumed to flow from hydrocarbon development has fueled "the growth of citizenship as new areas of social and economic life are brought under the calculus of rights" (Holston and Appadurai 1999: 11). Ironically, this extension of citizenship is built on the perpetuation of difference. Dennie Lennie, the director of the Inuvialuit Development Corporation, stated this view clearly: "Now people [Inuvialuit] are prepared, and pro-active in seeing development in our region, so we're ready to move ahead" (Canadian Broadcasting Corporation 2000).

Postscript

The first drafts of this chapter were written in the summer and fall of 2001 and a final revised version went to the press in the spring of 2004. There is always a danger, when writing about an unfolding event, that what was true or timely when originally written will cease to be so when finally in print. At the time of writing, a consortium of companies led by Imperial Oil was engaged in survey and engineering work for a Mackenzie Valley natural gas pipeline and was conducting the environmental studies required as part of the permitting process for the megaproject. In April 2005 a casual observer might have gotten the idea that the 1,220-kilometer, C$57 billion project was about to run off the rails. Under pressure from regulators and from environmental and native groups Imperial Oil announced a halt to all work on the pipeline. While there had been hints for some time that the political questions surrounding the benefits and costs of the pipeline had not been solved, the issue that brought the matter to a head was a demand by the native participants (whose lands the pipeline would cross) that the corporations commit to financing health, education, and other social programs in native communities. Stephen Kakfwi, a Dene leader who had succeeded Nellie Cournoyea as premier of the NWT and who is now a negotiator for the Sahtu First Nation, reminded everyone that citizenship is the issue that must be solved before a pipeline or any development project can go forward. Kakfwi was widely reported to have declared: "There's no way we're going to remain the poorest people in Canada when there's a $7-billion project going on here [on our land]" (cited in Ebner and Brethour 2005). By midsummer 2005 a deal was apparently in hand with the federal government, not Imperial Oil, agreeing to fund the social programs. The plan to build the pipeline may still unravel, or if it is built, it may not deliver real benefits to native communities; but there should be no doubt that the native peoples living along the pipeline route will accept nothing short of full citizenship in all its forms.

Notes

1. The Maple Leaf and the Alaska Highway pipelines were backed by some of the same players. Detail about expenditures is from http://www.arcticgaspipeline.com/History-Projects.htm, accessed July 27, 2005.

2. This was tense period in Canadian nation-building. Ottawa perceived external threats to its sovereignty from U.S. activity in its arctic waters and internal threats to sovereignty from Quebec separatists.

3. Several years earlier Sachs Harbour residents unsuccessfully attempted to prevent seismic

exploration on Banks Island, fearing that their community would become "another welfare town, robbed of its independence and overrun by outsiders" (Usher 1971b: 47).

4. Inuvialuit, along with Gwich'n Indians, signed an agreement-in-principle in April 2003 for limited regional self-government. The specifics of ethnic governance structures, however, remain unclear.

5. Letter from the people of Sachs Harbour to the Commissioner of the NWT, NWT Archives G79–003, Box 266–19.

6. This figure is equivalent to one-half of the total cash IRC received from the federal government as part of the land claims settlement.

7. Qallunaat are whites.

SEVEN

Cultural Survival and the Trade in Iglulingmiut Traditions

Nancy Wachowich

The Social Life of Dogs

It was the end of January 1997, dark season in Canada's eastern High Arctic community of Igloolik. The wind was blowing. I had my parka hood up and my head down as I disembarked from the airplane and made my way across the tarmac toward the terminal. Behind the windows, a group of Inuit stood waving at relatives. The sound of barking and howling husky dogs carried on the wind. For a moment the scene was reminiscent of archetypal descriptions of the arrivals of arctic anthropologists to *Nanook of the North* fieldsites—wind, snow, ice, cheerful greetings, howling dogs. Almost. But then I located the source of the howling. On the tarmac beside the luggage to be boarded for the return flight south was a pair of portable kennels with two sled dogs shifting restlessly inside. These huskies, I was told, were being shipped south to Iqaluit and then to Ottawa. Upon arrival in the nation's capital, they were to be euthanized, stuffed by a taxidermist, and transported back to the Arctic, this time to the neighboring settlement of Pond Inlet, where the dogs would be attached to a *qamutiq* (sled) and displayed as "traditional Inuit sled dogs" in that settlement's Nattinnak Tourist Interpretive Centre (fig. 1).

Sled dogs were once essential to Inuit survival. They were used for transportation, hunting, and in extreme conditions, food. The Inuit move into permanent settlements in the 1960s and the introduction of the snowmobile a decade later altered the use-value of dogs. Today some dog teams are kept by the small number of hunters who supplement their incomes by working as outfitters for recreational polar bear hunters from the South.[1] A few

7.1. Material culture exhibit and stuffed dogs in Nattinnak Tourist Interpretive Centre, Pond Inlet, May 2001. Photo by Nancy Wachowich.

other teams are used to teach dogsled skills to the young, to compete in the annual Nunavut Quest dog team race, or sometimes to lease to production companies crews shooting films, videos, and television commercials with an Inuit theme. The caged dogs on the tarmac that day had belonged to an older Iglulingmiut hunter who had recently died of cancer. After the funeral his widow had answered a request aired on the community radio by a Parks Canada agent seeking to purchase dogs for Pond Inlet's new interpretive center. In accordance with the Inuit custom of quickly disposing of the belongings of the dead, she sold the animals for what she considered a substantial amount of money. From the widow's perspective the dogs were no longer needed as part of a working team and could thus be converted to cash to pay household bills and buy food, ammunition, and fuel for her family. From the perspective of Parks Canada officials, the dogs symbolized Inuit traditional culture and a legacy of lives spent on the land.

Sled dogs, alive or stuffed, have become part of a paradoxical set of representational practices that, on first consideration, seem strangely disjointed from material realities in the North. The process through which these two living animals were transformed from working sled dogs to stuffed artifacts represents a larger series of symbolic transformations taking place in Inuit communities. In their purchase, death, and taxidermy the economic, physical, and semiotic value of these dogs was altered. Their social worth in the subsistence cycle reworked, they were awarded new value as material symbols of a past way of life to be shown to arctic cruise ship passengers, adventure tourists, and other visitors to Pond Inlet. Stuffed dogs have become part of the transnational circulation of objects and images perceived to be representative of Inuit culture. They have come to stand for a complicated and often conflicting set of dialogues concerning Inuit history, culture, and identity.

The Institutionalization of Tradition

This story of the sled dogs is the first of several case studies in this chapter illustrating how Inuit practices have been awarded cultural value as traditions, as artifacts, and as commodities produced both in and for local and transnational networks of exchange. In Igloolik a movement initiated by early ethnographers to record and preserve Inuit culture gathered momentum in the context of settlement life with the construction of a stone igloo cultural center, the development of local bureaucratized community projects involving traditional knowledge, and the contemporary cultural revitalization efforts by Inuit videographers. Since the early contact period, southerners have reinforced idealized and exotic notions of the remote and pristine arctic environment and the authentic Inuit who inhabit that landscape. Simultaneously Inuit themselves have worked at appropriating this "imperialist nostalgia" (Rosaldo 1989) in their own objectified self-representations. In their meetings with outsiders Iglulingmiut, subtly or sometimes not so subtly, draw upon western notions of an idealized Inuit past and use these iconic categories in their own cultural productions as a way to communicate social agendas.[2] In the past Inuit hunted for the animals, upon which they literally subsisted. Today the integration of Inuit into larger social and economic networks has created a new social environment that brings the politics of land claims, environmental protection, sustainable development, hunting rights, and intellectual property, among other things, into discussion. This has led to the articulation of a new or renewed understanding of subsistence in arctic communities (Freeman 2000; Hensel 1996; Smith and McCarter 1997; Wenzel 1991), an understanding that incorporates a variety of "ideational practices" (Wolf 1999). Such practices have various manifestations and, as the taxidermy of sled dogs demonstrates, can often emerge in the most unconventional forms. To ensure their economic survival in the contemporary arctic environment, Inuit must incorporate into their established harvesting activities what might variously be understood as a "hunt for tradition" (Fienup-Riordan 2000) or a "hunt for identity" (Rasing 1999). Today Inuit must hunt for their cultural, historical, and economic presence in the world. Like hunting for animals, however, the hunt for tradition often involves elusive quarry. As other contributors to this volume illustrate (see Searles and Graburn, in particular), expressions of the past are continually produced, objectified, and institutionalized as conscious models in processes of identity construction.

Definitions of Inuit cultural traits change shape as they are inscribed with such western notions as cultural heritage, history, modernity, science, technology, nationalism, and of course primitivism. Current and highly politicized debates in Nunavut government circles over efforts to institutionalize Inuit traditional knowledge or *Inuit qaujimajatuqangit* (daily referred to as IQ) draw these dialogues into a public arena as classifications of traditional Inuit gender roles, environmental protection, and community authority become the subject of ongoing vigorous debate. But key questions remain unanswered: what are the specific social relations and practices that bring about the reformulation of certain activities from the past as traditional? What changes have been instituted in Inuit social and political life since early contact with outsiders such that elements of Inuit culture (such as working sled dogs) can enter different domains of value and be transformed into cultural artifacts? Finally, what insight could an examination of this process offer to anthropology?

Traditions convey and codify cultural differences and enable historically marginalized people to mark their paths through modernity (Clifford 1997; Fienup-Riordan 2000, Mauzé 1997). They are born of the colonial encounter. Iglulingmiut elder Emile Immaroituk explains: "We didn't talk about traditions in the past. There were no other cultures here with us and we didn't think about preserving anything because we were living it. It was all we had. We were living it" (interview with the author, November 22, 1997).

Like Immaroituk, anthropological studies have also addressed the modernist roots of the category "tradition." They explore the process through which often mundane, utilitarian tools and cultural practices are awarded value as traditional (Appadurai 1986; Cruikshank 1998; Ginsburg et al. 2002; Miller 1995; F. R. Myers 2001; Phillips and Steiner 1999; Thomas 1994, 1999; Turner 2002). This literature attests to the growing trade in traditional culture—a trafficking of cultural capital through different semiotic systems, across cultural, national, and transnational borders, and in and out of commodity status. In order to survive as hunters in the modern world—a world that witnesses an unprecedented mobility and interpenetration of cultures—Inuit have come to use a variety of media to lay claim to their own historical vision and promote themselves and their culture as distinct. And yet, like indigenous peoples around the world, the Inuit find themselves in a predicament when forced to operate within the same frames of reference that have assured their marginalization since first contact. A current debate among indigenous media scholars centers on whether the appropriation of western media tools and epistemologies assist (Ginsburg 1991; Turner 1992) or restrict (Weiner 1997) indigenous peoples in their efforts at cultural rehabilitation. These debates bring issues of authenticity, "Faustian contracts" (Ginsburg 1991), and what I consider largely irrelevant concerns about cultural corruption and "ersatz anthropology" (Weiner 1997) into vigorous discussion, reflecting long-standing anthropological concerns about the changing status of culture in its progressively more objectified and negotiated states. What seems a more serious and pressing issue for Iglulingmiut, however—more than that of authenticity—is that of political efficacy as Inuit press their rights to self-determination within multicultural Canada. Cultural difference continues to be defined using western visions. It is acknowledged and legitimized only insofar as it conforms to western frames of reference (Clifford 1988).

Anthropological Paradigms and the "Remote Iglulingmiut"

Most of the field research for this chapter was undertaken during my 1997–98 stay in Igloolik, Nunavut. This community lies on an island in the Northern Foxe Basin approximately 3,400 kilometers north of Montreal and a one-and-a-half-hour flight north of Iqaluit. What drew me to this settlement (and away from my previous fieldsite of Pond Inlet) was its reputation among ethnographers and in contemporary arctic circles as a particularly remote and traditional settlement in the eastern High Arctic. As more than a decade of discussions of the politics of historiography in hunter-gatherer studies has taught us, anthropological reporting about remote and bounded communities is seldom politically or academically neutral.

Explanations provided for Igloolik's reputation as a remote and traditional place most often point to its relatively recent history of contact. Pack ice in the Northern Foxe Basin kept many European explorers and whalers from reaching the region. The first recorded contact between qallunaat and Iglulingmiut occurred in the early nineteenth century when Captains William Parry and George Lyon, along with 150 crewmembers from the British Naval Expedition, spent the winters of 1822–23 and 1823–24 on

Iglulingmiut lands. There the Englishmen lived among an Inuit population that Parry estimated to be between three and four hundred (Parry 1826: 549). Parry and Lyon both chronicled their dealings with what they considered an isolated polar group. Yet Igloolik Island was a frequented site; it was a nexus of overland travel for Inuit groups around the region during the eighteenth and nineteenth centuries (Stevenson 1997: 269) and, with its proximity to one of the largest walrus herds in the world, perhaps earlier. Metal utensils and meat trays were already in use when the explorers arrived (Parry 1826: 503; Lyon 1824: 346 cited in Mary-Rousselière 1984: 443), and a trade in meat, furs, metal, and wood quickly developed between crewmembers and the Inuit village settled around the British vessels. Inuit also drew upon European aesthetic classifications of their culture to produce souvenirs and Inuit cultural artifacts for crewmembers. The Inuit, wrote Parry, "brought with them a great many little canoes and paddles, sledges, figures of men and women, and other toys, most of them already bespoke by the officers and men, and the rest for sale" (1826: 173). Cultural difference and uniqueness, for nineteenth-century Iglulingmiut, became something marketable.

Anthropology's development as a modern, scientific discipline, and in particular Franz Boas's inaugural 1883–84 fieldwork in Canada's eastern High Arctic, is equally responsible for popular characterizations of the Iglulingmiut as a pristine aboriginal people. Boas's original goal had been to sail from Germany to the whaling station at Cumberland Sound. There he had hoped to find Inuit guides who would take him to the west coast of Baffin Island, across Fury and Hecla Strait, and "on [to] the shores of which the Iglulik band of Eskimos have their residence" (cited in Müller-Wille 1998: 40). To Boas the Iglulingmiut promised to exhibit a more thorough adaptation to their natural environment than those groups who had been living among whalers or who had more contact with explorers. He believed that geophysical and ethnographic data from this "isolated" and "pure" group would demonstrate early states of Inuit cultural development. Boas's plan to reach Iglulingmiut territories was never realized. Pack ice, poor weather, and disease among the dogs confined his fieldwork to short trips around Cumberland Sound, a region where the resident Inuit had had over a hundred years of contact with whalers (Cole and Müller-Wille 1984: 45–51).

Boas did not return to the Arctic after 1884 but instead moved his fieldwork to the northwest coast of North America. However he continued to study the polar regions from his post at the American Museum of Natural History, hiring field hands, such as American whaler George Comer, to collect data and artifacts. Before Comer's arctic voyage of 1900–1902 Boas presented him with a shopping list, requesting, among other things, items and data from the "remote Iglulingmiut" (Ross 1984: 148–49). Comer's subsequent collecting for Boas during the voyages of 1907–1909 and 1910–12 focused on data pertaining to the Inuit body (plaster casts of Inuit faces and body parts as well as skeletal material). The Iglulingmiut were of value to Boas's theories about cultural diffusion.[3] In the museum Boas depicted the Iglulingmiut as exhibiting the pure form of Inuit culture.

When Knud Rasmussen and members of the Fifth Thule Expedition arrived in the Igloolik region during the winter of 1921–22, the Iglulingmiut were experiencing considerable social and economic upheaval. Overhunting by whalers on the edges of their territories had depleted the game. Also, the early twentieth century saw the arrival of non-Inuit traders, missionaries, and eventually Royal Canadian Mounted Police as permanent residents of the North (Grant 2002). A popular account of this same expedition by explorer Peter Freuchen describes alcohol consumption and square dancing at local trading posts (1935: 385–86) as well as a Christian syncretic religious movement in the Igloolik region in the 1920s (1935: 385–90). Yet Rasmussen's scientific monograph detailing the symbolic culture of the Iglulingmiut (Rasmussen 1929) and that of his colleague archaeologist Therkel Mathiassen (1928) reporting on the material culture make little mention of these social changes. Rasmussen was, in fact, searching for indications of a "primordial Inuit religion" evidenced in the oral traditions and material artifacts of Inuit shamans. He envisioned the Fifth Thule Expedition as a chance to "travel back through time" (Sonne 1988: 24) to the barrenlands of the Canadian interior, which he believed were inhabited by descendants of the "original Inuit" (Burch 1988; de Laguna 1994: 14–15). Beginning this journey among the Iglulingmiut, Rasmussen described his meetings with Iglulingmiut families of the 1920s as being "transported to another age; an age of legends of the past" (1927: 5), one in which "despite their tea and flour and incipient enamel-ware culture . . . as regards their view of life and habit of thought" the Inuit were "little changed from their ancestors of ages past" (1927: 8).

A secondary goal of Rasmussen's ethnographic work had been to define and classify Inuit culture groups. While historic evidence of seminomadic movement and migration as well as intermarriage between groups made this spatial demarcation a nebulous task, Rasmussen nonetheless distinguished the "Iglulingmiut" from two other culture groups in the region, their neighbors the "Aivilingmiut" and "Tununermiut." He institutionalized the bounded category Iglulingmiut as an object of study for western science (Saladin d'Anglure 1988: 72–74).

The post–World War II era brought welfare colonialism to the Canadian North (Tester and Kulchyski 1994). Images of remote and pristine culture groups were conjoined with equally pervasive western notions of Inuit culture on the brink of collapse. Inuit traditions, inventoried in the early ethnographic accounts, were newly cast in arctic anthropology not only as mechanisms for adaptation and survival but alternatively as forms of filters or brakes, "an inertial force influencing Eskimo activity vis-à-vis the non Eskimo world" (Riches 1990: 72). As post–World War II government policies of northern development were implemented, Inuit were incorporated into the Canadian welfare and education systems. In an effort to inform effective policy making in the North, many arctic anthropologists turned from making cultural inventories to studies of acculturation.

Iglulingmiut families living in the newly created settlement were more accessible as scientific subjects and informants than they had been in the past. Settlements in the Eastern Arctic were considered by many as microcosms of southern society, exhibiting skewed political and economic relations between Inuit and qallunaat (Brody 1975; Paine 1977). The late 1960s and 1970s saw increasing numbers of administrators and scientists traveling to Igloolik. A new colonial/research environment in the North developed that altered Inuit forms of cultural production. Visiting social scientists flying in and out were less reliant on the Inuit for their physical survival than their predecessors had been, thus weakening the bartering power of the Inuit informants and subjects. Settlement-bound Inuit were also more readily available than they had been in the past to provide information for acculturation studies, surveys, questionnaires, and extensive interviews related to topics such as food consumption, health and social issues, land use, technology, sharing networks, and kinship patterns. Research in Igloolik reached a pinnacle between 1968 and 1972, when dozens of western scientists working as part of the International Biological Programme Human Adaptability Project based their Canadian Artic fieldsite in Igloolik and collected social science and biometric data from the majority of the local population (see Katsak in Wachowich et al. 1999: 174–77). As a result, mundane and utilitarian cultural practices from their previous life on the land (such as dog team travel, hunting, snowhouse building, sharing, and skin sewing) were awarded new symbolic, moral value as Inuit traditions by ethnographers and colonial administrators alike. Traditions became standards against which to measure social change in the context of settlement life; their preservation was cast redemptively against the threat of assimilation into the modern western nation.

By objectifying, classifying, and assigning relative value to presumably traditional Inuit cultural practices, arctic anthropologists since Boas and Rasmussen have engaged in the construction of the Iglulingmiut as a people to be studied. Arctic anthropology's development as a discipline has helped transform the tundra, the Inuit, and their material culture into objects of investigation for science. In the face of this cultural intrusion, Inuit creatively transformed these symbolically laden traits into politically effectual emblems of the contrast between Inuit and qallunaat worlds (Briggs 1997; Graburn, Searles, this volume).

Tradition as a Domain of Value in Igloolik: The Cement Igloo

The early 1970s were a time of profound change for the Iglulingmiut as the last families moved from their camps on the land into a government-built settlement. The Anik A satellite was launched at this time, providing telecommunications to settlements across the Canadian North.[4] A new professional class of young Inuit nationalists arrived back in the settlement—graduates of residential schools and assertively trained in western modes of thought. In Igloolik and across the North, a movement began to redress assimilationist government policies and to revalorize Inuit past lifestyles. In 1972, at the instigation of the resident Oblate Catholic priest/administrator and various Inuit community leaders, a formal elders group called the Inummariit Society was founded in Igloolik with a mandate to preserve Inuit traditions.[5] This cultural consciousness was afforded textual representation through the publication of a compilation of serials called the Inummariit Collection.

The physical landscape of the settlement was also transformed when the Inummariit Society began constructing a two-story igloo-shaped building of stone and cement in the center of the Igloolik (fig. 7.2). Named the Igloolik Cultural Centre and completed in 1972, the cement igloo was equipped with cabinets and shelves and was used as a museum exhibition space for hunting implements such as harpoons, bladder-floats, knives, skin clothing, qulliit (stone lamps, sing. qulliq), and other tools that Inuit had stopped using when they moved into the settlement. Qallunaat visitors to Igloolik interested in learning about Inuit culture were directed there. Elders were solicited to hold workshops for these visitors and for locals inside the igloo, where they would tell stories and explain the practices that had once been a part of their everyday lives on the land.

A number of individuals expressed feelings of sadness and loss at seeing one's culture packaged and displayed. One Inuk told me about visiting the Cultural Centre and finding the qulliq that her grandmother had donated in the late 1960s when her family finally moved in from the land. "It was a nice big black stone qulliq," she said. "It was really, really nice." She recounted how on her return from boarding school in Ottawa in the summer of 1973, she felt a chill run down her spine when she saw her grandmother's qulliq in the Cultural Centre, sitting cold and positioned beside others of various sizes and shapes on a shelf. Just a few years earlier, she said, she had watched her grandmother carefully tending this same qulliq's flame in their tent (Author's fieldnotes, November 13, 1997). The lamp, once used to heat a home and to cook food for a family, was awarded a new use-value as an artifact of times past.

The Igloolik Cultural Centre igloo was a designated space in the local landscape where attempts were made to venerate Inuit traditions. Yet the erection of this stone igloo-shaped museum, like the creation of other intercultural sites, was not without its ironies. Museums, permanent cement structures, and the valuation and display of material goods are extrinsic to this formerly seminomadic people; they conform more to western historical visions of the Inuit as a museum culture than they do to contemporary social realities in arctic communities. Graburn describes the similarly short-lived igloo-shaped wooden museum in Puvirnituq (1998a, this volume). Soon after it was built, the Igloolik Cultural Centre was declared a white elephant. Made from the wrong materials for the arctic environment, the building was nearly impossible to heat. Its stone walls frosted over and blackened with use of the Inuit qulliit. Visitors complained that the building was cold, drafty, and damp. Skins dried or rotted in this environment. Few local Inuit spent time at the site.

As the 1970s and 1980s progressed, and the first generation of Inuit born and raised in the settlement reached adulthood, it was no longer in Inuit interests to suggest or to show that theirs was a museum culture. Paramount for Inuit in their land claims negotiations was their ability to demonstrate a unique and living relationship to the environment. Land increasingly became the prevailing symbol of Inuit cultural identity, and the contemporary and ongoing Inuit relationship to that land was precisely the feature that distinguished them from qallunaat.

A few years after the Igloolik Cultural Centre opened, the missionary who

7.2. The Igloolik Cultural Centre. Reproduced with the permission of the Missionary Oblates of Mary Immaculate, Diocese of Churchill, Hudson Bay.

had initiated and administered the project moved to another community, and government funding was withdrawn. Without southern financial backing, the Inummariit Society disbanded and the stone igloo was boarded up. Tools and artifacts were retrieved and either stored or put back into use by Iglulingmiut families. Soon the building began to disintegrate, and the structure became a climbing and play area for local children. When a falling section of roof fatally injured a young child, the community council declared the site hazardous and sent in wrecking crews. The site remained vacant until 1995, when Igloolik Isuma Productions constructed their office and studio on the empty lot.

Bureaucratized Settlements: Exhibiting Lived Relationships with the Land

Inuit political movements of the 1970s and 1980s made it increasingly important for Iglulingmiut to exhibit nationally and internationally that they were an adaptive people, a people whose age-old hunting culture remained alive and well in the context of modern settlement life. In the 1980s a second Igloolik elders' organization, the Inullariit Group, was formed with a new mandate to preserve and maintain Inuit traditions. Administered by John MacDonald, a long-term non-Inuit resident of Igloolik (and director of the Igloolik Nunavut Research Institute), and a local committee, the Inullariit Group was incorporated as a society in 1993. This designation gave them legal power to solicit government and private funding in order to collect, inventory, preserve, and exhibit their cultural past in an increasingly bureau-cratized Canadian North.

One of the first projects initiated by the Inullariit Society was a com-prehensive oral history project, which today includes close to five hundred interviews. The oral histories have been translated into English, transcribed in both Inuktitut and English, and stored in a computer database program. They document Inuit cultural practices from the past, such as hunting, sewing, skin preparation, child care, Inuit forms of social control, dietary practices, astronomy and Inuit cosmology, land navigation, kinship, dic-tion, and geographic data, among other things. Stored in Igloolik (with copies sent to the Northwest Territorial Archive at the Prince of Wales Northern Heritage Centre archives in Yellowknife), key-word search tools allow the database to act as an encyclopedia of Iglulingmiut traditional knowledge. Since 1994 the Inullariit Society has also operated winter and summer survival and land skills programs in which elders accompany young people to hunting camps to teach land skills (hunting, navigation, skinning, butchering, skin processing, collecting moss and lichens, and the production of shelters and tools).[6] Other related programs include drum-dancing classes, skin preparation and skin sewing workshops, igloo build-ing classes, and Inuit navigation workshops (fig. 7.3). Inuktitut Language Week is held annually with workshops and radio phone-in programs pro-moting proper Inuktitut diction. Language Week coincides with the late January celebration called Qaggiq: The Return of the Sun, when a large cer-emonial igloo is built and drum dancers, square dancers, and throat singers perform in conjunction with a fashion show of traditional skin clothing and speeches by elders and politicians.

These projects bring community members together to focus on cultural revitalization and allow young people to participate in aspects of "tradi-tional" life that they might otherwise have missed. The sustained variety and continuation of these programs is a testament to the commitment of the members of the Inullariit Society, who are constantly rallying not just com-

7.3. An Inullariit igloo-building class on the hill beside Igloolik,
May 1997. Photo by Nancy Wachowich.

munity members but also outside agencies for assistance. None of these
activities would be possible without external financial support. Inullariit Society administrators prepare grant proposals in response to funding initiatives established by government and private organizations. Successful bids
translate into yearly endowments to the society, the income from which is
distributed to Iglulingmiut staff and participants in the workshops, classes,
camps, radio phone-in programs, and annual celebrations. At the end of
each fiscal term, the required reports are generated by the Inullariit Society
and circulated in Nunavut and the South, describing the success of this
"traditional" Inuit community in adapting to social change and strengthening their relationships with their physical environment as well as with one
another. These hybridized productions exist as memorials to the not-too-
distant traditional past made to speak to the increasingly bureaucratized
present.

Consumers of this new Inuit cultural capital are first of all Inuit youth,
who may not have the cultural knowledge that elders think valuable and yet
must be taught ways to assert future Inuit rights as a traditional hunting
people. "To learn the way of becoming an Inuk, that is the reasons they
[the youth] came to this area. I tried to advise them regarding that," wrote
Iglulingmiut elder Arsène Ivalu in a 1996 government report describing the
lessons he taught at a summer caribou-hunting land skills camp (Inullariit

Elders Society files, 1993–97). Secondary consumers are journalists, teachers, and scholars with an interest in Inuit cultural history. Government funding agencies and charitable organizations are mediators in this production cycle, uniting the social needs of Iglulingmiut with the ideological needs of northern and southern (taxpaying) populations. Popular and political imaginings of the North (see Grace 2001) replace images of strife or welfare colonialism (see Tester and Kulchyski 1994) with affirmative tales of a strong and sovereign Canadian Arctic.

In January 2000, in recognition of the volume of traditional knowledge compiled by the Inullariit elders, the society won the government of Canada's 1999 Northern Science Award, an honor most often awarded to university-based scientists.[7] At the award ceremony Arsène Ivalu, then president of the Inullariit Society, used this national forum to promote his group's mandate. Addressing the assembled audience of politicians, administrators, scientists, media personnel, and Iglulingmiut and speaking through a translator, Ivalu declared: "The culture is not being shown enough. . . . The thing is it's not dying at all because we are going to make it continue" (McKibbon 2000). By appropriating western strategies of cultural preservation and by deploying the rhetoric of spectacle and display within his speech, Ivalu drew upon a modern history of colonial encounters with scientists, administrators, and many other southern interfaces in order to promote the preservation and rejuvenation of Inuit cultural values. By "showing" their culture, the Inullariit Society, he pledged, acts as a brake to what many outsiders perceive as Inuit cultural deterioration. Through his engagement in this intercultural dialogue, Ivalu rallied financial and political support for the Inullariit salvage and cultural rehabilitation projects. This would ensure that his family and community would acquire necessary endowments to "show" their culture into the twenty-first century.

The Inullariit Society workshops have been fostered by a unique set of social relations different from those existing in the generations before the move into settlements. Stone igloos and workshops that teach Inuktitut language, land skills, and performance arts emerge as new forms of Inuit customs, rituals, values, institutions, and social relations. This contemporary network involves innovative technologies, actors, and commodities and marks Inuit assertions of their history and identity in the cultural present.

The Media Value of Inuit Images: Filming Life on the Land

The development of independent film and video in Igloolik has further projected Iglulingmiut identity politics into international arenas. Igloolik Isuma Productions was founded in 1988 and incorporated in 1990 by four independent video makers living in Igloolik (three Inuit and one qallunaq). In 1991 Isuma also established a nonprofit sister organization, a video cooperative called the Tariagsuk Video Centre (also known as the Women's Video Workshop). The body of work produced by these videographers is extensive, ranging from small-scale community-based Inuktitut videos and footage of community events to broadcast-quality television programs, short arthouse films, and most recently the internationally celebrated feature film *Atanarjuat: The Fast Runner*. During my 1997–98 stay in Igloolik I assisted Isuma's videographers in the production of a series of programs aired on local television entitled *The Qallunaat Project*, illustrating nineteenth- and twentieth-century European worldviews at the time of early European-Iglulingmiut culture contact. I also conducted a review of their film archives documenting a decade of footage of Iglulingmiut cultural practices— hunting, traveling, dog teaming, marine navigation; wielding harpoons, spears, and knives; tool construction, operating rifles and outboard motors, butchering meat, tending qulliit, processing and sewing skins, and raising children—along with scenes and events from contemporary settlement life.

Igloolik Isuma's media making has been depicted as part of a history of visual aesthetics of Inuit cultural forms reaching back to early colonial photography in the Arctic (King and Lidchi 1998) and Flaherty's 1922 *Nanook of the North*. While their films seem to conform to dominant media formatting—they program their pieces as serials, short films, feature films, etc.— their modes of production and aesthetic expressions simultaneously challenge these stereotypes and illustrate elements of the videographers' own Inuit and alternate media perspectives (see Ginsburg 1994; Turner 1991, 1992).

Igloolik Isuma films look different than most television, documentary, or Hollywood productions. This is partially due to the particular technology they use, but it is also the result of the particular subjects they frame and the videographic techniques employed. Long shots that picture people moving in a vast landscape and real-time filming techniques offer visual and temporal perspectives reminiscent of those held by Inuit hunters and travelers on the land. The dramatic reenactments of traditional life on the land add to this effect, suggesting an intimacy between actors and between subject and audience that makes many audiences think they are viewing a documentary rather than a work of fiction. The realistic effect is also due to the social process of filmmaking employed by Isuma. For example, during the shooting of a series of dramas that were set in the Igloolik region of the 1940s—the 1988–93 *Qaggiq Trilogy* and the thirteen-part 1994 *Nunavut Series*—each Iglulingmiut actor was encouraged to play his or her *atiq* (namesake). Actors improvised scenes by acting and reacting according to the characteristics and social relationships of the previous person who held the name, the person's whose soul an individual is said to share. Actors young and old thus played themselves, as they had existed in the 1940s. As was explained to me by filmmaker Paul Apak Angilirq, actors were both acting and "living through" their previous relationships to one another and to the land (Interview with the author, April 16, 1997).

Igloolik Isuma Productions deliberately employed Iglulingmiut perspectives on vision, time, mortality, and social and environmental relatedness in the filming of their early historical reproductions, for example the *Qaggig Trilogy* and the *Nunavut Series*.[8] By doing this they created a new social reality that brought these traditions to life. These living fictionalizations (a term they use) exist as reproductions, but on another level the actors are actually hunting, sewing, traveling, and answering to their Inuktitut names while living in camps with the camera running. Varied sites of screening and reception of these images infuse their programs with multivalent meaning as Inuit hunting implements, clothing, and cultural practices take on alternate meanings as tools, as artifacts, as art, or even as Inuit kitsch, depending on whether the programs are aired on local Igloolik or public broadcasting systems, at international film festivals, in museums, or—with the release of *Atanarjuat: The Fast Runner*—at mainstream movie theaters. Assorted audiences process these images using differing frameworks of understanding. Consequently the media value extrapolated from Inuit traditions varies.

Part of the attraction of western visual media to these Iglulingmiut videographers, besides the obvious community benefits, is that media offers them a wider network of national, international, and cosmopolitan audiences for whom they can project the image of a continuing Inuit presence upon the landscape of the North. For the Isuma producers the visual documentation of contemporary Inuit land-based practices, and of the assertion of control over their own self-representations in this communication age, is a sharply politicized manifesto. Zacharias Kunuk declares: "How else could we build igloos for the film, sew clothing, make harpoons and run dog teams if our culture had died out? How could a cast and crew of sixty professional Inuit make a movie in Igloolik if we were all dropouts and drunks? *Atanarjuat* shows a national TV audience our culture from an Inuit point of view, not as victims but with the skills and strength to survive 4000 years with our identity intact. Inuit culture is alive; that is our statement, not yours" (quoted in Cousineau 1998).

The fusion of western and Inuit visual media practices allows Isuma videographers to present exclusive renderings of Inuit history and identity that are otherwise difficult to articulate within western frameworks of understanding. Through film, Iglulingmiut assert their authority over both the medium and the message of cultural survival. The breadth and impact of their media practices provide further insight into the institutionalization of Inuit traditions.

Social Science Research and Inuit Modernities

All of the cultural programs currently running in Igloolik are part of the cash economy, supported by endowments, small grants, or technical support from government and private organizations. Administrators, researchers, elder advisors/instructors, storytellers, translators, transcribers, actors, dancers, singers, facilitators, artisans, technicians, participants in workshops and summer camps, and extras on the film set all receive payment for their participation in these projects. Grants also cover the cost of transportation and equipment. The paradox inherent in this financial and cultural exchange is that while people are increasingly promoting themselves as traditional hunters in the modern world system, it is nevertheless the case that without the added income from these projects, many Iglulingmiut would be unable to afford to buy snowmobiles, guns, and gasoline in order to hunt on the land (or to own or rent homes, pay taxes, travel, or purchase heating oil, electricity, municipal services, food, clothing, etc.). Representations of Iglulingmiut land skills, life skills, and hunting practices in material, textual, and video varieties have imparted to Inuit hunting practices new economic, social, and symbolic value and have thus encouraged their perseverance.

The successful production and marketing of objectified Iglulingmiut land skills and their circulation through modern networks of information and exchange reinforce Igloolik's reputation as one of the last bastions of Inuit cultural traditions in Nunavut. Nunavut government offices aimed at cultural retention, such as the Nunavut Social Development Council, the Baffin Cultural Institute, and the Nunavut government's Department of Culture, Language, Elders and Youth, were established in or moved to Igloolik in the 1990s. Iglulingmiut elders, recognized as expert consultants in IQ, have been appointed to boards and flown to meetings outside Igloolik. Igloolik Isuma's short films have been televised increasingly on networks such as the Knowledge Network and Bravo and added to film collections in museums, galleries, and universities. The 2001–2002 international release and acclaim of Isuma's feature film *Atanarjuat: The Fast Runner* sent Igluling-miut producers, directors, and actors to film festivals, award ceremonies, and conferences in cosmopolitan centers of North America, Europe, and Asia to present the film and accept awards.

Environmental barriers such as pack ice, blizzards, and ice squalls and the threat of starvation and frostbite kept many early explorers and early anthropologists from reaching Igloolik, thus distinguishing it as a remote and pristine place in the western imagination. As contemporary anthropologists we face different and equally pervasive boundaries around our research practices as we attempt to navigate the often complicated terrain of arctic fieldwork in the twenty-first century. Our practices now intersect with the politicization and commodification of Inuit cultural productions and with the motives and practices of other culture seekers: tourists, filmmakers, journalists, curators, administrators, etc. The Canadian Arctic has become a politically charged environment for social science research.

Meetings between Inuit and academics over the past three decades have witnessed an increased and formalized attention paid to the power and politics of social science research, to the definition and administration of intellectual property rights, and to efforts at developing collaborative research strategies (Wenzel 1997). Moreover, the tensions between southern and local research initiatives endure as Inuit stories of the "freedom of exploitation" by social scientists seeking "to exploit Inuit knowledge" for professional gain have been made part of public discourse (Flaherty 1995: 179). Well-intentioned but highly bureaucratic university and Nunavut ethical review committees and licensing procedures, as well as rising honoraria payments, have created a new social climate for anthropologists; one with a very different set of social and environmental boundaries than those that formerly existed.

Igloolik's reputation as a traditional place has been conscripted into Iglulingmiut assertions of their identity as hunters in the modern world. As a result hunting has taken on new meanings in this process and intersects with broader questions of authenticity, cultural politics, and cultural survival of the world's hunting and gathering peoples. In a recent paper Robin

Ridington (2002: 116) raised a set of rhetorical questions about aboriginal authenticity among North American First Nations: "Are aboriginal people from hunting and gathering traditions who eat pizza (or those who have law degrees or teach at universities or write novels or practice in the visual or dramatic arts) no longer authentically aboriginal? Must we relegate them to the status of former hunter-gatherers?".

It may be true, as Ridington points out, that definitions of hunting and gathering peoples drawn "too closely to 'authentic' aboriginal activities" may result in defining them right out of existence (116). In this same vein, some arctic anthropologists have argued that subsistence is a wider category than has previously been acknowledged. Subsistence, it is surmised, must extend beyond concepts of the ecological and the material to incorporate the social exchanges, values, and actions that are part of modern hunting communities (Dahl 2000; Fienup-Riordan 1983, 2000; Nuttall 1992; Wenzel 1991). Hunting and gathering relate to a specific economic mode of production, but they also entail the reproduction of a set of values and "forager modes of thought" (Barnard 2002) in the contemporary world. Iglulingmiut have resourcefully maintained their roles and status as hunters in the present day even when the "giving environment" (Bird-David 1990)— the Canadian Arctic and beyond—is one in which stuffed dogs, stone igloos, workshops, and film sets exist on equal grounds with snowmobiles, tents, and rifles as forms of hunting technology.

Acknowledgments

I would like to express my sincere thanks to a number of people in Igloolik who helped me understand this culture-making process. Among them are Paul Angilirq Apak, Meeka Aqqiaruq, Norman Cohn, Emile Immaroituk, Arsène and Madeline Ivalu, Zacharias Kunuk, John MacDonald, and Leah Aksaajuq Otak. Thank you to Apphia Agalakti Awa, Rhoda Katsak, Sandra Omik, and Phillipa Ootoowak in Pond Inlet. I am grateful as well to David Anderson, Patricia Badir, Julie Cruikshank, Aaron Glass, and John MacDonald for their helpful comments and suggestions on earlier drafts of this essay. This research was funded in part from grants from the Canadian Circumpolar Institute, the Canadian Northern Scientific Training Program, and a doctoral fellowship from the Social Sciences and Humanities Research Council of Canada.

Notes

1. Nunavut territorial law requires recreational hunters to hire an Inuit guide and use a dog team when hunting polar bear.

2. While the term *southerner* is arguably more appropriate for accounts of arctic culture contact, I deliberately use *westerner* to flag resonances with broad-scale historical, political, and ideological relations between indigenous peoples and colonial empires.

3. Iglulingmiut data were of particular value in evolutionary debates of the period. The skulls of eastern High Arctic Inuit, noted by phrenologists of that period for being particularly long and high (McGhee 1996: 16), were compared with skulls found in Upper Palaeolithic caves, the hypothesis being that the Inuit were stone age survivors (de Laguna 1994: 10). During those voyages Comer made and collected 220 casts that were said to represent ten groups of Inuit; these included 177 casts of Inuit faces, forty-one of hands, and two of torsos (Ross 1984: 154). He also collected photographs, sound recordings of Inuit songs, dances, and tales, and skeletal material, including close to a dozen Inuit skulls (Ross 1984: 160–61). Many of these came from Iglulingmiut (Saladin d'Anglure 1984: 177).

4. Residents in Igloolik voted first in 1973 and again in 1978 to ban television from the community. In 1983, following the establishment of the Inuit Broadcasting Corporation, television was permitted in Igloolik.

5. Missionaries often acted as facilitators for the modernization process by translating for government officials and promoting the schooling of children in church-run residential schools and federal day schools. Yet inherent contradictions in the missionary enterprise (see Thomas 1994) are well recorded in such efforts as well as in the published lamentations from that period regarding the loss of traditions and increased westernization of Inuit life (Mary-Rousselière 1972, 1974, 1976–77).

6. A 1994 Inullariit proposal for this program declared: "The loss of 'land skills' means more today than not being able to function effectively while hunting, or being unable to prepare skins for clothing; it is a loss of cultural pride and dignity" (Inullariit Elders Society files, 1993–97).

7. It was declared at the ceremony that indigenous traditional ecological knowledge (TEK) had been put on par with scientific knowledge. The irony here is that advocates of indigenous knowledge are compelled to adopt the frameworks and rhetoric of science in order "to challenge the Western scientific perspectives they see as influencing their lives and placing an imposition on their rights to self-determination" (Nuttall 1998b: 89).

8. *Atanarjuat: The Fast Runner* was set in the Iglulingmiut precontact period. Actors were working from a script, and many of the characters in the original oral versions of the tale did not have namesakes in the settlement. The directors thus decided not to employ this atiq acting method for the film.

EIGHT

Culture as Narrative

Nelson Graburn

The immense changes leading up to the 1999 establishment of the Nunavut Territory in Canada have challenged Inuit there to redefine themselves and their place in the world. In doing so, Inuit have come to question the ways in which they are uniquely Inuit and by what means they remain Inuit.

This chapter focuses on the ways Inuitness (*inunguniq*, the quality of "being Inuit") is challenged, changed, fractured, and reinforced in today's formal and informal institutions.[1] It focuses particularly on the ways that the *qallunaat* are part of shaping and enabling the Inuitness of Inuit. Inuit are concerned—almost hypersensitive—about the survival of "their culture" (Graburn 1998a) and thus very self-consciously engaged in conversations about and pursuing activities aimed at ensuring the perpetuation of their culture. This dramatically changed nature and context of cultural transmission provokes questions about the nature of the Inuit culture being transmitted. Thus this essay problematizes the nature of the culture being transmitted and, of course, the anthropological uses of the concept of culture.

If we consider even partially the relevance of MacLuhan's aphorism that *The Medium Is the Message* (1967), then we have to consider that the various channels by which this as yet vague information called "culture" is transmitted are as important as the information itself. On the other hand, we could show that MacLuhan was wrong or overemphasized the nature of the channels. The MacLuhanesque approach would then have us believe that "modern" culture—now equated with "global" culture—is that which is transmitted and supported by a huge variety of personal, institutional, and technical mechanisms, totally different from those "local" cultures transmitted and kept in conversation by direct personal oral, visual, and tactile channels. If this is so, we have to ask whether "modern" Inuit culture is like a local dialect or a subculture of the modern world-system global culture.

Unself-Consciousness and Self-Consciousness of Cultural Transmission

In earlier eras the transmission of uniquely Inuit culture occurred by example through intimate child rearing and living, transmission often being between older and younger generations of the same gender. Such mechanisms, typical of most community-based, nonliterate, and "nonmedia" societies, have been well described (Briggs 1970, 1998). For several generations even the most remote Inuit were aware of the existence of qallunaat strangers. They were probably unaware, however, of the family life or intimate culture of the newcomers. [2]

Many Inuit later confessed to me that at the time of my first sojourns in the Arctic, they still believed that qallunaat were not like them as human beings but were a different, perhaps spiritually more powerful kind of entity. Except that Inuit had already become "Christian" and were using imported technologies such as guns, tea, flour, and sometimes cloth clothing, the "choice" of large-scale cultural change was not immediate. Nevertheless, the very knowledge of another way of life and the cultural changes undertaken introduced a heightened self-consciousness among Inuit about their own culture. Qallunaat culture formed a mirror by which Inuit were able to see and compare their own culture. The very self-consciousness about difference may have worked to erode some aspects of Inuit traditional culture.

The chapter by Peter Kulchyski in this volume usefully reminds us that "culture" is far from being constituted by an array of traits that can be selected or "saved" at will. His particular example, the "conversation" carried out between Inuit in facial expressions, is learned by very young children and becomes what in modern parlance is part of the individual's *habitus* (Bourdieu 1977: 78–87); that is, an acquired, almost subconscious set of behavioral dispositions inculcated by social experiences. Acquired bodily dispositions such as walking, squatting, eating, and so on, sometimes called *hexis* (Bourdieu 1977: 78–87; 1993: 105), are parts of this tacit "grammar of performance" just as turn taking, breathing, or tone inflecting are parts of culturally or idiosyncratically acquired rules of conversation.

Bourdieu's theory of cultural transmission, in which he focuses on cultural reproduction rather than change, lies at the core of his *Practice Theory* (1977). Here he rejects not only naïve functionalism but also the existence of objective "social structures" that can be transmitted from generation to generation. Rather, culture is transmitted through practices that, though perceived consciously, become habits which in his metaconcept of habitus are then tacit or unconscious. Referring to a certain kind of cultural competence he explains: "Since . . . competence is the product of an imperceptible familiarization and an automatic transferring of attitudes, members of [these] classes are . . . inclined to regard it as a gift of nature . . . as *becoming natural*. Culture is thus achieved only by negating itself as such . . . to become second nature, a habitus" (1993: 234). At another point Bourdieu (1977: 78–79) suggests that the unconsciousness of these cultural and bodily dispositions is nothing but the forgetting of the context of acquisition.

But anthropologists or others, such as Inuit, who are exposed to strangers can notice and learn dispositions on purpose, like actors, as well as unconsciously.[3] Hence we have the paradox that cultural and bodily dispositions (including the linguistic and metalinguistic) that normally and traditionally were matters of habitus can come to consciousness and can be specifically selected for preservation by sensitive members of a threatened cultural group. Thus attitudes and behaviors that are or were at one time normally practiced unconsciously can become conscious and subject to preservation efforts at another time or by other members of the same group.

Self-Consciousness in Family and Group Settings

Awareness of the erosion of Inuit traditional culture and language arose across the North in many ways and was experienced differently in different areas and even by particular individuals. Those Inuit who were taken south for tuberculosis treatment or for education or other reasons often got to know white people "as people" and to visit their homes and see their families. From the 1950s on their tales were spread far and wide, and by the 1960s almost all Inuit knew someone who had lived in the South.

This intimacy and the "education" of those who had lived "down South" brought up the possibility of speaking English not just as a limited-purpose trade language but as a true alternative. Also by the 1960s, with the growth of media such as radio and written information as in schools, Nunavut Inuit began to hear that Alaskan Iñupiat and other Inuit were in danger of losing their language. One result was a conscious movement to preserve the language through various political actions in the Eastern Arctic, including having the first years of schooling conducted in Inuttitut.[4] Eventually some adults, even if bilingual, consciously started speaking Inuttitut to children all the time. As reported by Dorais (2002) adults may make a self-conscious point of talking Inuttitut with other adults in front of children to set an example. Some families insist on putting on or leaving on the TV and radio programs in Inuttitut. But even with a high degree of self-consciousness and commitment, there are problems: Inuttitut teachers themselves admit that they do not always speak Inuttitut to their kids at home (Graburn and Iutzi-Mitchell 1992).

In regions where the Inuttitut language is not used much, other traits or expressions of Inuitness, such as whale hunting (Freeman 1998), rights to subsistence hunting and gathering and the consumption of Inuit foods (Lee 2002), traditional dress, or the Northern Games are defended as icons of Inuit culture.

During my fieldwork in 2000 I observed conscious efforts to continue eating and, importantly, to get children to eat niqituinak—that is, an Inuit diet or particular Inuit foods. These foods include some that are iconically inuttitut, such as maktak (whale skin and blubber) or qisaruaq (the chewed cud in the caribou's stomach), but also specifically Inuit ways of processing foods: igunak, aranaq (fermented in oil); frozen (quak); with rancid seal oil (misiraq); and above all mikijjipuk, uujungituk (raw). [5] Of course most Inuit are not purists, and novelty cuisine is common, for instance combining cooking methods and Inuit foods, such as cooked maktak or freezing qis-aruaq with small chunks of caribou steak inside the stomach in the kitchen freezer—delicious.

Inuit uniformly reported that if you do not get children to eat raw meat by the age of three, they never learn to like it. Adults told me that they themselves missed the opportunity when young, possibly because of lack of "country foods" in their family then or because they were in hospital down south, and thus they cannot eat raw meat. At the same time they wonder how I, raised in England until the age of twenty-one, could have come to enjoy it. Most Inuit children are accustomed to store-bought foods from an early age, so teaching a child to eat raw meat becomes a concentrated effort, in which some relative, perhaps a grandfather concerned with the loss of culture, tries to get the child to eat, chew, and swallow while other family members look on anxiously.

It should also be said that the way food is distributed and eaten is an important and sometimes iconic Inuit cultural trait. By this I mean the sharing of "mass foods" (i.e., foods that have been obtained in large chunks, such as caribou or white whale, or smaller species obtained in large quantities, such as murres or char; cf. Graburn 1969a: 68–72). The sharing is a division that first takes place once the hunters arrive at the home community, often outdoors, and later the sharing that takes place inside dwellings when the extended family or wider community group is invited to come and eat—and to take away some food. These sharing episodes are doubly inuttitut because not only do they differ from the qallunaat customs of sharing within the nuclear family and ubiquitous buying and selling of food, but these rules usually apply only to recently killed or raw (including *igunak*) foods. The traditional male-female, child-adult rules of distribution and consumption are not usually obeyed for cooked foods. However, the still common sight of families and friends squatting beside large flayed seals on cardboard sheets on the floor may not be a self-conscious move to preserve Inuit culture but rather may be a normal way of partaking of game procured on a large scale. In either case, the act of eating would be *nirituinariaq*, an ordinary/traditional way of eating, something that may indeed be rare for members of today's younger generation.

We may consider briefly the contemporary wearing of clothes, which, like eating, is a necessity but can still be carried out in traditional ways, for example by wearing *kamiik*, sealskin boots, or in modified-traditional ways, such as wearing a cloth or a duffel wool *amautik*. And yet both adults and children usually wear store-bought clothes and boots these days. However clothes differ somewhat from foods in that they are most visibly a marker of claimed ethnicity in multiethnic situations, especially at ceremonies held in and outside the North. For instance Inuit writer and filmmaker Minnie Aodla Freeman always wears what she calls her "going to meetings" light cloth amautik-shaped parka when she is "on duty" as a representative Inuk. And at the 2001 British Museum conference on arctic clothing, when asked why she was wearing and displaying a cloth amautik with shiny bias binding tape and using spoon heads as decorations, Avataq staff member Taqulik Partridge answered: "We do not have to wear exactly what our parents and grandparents wore in order to represent Inuitness; we can use new materials and modify patterns *as long as we are recognized as different and Inuit*" (emphasis added).

Heroic Individual Efforts

While all Inuit have long been aware of changes in their lives, and have welcomed many of them, there are a few individuals who through particular circumstances, strong feelings, or the desire to be recognized for their leadership have made great efforts to preserve what they saw as threatened aspects of their culture or aspects they saw as extremely important and worth the effort of preservation. I will only discuss a few examples because I have already written about them at length (Graburn 1998a). These preservation efforts have included aspects of nonmaterial culture and language and, in a few cases, material culture too. Older people, in these cases usually men, regretted the loss of knowledge about traditional beliefs such as legends, stories, and history of particular people and places and of individual ancestors.

An early preservationist was Peter Pitseolak. In his youth he recognized that things were changing so fast that his grandchildren or perhaps even his children would not know the legendary and real stories of the past and would not know about some of the practical aspects of life, such as traditional hunting methods and traditional clothing. And as was common among those Inuit who made efforts at preservation, he used nontraditional methods to do so. Perhaps he exemplifies Inuit at the bridge point who have learned enough of the new technologies of preservation to apply them to "traditions," whereas many other *inutuqait*, elders, may have been equally concerned but used traditional channels such as oral transmission, exhortation, and *suangajuk*, "blaming sessions" (Graburn 1969b). As is well known, Peter Pitseolak used photography to record members of his community— their clothes, houses, and family groups—as well as directing the photography of didactic scenes of hunting methods and of local legends (Pitseolak and Eber 1975). In addition he wrote notes and stories about the community, using Inuttitut syllabic script, as records for posterity, for entertaining his friends in person and over CBC radio, and to show the local—especially new—qallunaat that he was the man who kept the records for the community.

Many Inuit recorded events, activities, and people who mattered to them in the commercial arts, mainly in their sculptures and prints. These art forms, recent innovations in fact, were didactic in at least two ways—while being made, displayed, and stored in the North they informed younger generations of important stories and events remembered by older artists in their areas; and eventually they told qallunaat buyers and audiences down South a version of these same stories. And as most stories are not cross-culturally self-evident, many artists, especially Davidialuk Amittuk and Joe Talirunilik, both of Puvirnituq, wrote the stories in syllabics on the base of the sculptures, on the face of a block print, or on separate pieces of paper that they hoped the qallunaat gallery owners would translate into English and display alongside the art objects. Of course the subject matter of their arts reflected what they thought important and what they knew (cf. Saladin d'Anglure 1978). Davidialuk emphasized legends and stories he had heard from his stepfather, the great storyteller Juanasialuk, whereas Joe Talirunilik depicted the stereotypically traditional life that he had led and the unique story of the adventurous migration by *umiak* (open skin boat) of his starving family and friends from the islands in Hudson Bay. Other knowledgeable elders may have also attempted to conserve stories in their arts, but they may not have been so recognized by me or other qallunaat as they were not so forceful in making their purpose clear, or perhaps the stories told were more subtle and unknown to us.

Tamuusi Qumak, late of Puvirnituq, was an activist throughout his life. He was one of the core founders of the Povungnituk Cooperative that led to the founding of the Fédération des Coopératives du Nouveau Québec, a major effort to allow the Inuit of Nunavik to be masters in their own house economically and politically. As such he was close to the community centers of power and hence felt empowered. He worked with the Inuksiutiit Katima-jiit (of Laval University) to produce a number of books in Inuttitut recording traditional Inuit habits and skills. He saw that the way the language was used was changing fast, even in a monolingual Inuttitut-speaking commu-nity, so he methodically collected words of the "real language" from older members of the community. Later with the help of Louis-Jacques Dorais of Inuksiutiit Katimajiit his handwritten cards were transformed through an electric typewriter and computer into a large dictionary of Inuit words, all defined in Inuttitut using syllabic script (Qumak 1990). Tamuusi hoped that this dictionary would be used in schools to preserve the language.

The culmination of his cultural preservation efforts came in the 1980s when he got community council permission to take over the abandoned igloo-shaped wooden office of the failed *caisse populaire*.[6] He appealed to the community and went around collecting material items that were no longer in use and mementos of past members of the community. He said time was like a vast river carrying everything in their culture out to sea to be lost forever. So he built a *saputik*, a weir, to catch all these things before they were lost. Saputik was what he called the little dome-shaped museum. In it he deposited items of hunting and igloo-living material culture that were no longer being used, such as wooden bows and arrows, sealskin floats, a kayak, and old clothing. He also displayed soapstone sculptures made by *inutuqaat* and photographs of past times and of the community's former inhabitants. Most of these bore handwritten labels, many of which were personal—"Iyautik's last kayak" or "Pualuk's grandmother's amautik"— rather than neutral descriptions such as "kayak" and "amautik." He also kept archaeological specimens found by local people. Unfortunately after his death the key to the building was lost, and by the time the museum was opened the next year, many of the objects had succumbed to mould and other severe damage.

Institutional Efforts Resulting from Self-Consciousness

With the establishment of Nunavut, Inuit have become very conscious that the new institutional arrangements for governing Inuit society, which are novel and in some ways "un-Inuit," are potentially erosive. Rather than people thoughtlessly following every aspect of the imported structures they have taken over, there is a government initiative to operate the governing structures according to Inuit *qaujimajatuqangit* (note the modifier *tuqa*, meaning "that which was, elderly," discussed later); that is, "according to Inuit traditional ways/knowledge." In my experience in Iqaluit, most functionaries were aware of the directive but were not clear about how to implement it. Further, the problem of teaching traditional knowledge has been pointed out by Rasmussen (cited in Tester 2001: 352): "The education that takes place in a community, or in context, is different and Rasmussen seriously doubts that Inuit education, which teaches *Inuit Qaujimajatuqangit* (traditional knowledge) can ever happen in a classroom. He warns Inuit to beware of the idea that what is best done by society at one time, is now best done by the book; that titles which frame words like emotional literacy, spiritual literacy, scientific literacy and sexual literacy 'spread the fantasy that alphabetized understanding is synonymous with competence and attunement' (2000: 55)."

In many areas language change and fear of language loss have led to full-scale political efforts to pressure governments and school districts to institutionalize the use of the Inuttitut language in early schooling. This has been successfully instituted in most schools of the eastern and central Canadian Arctic, making sure that children are taught in Inuttitut for the first four grades. The effort has been aided by programs that encourage Inuit to be educated and certified as teachers. Dorais (2002) and others have noted, however, that despite the use of Inuttitut in school, children frequently switch to English among themselves outside school.

Many personal and institutional efforts to mitigate the effects of the overwhelming use of English in broadcast media have led to successful policies to have radio and TV programs in Inuttitut. Television especially was attractive to Inuit children, who sometimes "watched the lines" before regular broadcasts were available and who were able to shout out phrases from commercial advertising even before they were able to converse with their families in Inuttitut (Graburn 1982). However, heroic efforts by Inuit in many areas in the late 1970s, particularly Taqramiut Nipingit of Salluit, persuaded the federal government to set up training programs in broadcasting skills. Inuit wholeheartedly embraced the opportunity to produce their broadcast media. The growth of the Inuit Broadcasting Corporation (IBC) is brilliantly rendered in the video *Starting Fire with Gunpowder* (Tamarack Productions 1991) made by the Inuit about their own mastery and use of television broadcasting.

This same self-conscious effort to retain control of information and make it available to monolingual Inuttitut speakers has long been visible in journals such as *Inuit Ullumi/Inuit Today*, the organ of Inuit Tapirisat (now Tapiriit) of Canada. However it was rather surprising that the useful journal of political and land claims information, the *Inuit North*, was available only in English.

Cultural Centers and Museums

Many communities in the North have developed cultural centers and museums (Graburn 1998a). These are usually dual purpose, informing non-Inuit visitors from the South and encapsulating the recent history and changes in Inuit culture and demonstrating particular skills to school children. Most of these rather impressive facilities (e.g., the Unikkavik in Iqaluit, the Pularakvik in Kimmirut, or the Parks Canada building in Pangnirtung) present a fairly stereotyped exhibit of traditional Inuit life as nomadic hunters close to the natural environment, which may be well displayed with stuffed animals and birds. To their credit the museums all also present a story of change, through both the modernization of the hunting life with snowmobiles and powered boats and entirely new aspects of life in more urban communities (see Wachowich, this volume). Most of the labels are bilingual, but in many cases only older Inuit can read them, and they are not commonly visitors. Contents may also include Inuit artwork old and new, photographs, and illustrations. Interesting dwellings known as *qarmat* (spring residences with snow walls and canvas—previously skin—roofs, or previously semi-subterranean houses with skin roofs) seem to have become iconic of the traditional Inuit life of the recent past in the Eastern Arctic.

Among local people school groups are common users. Elders with specialized knowledge are brought in to explain things to the youngest generation. They are told that they are being taught their history or their heritage, games may be played identifying objects or species on display, and stories may be told (by adults or children) relating to the exhibits. Obviously these are self-conscious attempts to transmit aspects of Inuit culture.

Schools and Colleges

Education at the postsecondary level is relatively new in the Canadian North, but within Nunavut there are now branches of Arctic College in almost every community, and there is a substantial central institution in the capital Iqaluit. Most of the instruction concerns skills for employment, but Arctic College seems particularly willing to entertain contributions from residents and visitors (such as myself) about all aspects of Inuit culture, particularly putting the young adult students in touch with the recent and distant past. Above all there is the Inuit studies program, which has run a special set of courses in Iqaluit and elsewhere, aiming through the Interviewing Inuit Elders program to "save" or recover many aspects of traditional Inuit culture known only to a generation of older Inuit who are passing away fast. These courses are not only "salvage anthropology" (e.g., Saladin d'Anglure 2001, on cosmology and shamanism), but they bring young Inuit into the interviewing process so that they may become informed about the culture and history remembered and become skilled investigators of their cultural past. Here the younger people are directly engaged in the oral tradition as memory for the most part rather than as performance.

The books themselves may not be read by many Inuit for a long time, a problem I see for many comparable works, such as Petrone's comprehensive *Northern Voices: Inuit Writing in English* (1988). Also produced at Arctic College is a possibly more accessible Memory and History in Nunavut series, bilingual in English and syllabics. The first in the series, *Representing Tuurngait* (Laugrand et al. 2001) is an example of recovery of cultural knowledge (see next section). It presents information gathered by the Reverend Peck on *tuurngait* (spirits) and stored for a century in the South, now illustrated by drawings made by Inuit at later dates. In some ways it is comparable to the much more widely read bilingual book *Eskimo Stories/Unikkatuaat* (Nungak and Arima 1969), containing stories recorded from Inuit to accompany photographs of soapstone sculptures that were stored in the South.

In many areas there are also "camp programs," bringing together elder and younger generations for a few days or weeks in the summer. These are self-consciously designed to transmit the traditions of life on the land, and some are arranged as therapeutic or correctional efforts for wayward young people in the urban communities. This seems to send signals that what is "good" about Inuit culture is (and of course, *was*) camp life on the land, not what people do in the urban milieu. This nostalgia for such a lifestyle is characteristic of modernity and quite the opposite of the situation in the 1940s and 1950s, when many of the Royal Canadian Mounted Police forced Inuit to remain on the land and forbade them from living in settlements unless they had full-time employment (Willmott 1961; also Tester and Kulchyski 1994). At a very different level, there are now commonly exchange programs with southern schools. When the Inuit children attend school and homestays in the South they no longer feel the invisible barrier of Otherness that held them back in the 1950s and '60s, and they are proud of their unique and rich heritage, which they have already been made aware of growing up in the North. They can feel themselves, both as hosts in the North and as guests in the South, to be transmitters of their own culture to outsiders.

Recovery of Cultural Knowledge, Artifacts, and Properties

Some aspects of Inuit culture have not disappeared with the loss of elder generations but have been lost to qallunaat people and institutions in the South. The stories, souvenirs, and photos that generations of qallunaat have casually or carefully taken out with them are sometimes recoverable. At a conscious level Inuit organizations such as the Inuit Cultural Institute (ICI) and Avataq, the Cultural Institute of the Nunavimmiut, are making efforts at repatriation somewhat comparable to those of the Native American Graves and Repatriation Act (NAGPRA) in the United States. Most obvious targets of this repatriation are archaeological objects. In Canada, however, if objects are taken back, there is a feeling that there must be institutions to conserve and store them; uses for display and education of the people of the North about their own past may come sooner or later.

More important to ordinary Inuit are old photographs, which may have been snapshots and souvenirs for the qallunaat visitors in the past but which for Inuit may be the only images of lost loved ones. I have been asked for pictures and have distributed to many Eastern Arctic communities photographs taken over the past forty-four years (Graburn 1998b), in the form of poster prints, albums, single prints, and CD-ROMs. Old photographs collected and preserved through institutions such as Avataq may not immediately return to their subjects' friends and relatives, but they are made available to Inuit on demand, both for illustration or publication and for distribution to the relevant community members.

A more specialized form of knowledge, genealogical knowledge, recorded by anthropologists and missionaries, is another highly desirable tool to link with the past and is sought after by communities and cultural centers. When given back, the knowledge may be shared with community members and used in schools and publications. Even more specialized are toponymy and anthropologists' maps (see Müller-Wille and Weber Müller-Wille, this volume). These have been used for land claims and for reconstructing past demographic movements and ecological relations, and above all they have assisted in the creation of new official maps renaming the land's features with Inuttitut designations.

Finally, transmission of culture through and with qallunaat is part of the real fabric of Inuit cultural history, because qallunaat as real persons have been part of the community fabric of all Inuit living today. *Qallunaqalauktin-agu*—the time before white people came—is by now only a kind of origin myth, passed on by word of mouth. Knowledge and photographs in books, reports, archives, libraries, and magazines in the South can be used to stimulate, refurbish, revive memory.

Being a "Real" Inuk

For some decades the matter of Inuit identity has been more and more overtly problematized, for both Inuit and non-Inuit. The displacement of the prototypical or "ideal" being-Inuit from central to marginal can be traced through the changing labels of Inuit identity used in everyday discourse in the eastern and central Canadian Arctic (see also Dorais 1988 for a discussion of Inuit ethnonyms at an earlier historical moment).

In the relatively unproblematized distant and recent past, until about thirty or forty years ago, there were clear distinctions made between Inuit and non-Inuit, primarily qallunaat and in some areas Indians, known as *allait* or *irqilliit*. However, cultural changes were not unnoticed, and as the Inuit came to live in a world that was not overwhelmingly traditional, those things that they identified as their own by tradition, not as borrowed from outsiders, were marked by the suffix -*tuinak*. [7] At first -*tuinak* meant "ordinary," and later it gained the added connotation of "real" (i.e., not borrowed).

An example of the changing sequence of expression might look like this: *Umiak* = skin boat, rowed and paddled (vs. *umiajjuak* = huge boat, white-man's boat, ship); then *umiatuinak* = skin boat, rowed and paddled (vs. *umiak, umiarak* = small wooden boat, used by Inuit, of roughly the same size and scale as umiatuinak). Eventually umiatuinak ceased to exist and boats made of wood or other nonskin material were unproblematically umiak. Related to this series would be *qayak* = kayak, then *qayatuinak* = Inuit made, skin kayak (vs. *qayariak* = canoe, made of canvas or fiberglass and wood imported or made by Inuit or by Indians at Kujjuarapik).

The parallel term *inutuinak* (in some areas *inullutuuq*) came into use in the 1950s and '60s to refer to Inuit in the sense of ordinary, "just an Inuk" (Schneider 1985: 87). It might have been used, for instance, when my wife, a Japanese American, served as a teacher in Puvirnituq in 1967–68. When she wore a parka, Inuit said she "looked like an inutuinak." This term *inutuinak* was opposed to *qallunak* or *qallunatuinak*, as in, "Lukasi Kanajjuak looks like a qallunak!"

This was during a period when Inuit life was changing rapidly through government intervention, with the majority of Inuit moving into settlements and eventually permanent wooden houses. Social scientists such as Bill Willmott (1961), Frank Vallee (1962), and Vic Valentine (pers. comm.) began to write about the two lifestyles of the Inuit—the *nunamiut* who still lived in impermanent dwellings, hunting and trapping on the land, and the *kabloonamiut*, who lived in permanent houses in villages and depended more on wage employment, relief, and commercial arts, though many still hunted and trapped. After all Inuit became village or town dwellers, the way of life rather than appearance gained salience, and the "realness" of Inuit became marked in another way, reflecting full participation in such a life.

The term *inummarik*, plural *inummariit* (in some dialects *inullarik*) originally meant "adult, in the prime of life," versus *uviqaak*, meaning youth, or *ituk/ningiuk*, meaning old man/woman, or even *inutuqaak*, a formerly active Inuk, an Inuk "retired" from the prime of life. But in the 1960s and 1970s the term *inummarik* came to mean "a real Inuk," someone who lives an inuttitut life, not like a white person (cf. Brody 1975). The connection between the two meanings, between life cycle time and the passage of historical time, is easily seen in the following statement by a middle-aged man in Kamanijjuak (Baker Lake) in 1976: "Before the white people came, we used to be adults (inummariit). We lived by hunting all over the land coming and going whenever we wanted. Sometimes life was good and sometimes it was bad, but we could do what we wanted. Now the whiteman is here, we are only children— even though we may not have such difficult times, the government does everything for us, just like our parents" (cf. Searles 2001b: 111, note 5). In the 1970s younger people, and then everyone, began to label old hunters and their spouses—often those who stuck it out and "retired" to villages, or still attempted a fully land-based way of life from villages—as inummarik, "real Inuit," versus Inuit who do not live like them.

The last step of displacement is signaled by the use of the suffix -*tuqaat* (formerly, used to be) as in *inutuqaat*, meaning a former "real" Inuk, which is generalized as the neologism "elder," someone who has passed through most of life and presumably picked up enough wisdom to be a guide for younger generations. As Searles (this volume) points out, Inuit identity even among Inuit seems to be based almost solely on the image of Inuit as hunters (cf. Nuttall 1998b). And as Searles (this volume) and Stern (2001) have stated, this male-centered view may have been aided and abetted by a century of anthropologists' writings.

What Is the Contemporary Inuit Culture Being Transmitted?

Canadian Inuit now live in small and larger villages and towns across the North and thus remain identified as peoples of the Arctic. However, thousands of Inuit now also live in the South, in *qallunaani* (white man's land). As Kishigami (2002, this volume) has recently pointed out, for people living or traveling in the South or in multicultural situations in the North, the meaning of Inuit identity includes demonstrating Inuitness to qallunaat, but it probably also includes demonstrating or bringing higher consciousness to themselves and the practices they wish to maintain as Inuit. Briggs (1997) has suggested that those characteristics consciously chosen, which she calls "emblems," are different from those displayed unconsciously in former or more homogeneously Inuit situations. This parallels my suggestions earlier in this chapter about the raising to consciousness of much that was culturally tacit. What was in the cultural habitus in the North often weakened and was consciously supplemented by selected iconic traits. Living in the South, especially, raised problems for people who were stereotyped as or believed they were essentially hunters.

Eric Tagoona (1979: 18), who was then working as a land claims negotiator, stated in a radio broadcast: "While I'm working in Ottawa, I'm not a real hunter, I'm too educated, I'm nothing unless I'm using my life as an Inuk. Like I'm an Inuk even if I've been to school and even if I'm working in Ottawa." The hunter metaphor has been perpetuated consciously and unconsciously. The term *maqaituk*, which used to mean "gone out hunting," has come to mean gone away to work, especially for short trips as when politicians go to conferences. Zebedee Nungak, then president of Makivik Corporation, declared at a 1996 conference in London on the history of arctic photography that he had "speared a big one, and was coming home with" a $10 million legal settlement from the government over forced relocation of Inuit in the 1950s.

In the past forty years of growing multicultural awareness, Inuitness is often a set of fragmented and contested suppositions, which are constantly changing. Inuit know what outsiders expect of them and are sometimes careful not to appear to be following this stereotype. For instance, Ruby Arngna'naaq (1978) argued publicly with the artist-writer Alooktook Ippelie:

> Alooktook sounds as though he is flustered by the fact that the "sweet smiling peoples of the far North" would be involved in a dispute. Really! . . . Do not forget, we are human beings who show anger, joy, suspicion, relief etc. You see, Alooktook, I live to break the myth about us. After all we are humans, with all the usual human qualities and human faults. We just happen to have our own way of showing these faults and qualities. And, because we are human, we err, misunderstand and see different points of view depending on your experiences and your acquaintances." [Alooktook agreed: "I too dedicate my work and life to break the 'myth' about the Inuit."]

A number of Inuit writers (e.g., Freeman 1978) have detailed the discovery process when exposure to Otherness has challenged their presumptions and defined *for them* their culture *at that moment*. On a group level, the Inuit who were invited to Ottawa for the Week of the Inuit in 1972 claimed that they were the artists of the world and they wanted the government to stop qallunaat from making and selling any art, because qallunaat could always get other jobs like being bus or taxi drivers at a time when, presumably, there were few employment opportunities for Inuit in the North.

For generations growing up subject to this cacophony of messages and conflicting opinions, life ahead is very unclear. While many Inuit believe that they have been forced to abandon their former lifeways by the government's schooling and housing programs, many despair at ever matching white people in "town living." Paulussi Inukuluk of Pond Inlet remarked: "Using that little pencil. Hard going! Whites are amazing. They do so much work that doesn't look like work at all. And, I thought, even if I learn things at school I'll never be a real white man" (quoted in Brody 1987: 24).

Perhaps it would be easier for young people if their ancestors were demystified and, as Ruby Arngna'naaq suggests, shown to be humans just like anyone else. Though it is no longer fashionable to talk about the sins of the ancestors, their humanity and their vicissitudes have been recorded by Inuit (Pitseolak and Eber 1975; Nungak and Arima 1969; Igloolik Isuma Productions 2000) and qallunaat alike (see Graburn 1968). If we look closely at the iconic "real" Inuk, the image turns out to be both mythic and mythical—a rigid, outdated, and inaccurate model, usually put forward by someone claiming to be an authority, like a museum curator. Yet today even the nature of Inuit qaujimajatuqangit is being challenged by younger Inuit, who may have different notions of what makes a real Inuk. For them a real Inuk must neither be judged by the standards of an earlier era (cf. Moller 1992) nor be held up as a mythical and misleading model unobtainable today.

Notes

1. For the most part I have tried to follow the orthography of Schneider, which generally follows the spellings adopted by the Kativik School Board of Nunavik (1985: vii–viii). These Nunavik spellings differ in small ways from those proposed by the Inuit Language Commission (1976), which are now in common use in Nunavut.

2. This statement would have been true much earlier for Inuit in some areas of the Eastern Arctic. For instance, whalers began to visit Cumberland Sound in 1839. The Inuit got used to trade goods and learned some English, and some even visited the lands of the whalers. They were also visited by ethnographer Franz Boas in the 1880s and missionaries arrived soon after. Though whaling declined, permanent posts were set up by the Hudson's Bay Company, the RCMP, and the Anglican Missions in the 1920s.

3. I first learned of this at the age of ten. After a week staying at my grandmother's house in a village far from my home, I went with my mother to the railway station to leave. On the platform I met a bunch of local boys with whom I had spent many happy hours during the week "train spotting," so I turned to talk to them to say good-bye. When I turned back to my mother she exclaimed, "Do you know that when you spoke to those boys you completely changed your accent and I couldn't understand a word you were saying!" Of course I did not know, until that moment. I probably also changed my bodily mannerisms.

4. Schneider (1985: 87) spells the Inuit language phonetically as Inuttitut and gives the currently most common spelling, Inuktitut, as an alternative. Interestingly, the spelling Inuktitut is used on the book's cover.

5. In addition to being the name of the Inuit language, inuttitut (all lower case) means "like the Inuit [do]."

6. *Caisses populaires* are credit unions in francophone sections of Canada. In northern Quebec caisses populaires were among the many southern institutions introduced to acculturate Inuit to Canadian modes of citizenship.

7. Postbase -tuinak, from morpheme -tu = it/that is, and -inak = just a/the only.

NINE

six gestures

peter kulchyski

more than one hundred years after franz boas traveled to and wrote about inuit of cumberland sound in *the central eskimo*, it is possible to suggest that the descendants of the people with whom boas worked still have something to teach. boas's work made a number of significant contributions, not least in advancing the concepts culture and cultural relativism upon which the professional discipline of anthropology rests. in these times, as the concept culture comes under threat from hybridity theorists on the one hand (cf. clifford 1988) and from its own defenders on the other (cf. sahlins 2000), it perhaps worth reminding ourselves that of all the great appropriations made from so-called primitive peoples, the concept culture may be the most significant and, contemporary trends notwithstanding, the most enduring as well.

the latter point deserves emphasis: the concept culture or the idea of culture existed in the european context until the mid-nineteenth century as a notion of growth, refinement, the attribute of so-called civilized society (the idea of what it means to be "cultured") until exposure to varieties of non-europeans raised the possibility of alternative civilizations. more critically, conversations with some of these non-europeans who could talk about their "ways," their "laws," their "forms" as distinct from those of their neighbors placed one firmly on the path that leads to a fully articulated notion of cultural relativism. the proper name boas fits here as a marker for one point in this dialogue. among the things modernity and postmodernity may rest upon—as firmly for example as cubism in painting may rest upon the artistic productions of african mask makers—is a concept culture that derives from the heart of that which modernity defines itself against: primitivism.

the teachings of those to whom boas talked, inuit of cumberland sound, are not therefore confined to the area of exotic curiosities but lead rather straight to the center of what appears to define significant social values upon which the most so-called advanced societies rest. this social value, the concept culture, remains critical inasmuch as it allows for non-essentializing descriptions of social difference. hence, although for example hardt and negri, citing etienne balibar, have argued that culture is made to fill the role that biology had played (2000: 192) and that "imperial racist theory attacks modern anti-racism from the rear"(191), the concept culture to which they refer is one that moves in an essentializing direction ("from the perspective of imperialist racist theory . . . differences between cultures and traditions are . . . insurmountable," 192). jettisoning the concept culture leads directly to abandoning any notion of social difference ("there is no outside," is the hardt and negri claim, 186–90) and ultimately abandoning any form of cultural politics: totalizing theory at this point places itself dangerously close to totalitarian ends. we have reached the other end of the world from cumberland sound.

boas's legacy was a concept of culture constrained by a variety of ideological mechanisms. the central eskimo was itself expressive of a totalizing paradigm, an attempt to represent the totality of a particular culture, which for good reason is in question these days. similarly, boas's work relied heavily on the material expressions of culture, culture as it is embodied through things. although he assiduously collected stories and other aspects of the social and ideological side of culture, material objects, technology, held a peculiar fascination for boas and his approach.

while paying the necessary tokens of homage to this founder-father-figure, what follows attempts to burrow within, to work the concept culture in a slightly different direction, a direction that resists totalizing encapsulation and that resonates with the indiscipline of native studies, itself a bastard child of anthropology. perhaps it may be described in proper poststructural philosophical fashion as a supplement: as native studies supplements anthropology and thereby problematizes it, this work may be a supplement to the work of boas. boas had the great advantage of working with inuit in cumberland sound who were in the full florescence of their culture, surrounded still by technologies of their own making, largely independent and self-sufficient, on the cusp of colonial relations. one hundred years later the inuit of cumberland sound, settled in the village of pangnirtung, continue to create vibrant and unique cultural forms, to inspire visitors, to offer lasting lessons for those who chose to pay attention. they have also had over a hundred years of colonialism and are immersed in untangling the colonial project.

methodologically this analysis works around an attempt to articulate critically or bring together tendencies in contemporary social theory with community-based practice. the practice involves "going there" as geertz (1988) would have it, visiting, listening, talking, waiting, assisting: mimetically adopting to the extent possible the norms of community life. at the same time it involves reflecting upon and reading what one encounters with an attention to particular issues that seem to constitute community itself. in some misshapen way this could be placed under the rubric of what are conventionally called participant-observation and fieldwork. however, to the extent that two forms of reading practice—the diacritical, which involves bringing together disparate texts, and the deconstructive, which involves questioning strategic dualisms and calling into question the metaphysics of presence—are brought to bear, and to the extent that both the terms *observation* and *participant* can be brought into question, it is preferable to characterize this as an ethics of reading.

furthermore the notion of fieldwork presupposes a degree of opposition between "here" and "there" that may no longer be tenable (also *pace* geertz). nevertheless there remains a need for understanding dominance— the terms *dominant* or *western* culture act as markers—and resistance. dominance, or the dominant culture, is that which is complicit with or more actively carries on the work of totalization. resistance signals the field of that which is still to be totalized. the concept or practice of "bush work" might be a substitution for "fieldwork" particularly suited to the indiscipline of native studies. one goes into the bush carefully following the lead of the hunters or guides taking one there. to get "bushed" is to undergo an epistemological crisis sparked by the mimetic embodiments that too long an exposure to one's guides provokes. as a methodology, bush work involves opening oneself up to the ethics of the other, reconstructing one's naming practices (exploding the concept of unnamed native informants), placing against the debased institutional ethics an operative, working (or working-through) ethics. since bush work involves simultaneously working with a notion of cultural alterity (the other is different) and the mimetic faculty (through which the other can be a part of us), it always involves a critical negotiation. dominick lacapra has argued that "the comprehensive problem in inquiry is how to understand and to negotiate varying degrees of proximity and distance in the relation to the 'other' that is both outside and inside ourselves" (1985: 140). as pangnirtung is outside and inside us, so we too remain outside and inside pangnirtung. reading the language of gestures in order to situate analytically these relations of, these oscillations of, dominance and resistance is in this context the work, or working through, of bush work.

the protocols of this work may be stated briefly:

(1) *culture here will be examined as it is practiced in contemporary modalities,* rather than as objectified in things. objectification and material embodiment still remain critical concepts but not in the manner practiced by boasian anthropology. by turning our attention away from things, we can pay closer attention to culture not as a residual element of some former purity but as an engaged and contemporary set of practices. the notion of practice, so central to raymond williams's (1977) cultural work (described as praxis by the sartre (1976) of *critique of dialectical reason*), itself directs us to activity rather than the things produced by activity.

(2) *culture is of interest as the expression and embodiment of values.* our interest is not in cultural diversity for its own sake or in culture as exotic other and mere difference for its own sake. particular values, for example egalitarianism or trust, are here valued. cultural practices circulate these values, many of which are under attack in the dominant social forms.

(3) *gestures and the language of the gestural are a key component of culture.* the habits of an individual may be read as a sign of some more deeply manifested trauma; the habits passed on through culture are equally signs of the deep structure of the culture, of the direction in which that culture works. these habits are often found in gestures, in material practices and actions of individuals, which, if they are reproduced by enough other individuals, are as much a sign of culture as is some esoteric technological form.

(4) *gestures are a writing with the body.* inasmuch as the gesture is a trace of a cultural value, inasmuch as the gesture is an active form of a culture in quotidian practice, it is a sign open to interpretation, a form of writing. but this form of writing inscribes with the face, with movements of the body: it is a writing with the body, embodied writing.

(5) *each gestural utterance may be ephemeral, but cumulatively or socially these gestures leave a significant trace.* the motion of hand or face seemingly disappears in the after instance of its practice, but having been, the

gesture is the latest page in a book of values. it embodies, reinscribes, recirculates the values that give rise to it. those values are its trace.

(6) *a gesture may as easily be hegemonic as it is emancipatory.* the salute to authority, the sign of the cross, most symptomatically the silence that greets the spectacle, these are all gestures that inscribe with the body an embodied subservience. there is nothing emancipatory about gesture *qua* gesture: but our interest in the material that follows is with gestures that move in emancipatory directions: signs of resistance to a totalizing field.

although he argues, in my view incorrectly, that gestures have disappeared from western culture by the end of the nineteenth century, agamben's "notes on gesture" remain a fruitful resource. the multiple forms of embodied subservience that circulate, although they inscribe hegemonic power rather than forms of resistance, still need to be understood within the language of the gestural. agamben does understand the "non-purposive" nature of gestures, arguing that the gesture is the exhibition of a mediality: it is the process of making a means visible as such (2000: 57). this leads him to conclude that politics is the sphere of pure means; that is, of the absolute and complete gesturality of human beings (59), a startling formulation and one that wholly accords with the analysis that follows.

i. the facial yes and no

among contemporary inuit of pangnirtung, the word *yes* in inuktitut and the word *no* are facial gestures. yes: one raises the eyebrows, opens the eyes wide, perhaps with a smile. this does not need to be accompanied by the ii (pronounced: "ee"), which may or may not supplement it. no: one furrows the brow, squints, wrinkles the nose, perhaps with a frown. ame papatsie told me to pretend i was looking into the sun. one may or may not accompany this with the verbal *ahka*. in both instances the facial gestures are seen more often without verbal supplement than the verbal is heard without facial gesture (the latter does not seem to happen with older inuit). this most basic of linguistic elements, the affirmation/denial binary, is here facially inscribed.

we are reminded of the fact, whenever a simple ii or *ahka* is called for, that inuit culture is what used to be called a "face-to-face" culture. as the established order lurches toward ever more mediated forms of communication and abstract modalities of representation, ii and *ahka* recall the ethics of embodied interaction. the intricacies of communication in a face-to-face setting are lost in the vastly advanced, supposedly communicatively competent dominant culture. saving face as a cultural practice remains critical in contemporary pangnirtung: one is not going to move on and teach in a different (better?) department, leaving behind all those one has publicly "dissed." in pangnirtung one has the embodied sense that one's great great great to the nth degree grandchildren will very likely be interacting with the great great great to the nth degree grandchildren of one's neighbor. best to ensure, even when one has something "up" on them, that they save face.

the ii and *ahka* also tell us a lot more about the performative dimension of language than several volumes of contemporary linguistic theory. in pangnirtung the performed utterance conveys extraordinary nuance. the ii for "do you want a chocolate milkshake?" likely resonates somewhat more than the ii for "can I hold that for you?" the *ahka* for "do you want to wear these wet woolen socks?" is likely more forceful than that for "can I add more cream to your coffee?" the frowns and smiles that may accompany ii and *ahka* already begin to mark this. utterance here is performed utterance, expressiveness itself is prized: we are a long way from the formally rigorous professionally nonaffective language of the american anthropology association, for example.

the performative and face-to-face dimensions of ii and *ahka* may be seen in another aspect of this form: inuit culture can certainly involve the ii that means *ahka*, the yes that means no. "can i interview you?" "ii, but not today, try me tomorrow." tomorrow it turns out that you have gone "onto the land" for three weeks. ii can be performed in a manner that broaches its exact opposite meaning. can outsiders be trained to read for this degree of nuance?

ii.

ahka.

ii. the handshake

although this gesture is not as widespread as it once was, nevertheless in pangnirtung today one can still find the "typical" inuit handshake. we meet. we greet. we reach out our paws and touch. we shake once. we let go. once and only once. while ii and *ahka* are linguistic facial gestures that can take place between strangers, the handshake is a gesture between friends, perhaps a gesture that inaugurates friendship itself. in this latter sense (as inaugural), it may then be a more general marker—of community relation rather than friendship. the commonplace practice of going around a room greeting and shaking hands with everyone one encounters seems not to acknowledge existing or potential friendship so much as a more genial, less intensive membership in community. here a more direct instantiation of face-to-face culture is inscribed.

in this gestural moment, what is absent deserves notice. what is absent is the repetition, the shaking of hands or the danger of shaking hands past some appropriate duration in order to mark the rough social distance or nearness of participants: the shaking shaking hands that say "i'm really really so very very glad to meet you I just want to keep this moment going on and on because that way you'll know how so very very very glad I really really really am." what is absent in the inuit handshake is the flourish, the repetition that lies: "i'm shaking your hand so much so you won't know that the contract you're signing is going to dispossess you."

the pangnirtung handshake leaves no room for the flourish and in this case no room for nuance or degree. it marks a social binary: friend or not friend (or part of the community, not part of the community). depending on where one stands in that binary one can work through the nuances that will follow. but friend or not friend is the starting point, and the starting point is marked by a direct gesture: the handshake. more will not make or mark better or stronger or closer friends. and once one starts on the path to more than one handshake one is caught in a deep ethical dilemma: how and when can I stop? "did I shake her hand as much as I did the dean from cornell? oh dear."

marcel proust, whose letters appear to me to be vastly underrated and who had more than one thing to say in them about friendship, managed to end every letter with a flourish, a unique gesture marking his particular affection for the addressee (1983). we humble scribes who follow, can we measure up? pangnirtung forestalls the creation of this problem with a clearly—forcefully—circumscribed limitation.

the handshake.

iii. the unannounced entrance

"who is knocking at the door?" someone knocking in pangnirtung is most likely a social worker (perhaps coming to scoop up the kids) or a police officer, who by legal statute must obey the law of the threshold. local people visiting one another simply walk in, sometimes calling out the name of the occupant they want to visit, or else simply making themselves at home until the occupant chooses to appear. when i ask inuit elders in pangnirtung how this came to be, they reply quite sensibly that one could not "knock" on a tent or an igloo.

there is an extraordinary social practicality to this gesture. let us assume it is winter. why should we tax our guests (assuming we want them to visit and thereby save us the trouble of walking) by leaving them outside our door waiting as we put the baby down, waiting as we wipe our hands with the half soaking dish towel, waiting as we turn down the tv, and still waiting as we run to the door in order to discover a frozen chunk of ice surrounding our dear friend? similarly, should we be so brave as to venture out on a visit, why tax our host by assuming we are so important that they should put the baby down, leave the dishes, turn down jerry springer right at the critical point when the mother is going to break down and confess that her son's obesity was the result of her own neurotic affection, and run to the door in order to open it for us (an action, after all, we are quite capable of engaging in on our own)?

in pangnirtung as in many another northern community, every door is an open door for the most part (unless the occupants are out overnight or for several days). in this gesture, the displacing of the threshold, we find a tangible embodiment of a value critical to communities that deserve the name community, a value that is found only as a hollow shadow of itself in a dominant culture whose dominance presupposes the destruction of this once common social attribute: the value of trust. in pangnirtung every private space is, however temporarily, a potential public shelter.

if gestures can be characterized as a writing with the body, then this gesture may be said to be emblematic of what i would call embodied deconstruction. the whole binary of public and private social relations, the instantiation of possessive individualism that continues to ground the established order, is challenged by this practice. the threshold as marker of the private, as legal guardian of the possessions, the threshold as limit before which even Law trembles, this threshold is entirely destabilized in pangnirtung, overturned and displaced in a parallel manner to the way in which deconstruction itself wants to overturn and displace a variety of metaphysical binaries. embodied deconstruction: rewriting the law of the threshold through movement of the body.

the unannounced entrance.

iv. the gift of food

having got ourselves in and shaken hands, what is to come next? we will sit at the table and wait for the famed tea and bannock (in pangnirtung, pulauga). and more often than not, nothing happens. there is the tea, sitting in a clear glass coffee urn on the stove, warm and inviting. and nearby on the counter, surrounded by a setting of scattered crumbs, some still warm pulauga, vague traces of steam rising from it, a tempting vessel filled with raspberry jam on the table at which we sit. our hosts are happily lathering the jam onto pulauga pieces that sit in front of them, sipping tea as they do so. on a sheet of clear plastic, on the floor, some muktuk perhaps, or seal meat. so close, and yet so far. in inuit houses, unless the hosts are accustomed to the strange habits of the qallunaat, one could wait a long time to be served. a long time. if one is hungry, why not help oneself? if one is thirsty, why not find a cup and pour some tea? again, why tax one's hosts by making them serve you? why tax one's guests by making them wait for you to anticipate their needs? instead, when visiting in pangnirtung, it is polite to find a cup, pour some tea, cut or break off some pulauga, try some of the seal or char or muktuk on the floor, and perhaps smile a thank-you as one enjoys it.

much has been written about sharing practices of gathering and hunting peoples. those sharing practices continue. the rules of generalized reciprocity that sahlins (1976) described in *culture and practical reason* remain viable: the closer the social proximity, the more likely sharing behavior will be practiced; the more necessary the item, the more likely it will be shared. hence even visiting researchers—surely the lowest form of social life in the whole arctic—get to help themselves to pulauga.

greenlandic inuit communities often impress visitors with how "traditional" they are by the fact that the recognizable forms of traditional technology are still used. most communities have a local bylaw that forbids motorized hunting within a specified radius, ensuring that game stays closer and dogsleds and kayaks remain in use. hunters can sell their game at local markets and get money to buy the bullets and other equipment they might need. there are no such bylaws in baffin inuit communities. in pangnirtung, it was a scottish teacher who for many years had one of the only dog teams in town, and the few local inuit who use kayaks do so for sport. but it would be a great shame for a hunter if she were to sell game to other local people. so which would qualify as more traditional, the technology or the values?

the tea and bannock we will eat on our visit are in my view a kind of sacrament, one of the few places where we can encounter the sacred as part of everyday life. this points to another temporality of justice: where generations will repeat themselves, problems of justice can be given the time they need to resolve themselves. in the crassest of terms: i will feed you today because i may not be so successful tomorrow, and i may then have to rely on your better luck or skill as a hunter. and if you have less skill, perhaps one of your children will have more. sooner or later these givings and takings will balance out. on a more abstract level the aporia that derrida points to in his essay on justice is at least indefinitely deferred, if not resolved. derrida writes that though "justice is always required immediately, 'right away' . . . it cannot furnish itself with infinite information and the unlimited knowledge of conditions, rules or hypothetical imperatives that could justify it" (1992: 26). but in the social context of pangnirtung, where one's children's children's children will meet one's neighbor's children's children's children, justice may not be required right away—justice may indeed give itself unlimited knowledge of conditions. the next generation, or the one after that, can resolve the problem if need be: in the very process of the passage of generations justice may unfold. derrida's aporia respecting justice (it must be timely/it must take time) is here imploded. what is given will come back, what is taken will be returned. in the time that is given. if not in my time, in my children's. or my children's children's. so i may give food. i may take food. i may, through this giving and taking, bind myself in a small way and free myself in a small way.

the gift of food.

v. the kiss

in the movies this is famous: a clashing of cartilage as two noses smash together as if the two determined partners were watching opposite tennis games. the kiss moves us from the space of friendship to the space of intimacy: the spaces created by lovers, by parents and children. this kiss (kuni) is a gentle touch of the nose to cheek or nose to nose. when an adult or parent does it to a child, it is accompanied by a "snuffing," as jean briggs so accurately describes it. when a child does it to a visiting researcher it needs no accompaniment but the warm glow of affection.

briggs's inuit morality play (1998) calls attention to parental versions. she distinguishes between niviuq, communicating tenderly with a child, and aqaq, to speak, sing, or chant tenderly to a small child. the stereotype works precisely to the extent that it lies: it cannot conceive of the tenderness associated with this form of intimacy, of the gentle softness which itself may slide to more erotic modalities.

here, at least, we are far from gogol's famous phallic nose. and once again we are in the face of a face-to-face culture. the kiss invites speculations: does the use of the nose mark an attention to displacing the oral phase, a direction away from appropriating the world with the mouth to a notion—

a markedly social notion—that other elements of the body are figured in affective gestures? that is, it may be that this form of kiss, particularly for young children, serves notice that the mouth and its all-consuming, appropriative dimension must be bypassed if the social—at least a social that deserves the name of community—is to be achieved.

or shall we speculate in precisely the opposite direction and suggest that —perhaps for lovers as opposed to children—the nose-kiss, kuni, turns us away from the ear and mouth, those indicators of speech, toward the scent of the other as a more deeply embodied gesture of trust? it is not the grain of the voice that draws us to him but a deeper sense of the body, a more intimate calling.

perhaps even our speculations are swept away, our critical faculties defied, by the intimacies that circle, invite, and foreclose in the warmth of this most tender of gestures: kuni.

the kiss.

vi. the smile

walking down the dusty road from downtown to uptown pangnirtung, climbing the hill in the stark bright mid-afternoon sun, i am hot and tired. an elderly woman walks in the other direction and our paths cross. our eyes meet and both our faces break into rich welcoming smiles. we have never met before and may not again. we both keep walking. the inuit smile, also stereotyped as emblematic of "the smiling inuit," is an extraordinary gesture.

the smile of public life in dominant culture is a smile that lies. it says "have a nice day" or "welcome to walmart." since agamben turns our attention to the connection between film and gesture i will draw upon an example from film: in a scene in a buster keaton movie (*go west*?). keaton, the man with sad eyes who never smiled, sets up a gag in which his character spots his opponent cheating in a card game. he abruptly and self-righteously announces this fact, which prompts the opponent to pull a gun and say, "smile when you say that." keaton's attempt to draw a frightened smile out of his malleable face is more than a source of amusement: it is an allegory of modern life. we smile under the gun.

the smile one gets and gives on the road in pangnirtung, or wherever we encounter someone, has to be deeper, has to communicate more. a small, tightly drawn half smile, a "have a nice day" smile, will not work. in my view there are millennia of knowledge, the genius of a culture, embodied in this daily practice. it signals an initial happiness at seeing the other, an openness to the other: an initial willingness to appreciate the other. it places us within the generosity of the appreciative mode and pulls us out of the symptomatic suspicion of the (conventionally) critical. it indicates that one has some residual energy left, whatever burdens one carries, to lift the other's load emotionally and have someone else lift one's own load. one can carry one's burden and still have an excess, a surplus, a residue that one can offer.

once we enter the space of these smiles we can begin to estrange ourselves from the world where no one smiles. the normality of the not smiling that goes on between strangers in contemporary cities is a symptom of the neurosis of dominant culture. but we must not smile in cities, lest we be taken for neurotics or psychotics ourselves. and of course between women and men the smile can be taken for invitation. remember the faces of the people in the slow-motion, busy-street-at-night sequence in *koyanisqaatsi/life out of balance*. think the danger, then, of smiling in contemporary culture.

the smile in pangnirtung does not mean that one is happy. it means that one can carry one's burdens. my friend kayrene nookiguak (now kilabuk) tells me, smiling, that a child has gone missing in nearby kikiktarjuak. it appears that the elderly grandparents were looking after the child. the grandmother had a heart attack and was medevaced out. the grandfather had not been able to give the eight-year-old child much thought and had not noticed for several days that the boy was missing. they search for the child for days. each day she reports, through a smile, their lack of progress. some time later kayrene tells me that the body has been found. "so," she says to me, "you see what things are like in our communities," through a smile. through a smile.

the smile.

last thoughts on six gestures

all of these gestures are embodied inscriptions that circulate in a culture where trust, as a value, continues to have some operational meaning. the strangeness of these gestures is itself a symptom and marks the suspicions that must ground cultural forms based on possessive individual property relations. of course the very historical moment when this reflection is being produced is one in which precisely trust itself is being liquidated. post 9/11 bears also the burden of being the signifier of an increase in the mechanics of suspicion: totalization and totalitarianism in a new and dangerous proximity.

if a culture embodies values, if a gesture articulates these, then a reading of gestures can give a sense of a culture. the dominant culture works so as to reduce communities to the mere accumulation of isolated individuals. the gestures produced by these individuals mark their homogeneity. community becomes structured around consumption: my affinity in this sense is for those who also like the music of lucinda williams, who watch *law and order*, who wear guess jeans—my gesture is to wear the t-shirt, turn up the music, sit silently and urgently hiss at those who want to talk in the theatre when the film has started. as seinfeld ends its run, my community dissolves and refigures itself around whatever. the fashion logic that commands consumption will tell me. these communities of consumption are so structured as to be vacated of political content. commodified culture expresses and articulates the values of possessive individualist communities. this modality of community is dominant in the world today and it is totalizing. hybridity theories would like to tell us that this is a good thing, or at any rate inevitable.

pangnirtung is one of the markers for the possibility of something else. constructed itself by, and therefore thoroughly implicated in, colonial processes—the fact of settlement itself being one of the most pervasive forces of totalizing power for gathering and hunting peoples—the people of pangnirtung are no strangers to trauma. both the trauma of colonization itself and the trauma of compulsive repetitions of its original violence are too much a fact of daily life in pangnirtung to allow for an unreflective, romanticized utopian fantasy projection. and yet. but. however. gestures— the habits of everyday bodies doing everyday things in pangnirtung—signal and point toward what are not only remnants but new inventions, new ways of reinscribing social bonds that deserve the name community precisely because they are social bonds: what holds people together rather than what tears them apart. pangnirtung as a contested site, a battleground in the war between a totalizing power and the possibility of detotalizing socius or at least of social relations that, in order to remain apart from the totalizing field, must resist it.

imagine that the word *community* meant something more than a mere group of people randomly collected (the serial collectivity, to use sartre's formulation). imagine that the community had to be built every day, rebuilt every day, could not be taken for granted but was in fact the object and direction of daily activity. imagine that your work and play, your giving and taking, played a role in building or unbuilding that socius. perhaps gestures like these would provide one with a fair starting point. perhaps the coming community comes in these forms of expressive embodied writings and embodied deconstructions. imagine.

perhaps.

TEN

The Ethical Injunction to Remember

Lisa Stevenson

John Amagoalik, chair of the Nunavut Implementation Commission, once asked: "Will the Inuit disappear from the face of the earth? Will we become extinct? Will our culture, language and our attachment to nature be remembered only in history books? . . . If we are to survive as a race, we must have the understanding and patience of the dominant cultures of the country. . . . We must teach our children their mother tongues. We must teach them the values which have guided our society for over thousands of years. . . . It is this spirit we must keep alive so that it will guide us again in a new life in a changed world" (Nunavut Social Development Council 1998: 1).[1]

Disappearance, extinction, the inability to survive as a race—these are the anxieties of an Inuit modernity. They lie at the fuzzy border between cultural and biological extinction. What is clear is that Inuit have begun, in particular contexts, to think of themselves as "a people," and that *they have become a people in the face of the possibility of extinction.* Amagoalik describes his telling childhood memories of listening to the voices of non-Inuit conversing: "There was always agreement between them that Inuit could not survive as a people. . . . What disturbed me . . . was the fact that they were so casual when they were talking about the 'death of the Inuit culture' " (Amagoalik 2000: 138). Of course, the various kin groups living throughout the Arctic that we have come to know as Inuit have always had a rich sense of tradition and of their connection to other Inuktitut-speaking people. But the political category Inuit—the idea that these kin groups were one people, the Inuit—is partly a response to a shared colonial history that elided the differences among native groups.

Over and over again young Inuit are urged by their elders to remember their language, their values, and their traditional ways of life. The alternative is unthinkable—they are threatened with their own disappearance, even extinction. Yet there are no historic dates of battles or names of past leaders to be scribbled on the backs of crib sheets in order to prevent this fate. Instead young Inuit are supposed to remember and recreate something that is hard even to put into words, something that Amagoalik calls "spirit" and others have called a "form of life," or even "mythical life."

While expressed with increased urgency, this concern with the disappearance of Inuit culture is not new; in fact it coincides with the emergence of anthropology as a discipline. It was among the Inuit of Cumberland Sound that Franz Boas, sometimes called the father of North American anthropology, inaugurated what anthropologists have come to call "salvage ethnography." His efforts to document traditional Inuit culture before it disappeared forever, while maligned by critics as atheoretical, resulted in the compendium *The Central Eskimo*, which has become the "encyclopedia of the Inuit in Cumberland Sound" (Müller-Wille 1998: 16). Describing his travels by dogsled in 1884 Boas wrote nostalgically: "I saw quite a number of old men and women who remember the old time thoroughly, when they were more numerous and no white men visited their land, when they hunted the whale and pursued the deer with bow and arrow only" (cited in Collins 1964: vii–viii).

For better or worse, this concern with remembering "the old time" follows Inuit studies to the present. We are still collecting stories from elders, creating databases and museums, trying in various ways to preserve the past. Today however, it is no longer just outsider anthropologists who are scurrying to document fading traditions. The Inuit themselves are centrally involved in the endeavor to create and sustain memory by recording interviews, collecting photographs, curating museums, and encouraging their children to learn traditional ways (Graburn 1998; Oosten and Laugrand 1999; Pitseolak and Eber 1993; Ungalaaq 1985). It seems that "a new awareness is developing in which Inuit take pride in their past and their culture" (Oosten and Laugrand 1999: 4).

One effect of this developing interest in cultural history is that even the most intimate and prosaic forms of memory have become linked to projects of recuperation, cultural survival, and ethnic heritage. A second result is the palpable anxiety connected to a perceived loss of cultural memory. This loss is often expressed as an ethical quandary like the one Amagoalik posed: *Remember or risk becoming extinct.* It boils down to the conviction that what should be remembered by young Inuit is not being remembered.

This failing is sometimes explained by a lack of interest on the part of the younger generation and sometimes by the absence of opportunities to participate in traditional activities. There are both individual and institutional attempts to address perceived cultural memory loss. Mothers take their children fishing and feed them country food. Grants are written to secure funds to allow Inuit elders to take groups "out on the land," to engage children who would not otherwise have the opportunity to participate in "traditional" activities. Government employees struggle valiantly to incorporate Inuit traditional knowledge, *Inuit qaujimajatuqangit*, into various levels of the new government. Remembering is seen as a safeguard to existence of an Inuit people, but it is the memory of a way of life rather than a set of historical events that shores up Inuit identity.

Why Remember?

In published interviews Inuit elders often speak to the question of why they believe it is important that their personal stories be told. They point to the need to preserve the Inuit culture or way of life for future generations. For example, anthropologist Nancy Wachowich describes her first meeting with the elder Apphia Agalakti Siqpaapik Awa: "She told me that she was eager to record her life history because she wanted the younger generations to learn and remember how Inuit used to live. She looked at me intently that first afternoon and, pointing to Lucy and then a group of small children playing outside the window, she said: 'I want to let them see what our lives were like back then. I want them to see what it was like for us. I want them to know' " (Wachowich et al. 1999: 17–18).

On one level Awa is telling her own personal life story. On another level she uses the first person plural to describe the subject of her recollections: "I want them to see what *our* lives were like. I want them to see what it was like for *us*." Who constitutes the "us" in Awa's formulation? How are the lines of community and cultural identity drawn?

In the foreword to a manuscript entitled *Inuit Life Fifty Years Ago: Recollections of Martha Angugatiaq Ungalaaq*, David Owingayak, the director of cultural/traditional affairs at the Inuit Cultural Institute, remarks that "in the spring of 1981, the Inuit Cultural Institute embarked upon a project to record and publish the reminiscences of Inuit from the Canadian Arctic as a way of preserving the knowledge of the older generations before it was lost forever" (in Ungalaaq 1985). It is clear that one hundred years after Boas the desire to salvage the disappearing knowledge of the Inuit persists—but in this case it is Inuit who are doing the salvaging. Like Apphia Awa, Martha Ungalaaq explicitly links her own memories to the continuation of her culture: "I am an old woman now, and I want to express myself for the sake of the younger people because I love them . . . Our culture must not be lost. Inuit and white people should help one another and co-operate on many things. . . . The Inuit way of living and what is happening today because of the coming of the white man are entirely different. So that Inuit will not become extinct like the Tuniit, let's be careful" (25).

In these two examples, culled from countless others, life stories are told not so much for what makes them unique or even unusual but precisely for their power to represent a way of life that is perceived to be disappearing. Notice the slippage in the title from the collectivizing "Inuit Life" to the recollections of a singular woman, Martha Angugatiaq Ungalaaq. What is the referent of the term "Inuit" in this context? Does Ungalaaq's narrative represent all Inuit of the circumpolar North, the Inuit of Nunavut, the Inuit living in Igloolik? Or does it represent yet another way of configuring Inuit community?

Certainly memory and cultural politics have not always been so closely linked for the Inuit. Jack Anawak, an Inuk who grew up living on the land and is currently a member of Nunavut's Legislative Assembly, has noted the way that Inuit archaeological sites, "while known, have been of limited historical interest to the Inuit, as they have simply accepted their existence as a part of their life. At times they utilize portions of them while out camping on the land. However, this attitude may be changing as outside pressures intrude which have resulted in a new awareness of these sites as key to preserving the past" (Anawak 1989: 48).

In Knud Rasmussen's accounts of the Fifth Thule Expedition (1921–24) we find examples of the earlier style of remembering Anawak describes. Rasmussen provides examples of songs and folktales in which Inuit elders simply express longing for their childhood. The song entitled "Ulivjak's happy reminiscences of caribou" provides a beautiful example of such nostalgia for the past that has nothing to do with a way of life disappearing, just the process of getting older:

> I call to mind
> And think of the early coming of spring
> As I knew it
> In my younger days.
> Was I ever such a hunter!

Was it myself indeed?

For I see

And recall in memory a man in a kayak;

Slowly he toils along in toward the shores of the lake

With many spear-slain caribou in tow.

Happiest am I

In my memories of hunting in kayak.

On land, I was never of great renown

Amongst the herds of caribou,

And an old man, seeking strength in his youth

Loves most to think of the deeds

Whereby he gained renown. (Rasmussen 1930b: 70)

In this song, as in many others collected by Rasmussen, reminiscing is an old man's pleasure and an end in itself. Ulivjak says he is "happiest" in his memories of hunting in a kayak, something he presumably no longer has the strength to do. The song expresses a nostalgic longing for a past to which the old man cannot return. In fact the past seems so foreign that Ulivjak even asks himself bemusedly, "Was I ever such a hunter! / Was it myself indeed?"

These are the memories of an old man, looking into the past as a way of consolidating his sense of self in the present. The burden of these memories is not so much to construct a viable "we" for the Inuit to inhabit but to tell a life story. There is a marked difference between recounting stories out of nostalgia or longing for one's childhood and a kind of self-conscious remembering for the sake of cultural preservation. Partly to distinguish between these different kinds of memory Pierre Nora (1989) makes the distinction between periods of time in which memory is a way of knowing, and therefore commemoration is unnecessary, and other periods in which the past seems to be slipping away and is therefore consciously commemorated. It is fair to say that the discourse around memory in Nunavut today is often centrally concerned with preserving Inuit culture for future generations.

Thus for Awa and Ungalaaq memory is conceived not so much in the singular and nostalgic mode as in the collective and the didactic. Interestingly, their immediate audience is not the youth they invoke and intend to educate—it is the anthropologist. The central role anthropologists and other academics play in the Inuit project of cultural recuperation should not be overlooked (see Graburn, this volume).[2]

While I was doing research in Iqaluit a document entitled "Being Inuk Is . . ." circulated via email. One entry stated that "Being Inuk Is . . . reading about your ancestors and relations in an anthropologist's paper." Yet there is always the uncanny sense that the ancestors in question might have understood that their descendants would later be reading their words. It seems that anthropologist as interlocutor is shadowed by a future Inuit "superaddressee" who will completely understand what the storyteller is saying and identify with the impulse that led to its telling (Bakhtin et al. 1992). Awa's superaddressee would be the generation of future Inuit who will benefit from and seek out the recording of memories, words, and ways of life. The anthropologist, as scribe, is being (politely) used.

Inuit Epistemology and Political Exigency

The slippage between an individual's life history and collective cultural memory is always an interesting one, but it is particularly so given that Inuit epistemology privileges firsthand, personal experience over information abstracted from other people, books, or other media.

Ethnographers describe an ability among Alaskan Yupiit and Canadian Inuit to accept dissonant versions of the truth especially when they are supported by personal experience (cf. Briggs 1998). The accounts of the Fifth Thule Expedition provide the following illustrative encounter between Rasmussen and a group of women whose rendition of a story he has challenged:

> We tell you only that which we know ourselves, and that which has been told throughout the ages in our tribe. You, who come from other peoples, and speak the tongue of other villages, and understand other Inuit besides ourselves, must know that human beings differ. The Harvaqutormiut know many things we do not know, and we know many things they do not. Therefore you must not compare the Harvaqtormiut with us, for their knowledge is not our knowledge, as our knowledge is not theirs. Therefore we tell you only what we know from our own villages. (Rasmussen 1930b: 111)

This reluctance to talk about things without a foundation in personal experience continues into the present. Elders involved in projects to preserve Inuit culture often refuse to speak of things of which they do not know firsthand. For example when asked to talk about tarriasuit, one elder replied, "I have heard of tarriasuit, but I have never seen them. . . . I've never experienced it, so I can't tell you about it. I don't want to tell you something I don't know about" (Tungilik and Uyarasuk, in Oosten and Laugrand 2000: 118).[3]

Oosten and Laugrand describe this disposition: "Inuit language and culture tends to set little value on generalization. Not the movement from the specific to the general, but inversely, the movement from the general to the specific is what is important. One should be precise in statements specifying time, place, subject and object. General statements are viewed as vague and confusing, whereas specific statements are seen as providing much more interesting information" (2000: 9). There is an underlying tension here: how can such epistemological individualism be reconciled with the current tendency to speak collectively of Inuit traditional knowledge, Inuit culture, and Inuit history?

It is my contention that the desire to situate personal memory in a cultural "memoryscape" (Nuttall 1992) cannot be understood without reference to the political developments of recent years. In fact I would argue that the transition the Canadian Inuit experienced after World War II from a camp life to a settlement life should be considered a "critical event"—an event transforming existing lifeworlds in a way that seems "almost hostile to the continuity of time" (Das 1995: 5–6).

To understand the Inuit fear of extinction (which seems somehow to cast the connection between memory and survival as a biological one) it is necessary to examine the totalizing nature of Canada's welfare economy—its desire to incorporate all Canadian subjects into a rational system (Paine 1977; Tester and Kulchyski 1994). The colonization of the Canadian Arctic was carried out according to norms that were driven by southern economies and was administered through the imposition of often inappropriate styles of life, such as the attempt to reproduce middle-class suburbs in the middle of the tundra (Jenness 1964).

As Robert Tookoome reminded me, "What people usually forget is that we only had contact for the last fifty years. That's a big change. It's like you [gesturing toward me]. It's like you're in 1800 and then you're translated to this way of life. You're not going to survive. . . . It's like you're driving in a car and get hit. All of a sudden the car keeps moving but you don't. All of a sudden these changes are happening and you're not grasping what's happening. When you're in an accident and all of a sudden you are just like spinning out of control. You have no time to think and to understand what's really happening. I think that's where we're at right now. It's that we don't really understand what's happening. We don't realize the significant impact that contact had on us."

Das suggests that after a critical event a new mode of action comes into being, which both redefines traditional categories and invents new forms of life. One of the *categories* that emerged from the transition to settlement life was precisely a cultural memory that would express and safeguard Inuit difference from Euro-Canadians.

The transition to a global Inuit identity was extremely rapid. In 1973 the first Arctic Peoples Conference was held and by 1975 a grant proposal to an American foundation stated: "We Eskimo are an international community sharing common language, culture, and a common land along the Arctic coast of Siberia, Alaska, Canada and Greenland. Although not a nation-state, as a people, we do constitute a nation" (Inuit Circumpolar Conference 2005).

In 1977 Eben Hopson, mayor of North Slope Borough in Alaska, called a meeting on the theme "Inuit under four flags" (Morin 2001: 32). The Inuit gathered at the meeting realized that while divided by national borders, they were confronting very similar social problems as a result of a shared colonial history. At the meeting they deliberately chose for themselves the enthnonym *Inuit*, which means "people, or human beings," forgoing the more regional ethnonyms (such as Eskimo, Yupik, or Kalaallit), none of which had the same unifying sense. Three years later Eben Hopson founded the Inuit Circumpolar Conference, which continues to be a force in Inuit politics today. Once again the preamble of the ICC emphasizes the unity of the Inuit as a *people*. It recognizes:

> That we, the Inuit, are an indigenous people, with a unique ancestry, culture and homeland;

> That the worlds and sub-areas which we use and occupy transcend political boundaries;

> That due to our historical inheritance and use and occupancy of our homeland we enjoy cultural rights unique to indigenous peoples and share common traditions, values and concerns. (Inuit Circumpolar Conference 2005)

No longer would the Harvaqutormiut, to take just one example, claim to be essentially different from other tribes, as they did in the 1920s. Instead there is a growing interest in a more global Inuit identity, one that can be parlayed into political gain in the arena of Canadian and international politics. The emergence of this group identity represents a radical shift from the time when an individual's allegiances were to an extended family network

(Hicks and White 2000). Marybelle Mitchell puts it succinctly: "Inuit did not perceive themselves to be a distinct ethnic group, nor were they officially recognized as such until the 1970s when the necessity of signing treaties made definition of the category urgent" (1996: 134).

Put differently, it is possible to suggest in line with Kulchyski (this volume) that we could describe a transition from a face-to-face culture to one that now imagines a certain kind of ethnic, cultural, even spiritual kinship with faceless others. While Kulchyski's intent is to document the way elements of a face-to-face culture persist in the present, I want to emphasize the way that certain memory practices provide support for this new way of imagining Inuit community. The imagined Inuit community is not to be understood as a step in the modernizing process (Anderson 1991) but as a strategy to gain political recognition and strength (cf. Kelly and Kaplan 2001).

The Road to *Inuit Qaujimajatuqangit*

In the latter half of the twentieth century Inuit have frequently had to speak with one voice to achieve political goals. The formation of the new Canadian territory of Nunavut stands out as a particularly successful example of Inuit political organization. Negotiating for the Nunavut land claims settlement entailed setting aside differences *within* Inuit culture and locating difference, at least the politically salient difference, between Inuit culture and everything non-Inuit. It was by drawing on an argument of cultural difference that Inuit leaders attempted to secure aboriginal self-government for their people. In Rosemary Kuptana's words, "It is not our race in the sense of our physical appearance that binds Inuit together, but rather it is our culture, our language, our homelands, our society, our laws and our values that make us a people" (cited in Moss 1995: 70). To take another example, in 1996 Mary May Simon published a book entitled *Inuit: One Future—One Arctic*. Such a statement would have been unthinkable in Rasmussen's time. In order to have a political voice the disparate Inuit groups in the Canadian Arctic literally had to imagine themselves as a people, unified partially through their difference from the rest of Canada.

In the Canadian context, due to repeated attempts to address the question of Quebec's unique status within the country, the possibility of incommensurable cultures, knowledges, or political systems is a highly charged issue. Multiculturalism in Canada, as elsewhere, holds that ethnic difference should be understood within a horizon of common citizenship (Paine 1999; Taylor 1994). This leads to some apparent contradictions. For example, Inuit arguments for self-government were based on the notion of a nonethnic and public government in Nunavut within redrawn territorial boundaries that would ensure an Inuit majority for years to come (see Simon 1996 for an Inuit perspective on this issue). This was one way that Inuit ensured that their version of self-government would be palatable to a federal government concerned about the political implications of a separate form of government in Nunavut (Hicks and White 2000).

The land claims agreement did, however, recognize the need to "encourage Government to design and implement social and cultural development policies and programs appropriate to Inuit" (Government of Canada 1993: section 32.3.3). Thus the establishment of Nunavut was still seen as "a unique opportunity to address questions of our cultural survival with a renewed vigour and imagination" and an opportunity "to participate in the creation of a public government that truly reflects Inuit values, and that is genuinely responsive to Inuit needs" (Nunavut Social Development Council 1998: 5). But this new political entity, the "Inuit of Nunavut," needed a concept through which to imagine their community's distinctiveness from other communities within Canada. In 1998 the term Inuit qaujimajatuqangit (IQ) was coined to encompass "all aspects of traditional Inuit culture including values, world-view, language, social organization, knowledge, life skills, perceptions and expectations" (Nunavut Social Development Council 2000: 79). Jaypeetee Arnakak, who has worked to formalize the principles of IQ, wrote in an editorial to the regional newspaper: "Inuit Qaujimajatuqangit. To me these words have almost the same ring as 'Next year in Jerusalem' does to Zionists: like Judaism, the IQ concept is a binding force for a people; unlike Judaism, though, IQ was never written down" (Arnakak 2000). IQ has become the new way of imagining what it is that makes the Inuit a distinct political entity.

Thus in some sense the question of Inuit "difference" in governance was transferred to the realm of "Inuit traditional knowledge." In February of 2001 the Nunavut government created an IQ task force to determine the best way to incorporate Inuit traditional knowledge into its programs, policies, and services and to make government offices more conducive to the Inuit lifestyle. Since then IQ has become somewhat of a buzzword throughout Nunavut as Inuit strive to make their government distinctly Inuit. For many Inuit the success of the fledgling Nunavut government hinges on its ability to incorporate Inuit qaujimajatuqangit into policy and practice. Speaking of the need to preserve and use Inuit qaujimajatuqangit in the contemporary context one young Inuk writes: "Call me a visionary but I thought that's what Nunavut was all about!" (Inutiq 2001). In the absence of a wholly Inuit government, IQ has become the signature of the Nunavut government, encapsulating what makes the government specifically Inuit.

The mandate to codify and operationalize Inuit traditional knowledge or Inuit qaujimajatuqangit within Nunavut's government agencies is only one highly visible attempt to make collective and thus to standardize Inuit knowledge and memory across a range of communities. Cultural memory had become the *sine qua non* of Inuit identity and the binding force of their community.

Inuit Youth and IQ

One of the ironies of the focus on Inuit qaujimajatuqangit is that since the 1950s and the move to permanent settlements around schools, hospitals, and government buildings, increasing numbers of young Inuit do not have access to what are considered "traditional" Inuit activities (see Searles, this volume). Therefore Inuit youth today are often perceived to be lacking the right kind of experiences or memories—memories associated with being on the land, hunting, and living in camps as their ancestors did in previous generations. As one young man complained to me, "You don't know how many times I've been accused on not being a real Inuk!"

How are young Inuit to gather the values and knowledge they are perceived to be lacking? It is not by merely listening to stories. In *Capturing Spirit: The Inuit Journey*, a suicide prevention video produced in northern Quebec, several recommendations are made. At the end of the video the narrator announces: "Here is a list of ideas or tips which the viewer should be able to take away after viewing the film." The first tip is: "Practice traditional activities such as fishing, hunting, camping or spending time with an elder" (Makivik Corporation 2000).

Over and over again the need for a personal experience to go along with the story is emphasized. Stories in and of themselves are like empty shells of knowledge. A suicide counselor in Pangnirtung told me that "the youth don't understand why they are called Inuit and not living on the land. To them, being Inuit is just a story."

Maurice Leenhardt, an anthropologist and missionary among the New Caledonians in the early twentieth century, made a similar distinction between a living myth and a cold story. "The myth does not exist that is not the ever-renewed revelation of a reality which so imbues a being that he makes his behavior conform to it. Short of this, it slowly hardens into a story which will become cold one day" (1979: 192). In fact Leenhardt suggests that we have been taken astray by the etymological development of the word *myth*. Naturally we ethnographers have been ready and eager to record "myth" in the form of stories or narratable experience because it can be written down or recorded on cassette and packed off to the researcher's university for further study. Leenhardt cautions against the assumption that narrative is essential to myth. He writes: "Now is a good time to separate the etiological myth from these lived myths. It is set apart from them because it does not so much express an event or human reality as it manifests the attempt by the intellect to explain origins and fix customs" (1979: 193). Lived myth, for Leenhardt, is an orientation in the world, a way of seeing and feeling that conditions all experience. It is not, therefore, a certain set of facts about Inuit ways, or knowledge divorced from a particular context, or even knowledge for the sake of self-aggrandizement. Inuit adults still want their children to be Inuit in the old way, through experience rather than through stories.

An Inuit staff member in the Baffin Correctional Centre in Iqaluit described the dilemma of the younger generation who are expected to know traditional ways: "I have thirty-year-olds in here who have never seen a seal. I have the feeling that they know something, but they don't. My ten year old knows more than they do." His partner chimed in, "You've seen those macho guys who are really kittens on the inside, they are embarrassed that they have lost their traditional ways."

What would it mean to "know something" in this context? Why does the director of the land program assume the young men in his care know something in the first place? It is perhaps because they speak Inuktitut, have grown up in predominantly Inuit communities, have Inuit names? Yet they do not seem to have the right knowledge, the *experience* of seal hunting, which has been described as "the practice that has kept our people alive for thousands of years" (Anilniliak 2002).

Ethics and Memory in Nunavut

It is this emphasis on experience that has led me to identify an ethical injunction to remember among Inuit in Nunavut. I use the term *ethical* in a technical and not in an everyday sense. In our everyday language we often conflate ethics and morality, which leads to thinking of ethics as a moral code. Instead I am starting from Aristotle's definition of ethics as "knowledge for the sake of oneself" (Gadamer 1987: 120). For Aristotle practical wisdom could not be achieved by learning general rules. From his perspective, instead of a rigid code for determining right from wrong, ethics might be considered a series of skills one learns by practice.

Michel Foucault, taking his cue from the Greeks, also puts the emphasis on practice rather than code. He wrote simply: "I think that ethics is a practice, ethos is a manner of being" (1997: 377). Furthermore, Foucault highlights the way that ethics and the self are connected—he points out that ethics is linked to a way of taking care of the self, a way of transforming the self in order to live the good life, however that good life may be conceived. At one point Foucault referred to ethics as "the kind of relationship you ought to have with yourself" (1997: 263).

Therefore ethical knowledge is not knowledge for its own sake, or knowledge divorced from a particular context, but rather knowledge that will transform the self. For instance when the land program at the jail attempts to provide a certain kind of experience through which participants can transform themselves according to Inuit cultural values, it is providing space for ethical transformation of the self.

Why I want to call certain kinds of memory ethical may become clearer when contrasted to another form of memory, traumatic memory. In the literature on the subject, a different conception of memory emerges: it is to be understood that survivors of trauma (such as concentration camp survivors or torture survivors) cannot not remember—that is, survivors of trauma bear the burden of memory, one they may often wish to escape (see especially Caruth 1996). In some sense what we often think of as agency is complicated in this traumatic understanding of memory, because memory actually forces itself upon the survivor from the outside, as something at once personal and foreign, at once recognized and unwanted.

In contrast, the kinds of memory we are concerned with in this chapter are memories that are produced through self-consciously engaging in particular kinds of activities and transforming oneself in the process. Thus a young Inuit girl who cannot speak Inuktitut tells me she wants to do more Inuit things, like going camping. An older Inuk man tells me in frustration that we have got to "acknowledge that there's other ways of coping with life. Instead of romanticizing everything about IQ and all that crap. Instead of romanticizing it and making it a phrase word, fucking implement it. Make it real." The key point here is to conceive of ethics not in terms of abstract moral precepts that an individual ought to *follow* by virtue of being human but as referring to a particular way of *becoming human* that results from working to transform the self. One becomes human through a series of transformations rather than proving one's humanness by following a moral code.

Foucault names the efforts made to transform (and in a radical sense create) the self "technologies of the self." He writes: "In all societies there is another type of technique, techniques that permit individuals to effect, by their own means, a certain number of operations on their own bodies, their own souls, their own thoughts, their own conduct, and this in a manner so as to transform themselves, modify themselves, and to attain a certain state of perfection, happiness, purity, supernatural power. Let us call these techniques 'technologies of the self' " (1997: 177). Ethics in this sense is not primarily about knowing how to distinguish between absolute good and evil but about the way knowledge transforms the self for a certain end.

Relatively little has been written within Inuit studies on what Foucault calls technologies of the self. However there are several notable exceptions. Stairs (1992: 117) examines what it means to be *inummarik* (a most genuine person), concluding that it is "a lifelong process of developing correct inter-action . . . with people and animals, community and environment." Searles (2001a) examines some of the micropractices involved in raising a child to be a "real" Inuk, including providing frequent opportunities for children to eat land food while not squelching their independence and ability to make their own choices. Briggs (1998) writes extensively on the way the emotional life of Inuit children is shaped by specific parenting tactics that develop a sense of the world as a dangerous place. In this chapter I would like to suggest that Inuit practices of remembering have become an Inuit technology of the self.

I was first confronted by the way memory is a technology of the self while attending a "healing camp" on the land that was designed to give single mothers a chance to take their families camping. There was very little sched-uled, and activities arose spontaneously; at high tide some decided to go fishing, others went hunting, and the children scrambled around on the rocks behind the camp or followed after a favorite adult. One night in my tent while my friend was preparing her two young boys for sleep, she com-mented: "It is good for them to be here, they will learn to long for it when they are older." I was struck by her words "learn to long." We can see a mother self-consciously trying to instill longing in her sons by exposing them to traditional Inuit activities. Is this possibly a way to think about memory as ethics—as bearing a relationship to the creation of longing? The memories that adults are trying to instill in their children are not simply the result of having lived a long and good life but are now something one must actively strive to create, the result of a certain kind of discipline one assumes, and actions one takes. That is why I have been calling them ethical. Interestingly, it is in the realm of ethics that the two forms of memory discussed at the beginning of the chapter—didactic and nostalgic—merge. The point of telling stories of the past is to encourage young people to recreate those experiences for themselves, so that they too can one day be nostalgic for the time when they hunted caribou.

Jaypetee Arnakak describes the dilemma he and his co-workers faced in the Department of Sustainable Development at the time the term IQ was first being developed. They wanted to make sure that in the frantic process of commemoration, the Inuit way of life did not become one of Leenhardt's "cold stories" but remained instead an ethical orientation to the world. To conclude with Arnakak's words: "In fact, IQ is a living technology. It is a means of rationalizing thought and action, a means of organizing tasks and resources, a means of organizing family and society into coherent wholes. . . . Trainees (myself, Peter Ittinuar and Joe Tigullaraq) deliberately tried to keep IQ from becoming an official policy, knowing that separating IQ from the contemporary realities renders something that is profound, enriching and alive into something that meaningless, sterile, and awkwardly exclusionary" (Arnakak 2000).

The concept of a pan-Inuit cultural memory embodied in IQ is a relatively new political construct inescapably linked to other political developments. In addition one of the most important technologies of the self in Nunavut today is the *practice* of remembering. Finally, I want to argue that memory in Nunavut has become an ethical injunction; that a certain kind of remembering is not just something that happens—an accidental by-product, as it were, the result of living a life, the residuum of time passing—but rather something that as a young Inuk you are encouraged to make happen, that you are called upon by others to produce in yourself. It is a warning, a command, an injunction: "Remember!" Of course this ethical challenge is not always explicitly expressed, but it is felt nonetheless. Remembering the past is understood to be the key to Inuit cultural survival. Among the Inuit of Nunavut in particular, it is possible to say that memory and ethics have become indistinguishable.

Acknowledgments

The research for this chapter was made possible by the William E. Taylor Award, Canadian Museum of Civilization, Ottawa; the Hewlett Pre-dissertation Fellowship, University of California, Berkeley; a Hornaday Grant from the Centre for Peace and Wellbeing, Berkeley; a Social Science Research Council International Dissertation Research Fellowship; and a National Science Foundation Dissertation Improvement Grant. The ideas explored were presented first at the International Congress of Arctic and Social Sciences held in Quebec City in May 2001 and then at the Social Sciences and Humanities Research Council Occasional Conference on Inuit Memory and History in November of that year. I am very grateful to Susan Sammons, who provided me with the crucial office space that enabled me to write this chapter. I also want to thank Pamela Stern, Peter Kulchyski, Lawrence Cohen, and Scott Hutson for their thoughtful readings of and insightful comments on this manuscript.

Notes

1. The Nunavut Implementation Commission was the organization overseeing the arrangements leading up to Nunvut's creation on April 1, 1999. It was composed of nine members appointed by the government of Canada.

2. I do not want to imply that both forms of memory were not available in both time periods—they may have been. I simply want to argue that the culturally privileged mode of remembering in Nunavut today has become the didactic.

3. A *tarriasuit* is an invisible humanlike being that can make itself visible to people.

PART 3

Reconfiguring Categories: Place

ELEVEN

Inuit Place Names and Sense of Place

Béatrice Collignon

Place Names and Arctic Anthropology

Among early arctic scientists, Franz Boas was the first to pay attention to indigenous place names. He stated that indigenous place names should be recorded on official maps and vigorously denounced explorers and whalers alike who felt free to baptize any place they wanted and ignore Inuit toponyms. Unlike foreign names, he argued, Inuit place names fitted the landscape perfectly (1885: 51, cited in Cole and Müller-Wille 1984: 52).

During his year of fieldwork around Cumberland Sound on Baffin Island (1883–84) Boas carefully recorded and mapped 930 place names, a project discussed in detail by Müller-Wille and Weber Müller-Wille elsewhere in this book. Their comparative study conducted a hundred years later offers important insights into the dynamics of place names and of Inuit geographic knowledge.

Most arctic anthropologists who followed in Boas's footsteps recorded some local toponyms in the field but never conducted systematic surveys. They saw place names as one means, among others, of getting acquainted with the territory of the Inuit they were studying. Place names were part of what traditional anthropology considered the general background data all anthropologists should collect during the first weeks of fieldwork, before moving to the research itself. In the late 1960s anthropologists Saladin d'Anglure and Dorais broke with that practice and conducted a broad place name survey among the Inuit of Nunavik (northern Quebec). Yet their prior interest was neither place names nor geographic knowledge. Their collection was neither published nor analyzed.

Thus it is perhaps not surprising that it took someone with a background in both cultural anthropology and geography to look at place names for their intrinsic value. In the late 1970s Müller-Wille put toponymic survey-ing at the center of a research agenda that linked together toponyms and knowledge of the land. Contesting the official representation of Inuit land conveyed by official maps (published in Canada by the Department of Natu-ral Resources), he advocated for the recognition of Inuit toponymy, arguing that "in their complexity [place names show] an intimate knowledge of the land that the existing maps do not provide" (Müller-Wille 1987: xii). Müller-Wille's main collection covers the whole of Nunavik. It was published first as a gazetteer in 1987 and then as a set of 1:50,000 maps in the 1990s. The latter are in current use in Nunavik.

Müller-Wille's surveys were conducted with the intention of recording knowledge that was feared to be quickly disappearing as elders passed away. The loss of traditional place names was presumed to be one of the many consequences of the settling down process of the 1950s and 1960s. Both researchers and elders worried about such a situation, and in many com-munities the elders often requested that toponymic surveys be conducted to ensure that their knowledge would outlive them. "Throughout my work on place names with the Inuit I found that their concern was the same as in Aivilik (Repulse Bay): to transfer the knowledge of their land with its place names into a form that would ensure its continuation with future Inuit generations and project a true image and identity of the land" (Müller-Wille 1987: xii).

Toponymic survey projects in the Canadian Arctic also gained the support of Inuit politicians. From a geopolitical perspective, putting Inuit names on the maps was seen as an efficient way of asserting Inuit rights to land and a strong act of Inuit empowerment. Toponymic surveys are also often presented as a useful tool for preserving the ability of younger Inuit to travel on their land. The assumption was that place names are part of a wider knowledge related to traveling and hunting. It is common to hear Inuit asserting that if you know the place names, you cannot get lost:

> Land marks were also observed in naming places. All land features like hills, lakes, rivers, islands, peninsulas and bays were given names. Young people today do no longer observe these geographical features nor do they use their names. . . . People travelled long distances without maps using place names and stories behind them. (Johnny Epoo, president of Avataq Cultural Institute, cited in Müller-Wille 1987: x)

It's good that you are writing our place names on the maps. It will be useful to us. There are many names we don't know, and so we don't go hunting and traveling far from the settlement. If you know the names you don't get lost so much; it's easier. (Inuinnait man, twenty-nine years old, author's fieldnotes, 1991)

In the early 1990s anthropologist Mark Nuttall looked at place names from a rather different perspective. His main goal was to study the sense of belonging, locality, and continuity; that is, the system of values that are important for contemporary Inuit identity in northwestern Greenland. He was therefore interested in the way Inuit view their landscape and develop a relationship with their land. The physical environment, he stated, is not only "action space" but also "thought space" (Nuttall 1992). He recorded some thirty toponyms of the Kangersuatsiarmiut territory, in a nonsystematic survey. These place names made him realize "it did not seem enough to just record land use sites, there were additional layers of meaning to understand" (Nuttall 1992: 49).

According to Nuttall, Kangersuatsiarmiut's toponyms fall into three main categories, depending on their meaning: names that refer to physical features, names that reflect analogy, and names that inform about land and sea use (the majority of the names collected). But what really matters, he argues, is that place names are multidimensional: they carry much more meaning than just that of the name itself. They have a "hidden meaning" that expresses itself in Inuit memory and in storytelling.

> Whatever place names say about geography, analogy or subsistence activities, however, many have an additional layer of meaning. It is precisely that which is hidden and invisible in the land which is often neglected. Stories and myths unfold against a geographical backdrop. Events, whether contemporary, historical or mythical, that happen at certain points in the local area tend to become integral elements of those places. They are thought about and remembered with reference to specific events and experiences and it is in this sense I refer to landscape as a memoryscape. Memories take the form of stories about real and remembered things. They cannot be separated from the land even though place names do not immediately reflect such stories. Some place names may be mnemonic devices, triggering a collective memory of an event that has significance for the community. (Nuttall 1992: 54)

Studying Inuit Geographic Knowledge

In 1991 I began a research project on Inuit geographic knowledge, focusing on the Inuinnait (Copper Eskimos) of the western central Canadian Arctic. My particular theoretical interest as a human geographer was in nonscientific geographic knowledge. A century earlier geography had positioned itself in the academic field as a contact discipline between natural sciences and social sciences. The emphasis was on the methods and theories of the natural sciences and, as a result, on places rather than on people. In the 1970s geography took a dramatic turn to become a social science, a unique revolution in the history of modern sciences.

From the beginning of modern geography in the 1880s both human and physical geographers stressed the importance of fieldwork. Robic (1991) has shown how scientific geographic knowledge often relied on local— "popular"—knowledge for basic information, using it also as a kind of field-proof to confirm more theoretical claims. But the knowledge itself, as a global and organized set of information, was either despised or ignored. My research was consequently aimed at demonstrating that a nonscientific knowledge was indeed a real knowledge and not just loose pieces of information. Although this sounds obvious today it was not the case just a decade or so ago, when the word *knowledge* itself was seldom used in the realm of the nonscientific. That was before traditional ecological knowledge (TEK) became a major topic in anthropology. Advocating for full recognition of Inuit geographic knowledge, my work also aimed at developing Inuit empowerment through the recognition of the value of their own knowledge.

In the "Anglo" social sciences such research would certainly have been fostered by postcolonial studies, and one might expect here a discussion emanating from a number of quotes from well-known geographers and anthropologists. French academia, however, does not have such studies, and although I have become familiar with the literature over the years, it was not part of the theoretical background from which my research agenda stemmed.[1] From the beginning, in the 1960s and 1970s, French social sciences have been greatly influenced by the works of Roland Barthes and Michel Foucault, which rapidly became mainstream references. From the early 1980s Pierre Bourdieu on the one hand and Raymond Boudon on the other became major sources of theoretical constructions. This has not been true of postmodern theory in general, however, which to this day remains quite marginal in France. Although some authors, such as Jacques Derrida, a poststructuralist rather than a postmodernist, have had a definite impact through the practice of deconstruction, the general bulk of postmodern theory has not pervaded the French academy the way it has in Anglo social sciences. Neither has feminist theory.

My research project demanded that I first find out what kind of information made up Inuinnait geographic knowledge; and then that I understood and showed how the various pieces of information were structured to form an efficient knowledge people can call upon when needed. Place names were obviously part of the information I wanted to identify and analyze. Since they had never been recorded in the western central Arctic region, my fieldwork (September 1991 to June 1992 and November–December 1992) included an extensive place name survey. I carried out the survey in the four communities where the Inuinnait (some three thousand in 1992) settled between the mid-1950s and the late 1960s: Cambridge Bay, Holman, Kugluktuk (Coppermine), and Umingmaktok-Qingaun (Bay Chimo and Bathurst Inlet).[2]

Holman was already familiar to me as I had been part of an archaeological dig thirty miles east of the community in the summer of 1980, along with local Inuit teenagers. I had also lived in the community from June 1986 to January 1987 when preparing my masters in geography. Of the four communities, three are today in Nunavut and one—Holman—is in the Northwest Territories (map 11.1). This odd partition is the result of the coming of Western Inuit—Inuvialuit—to the northwest coast of Victoria Island in the 1920s and 1930s (Condon 1994). Holman is therefore a mixed community of Inuinnait and Inuvialuit. Its population decided to join the Inuvialuit land claim agreement in 1984, which led to their remaining in the Northwest Territories after the 1999 division between the NWT and the new territory of Nunavut. The Inuinnait dialect—Inuinnaqtun—is the common language of all Holman Inuit fluent in their native language, although some individuals are also fluent in Siglitun or Ummarmiutun (see Nagy, this volume).

The place name survey extended from October 1991 to early April 1992. Staying in the area for over ten months gave me time to speak not only to those elders who were identified as knowledgeable about place names but to all the elders, men and women alike, who still had sound minds. I also interviewed most of the active adult hunters (and trappers) as well as the younger adults who were identified by others or by themselves as knowledgeable about place names. In contrast to that of Müller-Wille and Weber Müller-Wille (see their chapter in this volume), my goal was not only the quality of the place name set collected. I also wanted to assess how

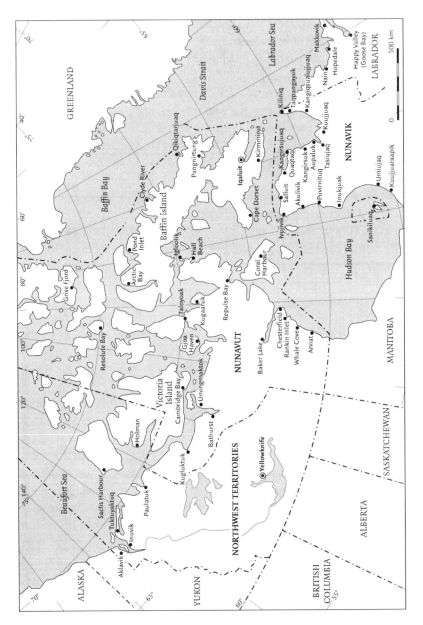

11.1. Inuit communities of Canada (NWT, Nunavut, and Nunavik).

toponymic knowledge is shared, or not, by members of a community, and how different individuals develop a personal knowledge out of a common background shared by the community as a whole. Sixty-nine Inuinnait volunteered in the survey, and I hired four local translators. The methodology for the survey followed Müller-Wille's (1985) and is discussed in detail in Collignon (2006). Although I encountered a few English place names given by younger Inuit to previously unnamed places, it is remarkable that most "new names" were Inuinnaqtun ones, expressing the vitality of toponymic knowledge.

Altogether I recorded 1,007 place names, on 1:50,000 scale maps where available (the whole mainland, a few parts of Victoria Island, and some inlets) and on 1:250,000 scale maps elsewhere. The coordinates of the 228 toponyms recorded on the latter could not be plotted accurately because the scale was too small. Therefore they do not appear on map 11.2, which shows the location of only 779 Inuinnait toponyms.

What's in a Place Name?

The 1,007 toponyms were first sorted out on the basis of the type of feature named. The typology built followed the well-known opposition between land and sea/ice described as early as 1906 by Mauss (1979) and separated inland and marine features (fig. 11.3).

The coastline was always a transitional space for the Inuinnait (Collignon 1993). Historically they would wait there for the ice to be thick enough to move their camps on it in winter; or for the land to "dry up" that so they could start traveling inland and hunt caribou in summer. Whether the coast should be categorized as an inland feature or a marine feature was therefore not obvious. Considering that the coastline was usually seen through the eyes of the sea/ice traveler, it eventually seemed appropriate to classify this as a marine feature, despite the oddness of such a categorization at first sight. Results showed that although inland features were more numerous, marine ones occurred in good proportion (40 percent). Lakes were the feature most named (fig. 11.4).

This typology reveals the kinds of features Inuit are more likely to name. It gives us a first glimpse of their way of looking at the landscape. Yet it is only a superficial glance and it fails to unveil truly enough about Inuit geographic knowledge and relationship to the land. This calls for another look at place names, from a different perspective.

Moving from the question "what" (features named) to the question

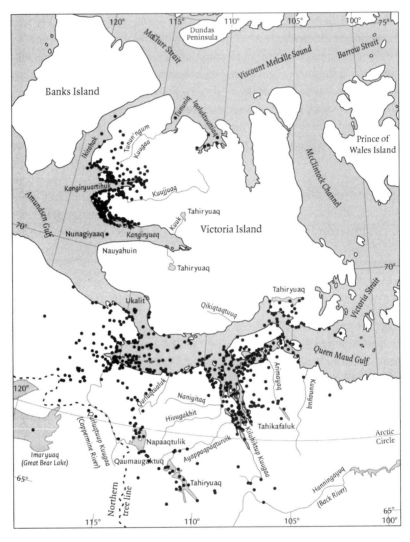

11.2. Spatial distribution of 779 Inuinnait toponyms (out of 1,007 collected).

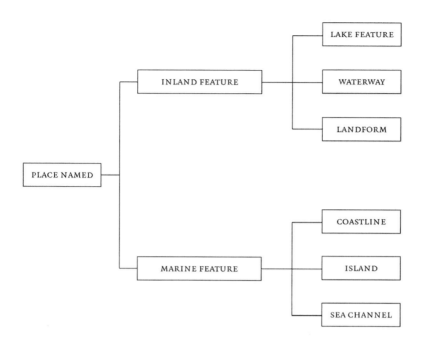

11.3. Structure of the typology based on the type of feature named.

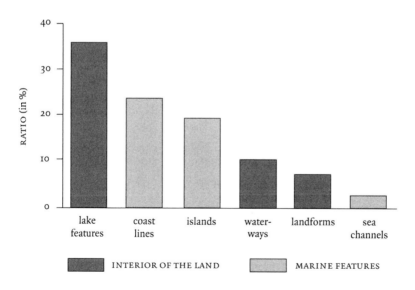

11.4. Distribution of toponyms according to the type of feature named.

"how" (words forming place names), a second typology was created based on the type of meaning carried by the toponyms. This sorting required a more complex typology, as one can see in figure 11.5.

Most of the toponyms recorded by Nuttall (1992) dealt with local land use. However, others who have worked on larger data sets (Holmer 1967, 1969; Le Mouël 1978; Goehring 1989) emphasize the descriptive quality of Inuit toponyms, of which a large majority relate to the natural environment. It thus seemed only logical to base my own typology on a major division between natural and human environment. Yet such categories derive from a western conception of the world that relies on a frontal opposition between Nature and Culture. They do not convey the Inuit conception of the world. Hence I later turned to two Inuit categories that seemed more relevant to this study: nuna and uumajuit. At the level of the human experience of the territory, nuna refers to the land in general, whether it is earth, ice, or water—salty or fresh. Uumajuit is a plural that refers to "game animals" in current conversation. Yet, as is often the case in Inuit language, the word has several layers of meanings, from the most specific to the most general. It therefore can also refer to all animals and, at its most general and abstract level, to all the living beings that are animated by a vital warmth and roam over nuna: the people, the animals, and all other beings, such as giants, dwarfs, etc. Unlike the westerners' opposed categories of "physical" and "human" environment, nuna and uumajuit are complementary. At an even more general level MacDonald (1998) shows that nuna encompasses all uumajuit: together nuna, qilak (the sky), and sila (the air) form the universe. In 1996 I visited Holman Inuinnait and took the opportunity to present the typology to some of them. I had the pleasure of hearing them comment on its relevance, explaining why in their view it made sense to sort the toponyms the way I had.

Results showed that although a majority of toponyms were related to nuna, the ratio between nuna and uumajuit categories was actually quite balanced (60/40; see fig. 11.6.). Within the nuna categories the proportion of place names built on morphologic analogies (e.g., uumannaq, "shaped like a heart") is striking.[3] Toponyms that refer to uumajuit are in fact more numerous than they appear on the graph. To realize this one has to look more deeply into the toponyms and reach their hidden meaning, to use Nuttall's phrasing.

I became aware of this hidden meaning through comments added to toponyms during the survey, especially those coming from the translators.[4] For example, a translator would give two totally different translations for the

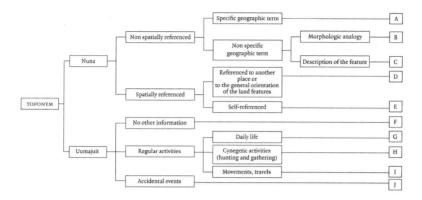

11.5. Structure of the typology based on the meaning of the toponyms.

same name: *Hiuqqitak*, "sandy and shallow place"/"caribou crossing place." Or a translation would prove radically different from the one I had been given for the same name by another translator: *Nilak*, "where the ice piles up"/"hard to cross," despite the fact that Inuinnait all speak the same dialect—Inuinnaqtun. Whenever I expressed my perplexity I would be told that, yes, the name means "where the ice piles up" but its *real* meaning is "hard to cross" because this is what people think about immediately when they hear the toponym *Nilak*. Similar explanations were given for *Hiuqqitak* and the like.

By spontaneously recognizing the multidimensional nature of Inuit place names, translators were stressing the situatedness of their geographic knowledge. Postmodern studies, postcolonial studies and feminist studies have shown that western science is a situated knowledge as well, although it is built on the denial of its situatedness as this was seen as a weakness (Lyotard 1984; Haraway 1991; Godlewska and Smith 1994). Inuit on the other hand are strongly aware of the situated nature of any knowledge and do not see it as problematic. Indeed they always take much care in expressing this quality, notably through constant contextualization of any piece of information they might share, a trend encouraged by the very structure of the Inuit language (Collignon 2006).

Names as Cultural Landscapes

The next question to arise was how to deal with those multiple layers of meaning. Should one of them be privileged and if so, which one? Which led to another question: what are place names for, apart from being a useful tool for the researcher?

197

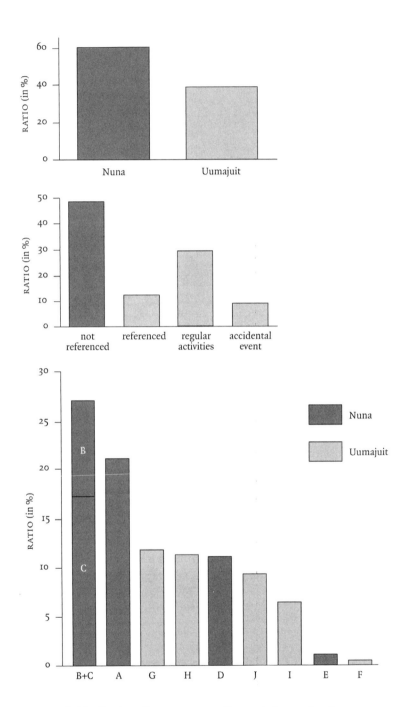

11.6. Distribution of toponyms according to their meaning. Letters A–J refer to the ten categories of meaning described in figure 11.5.

Only the Inuinnait could answer that question, and they did so in the course of the survey when elders uniformly claimed that *place names were not for traveling*. When I started my research it seemed obvious to everyone I could talk to in academia that place names were useful knowledge on which Inuit relied when traveling to stay on the trail and to avoid getting lost. Young Inuinnait shared the same view, as they repeatedly told me. Knowing your place names seemed to be a sort of insurance against the worst hazards of traveling: getting lost or breaking down and being unable to tell where you are because you do not know the place names in the surroundings.

Yet in the second week of the toponymic survey I met with an elder who knew only the place names for the area in which he had grown up, and none for the area where he had hunted and trapped for most of his adult life. As this seemed very odd to me I asked how he managed to travel without such precious knowledge. His answer was straightforward and did not surprise the translator at all: place names are not needed to travel. Following this interview, I made sure I asked everyone I interviewed whether he or she thought of place names as part of the knowledge related to traveling and if they were needed for traveling safely. The same negative reply was given over and over, both by those who knew a lot of place names and by those who hardly knew any. The extreme case was an elder from Cambridge Bay who knew only five place names but was famous as a hunter and traveler. In Kugluktuk the survey took place in the meeting room of the Hunters and Trappers Association, a building open to visitors. Some active hunters made a habit of coming to listen to other interviewees, especially when these were elders, as they were curious to learn the toponymy of areas where they hunted or trapped on a regular basis. Their attitude confirmed both the Inuinnait interest in toponyms and the very loose relation between toponymic knowledge and traveling knowledge. But if place names were not for traveling, what were they for? And why was it so obviously important to all the Inuinnait that they should be recorded and eventually recognized by the Canadian government as the official toponymy of the region?

My research on Inuinnait geographic knowledge made it clear that place names are a narrative about the land. They tell the story of the land and of its people, a story that emphasizes space rather than time, as is also clear from Nagy's analysis in this book. And it is for their quality as narratives, as holders of an essential part of Inuit memory, that place names should be recorded and passed on from one generation to the next. They are a major piece in the construction of a memoryscape (Nuttall 1992) out of the neutral landscape. This memoryscape could also be called cultural landscape, in a renewed definition of the latter. According to Carl Sauer (1925), who created the expression, cultural landscapes are the material expressions of cultures that have carved out natural landscapes to conform to their specific needs and values. [5] Historically Inuit people left hardly any conspicuous material sign of their presence in the landscape save for inukshuks (inuksuit) built here and there and tent rings and other evidence of their camps. Yet they do transform the landscape, if only intellectually, through the way they read it. Our tendency to think of place names as an operative tool for traveling instead of as a narrative through which a tight relationship to the land is built can be interpreted as a legacy of a tradition that emphasized the material culture over the intellectual one.

As narratives, place names are useful not for the action of traveling but for later telling the story of the journey. They enable the traveler to share the experience with kin after returning home. Place names are spoken at camp, in the igloo or the tupiq (tent), as often as on the land. They are words and as such they have a special power, much greater than the sometimes simple meaning they seem to carry at first glance: tahiq, "a lake," is never just a lake. It is always much more than that, as it is heard and understood within a rich context of land use and experience that its simple evocation triggers in people's thoughts. The chapter about Tatiik in Collignon (2006) clearly illustrates that. For the Inuinnait of Holman, the neutral descriptive name tatiik, meaning "the two lakes,"—is indeed a powerful one, which reminds people of the importance of fishing as a subsistence activity but also of the strong emotions linked to the regular occupation of a camp site over several generations. Place names appear as mediators between the land and the people as well as between the people themselves. They are one of the means through which the experiences of interactions with the land can be shared, and thus through which the land can be understood and become a human place where one can live a full life, not just survive.

Thus knowing place names obviously enriches the knowledgeable traveler's journey, since the succession of names along the trail unfolds the story of the long and complex relationship between the land and the people. And this explains why Kugluktuk's active hunters were eager to learn more toponyms from their elders: not to avoid getting lost but to deepen their experience of a land they travel on a regular basis. Yet on practical grounds, place names are not necessary: they are not part of what could be called the "traveler's survival kit."

Place names hold in themselves many stories of the oral tradition. Those

Table 11.1. Place names in collections of Inuinnait oral tradition.

Source	Number of stories collected	Number of stories mentioning at least one toponym	Total number of toponyms mentioned	Number of toponyms mentioned also collected in 1991–92 survey
D. Jenness 1914–16 (published 1924)	52	13 (25%)	17	13, in 10 stories (76%)
K. Rasmussen 1923–24 (published 1932)	51	6 (11%)	12	7, in 4 stories (58%)
M. Métayer 1958 (published 1973)	109	42 (39%)	50	33, in 32 stories (66%)
Collignon's 1991–92 survey (published 1996)	toponyms: 1,007	toponyms that triggered a story: 45	number of stories: 45	stories triggered also mentioned in at least 1 of the 3 collections: 44 (98%)

are either inscribed in the literal meaning of the name or in its hidden meaning. Some stories are mundane: picking berries, catching lots of fish, losing one's knife, etc. Others remind people of wise and not so wise land uses; for example, recalling starvation episodes as direct consequences of a wrong decision (such as spending the summer on an island instead of on the mainland: since the Inuinnait did not have sea kayaks, they could not leave after ice breakup had occurred). Others are related to a spiritual reading or understanding of the land and tell about magical or strange beings, good or evil.

This link between place names and oral tradition can also be approached via oral tradition. In stories, names of places where something happened are sometimes mentioned, as are names of regular campsites or meeting places. Some stories have a complex metaphysical meaning, such as the origin of death or clouds; others are stories of everyday life or particular episodes, such as starvation, murders, and meeting with other groups (Collignon 2002). So far Inuinnait stories of the oral tradition have been recorded in a systematic way in three historic collections (table 11.1), presented in detail in Collignon 2006.[6] Comparing these collections with the results of the 1991–92 place name survey shows important variation in the proportion of stories mentioning toponyms. It also shows great stability in toponymic knowledge through time, as 58 to 76 percent of the place names mentioned in a collection were also collected during my survey. This corroborates Müller-Wille and Weber Müller-Wille's findings discussed elsewhere in the present volume.

As some of those place names are found in several collections, we come to a total of seventy-two place names that either were mentioned in at least one of the three published collections and recorded during the 1991–92 survey; or were recorded during the place name survey and triggered a story that is found in at least one of the three collections. The story, in its recorded form, did not always mention the place name itself. The spatial distribution of those seventy-two place names as it appears on map 11.7 shows that they are located both at the core of the Inuinnait territory and at its margins, as if underlining its limits.

Inuit Geosophy and Sense of Place

As a narrative about the land, place names act like witnesses telling us about the relationship Inuit build with their environment. They express the Inuinnait view of the landscape and their own understanding of their land—that is, their geosophy or geographical wisdom. Geosophy goes beyond a practical and efficient geographical knowledge. It encompasses feelings, dreams, hopes, values, and beliefs. Although built on shared values, pieces of information, and representations, it is highly individual: each person slowly develops a geosophy through a lifetime. I mentioned earlier the important variations of toponymic knowledge among good hunters. As a group, the Inuinnait of one area recognize a set of place names as shared among them and therefore as legitimate. But as individuals some are interested in continuously developing their knowledge of this set, whereas others almost totally ignore the names. On top of that, some individuals develop their own personal toponymy. These were not recorded in my survey and were seldom mentioned—in those cases as family place names—rather than as individuals' place names. We need to acknowledge the diversity among the groups we study and with whom we work. Unlike scientific knowledge, theirs is not normative and allows for important variations, depending not only on gender and age but also, and perhaps more important, on individual personality. So far, social scientists have not been keen on working at such a level. Yet Nuttall's reflection on knowledge gathering (1998a) clearly shows how necessary it is to do so.

As a narrative about the land, place names also act as a major means by

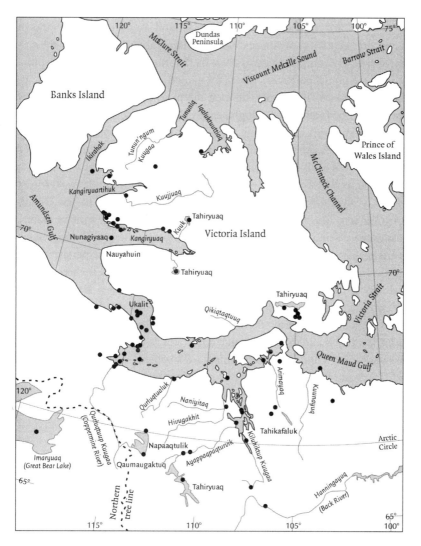

11.7. Spatial distribution of the seventy-two toponyms
mentioned in at least one collection.

which the Inuit build a strong sense of place and emplacement in their own land. But what kind of "places" are we talking about? Analysis of the collection of Inuinnait place names reveals that the emphasis is usually more on the relationship between one place named and others, named or not, or between a place and people, than on the place itself. Inuinnait geosophy appears to be founded on a high sense of context and relations, in which space and networks are indeed more important than places. The Inuinnait sense of place is in their relations to others, in the fluidity of the connected territory. This leads to a dynamic relation to places and identity, on which contemporary Inuinnait can rely to redefine their identity and their territory in today's world. What is important to them is not so much to have a place of their own but to have at their disposal a whole set of various places, with very different qualities, all connected together through the shared experiences of the various members of the community. In this perspective, it is as important that elders share their experience of places where no one ever goes any more, passing on stories and toponyms, as it is that younger people share their experience of being in Edmonton's arena watching the hockey game and cheering for the Oilers. These tales are both part of today's world, which is understood through both genuine Inuinnait knowledge and western knowledge. Even as Inuinnait lives become more similar to those of North Americans, the vitality of Inuinnait place naming expresses the continued vitality of Inuinnait geosophy.

Acknowledgments

This text is first the result of a long relationship of trust, respect, and friendship with the Inuinnait, to whom I am indebted in many ways. I thank Pamela Stern and Lisa Stevenson for inviting me to the 2001 American Anthropological Association session on "Boas and Beyond" and later to contribute to this book. I greatly appreciated their comments on the earlier version of this chapter, as well as their editing of my prose. The research presented was sponsored by a doctoral grant from the French Department of Research and Education, 1990–93. The Geographical Names Board of Canada through the Territorial Toponymy Program of the government of the Northwest Territories provided all the maps needed. The Inuinnait freely contributed to the project, giving their time and expertise. Research permits for fieldwork were issued by the Science Institute of the Northwest Territories, permit numbers 11165N, 12067R, and 12257R. All figures are the author's.

Notes

1. It should also be mentioned here that, unlike anthropology, geography did not take a structuralist turn, and the theories of Lévi-Strauss were never a great influence on the discipline.

2. On April 1, 2006, the official name of Holman changed to Ulukhaktok, meaning, "there are plenty of things [rocks] to make women's knives (ulu)." The name change occurred too late in the production process to correct the text and maps in this book.

3. Unlike most Canadian Inuit, Inuinnait write using only the roman alphabet. In this chapter, Inuinnaqtun words are transcribed following the standard roman orthography recommended by the Inuit Cultural Institute since 1976. Inuinnait themselves remained reluctant to adopt it until the late 1990s, favoring the orthography inherited from the Anglican missionaries.

4. Three of my four translators (aged thirty-one to fifty-eight) were women.

5. "The cultural landscape is fashioned from a natural landscape by a culture group. Culture is the agent, the natural area is the medium, the cultural landscape is the result" (Sauer 1925: 22).

6. The three are Jenness 1924, Rasmussen 1932, and Métayer 1973. "Oral tradition" is here limited to the stories told as such by storytellers, although anthropologists today agree that oral tradition encompasses much more than that. Life stories such as those recorded and published for Northern Inuinnait by Richard Condon (1996) obviously convey an important toponymic knowledge that would be worth analyzing.

TWELVE

Inuit Social Networks in an Urban Setting

Nobuhiro Kishigami

Both government statistics and anecdotal reports indicate that Canada's urban Inuit population is increasing. The demographic shift gained momentum during the 1980s as more northern-born Inuit relocated to southern Canadian cities (Kishigami 1999; Royal Commission on Aboriginal Peoples 1993). In 1991, 8,305 Inuit (approximately 17 percent of the Canadians who identify themselves as Inuit) reportedly resided in the largest Canadian urban centers (Statistics Canada 1994: 100; Centre for International Statistics at the Canadian Council on Social Development 1996). [1] This new urbanization foregrounds numerous changes in Inuit communities in the North as well as in the lives of the urban migrants. In the summer of 1997 I interviewed fifty-four Inuit living in Montreal on a variety of topics including lifestyle, contacts and interactions with family and friends still in the North, and importantly, social and economic exchanges with other urban Inuit.

Franz Boas argued that kinship was the primary organizing principle of social life in Inuit communities of the 1880s, observing that "the social order of the Eskimo is entirely founded on the family and the ties of consanguinity and affinity between the individual families" (Boas 1964 [1888]: 170). Inuit kinship, however, is not merely a matter of biological relatedness but depends on many other factors, such as physical proximity, naming, and regular social interactions. Despite the enormous social and physical reorganization of Inuit communities and economies in the latter half of the twentieth century, arctic anthropologists continue to describe the overriding importance of kinship as the organizing principle of social networks and social activities in contemporary arctic communities (cf. Burch 1975; Damas 1963; Kishigami 1995; Nuttall 1992; Wenzel 1981). To date little anthropological attention has been paid to the lives of urban-dwelling Inuit. However, the urban environment is markedly different—socially, culturally, and physically—from that of Inuit communities in the North, and thus we should expect Inuit living in cities to live markedly different lives than their northern kin. In this chapter I explore whether kinship is the main organizing principle of social networks and social activities of Inuit living in Montreal.

Research Methods

My previous experience in both Montreal and the eastern Canadian Arctic led me to select Montreal as a research site for examining the urban Inuit experience (Kishigami 1995, 1997, 2000). Montreal is an important service center for Inuit from Nunavik (as it was for the Inuit from the Baffin region of Nunavut until the late 1990s), and a number of Nunavik Inuit organizations are based in Montreal. Additionally, as an international student at McGill University in the 1980s I had the opportunity to experience Montreal as a nonwestern nonfrancophone outsider, which was not entirely dissimilar to the experience of recent Inuit arrivals in the city.

In the summer of 1996 before beginning this project, I visited the offices of several Inuit and native organizations in Ottawa and Montreal in order to explain my project and obtain their cooperation. In Ottawa the organizations included Inuit Tapirisat of Canada (now Inuit Tapiriit Kanatami), Pauktuutit (Inuit Women's Association), Inuit Circumpolar Conference–Canada, and Tunngasuvvingat Inuit (Inuit house). In Montreal I met with officials from Makivik Corporation, the Native Friendship Centre of Montreal, Chez Doris (a women's shelter), and the Kativik School Board. I conducted preliminary interviews with ten Inuit at the Native Friendship Centre and, based on this pilot survey and in cooperation with Caroline Stone at Makivik Corporation, developed a series of questions for a one-hour open-ended interview.

Using a snowball sampling technique, I contacted as many Montreal Inuit as possible between June 17 and August 8, 1997. In the end fifty-five people agreed to answer my questions (table 12.1).[2] Because it was summer, university students, who make up a significant portion of urban Inuit, were undersampled. Additionally, I did not interview anyone under the age of seventeen. While the sample cannot be assumed to be entirely representative of urban Inuit, it does include individuals from the full range of economic and social circumstances and thus provides a starting point for an examination

Table 12.1. Source of Inuit respondents to questionaire.

Chez Doris	7
Makivik Corporation	14
Kativik School Board	11
Native Friendship Centre	22
TOTAL	54

of social networks. The final sample included twenty-two employed Inuit, twenty-four jobless Inuit, and eight students.

Inuit in Montreal

The population of the Greater Montreal area is about 3.1 million. Montreal is a multiethnic, cosmopolitan city with a large immigrant population. Nonetheless French Canadians dominate the city numerically, politically, and culturally, and French is the dominant language.

Many of the current Inuit residents of the city originally arrived there from arctic communities in order to continue their education, for employment, or for medical care. Despite whatever intentions they had that the move would be temporary, many migrants ended up staying in the city. Inuit women, especially, left the North in order to escape shortages of jobs and housing, drug and alcohol problems of their own or of members of their immediate families, or threats of sexual and physical violence (Kishigami 1999). Their reasons for leaving the North are multiple and often tinged with ambivalence. As one woman told me: "I think that because there are many social problems in northern communities, many people move to the South to escape these problems. In Iqaluit, I have my family and friends, and good landscape for hunting. But the community is too small. People are always angry at each other and have drinking problems. On the other hand, I feel very comfortable in Montreal where there are a lot of supermarkets, grocery stores, restaurants, museums and amusement parks. I like to live in the South."

This generally positive assessment of life in Montreal was not universal. Another woman experienced the move differently: "I feel lonely in Montreal because I do not have my family in the city. It is too hot here and the city lacks native food. But I was physically and mentally annoyed by various kinds of social problems in the North. There were many gossips and was no privacy. So, I don't want go back to the North."

Regardless of their reasons for moving south, once they have arrived in the city many Inuit decide to stay in Montreal. Some who may have intended

Table 12.2. Characteristics of the sample.

	Male	Female
Employed	5	17
Jobless	10	14
Student	2	6
Mean age	33.1	33.2
Mean number of years in Montreal	4.3	8.9

to stay, on the other hand, return to the North soon after arriving in Montreal, and numerous others move back and forth (cf. Fienup-Riordan 2000).

In terms of occupation, Inuit living in Montreal can be classified into three categories: those who are employed, those who are not, and students (table 12.2). Limited or nonexistent fluency in French limits the employability of many Montreal Inuit, and thus the majority of Inuit with jobs in my sample were employed by one of the native or governmental organizations. The unemployed included those who were in Montreal for ongoing medical treatment, Inuit dependent on welfare, and the homeless. Young Inuit are enrolled in elementary, junior high, and high schools, colleges, or universities in the Montreal region.

In general Inuit employed by native and governmental organizations and those who are students live quite comfortably in Montreal. However, those without jobs manage to survive only through the support of charitable organizations and welfare. Jobless Inuit tend to pass their days doing nothing in particular, and many have substance abuse problems. For them urban life is also felt with ambivalence. As one informant noted, "I can get beer and drugs more easily in Montreal than in the North."

The average household size of those who participated in this study was 2.5 persons. The households consisted of single persons, couples, and couples with children. The average household size of the employed Inuit and students (4.5 per household) is larger than that of unemployed Inuit (1.48 per household). While five employed Inuit (23.8 percent of the employed) live alone, fifteen unemployed Inuit (65.2 percent of the unemployed) do so.

Given the urban setting, Montreal Inuit are unable to engage in subsistence pursuits such as hunting and fishing. However, they are able to, and often do, speak Inuktitut among themselves and sometimes share native food sent to them by northern kin. Although a few of the respondents reported that they produce soapstone carvings and other Inuit handicrafts in Montreal, there are few other ethnic distinctions between urban Inuit lifeways and those of other city dwellers in similar socioeconomic circumstances. Most of the Inuit migrants accommodate to existing urban institutions rather than attempting to maintain a northern way of life in the city.

The Inuit interviewed live scattered throughout the city rather than in ethnic community enclaves, and thus they rarely have other Inuit for neighbors. Except in the few cases in which the entire extended family relocated, each has very few kin in the city. One woman informant told me: "Nobody helped me in Montreal. So I tried to find a place to stay by myself." The lack of kin support has consequences. Women in particular often live with or marry non-Inuit, and as a result their children tend not to speak Inuktitut; in general they tend not to retain a specifically Inuit cultural identity due to a lack of opportunities to engage in specifically Inuit practices in Montreal (Kishigami 2002).

According to the 1991 aboriginal census (Statistics Canada 1994: 100), 455 of the 775 Montreal Inuit listed multiethnic identities. My interviews reveal that young Inuit raised in Montreal and Inuit who have a spouse or one parent who is non-Inuit tend to identify themselves as one of the indigenous people of Canada, Canadians of Inuit descent, or indigenous people of Quebec rather than as Inuit (Kishigami 2002; see Fienup-Riordan 2000: 151–68 for a different situation in Anchorage). Interethnic marriage and city dwelling in multiethnic situations may make intergenerational transmission of language and culture difficult (Kishigami 1999; see Sprott 1994; see also Fogel-Chance 1993 for a different situation in Anchorage).

Let me give four examples. The first case is an Inuk man married to an anglophone woman. He works for the Kativik School Board as an Inuit student advisor. Although he is in an Inuit environment from 9:00 a.m. to 5:00 p.m. during weekdays, the rest of his life cannot be described as Inuit. This man and his immediate family live in a suburb of Montreal. His children, who go to a local elementary school, do not speak Inuktitut but English and French and seldom eat native food at home. In short, his family leads a middle-class life largely indistinguishable from that of other middle-class Canadians.

The second case is a seventeen-year-old university student whose mother is Inuk and whose father is Québecois. The girl's family had moved to Montreal three years earlier from Kuujjuaq, a community in arctic Quebec (Nunavik), because her mother was transferred in connection with her job. The girl is Québecoise in appearance and does not speak Inuktitut fluently. She eats raw meat or fish only sometimes in an Inuit way at home. However, she regards herself as an Inuk. On the other hand, her younger brothers in Montreal understand Inuktitut but do not speak it. According to her, her brothers seem to regard themselves as Inuit and Québecois. It apparently does not matter to them whether they are Inuit or Québecois in their daily life in the multiethnic city.

The third case is an Inuk woman who moved south to Montreal with her Québecois husband about twenty years earlier. They had four children after their arrival in Montreal. The woman has a drinking problem, which contributed to her divorce from her husband after about nine years in the city. At the time of our interview she lived alone and was dependent on welfare. Her children, whom she was seeing only about once a month, lived with her ex-husband. One of the four speaks only French and regards himself as Québecois. The other three children, whose first language is also French, understand Inuktitut but do not speak it. These three consider themselves half Inuit and half Québecois.

The fourth and economically most extreme case is a homeless man. He was spending his days sitting in the exit area of the subway station or on a main street begging. He received free meals at a church soup kitchen or city shelter or at the Salvation Army. He slept in parks, at several public shelters, or sometimes at his friends' residences. In terms of his daily activities, there was no real difference between him and other homeless people from various ethnic backgrounds in Montreal. Except to a very limited extent in Iqaluit and Kuujjuaq, this form of homelessness does not occur in the North.

Social Ties of Urban Inuit to Their Native Communities

Inuit of Montreal maintain their relationships with their families, extended kin, and friends still in the North through telephone calls or by visiting one another. Seventy-five percent of the respondents reported making telephone calls to their home communities once a month or more. Air fares between Montreal and northern communities in Nunavik or Nunavut are prohibitively expensive, and the unemployed Inuit are seldom able to travel North.[3] The employed Inuit and the students, on the other hand, report that they are able to visit friends and family in the North fairly regularly. The majority of urban Inuit, nonetheless, maintain contacts with their family, other kin, and friends in Arctic.

Diet, Social Networks, and Resource Sharing in Montreal

Almost all the Inuit in Montreal originally from northern communities told me that they prefer Inuit food prepared in traditional ways to Euro-Canadian foods. For them "Inuit food" is any Inuit traditional food, such as caribou and seal meat, arctic char, skin parts of beluga whale, and so on, which are primarily eaten raw, frozen, dried, or boiled. Most also observed that their children and non-Inuit spouses, if they eat Inuit food at all, do not eat it prepared in the ways that would be typical in a northern community.

Not surprisingly, socioeconomic status makes a difference in terms of the consumption of Inuit food, and there are clear differences in meal content and the sites of meal consumption between the employed and unemployed members of the sample, with native food much more readily available to the employed.

Homeless and unemployed Inuit were forced to depend on several missions, the Salvation Army, Chez Doris, and the Native Friendship Centre of Montreal for almost all their meals. Chez Doris serves Inuit dishes to Inuit clients two Wednesdays each month. One homeless Inuk told me that he had his suppers at the Salvation Army and lunches at a downtown church from Monday to Friday, and that sometimes on Saturdays and Sundays when many charitable organizations are closed he had nothing to eat or drink except water.

Unemployed Inuit sometimes obtain Inuit food when they visit friends or relatives in town, and they occasionally ask northern relatives to send food to them by air cargo or via travelers, but these occasions are rare.

The employed Inuit I interviewed ate most of their meals at home. While a few consumed Inuit food almost every day, others ate these foods only few times a month. On average, the employed included Inuit foods in their diets at least once a week. When they wanted native foods, they made telephone calls to their parents, siblings, relatives, or friends in arctic communities requesting that the food be sent to them by air cargo. They are also in a better position to host northern visitors, who are likely to bring native food with them as gifts. The employed were able to keep seal and caribou meat and fish in home freezers and, by consuming the food in small portions, were able to stretch out their supplies. In addition those employed by Makivik Corporation or by the Kativik School Board shared caribou meat and arctic char for lunch several times a month.

In sum, poor Inuit living in Montreal ate less country food than did employed, better off Inuit. Because of limited quantities of Inuit native food in the city, food sharing and invitations to meals occurred only occasionally. Based on my observations and interviews with Inuit in both the North and South, food sharing is less frequently practiced in Montreal than in northern communities. The urban Inuit with whom I spoke attributed this lack of sharing to shortages of country food and infrequent interactions among the urban Inuit, who are widely scattered around Montreal (see Lee 2002 for a different situation in Anchorage), but it seems that another process may also be at work. In northern communities, food sharing is most common among kin (Kishigami 1995, 2004; Collings et al. 1998). Urban Inuit have very small networks of kin living locally.

Inuit in Montreal had not formed a distinct ethnic community in the city in the mid-1990s, and there were few places for them to meet and exchange information as Inuit.[4] Except for Inuit organizations such as Makivik Corporation, Avataq Cultural Institute, and Kativik School Board, Inuit in Montreal did not have any ethnically based groups. The Inuit I interviewed, including those who worked for Inuit organizations, have friends of many ethnic backgrounds and from a wide variety of activities. As they did not form a spatially separate community, individuals were left to create networks on their own. Rather than being based on ethnicity or even aboriginal status, the urban social networks appear to be personal and egocentric. Generally speaking, Montreal Inuit found it difficult to create and maintain arctic lifestyles and a particularly Inuit cultural identity.

In 1998 several Montreal Inuit decided to change the situation and held meetings to discuss the establishment of an urban Inuit organization. The organizers included employees of the Makivik Corporation, Avataq Cultural Institute, and Kativik School Board as well as a few Inuit dependent on welfare. An initial activity was an Inuit feast held at the hall of St. Paul's Anglican Church in Lachine (a suburb of Montreal) on a Saturday in November 1999. About 120 Inuit attended. Consequently the volunteer group decided to hold monthly arctic community–style feasts (Mesher 2000). By October 2002 the feasts had been held more than thirty times. The participants included not only Inuit from Nunavik but also Inuit from Nunavut and Labrador, non-Inuit partners, and children. Many of the most regular attendees were the jobless, but students and employed Inuit also attended the feasts. Interestingly, several urban dwellers became acquainted or reacquainted with distant kin whom they found among the other feast attendees and reestablished those relationships.

On March 29, 2000, an Inuit social organization called the Association of Montreal Inuit was officially established (Mesher 2000). There is no defined membership. Anyone who identifies himself or herself as an Inuk can belong, no matter where the participant originated. Makivik Corporation agreed to provide the association with an office and storage room. The aims of the organization include functioning as a center for information exchange and socializing and providing a monthly supper for urban Inuit. The regular feasts are organized by volunteers, and the association has succeeded in getting the fourteen Nunavik communities to supply native food such as arctic char, ptarmigan, eider duck, caribou, seals, etc. The Makivik-owned Air Inuit provides the shipping without charge. In return the association collects secondhand clothing, furniture, toys, sports equipment, and books for distribution in arctic communities, to be shipped to Nunavik communities by cargo ship in summer and by air at other seasons, such as Christmas.

The association also organizes a number of events in Montreal to promote cultural exchange between the Montreal Inuit and other Montreal residents. These events have included cultural exchange meetings with a Westmount Rotary Club and with the Boy Scouts of Montreal. In June 2001 members of the Association of Montreal Inuit marched together in the Aboriginal Day parade in Montreal. In November 2002 the association officially opened its own drop-in center in Dorval, a suburb of Montreal near the airport, and opened a combination Inuit art/clothing/food shop next to the center the following March. The activities of the new association enabled Montreal Inuit to begin to develop a sense of community.

Discussion and Conclusion

While Inuit society in the Canadian Arctic has been changing, the individual household and the extended family are still the most important units when it comes to hunting and fishing activities, summer camping, and food and meal sharing in contemporary arctic communities. With several exceptions, however, Canadian Inuit communities have populations smaller than one thousand, and the communities are physically isolated. Social interactions among the Inuit kin and neighbors within each arctic community are much more frequent and intense than among those scattered throughout the Montreal area (see Kulchyski, this volume).

My research on social change in Akulivik indicates that although hunting and fishing activities have declined drastically since the 1980s, individual food sharing practices and food distribution through the hunter support program of the James Bay and Northern Quebec Agreement contributes to the reproduction of the extended family and neighbor relationships as well as to a sense of being a community member and being Inuit. In contrast, "traditional" native food sharing seldom occurs in daily life in the city. When an Inuk get native food from the North, it is usually eaten by the recipient alone or with cohabitants and is shared only occasionally with Inuit friends in Montreal. One characteristic of Inuit social networks in Montreal is that relationships based on friendship are more important than extended kin networks.

Furthermore, friends come from a wide variety of contexts. Interestingly, however, a number of urban dwellers have become acquainted or reacquainted with distant kin whom they found among the other feast attendees and have reestablished these relationships. Some women who had never met in the North discovered that they were related and now call each other by the appropriate kinship terms.

As noted, most Inuit living in Montreal maintain relationships with their families, kin, and friends in their native communities by occasional or regular visiting and phone calls. There is a clear difference between employed Inuit and unemployed Inuit in terms of the frequency of visiting and telephone calls. According to many of the Inuit who responded to my survey, the relationship between an Inuk in Montreal and kin and friends in the native community functions primarily as a network for sending frozen caribou, arctic char, and seal meat south to the Inuk in Montreal. In this context, kinship still functions socioculturally between urban and arctic Inuit.

Although Inuit in Montreal practice food sharing less frequently than Inuit in arctic communities, the urban Inuit do still practice it occasionally. One feature of food sharing among the urban Inuit is that they share their native food not with kin but with their Inuit friends from other communities. While food sharing practices in the arctic communities are deeply related to reproduction of family and kin relationships, those in the city are connected to ties of friendship among Inuit from various communities. Unlike Inuit in the North, whose primary interactions and food sharing occur with kin, Montreal Inuit conduct most of their social interactions with other Inuit as coethnics. In other words ethnicity has become a substitute for kinship. Significantly, a new type of food sharing—that is, a regular feast organized by the recently established Montreal Inuit Association—has the potential to produce and reproduce social relationships within the Montreal Inuit community, based not on kinship but on friendship and the shared experience of living as an Inuk in Montreal.

Notes

1. There is a fairly large discrepancy between the figures reported for the number of urban Inuit in 1991 Aboriginal People's Survey and the Canadian census from 1996. The differences appear to be related to differences in the census questions on aboriginal origins (Saku 1999: 369). According to 1996 Census, the total population of Inuit in Canada was about 41,000, and about 2,600 people lived in metropolitan areas. The Inuit population of Montreal was reported to be 365 (Statistics Canada www.statcan.ca).

According to the 2001 Census, the total population of Canadian Inuit was about 45,000, of whom more than 5,000 lived in southern Canada. The Inuit population in Montreal was 435 (Statistics Canada 2003).

2. One person at the Native Friendship Centre was a visitor to Montreal, therefore he was excluded from my final sample.

3. Air Inuit (an Inuit-owned company) monopolizes all the flights between Nunavik and the South (Montreal and Quebec City).

4. Inuit can find or meet other Inuit in a shopping center near Dorval Airport, at a park near Atwater Metro Station, and at several pubs in downtown Montreal.

THIRTEEN

Inuit Geographical Knowledge One Hundred Years Apart

Ludger Müller-Wille and Linna Weber Müller-Wille

"Why is it that Germans had Inuit maps already in 1885 and till today Canada still has none with Inuit place names on it?"

Allan Angmarlik and Josephie Keenainak
Pangnirtuuq (Pangnirtung), August 4, 1984

Parallel events occurred one hundred years apart in the history of arctic social sciences in the Tinijjuarvik region on Cumberland Sound in Nunavut in the Canadian Eastern Arctic. Visiting researchers—Franz Boas in 1883– 84 and the authors in 1984—conferred with the local Inuit about the same places and sites. Among other topics, these encounters centered on the documentation of Inuit geographical knowledge and land use practices through place names. In both cases the research activities led to a list of toponyms and the creation of maps. These maps were either drawn by Inuit themselves or surveyed by the researchers using western cartographic means.

The 1883–84 event was the first attempt to record Inuit place names systematically and in their totality from oral tradition throughout a contiguous geographic region. The 1984 event was a review of that toponymic collection to validate the temporal depth and dynamics of Inuit geographic knowledge and to connect Inuit with their written ethnographic past related to topography and toponymy. It was also a cooperative effort to react to and fulfill priorities set by local Inuit residents and organizations to preserve, maintain, and enhance Inuit cultural heritage for future generations (Allan Angmarlik, pers. comm. and correspondence with the authors, 1984).

The juxtaposition and interpretation of these two events a century apart provide insight into the approaches and methodologies applied. Furthermore, comparison allows us to delve into how humankind constructs places within specific natural environments through the shaping of frameworks for understanding and knowledge. These frameworks change according to how spaces and sites are filled and organized mentally through human presence—the interchange between people and environment being in a constant temporal and spatial flux. In this context, the concept of critical topography (Bordo 2000) allows us to probe human-environmental interactions in temporal and spatial dimensions in which space, the landscape, is seen as a "witness" to events that permeate cultural memories situated in geography.

Inuit and Western Perceptions of Arctic Landscapes

The circumpolar arctic environment has been scientifically defined since the nineteenth century as treeless lands with areas of continuous ice as glaciers or sea ice, lying under permafrost conditions, with certain climatological and ecological characteristics. It has been the living space of the Inuit and their predecessors for several millennia. Cultural, linguistic, socioeconomic, and political expressions and institutions have been manifested and altered through the continuum of Inuit interacting with their environment in these lived arctic spaces. Life, culture, and nature for the Inuit, are clearly one and not separate; in fact, this is not at all unusual. However, it needs to be emphasized because the Arctic, the North, has often been interpreted from the outside as "inhospitable." This mental and practiced relationship of the Inuit with the environment is expressed deeply, for example, through place names, which provide detailed indicators of the heightened quality of human-environment interactions. The specificity of the arctic environment has been fully integrated in its totality by the philosophy of life and knowledge of the Inuit.

In western history, Europeans (Euro-Canadians) have been understood as the outsiders and intruders attracted to spaces beyond the reach of their own realms. For a long time the North and in particular the Arctic have held the notion of the Other—unknown, pristine, sublime, in sum Ultima Thule—its myth and magic there to be explored and conquered in colonial fashion, by prying the knowledge of places from the environment itself or from its aboriginal inhabitants. Their lives and livelihoods were often perceived and presented as an indescribable burden, a matter of pain in facing the inhospitable elements. Clearly, the Arctic was not the living space for European explorers and scientists but rather a playground to unravel the geographically unexplored through daring adventurism, through research into poorly understood natural and physical processes or into the astounding human adaptive strategies of survival by employing western scientific concepts and methods.

It was within this context that Franz Boas sought to meet the Inuit in the Canadian Arctic in the 1880s—an event with repercussions for both the Inuit and western scientists. For the Inuit of Baffin Island, Boas was the first of a continuous string of "visiting scientists" probing into their culture and identity. For western scientists, Boas's visit marked the evident emergence of arctic anthropology as part of cultural anthropology, then Inuit studies, and ultimately arctic social sciences (*Études/Inuit/Studies* 1984).

Boas Collects Arctic Place Names, 1883–1884

In 1883 Franz Boas—twenty-four years old and with a doctorate in physics, geography, and philosophy and an early boyhood fascination with arctic exploration—rode high on the first global wave of scientific rigor and co-operation focusing on the polar regions: the multinational First International Polar Year of 1882–83. This large research network in polar sciences conducted standardized and synchronized measurements and observations for one annual cycle at permanent stations placed in different locations throughout the circumpolar North and sub-Antarctica (Barr 1985). From September 1882 to September 1883 a German-run research station was located at Sirmilik at the head of Tinijjuarvik (Cumberland Sound).

In the wake of this station's activities Boas arrived in Tinijjuarvik in late August 1883 to begin his one-year research project into what he called "*the simple relationships between the land and the people*"—between the arctic landscape and the Inuit (Cole and Müller-Wille 1984, emphasis in original). During that year he resided at the Scottish whaling station on the island named Qikirtat (Kekerten) between late August 1883 and May 1884. This station became the base for his extensive surveying trips throughout the sound of Tinijjuarvik. The remainder of the time till early September 1884 he traveled to and along the western coast of Davis Strait (Boas 1885; cf. Müller-Wille 1998).

One of Franz Boas's main research goals was to produce a map of Baffin Island using the most modern tools of surveying available at that time. This task required extensive travels by boat and dogsled and on foot and the use of a theodolite to obtain as many bearing points as possible. In this task he was aided by his servant Wilhelm Weike (1859–1917) from Germany and by many Inuit—men and some women, whose commitment he obtained and compensated in kind by goods such as tobacco, imported foodstuffs, a rifle, or a knife.

From his first days in the Arctic Boas made it clear that he would get to know the land, sea, and ice with the Inuit by acquiring skills in their language, learning their place names while traveling with them extensively throughout the area and seeing and experiencing all named spaces and places in situ. His anthropological and methodological position on giving priority to aboriginal place names was resolute, and despite strong criticism from one of his habilitation thesis evaluators in Berlin (Kiepert 1886), he took a stance in opposition to colonial naming practices, which distorted and displaced aboriginal peoples' relations with their environment.

As Boas expressed it, "it is truly to be deplored if indigenous names get lost, because, like the Eskimo ones, they are so fitting; I have experienced such considerable anger, annoyance and inconveniences from numerous English names, and the absence of indigenous names, that the situation has prevented me from making use of the explorer's naming rights anywhere. It is certainly more valuable scientifically to preserve the indigenous names than to write names of all meritorious or not so meritorious friends à la Ross and Hall on bays and foothills" (Boas 1885: 51; from the German by authors).

In these methodological efforts the Inuit were the experts whose geographic and toponymic knowledge Boas began to record and map during his very first trip with Inuit, leaving Qikirtat to contact the German Polar Research Station at Sirmilik in early September 1883 (Müller-Wille 1998: 79–94). Later on he continued the surveys during intensive working sessions at the Scottish whaling station during the fall of 1883, which produced maps drawn by Inuit with lead pencils on carton paper and established lists of numerous locations and areas with Inuit geographical names (Müller-Wille 1998: 129–35). Toponymic and cartographic work became a constant aspect of Boas's work right until he left the Arctic. This effort resulted in a collection of 930 toponyms fully documented on his surveyed maps, covering both the sound of Tinijjuarvik and the eastern coast of Qikirtaaluk (Baffin Island) along Davis Strait (Boas 1885: 90–95, maps and sketches). These toponyms became for him the basis for the ethnological and geographical analysis of the complex system of relationships between Inuit and the arctic landscape (Boas 1885, 1888 [1964, 1974]). Examples are his discussion of the "influence of geographical conditions upon the distribution of the settlements" and of "hunting and fishing taboos" with respect to Inuit practices on land, water, or ice (Boas 1888: 460 ff. and 471 ff.).

The working sessions with the Inuit experts were considerable linguistic and cross-cultural challenges for Boas. He was a native German speaker and had had training in classical languages and French in school. He had also learned English, the lingua franca of the whalers, and some smattering of Inuktitut (the Greenlandic variety) on his own before the arctic sojourn. English was his main means of communication with the transient or over-wintering local whalers and, in particular, with the Scottish whaler and station manager, James Mutch, who was married to an Inuit woman and was fluent in Inuktitut.

Most Inuit who worked for the whalers and resided at Qikirtat at that time, both men and women, had also acquired a type of pidgin English, which Boas picked up as well. Mutch became Boas's main mentor and mediator for negotiating among cultures, languages, and people. Letters, diaries, and later publications make it apparent that Inuktitut became a major mental struggle for Boas and impeded his access to and understanding of Inuit culture. On October 31, 1883, he wrote in the letter-diary he kept for his parents and sisters: "I am now trying to collect information from the Eskimos about the country, and I spent the entire day drawing one or other of the maps. The language is quite abominably difficult!" (Müller-Wille 1998: 130). It would never be easy for Boas to work with Inuktitut; before and after his fieldwork the Danish linguist Hinrich Johannes Rink of Copenhagen, conversant with Greenlandic, helped Boas correct as many misunderstandings as possible and helped him cope with his linguistic frustrations.

The toponymic fieldwork methods Boas applied while working with the Inuit were a combination of systematic interview sessions consisting of obtaining and entering information on maps and lists or reviewing map sketches prepared by male and female Inuit experts. In addition his own geographic observations and geodetic surveys complemented the recording of Inuit geographical names and knowledge. Surmising from the diaries and names given by Boas, these map sketches were drawn by at least ten to fifteen Inuit, whose participation in the exercise was voluntary but who expected to receive compensation in kind. Participation was also based on Mutch's advice on whom the Inuit themselves considered to be experts. In retrospect it cannot be determined whether these mapping skills were attributable only to a small number of Inuit; however, the Inuit habit seems to be to delegate such tasks to individuals who clearly have this knowledge and who are trusted by the community—a circumstance that showed itself in the surveys one hundred years later. A modern analysis of these Inuit sketches confirmed the high proficiency of mental mapping among Inuit and showed the strong resemblance of their maps to maps based on techno-scientific methods—in scale and shape as well as content and style (Spink and Moodie 1972: 90–93; Müller-Wille and Weber 1984).

With these working sessions it seems that Boas had, in fact, mobilized the whole Inuit community of Qikirtat, including some women, to produce maps and a toponymic gazetteer. The following quotes describe this process well. On November 3, 1883, he wrote:

> The sketch maps are always valuable. The table is opened out and a large quantity of paper laid out on it. We and Mutch lie on the table and then the conversation proceeds, seven-eighths in Eskimo and one-eighth in English. In the morning Pakkak and his kuni [wife] were here, mapping Kignait and Padli for me. Since I am giving the natives tobacco for their maps, they are arriving on their own accord; thus in the evening Bob arrived with a grey blotter showing the Davis Strait coast from Padli to far to the north. (Müller-Wille 1998: 133)

A few days later he added:

> The amicable Eskimos are constantly coming and going here. Almost the whole of Kikkerton is engaged in drawing maps for me, from which I hope to get on the track of my questions. I have already achieved a good part of what I need to know, but can't imagine how much an effort is involved to drag all this out of these people. (134–35)

In assessing Inuit attitudes to these endeavors he noted on November 6: "It is better to question the Eskimos individually than several of them together, because it seems that they are shy in front of each other" (136).

At this point Boas's motives for concentrating so strongly on the acquisition of toponymic data can be questioned. Though his research program was multifaceted, from the outset it was driven by the scientific requirements for geographic exploration prevalent at the time. These included the collection of information on the natural environment, with little concern for the social dimension as contained in the toponyms. The main concern was to produce a map that would show the success of exploration, proving that, in fact, the land and waters had been discovered and visited by Europeans. In Boas's case this meant to improve on existing maps of the area. He was clearly trained and equipped for this task. Yet he also understood and stressed the fact that producing a map would require including the understanding of how the local people organized or "constructed" their environment through "use and occupancy," for which their own place names were the obvious markers and indicators for the "simple relationships between the land and the people." Hence his emphasis on mapping and place names. It can also be argued that this approach provided Boas with "easier" access to Inuit culture, given his limited linguistic capabilities, which might have restricted his ability to delve into other realms of life.

Despite all adversity, the results of Boas's cartographic and toponymic work, in combination with other ethnographic aspects of Inuit cultural heritage, are astounding and have withstood the rigor of later reviews by Inuit and others. Upon his return to Germany in 1885, Boas's research results were published in rapid succession with a full and detailed account of his travels and the physiography of arctic lands, the production of an outstanding map of southern Qikirtaaluk (1:600,000) with Inuit place names, using the Greenlandic orthography, spelled out and placed accurately next to their geographic locations, and finally a complete list of Inuit toponyms with translations into German (Boas 1885). In 1888 the map was reprinted as an appendix to *The Central Eskimo* (Boas 1974 [1888]), differing from the original publication in Germany with changes to the spelling of some of the Inuit place names. In the scientific community these alterations created confusion in the application of those names.

The map published in Germany in 1885 did enter into the body of the scientific literature and was keenly used by Canadian government scientists in the 1920s and 1930s; there was no better map produced for that area until then. One of these scientists, J. Dewey Soper, suggested the acceptance of some of the Inuit toponyms, mainly in the Greenlandic orthography included in Boas's list, by the Geographic Board of Canada in 1927–28 (Helen Kerfoot, Energy, Mines and Resources Canada, Ottawa, pers. comm., 1983). Thus a few of these selected place names were entered finally on maps of the National Topographic System and came to be part of the official and legal place names of Canada. Pangnirtung (Pangnirtuuq) was one of those names; its location, which was an uninhabited promontory on the fiord in the 1880s, was selected as the place of fur trading, government, and policing activities in the 1920s. The decision to accept a local name showed the respect that was given by these natural scientists to Inuit knowledge and heritage. By the 1960s this location had emerged as the central settlement for the Inuit from the various camps around Tinijjuarvik, and it has become the town where Inuit of the Tinijjuarvik region and their descendants live today.

Franz Boas never returned to Tinijjuarvik or the Arctic, although James Mutch, with whom he continued to correspond until the 1910s, kept him up to date about the Inuit with whom he had worked and traveled. This was the time when Aksayuk Etuangat (discussed later in the chapter) was a young adolescent. From the record it is not apparent if any of Boas's publications or maps reached the Inuit who had provided the geographic knowledge stored in them. This knowledge was a firm part of the western scientific tradition and eventually became a classic in cultural anthropology, *The Central Eskimo* (Boas 1888 [1964, 1974]), which is still widely read by students of the social sciences and has fixed the image of the Inuit for western societies.

The originals of the maps drawn by Inuit, whose names are indicated, either ended up in the Ethnology Museum in Berlin or stayed with Boas's personal and professional papers, now housed in the archive of the American Philosophical Society in Philadelphia—all in distant places and out of reach of contemporary Inuit, the descendants of those experts who worked with Boas.

The NUNA-TOP Project Review, July–August 1984

By the 1980s times had changed considerably in the Arctic. The Inuit of Canada and the circumpolar North had gone through developments that touched upon their livelihoods, settlement patterns, and rights to the land and its resources as well as redefinition of cultural identity through increased self-awareness and knowledge about their own conditions (see Tester, Stern, this volume). For many Inuit the preservation of knowledge of their own past—knowledge connected to the present and to be used for the future—had become of paramount importance for their empowerment to be themselves in their own lived spaces.

The ethnographic past that existed and lingered in western publications, museums, and archives held keys to the Inuit understanding of that past, combining it with the still available knowledge of their oldest generation, the elders. Toponyms are a small but nonetheless essential element of cultural heritage: they link people with their land. Thus it was only natural that the recording of orally transmitted place names became a priority for most Inuit and their organizations throughout the circumpolar North. Also, it was geographical knowledge, presented in the "Inuit Land Use and Occupancy Project" conducted in the early 1970s, that became the evidentiary basis of Inuit land claims (Freeman 1976).

In July and August 1984, one hundred years after Boas had left Qikirtaaluk (Baffin Island), the Inuit of Pangnirtung met Boas's Inuit legacy. Some who

encountered it were elderly, like Aksayuk Etuangat (1901–96), whose grandparents and parents had met Boas and told stories about him; and others
were young, like Allan Angmarlik (1957–2000), who had just found Boas's
The Central Eskimo and devoured it, finding through it a link with the dis-
connected past. The path to this encounter began for us in the early 1970s
through our involvement with Inuit of Naujaat/Aivilik (Repulse Bay) and
our recording of their place names. At that time the Inuit remarked that
their names for places did not appear on official maps. This early project led
to our NUNA-TOP surveys of the 1980s and 1990s, toponymic surveys that
covered all of what are today called Nunavik (the Inuit areas within Quebec
as well as offshore islands excluding Sanikiluaq, the Belcher Islands) and
Kivalliq (Nunavut and a section of northernmost Manitoba; Müller-Wille
and Weber 1982–95).

Furthermore, Ludger Müller-Wille had begun research on Boas's early
work with the Inuit, transcribing, translating, editing, and finally publishing Boas's original field diaries and letters (Müller-Wille 1998). Part of this
work included the transfer of Boas's collection of Inuit place names onto
modern maps. Once this was done, the next step was to take this collection
and the maps to the Inuit of Pangnirtung for a review of this historic data.

The NUNA-TOP research was conducted in Pangnirtung during the summer of 1984. After getting permission from the Hamlet Council and the
Hunters and Trappers Association and the necessary research permit, the
authors and a research assistant, Christine Mason, flew to Pangnirtung. We
were met at the airport by Allan Angmarlik, a local educator, in late July 1984.
Angmarlik had agreed to be our local research partner and liaison with the
community.

The survey methods developed for the NUNA-TOP projects (Müller-Wille
1984a) were applied. The stationary portion of the survey was conducted in
a public space (the school) with all map materials and documents available;
field trips were scheduled to sites such as Sirmilik, the former German Polar
Research Station (1882–83), and the Kekerten Islands, the historic whaling
station of the nineteenth and early twentieth centuries. The place name survey was announced on community radio. Working sessions were conducted
in both Inuktitut and English; they were public, and people who showed
interest could and did drop by.

Inuit experts were approached by Allan Angmarlik to join the sessions
individually or in groups of two or three people. Their selection was com-
munity-generated without any influence from us. It was understood that
the process of self-selection would entice the most qualified, respected,

and trusted Inuit to appear for interviews. In the end five Inuit men made themselves available to take on the responsibility for the community as a whole to provide for the full documentation of their toponymy as they knew it. The goal was quality and not quantity of people knowing names. All experts were paid for the time spent in the interviews.

The research team members, both Inuit and non-Inuit, had specific tasks assigned—interviewing, documenting and recording information on maps and sheets of paper, and moderating between the team and the community. After the sessions a progress report in both Inuktitut and English was submitted to the Hamlet Council, and the community at large was invited to a well-advertised open house as the last event of the survey in Pangnirtung. At this occasion the newly established survey maps and lists of names were presented in preliminary form for public review, corrections, and additions (Müller-Wille 1984b).

The basis for the 1984 survey was the 930 Inuit toponyms Boas had collected from the Inuit a hundred years earlier. Copies of his original maps, lists, and publications as well as the modern maps with these locations identified were taken to Pangnirtung and used during all working sessions and field trips. First, the Inuit experts identified Inuit place names and drew their spatial extent on unmarked map sheets (1:50,000 and 1:250,000), disregarding the toponymy printed on these maps. Once this was achieved, each named location and space was compared with names given to Boas for the same places. Each name was also recorded on separate sheets with all pertinent information related to the place, its history, the session, and the expert providing the name (Müller-Wille and Weber 1984). At the request of the Inuit, sessions were not recorded on audio or video tape, although photographs were taken at these occasions. Their explanation was that they did not feel at ease being recorded for future use by unknown people. In later surveys in Kivalliq in the early 1990s, Inuit insisted that recordings should be made, an apparent reaction to increased use of communication technology in Inuit communities.

The Inuit experts, five men ranging in age between fifty-one and eighty-three years (average sixty-three), became rather impressed by the data collection process. They expressed astonishment that Inuit place names known to their parents and grandparents existed on maps published in Germany in the 1880s which they had never seen. They knew and confirmed many of these names, indicating that the names had a continuum, but there were variations and lacunae in their contemporary knowledge. This led them to discuss the reasons such changes occurred in the toponymy. In no case did they discard or disregard "forgotten" Inuit place names; rather they were accepted as genuine Inuit knowledge that had been lost but had now been rediscovered and recovered for reintegration into the current Inuit knowledge as part of the overall cultural heritage.

Among the Inuit experts Aksayuk Etuangat, the oldest person in Pangnirtung at that time, stood out and was the link between distant past and present. Reviewing the names in the way described triggered his recall of his parents' and grandparents' stories of Inuit knowledge, including place names as well as tales about Boas and his sojourn among the Inuit. In fact, in Pangnirtung, Etuangat was considered to be one of the few bearers of the encyclopedic local Inuit knowledge with his vast experience in hunting, whaling, and traveling, encountering many people, Inuit and strangers. Of the Boas collection of place names he easily knew and confirmed between 35 and 40 percent. He remembered another 30 percent when they were mentioned or shown to him on the map to prod his memory, which then led to further identifications. The rest were names that had apparently disappeared from the current repertoire of Inuit toponyms and could not be retrieved with any local expert and thus remained as part of the historic record of Inuit life of over a hundred years before.

Furthermore, this survey showed intriguing variations in the geographic distribution of place names through time. The maps produced by Boas indicated high concentrations of names coinciding with intensive human activities in particular places at that time—for example, around Kekerten with its whaling stations and continuously used campsites along the shorelines of Tinijjuarvik, all sites that Boas frequented during his stay. In contrast, the toponymy of Pangnirtung Fiord was fairly sparse, just some fifteen place names obtained from Inuit experts, confirming that the fiord at the time was less frequented than, for example, Kignait Fiord, which was a major gateway to crossing the peninsula to Davis Strait. However, in 1984, after sixty years of Euro-Canadian settlement at the promontory of Pangnirtung and close to thirty years of modern Inuit habitation at the same site, frequency and occupancy had increased, resulting in a diversified toponymy of 135 names. The proliferation of names expresses the close human-environment relationship that had emerged in this specific region (Mason 1985)—an indication of the adaptive dynamics of place name systems.

At the open house in Pangnirtung at the end of the survey in August 1984, Etuangat and other Inuit were presented with maps and notes including personal names and photos copied from Boas's publications and papers. In most cases the Inuit viewers could relate to all these materials and immediately added further information on sites and people. The cycle had been closed; the connection with the past was established—a past that was glazed over by Christianization, which began in Tinijjuarvik in the 1890s, eradicating almost any connection with the deeper past. During these sessions Inuit stressed that regaining Inuit history, partly with the aid of western documents, is a vital step for Inuit to maintain cultural integrity.

Recapturing Lost Knowledge

The events and encounters described show that there are clearly two continua of knowledge: the internal Inuit one and the external western/techno-scientific one. The latter obtained glimpses of knowledge through the method of limited visits with some active participation, followed by retreat and sporadic revisiting. The knowledge obtained is meshed into the continuum of scientific endeavors, thus in most cases existing parallel to the internal body of knowledge. In this case the encounter of 1984 provided a rare opportunity for the merging of these continua. The authors cannot say what the direct repercussions of this process have been for individuals or the community.

In a broader context, however, it can be stated that the level of awareness concerning such connections among sets of knowledge—in this case toponymy—has risen in the public sphere in recent times. In the 1990s, as the establishment of Nunavut Territory and the government of Nunavut in 1999 drew closer, the issues of traditional knowledge, its preservation, and its inclusion into governmental policies were discussed (Anawak 1998). Here philosophical and cultural aspects of life were translated into political programs and actions that would shape the relationship among Inuit, their local government, the State, majority society, and scientific communities at large (Wilman 2002). This process is continuing, much of it in the public forum of debate over language and cultural heritage.

One example is the toponymy policy that the government of Nunavut has developed with respect to aboriginal or Inuit knowledge, *Inuit qaujimajatuqangit* or "of the Inuit, their things, that they have known for a long time" (Nunavut 1999a). There is a priority to maintain Inuit geographic knowledge as a fully recognized representation of how Inuit live in their own space—the Arctic.

Furthermore there is concern about who has power and control over the representation of cultural heritage as an integral part of daily life. There is also the issue of whether Inuit heritage should be recorded at all because its basis and validity lie in the oral transmission of knowledge and not in being written down and made available globally to anybody. Fixing it in written form might, in fact, destroy the essence of cultural distinctiveness. On the other hand there are voices stressing the fact that cultures, including the Inuit culture, do not exist in isolation; rather culture is dynamic and has emerged by drawing from within and beyond one's own community without delineating exact lines of separation. Observing the progressing debates and discussions in Nunavut, it is evident that practical decisions and compromises have to be made that truly allow people to make their own decisions about how their heritage and knowledge shall contribute to the cultural well-being of their people.

Acknowledgments

This chapter is dedicated to the memory of two *inummariit* (real Inuit) from Pangnirtuuq (Pangnirtung), Aksayuk Etuangat and Allan Angmarlik, who together devoted their time and energy to researching Inuit place names with the NUNA-TOP project in July–August 1984. Fieldwork in Pangnirtung and Tinijjuarvik was conducted under the Scientific Research Licence 1984/4087 issued by the government of the Northwest Territories and supported by a Social Sciences Research Grant (Faculty of Graduate Studies and Research, McGill University), the Northern Scientific Training Grant Program (Department of Indian and Northern Affairs), and Indigenous Names Surveys (St-Lambert, Québec). In July 2000 Allan Angmarlik's life was cut short tragically when he and his Inuit companion fatally crashed in his ultralight airplane in southern Qikirtaaluk while surveying the arctic landscape.

The toponymic materials have not yet been completely processed for publication and for officialization, a prerequisite for their inclusion on topographical maps issued by the Canadian federal or territorial governments. In 2003 initiatives to conclude these steps were taken with the Inuit Heritage Trust and the Territorial Toponymist, Ministry of Culture, Language, Elders and Youth, Government of Nunavut (Iqaluit, Nunavut).

This contribution is based on a paper entitled "Facing the Ethnographic Past: Inuit of Pangnirtung meet Franz Boas's Legacy 100 Years Later" and was prepared for the session on "Geopoetics and the Disaster—Media, Events and Site" chaired by Jonathan Bordo at the Annual Meeting of the Canadian Communications Association (Learned Societies Meetings) in Toronto on May 29, 2002. The authors are grateful for comments and encouragement by Jonathan Bordo, Pamela Stern, and Lisa Stevenson.

FOURTEEN

Iglu to Iglurjuaq

Frank James Tester

Among Canadian Inuit, the transition from igloos and tents to rigid-frame European-style houses (iglurjuaq) in the 1950s and 1960s severely challenged the methodological practices of anthropology, especially the environmental determinism characteristic of Boas's early ethnography of Baffin Inuit, *The Central Eskimo* (1964 [1888]), and the cultural ecology it foreshadowed (E. A. Smith 1984). [1] The introduction of housing—a social and political act on the part of the Canadian State—pushed anthropologists toward a different mix of ideas with which to understand changes in Inuit culture no longer determined (and it is debatable that any culture can be understood this way) by the resources (objects) and circumstances (geography) of the Arctic environment. Factors other than the physical environment and Inuit cultural practices were increasingly affecting Inuit lives as the colonial agenda of the Canadian state intensified. Boas's envelope has been difficult to escape, and the interpretive anthropology used to examine Inuit culture change in the 1960s was, arguably, equally flawed. [2]

Some anthropologists attempted to apply ethnographic and interpretive methods to the examination of Inuit living in newly created settlements. The result was a form of social psychology, whereby the mental processes and stresses associated with community living were described in light of what researchers knew, or thought they knew, about Inuit culture. Interpreting the data involved bringing into the mix assumptions about adaptation and the complex nature of urban environments borrowed—often unconsciously—from the researchers' understanding of their own contexts. Studies of Canadian Inuit living in Arctic settlements by Frank Vallee (1962) and John and Irma Honigmann (1965) are examples. In examining culture change and arctic suburbs, the conscious role of State actors—revealed by the content of official State and related documents as well as other edicts they produced—were largely ignored. How then, might we produce better explanations, giving due regard to the cultures of the colonized *and the colonizer* in understanding change? Such explanations, by their very nature, must always be incomplete fragments. In this chapter I argue the importance of paying attention to the textual means by which relations of ruling were (and are) created—as a source of information that nevertheless moves us in this direction—and as data essential to attempting an understanding of both cultural formation and emerging cultural practices. Ethnographic data, combined with a critical reading of text, move the project along.

The Modern Agenda

The history of housing policy in the former Northwest Territories of Canada is writ large with the struggle between housing as a market commodity and housing as a social good essential to Inuit health and welfare. Superimposed upon this are questions of form. What should Inuit housing look like? How are we to make the transition between traditional forms and functions and those that contemporary rigid-frame housing attempted to dictate?

These struggles emerged on the coattails of a period of high modernism, in the decade following the Second World War when faith in the modern, the scientific, and "the idea of progress" was relatively unshaken. Modern science and rational planning by the State had won the war. The precepts of modernity would also conquer squalor, disease, and poverty. These commitments were behind the idea of development and modernization ushered onto the world stage by U.S. President Harry Truman in a speech on January 20, 1949: "We must embark on a bold new program for making the benefits of our scientific advances and industrial progress available for the improvement and growth of underdeveloped areas" (cited in Esteva 1992: 6). In the Canadian Arctic the same logic informed a process slow to get off the ground. By the late 1950s, modernization of the eastern Canadian Arctic—for example, the presence of the Distant Early Warning (DEW) line, a mine at Rankin Inlet, and the collapse of the traditional trapping economy—convinced the State that modernization was an inevitable if not a desirable policy objective.

Modernization was synonymous with assimilation, and while assimilation was not a new policy, it took on new and increasingly economic forms. What had formerly been attempted with social edicts prohibiting certain kinds of behavior (traditional dances and ceremonies, raising funds for First Nations causes, etc.), and with prescribed forms of education, was now attempted by extending to aboriginal people rights of citizenship (the right to vote) and economic benefits, including housing provided by the State.

This chapter examines the period of transition from the physical forms characteristic of Inuit as hunter-gatherers—primarily tents, igloos, and *qar-maq* (sod homes, usually with a whalebone or driftwood frame roof, covered in sealskin and later in canvas)—to the built environment and rigid-frame housing provided to Inuit by the Canadian government, commencing in the mid-1950s and culminating in the Eskimo rental housing program initiated in 1965. In what follows I sample, in a manner admittedly incomplete, the historical record documenting this transition. In doing so, I treat the move from igloo to rigid-frame housing as a window through which we may debate theoretical and methodological considerations relevant to understanding social transformations in an age dominated by State and now by global institutions, in which rule is by fiat, text, and often by force.

Getting Started

The northern administration was not the first to introduce rigid-frame housing to Inuit. In the 1930s two well-known Inuit traders, Ikey Bolt and Angulalik, working with the CanAlaska Trading Company and competing with the Hudson's Bay Company in the Coronation Gulf/Chantry Inlet area of the central Arctic, imported wooden houses to the region. These got a mixed reception, not from Inuit but from *qallunaat* (non-Inuit) observers, who greatly feared that replacing the igloo and tent would contribute to the sedentarization of Inuit, would interfere with their ability to make a living hunting and trapping, and, paradoxically, would have disastrous implications for Inuit health. Here is Richard Finnie's 1940 description of one such building, erected in 1930 at Richardson Point in Starvation Cove:

> With the energetic aid of Angoojuk and his relatives, who by now had become fairly good carpenters, we practically completed the house. The double windows were weather-stripped and tightly nailed down, for Angoojuk cared more for snugness than for ventilation. The floor was covered with linoleum. Everything looked very neat indeed. But I reflected that it would not long remain so, as the house would be furnished and cared for in the manner of an igloo or tent. A seal-oil lamp would be used for cooking and heating. The place would soon be littered with raw skins, fish, meat and blubber, and the occupants would carelessly spill refuse and spit freely. A

tent is moved from time to time to get it away from the dirt and debris that accumulate within it, and a snow house cannot be occupied for more than a few weeks continuously before it glazes and becomes cold and damp; so these summer and winter shelters are automatically hygienic. Systematic sanitation could not be practised by these Eskimos—even if they were instructed in it—without radically altering their mode of living, and that would be disastrous. Therefore, Angoojuk's new house, of which he was so proud, would certainly be conducive to ill-health in its permanence and consequent filth. I felt guilty in being a party to its construction, the first white man's igloo ever owned by an Netsilik Eskimo. (Finnie 1940: 72–73)

Following this observation and admission, Finnie's text makes reference to Amundsen's exhortation in *The Northwest Passage*. Amundsen declares: "It must, therefore be the bounden duty of civilized nationals who come in contact with the Eskimo, to safeguard them against contaminating influences, and by laws and stringent regulations protect them against the many perils and evils of so-called civilization. Unless this is done, they will inevitably be ruined" (cited in Finnie 1940: 73). One such contaminating influence was later feared to be the idea of housing as a "right," a dangerous notion that would contribute to a state of dependency between Inuit and the State. References to unhealthy bodies and unhealthy minds are a key feature of struggles over housing between those acknowledging housing as a public good and others fearful about the State supplanting market logic in its provision. However, once "dependence" is deconstructed as a category associated only with State provision, the debate is revealed as one between those preferring dependence on the State and those favoring dependence on the vagaries of the market (and Inuit as wage laborers) for its provision.

Fear that Inuit enjoyment of a lifestyle and kind of accommodation other than their traditional ones would destroy the traditional economy, thereby generating dependence and a reluctance to acknowledge that the fur trade had permanently collapsed as the means of support, played a role in the failure of government officials to do anything about Inuit housing until the late 1950s. By then it was in a deplorable state.

Inuit housing had not been an issue during the 1930s and 1940s. Inuit lived much as they always had, in tents in summer and igloos in winter and, in areas such as Cumberland Sound, in qarmaq all year round. With some exceptions, Inuit camps were temporary locations with households built around the extended family. In the Cumberland Sound region of Baffin Island, the family consisted generally of a man, a woman, their unmarried children, perhaps adopted children and a second wife, and sometimes a son or son-in-law and a widow and her children (Boas 1964 [1888]). Similar patterns existed throughout the Arctic.

The Second World War changed some of this. Inuit were employed at military and communication stations at Cambridge Bay, Victoria Island; Fort Chimo, arctic Quebec; Coral Harbour, Southampton Island; Churchill, Manitoba; and at Frobisher Bay. In the absence of any alternatives Inuit built shacks around air bases and weather stations, a practice that continued into the 1950s with the spread of Cold War logic to the Canadian Arctic. American troops increased their presence in Frobisher Bay, Resolute Bay, in the High Arctic—to which Inuit were relocated in 1953—and at Churchill, Manitoba, just south of the NWT border. Elsewhere the contradictory forces of life on the land versus sending children to church-run day and boarding schools led to the growth of settlements that had previously been little more than missions, Hudson's Bay Company posts, and stations for the Royal Canadian Mounted Police (RCMP). Many parents refused to abandon their children to the unseen and unknown whims of qallunaat educators and instead became resident in the communities where the children attended school.

Forced to rely on their own ingenuity, Inuit scrounged lumber and other building materials from dumps. They built homes of packing crates, skids, and cast-off building materials—insulation, metal, and wood. They piled snow around their dwellings in winter to serve as insulation and lined the walls of snow huts with cardboard, paper, and wood. The idea that these so-called shacks were an improvement on igloos and tents is perhaps hard to accept. From a qallunaat perspective, cognizant of the health implications and given a different aesthetic view of housing and communities, it often appeared that Inuit had abandoned environmentally and culturally appropriate forms of housing for something with disastrous implications for their health and general well-being. It was a trade-off perhaps best understood in relation to the importance Inuit placed on being with their children, as compulsory schooling was introduced, and to the need to find alternatives to the trapping economy that had employed them for decades. Furthermore, not all self-made housing amounted to slum-style shacks. Some Inuit homes created with scrap materials were well built and comfortable, as observations by an adult educator sent to Resolute Bay in 1967 suggest (see later discussion).

But the house cannot be understood by itself. Walter Pokiak of Ikaluktutiak describes the seductive qualities of settlement living and permanent housing:

> Question: Why do you think so many people moved off the land, because the number of people living here in Cambridge Bay went way up? How do you explain that? Why did that happen?
> Walter Pokiak: The supplies were much easier to get. You know, the Hudson's Bay had the supplies, so the people would come off the land to do some of their shopping, sell their furs and move back out on the land. And then they started building more houses. Then they started moving in because it was warmer to live in a house than it was out on the land—like in a tent or an igloo.[3]

While there were exceptions, the historical record makes it clear that this move to settlement living, much of it around air bases and related facilities, was a disaster for human health.[4] A welfare officer visiting Igloolik in 1957 described the results this way:

> In this community we found a method of house construction that differed greatly from what we had seen on the rest of the patrol. The natives were living in snow houses, but these houses had been lined with boards, plywood, canvas and paper. The people had moved into these structures in September and had lived there ever since. They were dirty, wet and extremely poor form of housing [*sic*]. In some cases the soap stone lamp had disappeared and stoves made out of 10-gallon oil drums have been introduced. The Eskimos were burning wood and seal oil in these homemade articles which gave off more heat than the lamps and is one reason for the structures being so wet. Most of the clothing worn by the natives was trade goods and very few articles of native clothing were worn. The children in particular were very poorly clothed.[5]

Similar problems existed at Frobisher Bay, Inuit shacks having been constructed near the American air base where many Inuit were employed.

Meanwhile at the site of the Hudson's Bay Company store, about five kilometers down the coast, the Canadian government was trying to build a new community called Apex. This experience and a growing concern over the health implications of the shacks appearing in arctic settlements was to give rise in 1959 to the first arctic housing policy.

A Cog in the Machinery or Wrench in the Works?

In the Apex settlement Doug Wilkinson, the newly appointed northern service officer (NSO), started experimenting with Inuit housing. In the spring of 1955 as the new settlement was being planned, no provision had yet been made for Inuit housing. Inuit were expected to live in tents in summer and igloos in winter or to continue living in the shacks they had constructed near the base. Subsequently Wilkinson converted buildings intended as a cookhouse, a bunkhouse, and a warehouse into Inuit housing, adding a fourth house built of extra lumber.

The documentary record suggests that Wilkinson, who a few years earlier had celebrated traditional Inuit life with his film *Land of the Long Day*, was fully committed to the project of modernization, of which housing was the centerpiece. "Proper housing is an important cog in the machinery for developing a new social existence for the wage earning Eskimo, his wife and his family."⁶ He advised the senior administration that it would be best if Inuit purchased their houses, rather than renting them, having in mind the idea of "pride of ownership" borrowed from his own culture.⁷ According to Wilkinson, Inuit readily accepted rigid-frame housing, and where there was any reluctance, his job was to overcome it. However he also overlooked or attached little significance to Inuit resistance to behaviors and habits that he assumed followed logically from adopting permanent housing as a totalizing concept. Wilkinson's memos make obvious the expected role of housing in redefining all aspects of Inuit life.

In particular, his memos indicate the development of dependence on wage employment and a reordering of the concept of time: "I do not think there is much point at the present of expecting Eskimos to buy the materials for their homes f.o.b. Montreal and then either putting them up themselves, or having someone do the job for them on a private basis. The first Eskimos to move into the houses will be employees at the town and air base. They all work ten hours a day, six days a week. They have no time for house construction."⁸

In commenting on his historical experience with the problems of settlement living, George Porter of Gjoa Haven had this to say:

Question: So, when the community first started to come together in Cambridge Bay, what kinds of problems or issues were there? Were there problems with dogs, or problems with housing, or problems with water, or problems with garbage? What kind of things were people having to do? George Porter: Well, the houses started coming slowly. Right away, everybody didn't get a house. There was no problem with water or anything. It's the change; the way we lived and the way you people live. That's the problem. I'd call that a problem right there. People could not just do it right away. Why should I go to work? Why should I get up at eight o'clock every morning to go to work? I want to get up when I feel like it.[9]

Rather than address problems of a physical nature when invited to do so, Porter focuses on the reordering of time. This was an important aspect of modernization associated with having a house, having to pay for it, and subsequently being dependent upon wage labor.

Wilkinson in fact goes as far as attributing to Inuit the same modernist agenda underlying his approach to the provision of Inuit housing. It is thus not hard to understand how frustrated qallunaaq officials became when this agenda did not take hold among Inuit residents of arctic settlements. This in turn contributed to racism and the portrayal of Inuit as "lazy," "primitive," and "backward" Eskimos.

With a style that presages southern Canadian urban renewal efforts of the late 1960s and the idea of progress, the community of shacks Inuit occupied were to be replaced with houses: "Our primary objective should be to work for the day when Eskimos can drive DNA [Department of Northern Affairs] bulldozers through the present base village and obliterate all memory of the squalor and filth it holds. Some Eskimos are thinking of this already, others will think this way in the near future. When they move to the town they can bring with them the energies, the ambitions they may have. They can bring with them their memories of the village, but the village itself should be blotted out."[10]

How is such text to be understood? It is too easy to see this simply as an authoritarian exercise in relocation and assimilation. The shacks occupied by Inuit *were* a health hazard. Furthermore, Inuit had been living in these deplorable conditions for many years while working at the American air base created in 1941. Interviewed in 2001, Wilkinson pointed out that Inuit lived in many different circumstances in the 1950s. In the case of Frobisher Bay (Iqaluit) he argues that what happened was not so much about culture change (much of which he suggests had already happened) as about solving serious problems related to the provision of decent and healthy accommodation. At the same time he notes that some Inuit abandoned the village near the air base for tents erected down on the bay, some distance from the settlement, something that can be seen as a form of resistance against the accommodation—and culture change—they were being "offered."[11]

Resistance took other forms. In July of 1956 Wilkinson approached Ben Sivertz, chief of the Arctic Division of the Department of Northern Affairs, with a request from Inuit employed on the day labor program. They objected to eating three meals a day at the department mess hall and to paying sixty dollars a month for the privilege. The issue was clearly one of food preferences and eating habits, Inuit not being accustomed to or fond of the qallunaaq food, nor accustomed to eating three meals a day at specified times. Perhaps concerned about Inuit going home for lunch and not returning to work or not returning on time, Wilkinson suggested that they take only the noon meal at the mess hall. Inuit were not prepared simply to accept Wilkinson's suggestion without deliberation among themselves. He reports that "all the Eskimos got together and decided they would have only the noon meal in the mess hall."[12] Inuit also routinely left their jobs without announcement to go hunting. There were clear limits to working ten hours a day, six days a week.

Gender relations were also dramatically reordered with the move to rigid-frame houses and the end of camp life. While the household was now dependent to a considerable degree on predominantly male wage employment, the traditional roles of women in choosing the location for a tent, in preparing and sewing the skins for the tent or qarmaq cover, and in controlling the allocation of interior space were replaced by labor and decisions made external to the household. The role of women was redefined as a typically 1950s qallunaaq and suburban one. In a statement illustrating that Wilkinson had transferred to Inuit his own ideas (and perhaps experience) with meal preparation, he noted: "As well by having their breakfast and supper at home, they are with their families more, and their [sic] is more incentive for the wives to prepare meals for the families. With the husbands eating three meals a day in the department mess I have been afraid we might end up the summer with very healthy men, but with run down women, the latter neglecting to prepare proper food without the incentive of having to prepare food for the husband."[13]

Inuit made their own modifications to the houses with which they were provided. Simonie Michael, an Inuk employee working for the Department of Northern Affairs who lived next door to the Wilkinsons, took hammer and saw to his unit, changing the cold porch and storage to make it suit his purposes better.[14] At the same time there were prohibitions against doing so. At one point Wilkinson suggested modifying the design of the "512" homes sent north to incorporate the chemical toilet into the building by housing it in a small separate room adjacent the open kitchen/living room area and venting it through the stove pipe. This was advanced as an alternative to housing the toilet in the cold porch, where the contents froze and where opening the door to use it meant inviting cold air into the interior.

These innovations were not well received. John Nicol, chief of Works and Services, noted: "It is my understanding that it is illegal to tamper with government property and the officers concerned can be forced to reconstitute the building at their own expense." [15] Situations like this presaged the confusion that developed in the 1960s within an administration fearful of dependent relations and appearing to promote Inuit self-determination and "pride of ownership" while engaging in practices that clearly undermined Inuit ingenuity, initiative, self-esteem, and control. A critical reading of these texts suggests that Inuit control and participation were recognized only when these were no longer a threat to the "right way of doing things."

Both the NSO and Inuit at Frobisher Bay were caught in dilemmas not of their own making. The NSO was charged with putting a community together and was run ragged in the attempt. The powerhouse caught fire. Social relations among the qallunaat members of the new community were difficult. Ottawa took ages to respond to requests for equipment or changes in plans. The governor general and his entourage arrived for a visit. Pipes froze and equipment failed. While wanting to initiate a community council to involve Inuit in decision making, Wilkinson found that the practical demands of his job allowed no time for it. [16] This was an initiative that would have to wait until he was posted to Baker Lake a year later, where he helped create the first community council in the Eastern Arctic.

The idea of authoritarian rule must be placed in a context that permits observation on intent, consciousness, and behavior. For Wilkinson, events at Frobisher Bay must be understood with reference to his film *Land of the Long Day*, made a few years prior to his posting to Frobisher Bay, and also as revealed by his subsequent experience as a northern service officer at Baker Lake, where he initiated the community council. The problems with interpreting what was happening in this context are many. The northern service officer's role and behavior can be understood not only in terms of the cultural norms and role expectations associated with his own moment of history but also through material and other circumstances acting to limit and reorder his intentions—whatever they may have been. The commitment to modernity (like a commitment to hunting as a way of life) is a cultural "norm" within which Wilkinson's behavior becomes intelligible.

Inuit were caught in other dilemmas. The idea that living in tents and igloos was an idyllic form of existence can also be seen as a product—albeit of a different kind—of the same culture that celebrates modernism and progress. While contemporary researchers, mindful of the agendas of colonization and assimilation, celebrate traditional—and here the language itself is a problem—culture (and there is much to be said for doing this), doing so should not blind us to the fact that some of what modernism has produced makes sense relative to other developments in the modern world. Here is how Peter Irniq, the commissioner for Nunavut (2000–2005), describes his own experience of living in tents and igloos:

> Moving from an igloo to a tent was a good change—bright—and the smell of the new leaf, such as natural earth, was a welcome thing. But what about living in a tent until it was time to build an igloo, in late November, early December? I think, Inuit life was the hardest when we had to live out the fall season. When the days were getting shorter, we would finally light our caribou fat candle or small qulliq, only when it got really dark. This was to conserve the only light we had. I remember my mother would start sewing clothes sometimes in the evening when we would light the candle. That was because in the daytime, she would prepare the caribou skins that my father had caught.
>
> Then there was mid-October/November and part of December, when we were still living in a tent. The frost would become so heavy up on the ceiling of the tent that the flakes would start falling to our sleeping platform area. That was difficult, especially in the mornings, when we are getting up. Plus, our boots would be so frozen that we would have to put them on right away to thaw them out and dry them with natural body heat. That would take at least one half hour or so. We did this by walking around outside. I remember our tent would become pretty solid from the formation of the ice inside the tent, especially from the humidity from both the humans and the qulliq. [17]

From this account, it is not difficult to see that living in an igloo or tent and being engaged in wage employment, having to go to school, etc., might be difficult to reconcile. A house might make life easier. At the same time it is difficult to be part of settlement life, to have a full-time job, and be actively involved in hunting or trapping. This does not permit one to travel freely or to live where animals are found at different times of the year. Housing can thus be seen as both a product of circumstances acting on Inuit culture, as well as an original source of culture change.

Even with regard to daily routines, Inuit attempted to influence housing design, location, and the use of space. They blended permanent homes with traditional practices wherever possible. Graburn describes the result:

> The interiors of the houses are no longer arranged along the same lines as the traditional igloo, for the simple reason that there is no snow in a

wooden house to form the traditional sleeping platforms. Beds, raised off the floor, are in common use; most of them are constructed of wood but some are cast-off white man's cots. The beds are covered with the same mixture of caribou skins, blankets, sleeping bags and odd clothing that covered the sleeping platforms of the last decade. The Eskimos still make very little use of chairs and tables and most families eat squatting on the floor around the communal pot. (Graburn 1969a: 164–65)

The Policies and Practices

Wilkinson's suggestions about home ownership were taken seriously when the first housing policy was put in place in 1959. Houses were sold to Inuit, who were given a ten-year mortgage, or in the case of the disabled or those on social assistance, housing was provided at a nominal cost paid from welfare benefits. This policy was a complete failure. Most Inuit could not afford the payments, and many consequently continued to live in shacks and tents. Those who did purchase homes quickly fell behind in their payments as employment was sporadic, and other sources of income were few and equally unstable.

The cost of heating these plywood boxes was considerable. No attention was paid to family size in awarding a house to those on assistance. They were simply provided with the smallest and cheapest model of 280 square feet. The result was a proliferation of health and social problems.

By 1964 about seven hundred houses had been provided to arctic settlements under the 1959 low-cost and welfare housing program—rigid-frame (fig. 14.1), matchbox, and 512 designs—at a cost of $1.42 million.[18] Housing was a commodity and as such had to be affordable. However, even at a price discounted 40 percent below the cost of provision, Inuit could ill-afford a basic one room "cottage," as these plywood boxes were called in government reports.

Suddenly a social phenomenon largely missing from traditional camp life became a defining feature of northern settlements. Where Inuit 512 housing was stacked up against the accommodation of the Hudson's Bay Company manager or the RCMP—and increasingly a teacher, nurse, or NSO—Inuit housing announced to all that Inuit were poor. Poverty was created by a series of new social relations imposed on people who had previously defined difference in other ways. The house was more than symbolic. Inuit were defined as poor by housing policy. They were poor because, as a consequence of government policy, they could not afford a house. "A housing

14.1. Rigid-frame housing being tested in Ottawa. Source: *Eskimo Mortality and Housing*, Health Canada, 1960. Reproduced with the permission of the Minister of Public Works and Government Services Canada, 2004.

policy for northern Canada must be a policy for poor people. The vast bulk of Canadians in the north—almost all Eskimos, Indians and Metis—live in poverty. They will continue to do so for the next two decades. A great many can pay nothing toward their housing costs. Almost all the remainder can pay only a fraction."[19]

The policy that subsequently emerged in the mid-1960s was the product of a protracted struggle between those who saw housing as a commodity and those who defined it as a social good. In 1959 the Indian and Northern Health Service of the Department of National Health and Welfare, upset by the intransigence of the Department of Northern Affairs and National Resources in dealing with the public health implications of Inuit housing, decided to publish a document—primarily a photographic essay—showing the entire range of the Inuit housing experience, including the shack housing that was increasingly dominating the landscape of arctic settlements. The archival evidence suggests that the initiative was primarily that of Dr. John Willis, a principal health officer with the Indian and Northern Health Service.

Not wishing to be publicly humiliated, and wanting to be seen to be working for the betterment of Inuit housing, the Northern Administration Branch of the Department of Northern Affairs and National Resources agreed to participate and jointly publish the essay with the Indian and North-

ESKIMO
MORTALITY
AND
HOUSING

14.2. Cover of *Eskimo Mortality and Housing*, 1960. Source: *Eskimo Mortality and Housing*, Health Canada, 1960. Reproduced with the permission of the Minister of Public Works and Government Services Canada, 2004.

14.3. Shack housing in Eskimo Point (Arviat), 1956. Source: *Eskimo Mortality and Housing*, Health Canada, 1960. Reproduced with the permission of the Minister of Public Works and Government Services Canada, 2004.

ern Health Service. Entitled *Eskimo Mortality and Housing*, the text was first produced in 1959 and republished in 1960 (Department of Northern Affairs and National Resources 1960). The cover misrepresented the content as well as the intent (fig. 14.2). An igloo, backed by seven crosses, was juxtaposed with a frame house, complete with a smoking brick chimney (like none ever seen in the Eastern Arctic) with only one cross out front. But it was not the traditional igloo that was contributing to Inuit mortality. It was the shacks clustered about military and other qallunaaq institutions (churches, Hudson's Bay Company posts, RCMP detachments, DEW line stations) and a diet that, to some extent, relied on income generated by the arctic fur trade—an economy that collapsed in the 1950s.[20] In language, and now in pictures, Inuit culture and technology—which had worked for generations of Inuit—was portrayed as being of primitive form, contributing to the spiraling levels of mortality in the Inuit population (fig. 14.3). Nothing could have been further from the truth. However, departmental plans did not go unchallenged.

At a December 8, 1963, meeting of the Inuit co-operative in Igloolik, Inuit decided that plans to ship low-cost housing were unacceptable to the community. They rejected the idea of prefabricated houses and suggested that the department simply ship them the materials. Inuit would build their own homes, having decided that about five hundred dollars was all the average family could afford.

They looked over government plans and decided that the designs were inappropriate for the climate. They noted that all the windows should be on the south wall. The prefabricated units designed by the department had windows on the east and west sides of the building if the house was located such that the door was on the south-facing side. Inuit noted that the north side of their houses should be low and without any openings and suggested a redesign of the porch so that they could add to it with snow blocks, thus creating a larger porch that would protect the entrance. The bathroom and bathtub were identified as unnecessary and impractical expenses. Producing enough hot water to fill a tub was impractical. They suggested, reminiscent of the igloo, that the toilet be placed in the porch. Inuit were not about to have a qallunaat-designed house define them as poor, and their bodily functions were not about to be reassigned by government engineers.

In a letter to the administrator of the Arctic, they enclosed the floor plan of the larger of two sizes of house they wished to construct and a list of materials. They noted that twenty-two families were currently living in "icy shacks wich [sic] are an unhealthy source of tuberculosis, skin diseases and child mortality." [21] As a parting shot, the letter suggested that if the administration was unable to accommodate the community's wishes, they would appeal to the press, radio, and TV and "with aid of statistics photograps [sic] and slide in order plead urgency of action." [22]

The response of the northern administration was not entirely negative. The engineering branch agreed to look at the plans put forth by the cooperative and to attempt to incorporate the suggestions into a new design that was within the price range suggested. [23] The acting director pointed out that in order to qualify for the thousand-dollar subsidy attached to houses purchased under the low-cost housing program, certain standards had to be met and that any house receiving the subsidy would have to have engineering approval. Modern engineering—which by all accounts had thus far produced housing inappropriate to arctic conditions and unsuitable for most Inuit families—was presented as having standards so high that they might preclude the design and suggestions put forward by the Inuit cooperative.

Ultimately the department concluded that it could not provide the house suggested by Inuit at Igloolik within their price range and proposed instead to send a simpler design called a Tisigak, a suggestion with which the cooperative finally agreed.[24] Plans were made to ship four of them north. None of them arrived. By October Father Louis Fournier, the Roman Catholic priest in the community, was writing to Ottawa to express disappointment on behalf of the co-op. On investigation it was found that parts of the four houses had been offloaded at Igloolik, but the units were missing doors, windows, chimneys, and stoves. The panels and studs that did arrive were mistaken for maintenance material, stored, and used on other buildings.

In other situations houses were used in unexpected but adaptive ways, as the branch housing coordinator observed in this 1966 report: "I should mention that there was one case of a family in Coppermine who had just moved in from a camp and were given a three-bedroom house. At first they all lived in one bedroom and actually garaged their Snowmobile in the living room (where else can it be kept warm and clean?). Because of pressure and example from other Eskimos this family is now utilizing the house in a much better way, particularly taking into account their newness to the settlement way of life."[25]

The State, solidly in control of all aspects of Inuit housing, had the means to make Inuit conform to rules and regulations put in place to ensure "proper" use of the housing it provided. It was not alone in insisting that houses be treated as qallunaat intended. The Anglican bishop of the Arctic, Donald Marsh, urged that families not be permitted to move into government housing until they had demonstrated that they were capable of keeping their existing houses clean. Mr. D. Davies, branch housing coordinator for the federal government, responded: "Surely we have the right to let them move in and then if there is no sign of improvement or a downright refusal to co-operate, then we can move the family back to the small shack."[26]

At Resolute Bay Inuit scrounged lumber from the dump, rich with material cast away by the air base. They built themselves substantial houses, which were remarked upon by the community worker who arrived in 1966 to introduce Inuit to the government's new low-rental housing program— a young man who had recently graduated and had never built a house in his life. "The house models were used as visual aids, and it was really the use of these models that turned (the Inuit) on. Since they had built their own homes, they were interested in all manner of mechanical detail and I was often unable to supply an answer. (This continued to be a problem throughout my stay in Resolute Bay, in that these people were so sophisticated with regard to housing and construction practices, that I was often unable to supply them with a legitimate answer.)"[27]

Finally, while Inuit control of Inuit housing was contested terrain, the "turf" within the State was also conflicted ground. By the mid-1960s the health arguments advanced by the Indian and Northern Health Service, and John Willis in particular, were pitted against the "logic" of the market and those who argued that giving Inuit heavily subsidized housing would generate dependency relations from which the State would not recover. [28] A subcommittee set up to report on Eskimo housing programs waded into the debate, making the case for housing as a social good and not merely a market commodity. They addressed the argument that "the northern recipient would suffer character damage" and become "dependent" if helped too much and that subsidized housing for northern residents would constitute social injustice to other Canadians "who don't get free housing." [29] The committee went on to suggest that as far as subsidized housing damaging Inuit character was concerned: "Surely, in any case, it is more desirable to have a live and slightly disturbed Eskimo than a dead one." By the time they wrote this, a tuberculosis epidemic that broke out in Arviat (Eskimo Point) in 1962 had made the point for them. Housing that gave rise to disease and required medical evacuations, and in some cases years of treatment in southern TB sanatoria, was expensive indeed. [30] This economic reality was ultimately convincing.

The argument advanced against the idea that housing was free was well considered. Noting that housing anywhere in Canada was free only to the extent that the tenant made little or no direct, individual contribution, the authors argued that the community was free to chose to share the costs of housing among community members and that Canadians had endorsed such developments in the South. They went on to cite social housing projects in Regent Park, Toronto, and Pinecrest in Ottawa as examples, adding that residents no more receive free housing "than any other resident receives free police protection, or fire protection, or other municipal services." [31] The case for social housing had been made. Commencing in 1966 the government introduced a low-cost, rental-housing program that turned the provision of homes to Inuit in a different direction, at least for a few years.

Conclusion

This story is obviously incomplete. While the objective is that of achieving a totality—a whole or "complete" explanation—no such thing is possible, even if several books were to be written on the topic. There are other facts to uncover. There are alternative explanations for what has been presented. There are new ideas and theoretical positions to be developed in reaction to these. In other words, the process of attempting to understand a historical record is multiplied to infinity. Sartre defined this process of totalization as a *developing* activity; understanding and behaviors that make history (or attempt to make it or even understand it) and can never accomplish the totality toward which they are directed (Sartre 1976: 46). "However: anthropology will continue to be a mere confusion of empirical data, positivistic inductions and totalizing interpretations, until the legitimacy of dialectical Reason has been established, that is to say, until we have earned the right to study a person, a human group or a human object in the synthetic reality of their significations and of their relations to the developing totalization" (Sartre 1976: 823). Systems of *meaning* (significations) of Inuit and qallunaat in relation to one another, and *in relation to the totalizing attempts of the State* (and in a globalizing world, increasingly to non-State actors) warrant further study in a progressive anthropology of colonialism, in which concern for human dignity and freedom are posited at the heart of the enterprise. The history of Inuit housing is merely illustrative of a tiny fraction of this undertaking.

This seems to be an opening for postmodern claims about the impossibility of grand narrative and theory. Far from it. Certain *sensibilities* essential to the anthropology of colonialism are enduring and universal. Among others these include the logic of the welfare state; the "idea of progress"—indelibly attached to western capitalism; and the discourse of "dependency relations" associated with the colonial project, which I have attempted to deconstruct, at least in one application.

The danger in starting with this colonial discourse is one of overgeneralization; what Nicholas Thomas claims is a tendency to characterize colonial discourse "in unitary and essentialist terms, that frequently seem to do more to recapitulate than subvert the privileged status and presumed dominance of the discourses that are investigated" (Thomas 1994: 3). Archival documents in relation to *specific* instances of totalizing and colonial activity are important to challenging unitary and essential claims. The State is, in this instance, internally divided. For example, John Willis and his photographic record, understood in relation to developing material circumstances, contributed a great deal to internal debates about housing as a market commodity and housing as a social good—the latter being ultimately recognized in State policy. But even Willis was not a unitary force for progressive thinking about Inuit housing. In pointing the finger at Inuit-constructed "shacks" it is possible that Willis contributed to notions of "the primitive"; the images are contradicted by the historical record, which suggests that in many instances (i.e., Resolute Bay) Inuit built remarkable homes with few resources and were skilled in doing so. Furthermore, the totalizing behavior of the State and those who countered it cannot be adequately appreciated without regard to consciousness, and Willis, an important actor, cannot be appreciated fully without reference to what appears to have been a unique developmental experience. He was the son of Canadian missionaries to pre-Maoist China, something I have not explored here. Another person might have done less. Some did.

The 1960s work of John and Irma Honigmann in Iqaluit and Inuvik I have described as anthropology in the service of the State. The interpretive/ethnographic methods of these anthropologists were aimed at lawful understandings of human relations in a Parsonian or Weberian tradition. The goal is positivistic: the discovery of social facts useful to the management and regulatory functions of the State. Such work can be understood in relation to surveillance, something Foucault recognizes as essential to power, domination, and governing. It is a long way from this—arguably the legacy of Boas and the way much anthropology has attempted to establish dependable relationships between and among behaviors and environments—to a critical anthropology contributing to the liberation of colonized people and the diversity for which postmodernism claims to create a space.

Paradoxically, this cannot be done without reference to universal sensibilities that both inform and are discovered operating within specific and local projects, of which the early history of Inuit housing policy is one example. The reluctance of some State actors to fund Inuit housing adequately, and thereby to challenge its definition as a market good, is evidence that in relation to the welfare state, the so-called logic universally characteristic of capitalist economies cannot be ignored. Nor can cultural manifestations of the same: the idea of progress, the mandated place and role of Inuit women within this logic, etc.

What is discovered in a critical anthropology of colonialism, combining ethnographic research with a critical (meaning historically and ideologically informed) reading of text, is that the colonial project of modernity is a fractured one; it is dogged by internal contradiction, confronted with opposition, and plagued by material—including geographic, economic, and environmental—constraints that are absorbed in the totalizing moment. Resistance, change, and the reinvigoration of cultural diversity emerge as possibilities.

Notes

1. This chapter is based on research supported by the Social Sciences and Humanities Research Council of Canada. Photographs are taken from *Eskimo Mortality and Housing*, published in 1960 by the Indian and Northern Health Service of Health and Welfare Canada, and the Northern Administration of the Department of Northern Affairs and National Resources, as it was known at the time.

2. From the mid-1950s until Hugh Brody published *The People's Land* in 1975, Canadian Arctic anthropology overwhelmingly served (and was often funded by) the State, projecting itself as a useful discipline with a contribution to make toward resolving practical problems. Consequently, criticism of government policies and programs was severely muted.

3. Interview with Walter Pokiak conducted by Peter Kulchyski and Frank Tester, Ikaluktutiak, May 13, 1998.

4. Photographic and other evidence making the case was collected by the Indian and Northern Health Services of the Department of National Health and Welfare and the Northern Administration Branch of the Department of Northern Affairs and National Resources and published in 1960 in a monograph entitled, *Eskimo Mortality and Housing*.

5. *Extract of Field Report*, reported by P. B. Gorlick, June 10, 1957. The report is accompanied by a handwritten note: "Any projects in the wind for these dislocated people?" National Archives of Canada, Record Group (hereafter cited as NAC, RG) 85, vol. 1360, file 252–5/136, pt. 1.

6. Letter from Doug Wilkinson to Chief, Arctic Division, Department of Northern Affairs, Frobisher Bay, June 4, 1956, *Eskimo Houses—Frobisher Bay*, p. 2. NAC, RG 85, vol. 1267, file 1000/169, pt. 7.

7. In *Eskimo Housing as Planned Culture Change*, D. K. Thomas and C. T. Thompson (1972: 23) note that this "pride of ownership" was a key principle guiding Inuit housing policy from 1959 to 1965 when a new rental policy was introduced. However the ownership policy was also a financially convenient one and, had it worked, would have saved the State from having to make substantial contributions toward the cost of Inuit housing.

8. Letter from Doug Wilkinson to Chief, Arctic Division, June 4, 1956, p. 4. NAC, RG 85, vol. 1267, file 1000/169, pt. 7.

9. Interview with George Porter conducted by Frank Tester and Peter Kulchyski, Gjoa Haven, May 18, 1998.

10. Letter from Doug Wilkinson to Chief, Arctic Division, June 4, 1956, p. 4. NAC, RG 85, vol. 1267, file 1000/169, pt. 7.

11. Interview with Doug Wilkinson, Ottawa, Ontario, conducted by phone, November 20, 2001.

12. Interview with Wilkinson.

13. Letter from Doug Wilkinson, NSO, to Chief, Arctic Division, Department of Northern Affairs and National Resources, Ottawa, Frobisher Bay, NWT, July 16, 1956. *Meals for Eskimo Employees in Day Labour Mess*, p. 2. NAC, RG 85, vol. 1267, file 1000/169, pt. 7.

14. The Honigmanns (1965: 24–25) describe Simionie has having, by 1964, the most elaborate co-op house in Frobisher Bay. In fact Simionie was instrumental in organizing the first housing co-operative in the Eastern Arctic. Formed in 1961, the co-operative imported the first co-op houses to the community in 1962. Some Inuit even requested a garage for their cars.

15. Memorandum for the Director, Ottawa, June 25, 1956. *Eskimo Cabins, Frobisher Bay*. NAC, RG 85, vol. 1267, file 1000/169, pt. 7.

16. Interview with Wilkinson.

17. Correspondence with Peter Irniq, Iqaluit, Nunavut Territory, September 29, 2001.

18. *Report of Subcommittee on Eskimo Housing Programs*, June 26, 1964, appendix. NAC. RG 85, vol. 1911, file NR4/2–8.

19. *Report of Subcommittee on Eskimo Housing Programs*, p. 3.

20. We do not have reliable data on infant mortality and morbidity rates prior to the early 1950s. What the data from the early 1950s shows is a rate of about 250 per 1000—reminiscent of Canadian rates in the late 1910s. There is some evidence to suggest that rates were increasing in the late 1940s and early 1950s, a period that corresponds to the growth in shack housing. What rates were in the 1930s or early 1940s is unknown. However, this does suggest that shack housing, not igloos, was likely a contributing factor.

21. Unsigned letter from Igloolik, December 16, 1963. NAC, RG 85, acc. 1997–98/076, vol. 15, file 251–7/138, pt. 1.

22. Unsigned letter from Igloolik.

23. This was presumably $1,500 and not $500 (the $1,000 subsidy plus $500).

24. Memo for Director, from D. Davies, Branch Housing Co-ordinator, Ottawa 4, June 22, 1966, p. 1. NAC, RG 85, acc. 1997–98/076 140, file 690–1-1, pt. 1.

25. Memo for Director.

26. *Adult Education—Rental Housing Program—Resolute Bay, N.W.T.* n.d. NAC, RG 85, acc. 1995–98/076 140, file 690–1-1, pt. 1. From the context and other documents, it is evident that this was written late in 1966. The unknown author was one of the adult educators hired to do adult education about the new rental housing program introduced in 1966 to replace the low-cost and rental program introduced in 1959. The new policy was a rental one that made housing available on the basis of need (house size related to family size) and not solely on whether people were employed, and therefore deemed able to afford a house, or on welfare, in which case they were given a small unit. In May of 1966 the Central Mortgage and Housing Corporation granted the northern administration $169,000 to operate an adult education program to introduce details of the new housing policy and program to Inuit.

27. In the social construction of the issue of Inuit housing, the press played a role, at least in one article that received widespread attention, contributing to the image of Inuit as recipients of outrageously expensive benefits not available to other Canadians. In an article entitled "Plywood Village in Arctic May Become Eskimo City" published by Southam Press, Douglas Leiterman, at the time a colleague of Canadian broadcaster Patrick Watson, reported that putting "a roof over the head of 5 Eskimo families, to teach their children 17 English words, has cost the taxpayers of Canada, $250,000" (*Edmonton Journal*, April 10, 1956). Leiterman, who was doing anything but reporting news, went on to suggest that it would take another $250,000 to build ten more houses and to make blatantly racist remarks about Inuit residents of Apex. The $250,000 figure was pure fiction, but articles like Leiterman's contributed in a decidedly unhealthy way to debates about Inuit housing as a social good and necessity versus something that should be considered as a private good.

28. *Report of Subcommittee on Eskimo Housing Programs*, June 25, 1964, p. 8.

29. Part of the problem was that the social costs of poor housing fell on the budget of the Indian and Northern Health Service, while the costs of the housing itself were borne by the Department of Indian Affairs and National Resources.

30. *Report of Subcommittee on Eskimo Housing Programs.*

31. *Report of Subcommittee on Eskimo Housing Programs.*

FIFTEEN

From Area Studies to Cultural Studies to a Critical Inuit Studies

Pamela Stern

Anyone who has been reading anthropology recently might have come to the conclusion that the discipline and its primary object, ethnography, have come unmoored from the very places that formed the basis of the anthropological enterprise for so many years. Ethnographers of late have addressed such seemingly unconventional subjects as the state (Taussig 1997), organ transplantation (Lock 2002), embodiment (Martin 1994), international relations (Riles 2000), and international development (Ferguson 1994). Ethnographic studies of peoples and communities still dominate the discipline, but contemporary ethnographers recognize that more often than not, communities are fluid and transnational, that identities are mutable, and that the notion of culture itself is socially constructed. This paradigm shift for anthropology represents a generally positive response to the disciplinary crisis engendered in the 1980s by both postmodernism and the "writing culture" critique (Clifford and Marcus 1986; Fox 1991), the challenge from cultural studies, and with the end of the Cold War, the presumed obsolescence of traditional area studies.

Where does this paradigm shift leave anthropologists who do research in geographically, if not socially, bounded places and among peoples long imagined as isolated and exotic? Anthropologists doing research in Inuit communities sometimes feel that they are as isolated as the people they study are wrongly imagined to be. Nothing could be further from the truth, and comparisons of topics addressed in Inuit studies and the discipline of anthropology over the past 120 years reveal that arctic anthropology has remained in step with the larger theoretical concerns of anthropology. Like anthropology, Inuit studies suffered a crisis of confidence in 1980s that appears to have been resolved. For Inuit studies the crisis manifested itself mostly as hand-wringing about our supposed inability to contribute to the creation of social theory (Adams 1972; Balikci 1989; Riches 1990). [1] For the record, Inuit studies has led the way in a number of theoretical and methodological areas, including ethnographic film (Flaherty 1922), ethnic and tourist arts (Graburn 1976), and indigenous knowledge (Freeman 1979; Huntington 1992).

Inuit studies took a giant leap forward with the founding of the International Arctic Social Sciences Association (IASSA) in Fairbanks in 1990. The creation of this forum for the exchange of scholarly ideas about the peoples of the circumpolar North represents a healthy disciplinary and geographic broadening of the field. IASSA membership includes anthropologists, geographers, sociologists, economists, political scientists, and demographers. Importantly, the membership and conference participants include researchers outside the academy, especially northern indigenous social scientists, policy makers, and residents. In addition, the arctic culture area extends beyond North America to include the entire circumpolar North (Young 1992). The Inuit circumpolar North refers to the arctic zone from Greenland west to Chukotka. This geographic and analytic broadening reflects not only post–Cold War political possibilities but also social scientists' new understandings of the Arctic as a zone of geopolitical activity. [2] Anthropologists may still outnumber other social scientists in the North, but anthropology is also a different discipline than it was in the 1980s. Anthropologists now address questions of identity and globalization, and exposing relations of power has emerged as a central concern. We are more conscious of the relationship between research and governance. And the peoples we study read what we write. The questions of representation brought to anthropology by "writing culture" are especially salient within Inuit studies today. The changes, both disciplinary and geopolitical, have transformed Inuit studies as field of intellectual investigation from a component of area studies to a relative of cultural studies. But this is not enough if the field of Inuit studies is to remain intellectually and socially relevant. The issues raised and the research discussed in the preceding chapters are meant to point the way ahead to an engaged critical Inuit studies.

Inuit Studies as Area Studies

Histories of the field of Inuit studies usually begin with Franz Boas's 1883–84 ethnographic research at Cumberland Sound on Baffin Island. Boas was just one of the several ethnographers studying Inuit in the 1880s; however, the research of his contemporaries Gustav Holm in East Greenland, John Murdoch in northern Alaska, and Edward Nelson in the Bering Strait region are virtually unknown to anyone outside Inuit studies. Thus despite Boas's own infamous opposition to generalizing, the seal-eating, snowhouse-dwelling Inuit he described in *The Central Eskimo* (1964 [1888]) have come to stand rather imperfectly and ironically as the prototypical "traditional" Inuit culture.

Though Boas never returned to the Arctic, he exercised an influence on the field of Inuit studies that continued until very recently. Specifically, the historic particularism promoted by Boas and his cadre of students was compatible with delineated culture areas or geographically bounded regions with distinct ethnic or cultural foci. The "culture area" concept explained similarities among groups within a geographic region in terms of both diffusion and adaptation to the physical environment. Although the territory encompassed by the Inuit circumpolar North is enormous, until recently the peoples living in this treeless zone shared many items of material culture, spoke related and generally mutually intelligible languages, and had common cosmological beliefs. These common cultural traits are understood as the result of relatively recent common descent from the peoples archaeologists have labeled Thule Inuit.

Inuit studies (or Eskimology, as it was called until the 1970s) developed as the scientific study of the past and present peoples who inhabited the North American arctic culture area (Kroeber 1938). While most archaeologists now believe that the peopling of North America occurred in waves over a period of several millennia, this was not apparent to early archaeologists and ethnologists of North America. They did, however, recognize that the ancestors of modern Inuit, the Thule peoples, had arrived in North America much later than the ancestors of modern Indians. At the time of first contact with Europeans the linguistic and cultural differences between Mississippi Choctaw and Northwest Coast Tlingit were every bit as great as the differences between either group and Inuit, but through the historical processes of classification Inuit came to be regarded as ethnically and culturally distinct from other aboriginal North Americans (but also distinct from reindeer-herding Siberians). This ethnic division between Inuit and Indians, in many ways an invention of early academics, has had real consequences (in Canada, particularly) in government administration of and control over indigenous peoples and lands.[3]

The research of archaeologists, because of their interest in the origins and diffusion of prehistoric Eskimo cultures, reflected a slightly more integrative approach to the Inuit circumpolar North than did the work of ethnologists, who have tended to confine their inquiries to localized groups of Inuit. Thus the Fifth Thule Expedition led by Knud Rasmussen (1921–24) was unique in its inclusion of the Inuit circumpolar North from Greenland to North Alaska. The Fifth Thule Expedition greatly contributed to our understanding of the Inuit circumpolar North as a single culture area, but as Wachowich (this volume) points out, Rasmussen and colleagues were also instrumental in institutionalizing an ethnographic consciousness about cultural boundaries between geographic and linguistic subgroups of Inuit.

In addition to identifying cultural and linguistic boundaries that may not have existed, early ethnologists helped erase some that may have. Igor Krupnik observes that during the same era, the Soviet Committee of the North, a group that included prominent and well-respected northern ethnographers, delineated twenty-six distinct Siberian peoples as part of a national minority educational strategy. The Soviet policy of "one nation—one language" denied the existence of dialectal diversity within languages and thus forced Siberian Yupik speakers, among others, "to adopt *one* of their existing [three] dialects as a base to build their new identity and educational system" (Krupnik 1992: 196, emphasis in original; see also Burch 1980).

In the modern world academic research both informs and is informed by governmental practices. Nowhere is this more apparent than in the case of area studies. Area studies, which developed as the academic arm of western colonialism , flourished under the geopolitical (in)sensibilities of the Cold War. The strengths of area studies were also its weaknesses. Inuit specialists, like Africanists, or Asianists, are just that—specialists. In focusing narrowly on "their people" they sometimes lose track of the larger goal of social sciences—making sense of the human condition. Thus it becomes difficult, if not impossible, to make comparisons across regions or to validate (or invalidate) theories of human behavior.

More important, however, area specialists become too well schooled in the accepted and acceptable ideas about the peoples they study. Particular metanarratives of behavior, culture, or history become naturalized and remain unquestioned. Ann Allison (1994), writing about the gendered nature of work and social life in Japan, observes that it is too easy to ascribe the practices associated with a group of people to "Culture" and to forget about the role played by institutionalized and transnational relations of power. Certainly people's habitual actions are situated within particular cultural traditions, but they do not exist apart from the historically created (and re-created) patterns of social control. In the case of Inuit society, scholars have long attributed Inuit societal forms, values, and practices as cultural responses to the harsh arctic environment (Adams 1972; Boas 1964 [1888]; Briggs 1978, 1991; Mauss 1979). In particular, scholars have lauded the communitarian values associated with Inuit food sharing practices while ignoring the less egalitarian aspects of the institution (Collings et al. 1998). Pryor and Graburn (1977), however, demonstrate in a little-known paper that far from evening out food supplies, institutionalized food sharing tended to benefit those least in need.

Another persistent metanarrative about Inuit culture explains Inuit economy and society as revolving around male-dominated subsistence hunting (Balikci 1970; Brody 1987, 2001; Dahl 2000; Hensel 1996). Still another metanarrative seeks to locate current social problems in many Inuit communities in a collective emotional pain associated with the loss of Inuit cultural traditions and in rapid social and economic change (Brody 1977; Clairmont 1962, 1963; Klausner and Foulks 1982; Rasing 1994). I should note, however, that metanarratives about the disappearance of traditions, as well as generalizing the activities and perspectives of men to an entire population, occur in area studies generally.

Surprisingly perhaps, given our historically unquestioned acceptance of the region I am calling the Inuit circumpolar North as a distinct culture area, culture area–wide treatments of Inuit peoples and cultures have been relatively few (Birket-Smith 1959; Damas 1984; Graburn and Strong 1973; Schweitzer and Lee 1997; Weyer 1932 as well as Jenness's five-volume *Eskimo Administration*). Rather, scholarly writing about Inuit cultures and communities has been largely confined to descriptions of individual communities, regions, or political jurisdictions. Four decades ago Charles Hughes (1965) observed the existence of national traditions within Inuit studies. According to Hughes, these national distinctions had less to do with the nationality of the researchers than with the national jurisdictions in which Inuit live. In other words, there were national traditions within Inuit studies. For example, Hughes noted that the community studies so prevalent in Canada at the time he wrote were nowhere to be found in studies of Greenland Inuit. Significantly, these regional traditions within Inuit studies continue today, such that many of the researchers we approached to contribute to this volume—ethnographers with innovative approaches to understanding Inuit culture—had researched in Canadian Inuit communities. Inuit studies remains too compartmentalized. Inuit studies as area study can be divided into two distinct periods: a classic period inaugurated by Boas's salvage ethnography in Cumberland Sound, and a problem-oriented phase that began around 1950. The period between the 1880s and the 1920s is often considered a golden age for Inuit ethnography. The ethnographic monographs produced in this period (Birket-Smith 1929; Boas 1964 [1888]; Bogoras 1975 [1913]; Holm 1914 [1888]; Jenness 1970 [1922]; Murdoch 1988 [1892]; Nelson 1983 [1899]; Rasmussen 1929, 1930a, 1931, 1932; Turner 1894) are usually regarded as descriptive of Inuit cultures *before* they were changed by interactions with the agents of colonialism. As examples of ethnography these works are truly rich. Nonetheless, in their efforts to capture and record the "original" Inuit cultures, the ethnographers ignored abundant evidence of the social, economic, and demographic changes that had resulted from interactions with commercial whalers especially but also from contacts with missionaries, traders, and government administrators.

Little ethnographic research was conducted among Inuit during the 1930s and 1940s. One exception, Holtved's *Contributions to Polar Eskimo Ethnography* (1967), is of the same genre as the classic monographs of the previous decades. The end of World War II, which brought new forms of colonialism to the North and to Inuit, affected the ethnographic research conducted in the Inuit circumpolar North between the 1950s and 1980s. Unlike in some other area studies, the topics addressed by northern ethnographers tended not to be directly supportive of Cold War efforts.[4] Nonetheless, the Cold War and the militarist thinking it engendered were more important in reshaping arctic geographies and had more far-reaching consequences for Inuit communities than any previous colonial activities in the North. While northern ethnographers were not ignorant of effects of military activity in the North, they tended to treat it as background noise rather than as a major force in the lives of northern peoples.

The Cold War led to industrialization of the Soviet far East and to the relocation of ethnic Russians, Ukrainians, and others to work in the new factories. Whole cities were created in the Soviet far North. Iñupiat of Big and Little Diomede islands in the Bering Sea, accustomed to hunting in the waters surrounding their island and regularly visiting and sharing with family members living on the other island, were denied this freedom of movement after 1948. In the West the United States under the auspices of NATO built a series of listening posts and Distant Early Warning (DEW) line stations north of the Arctic Circle to provide forewarning of any Soviet missile attack. A few Inuit found employment as laborers at DEW line sites. Many others traded furs and handicrafts to the military men posted there.

The sites and their human sentries became sources of valuable recyclables but also of communicable diseases.

The Superpowers built military bases on Inuit lands. In Greenland twenty-seven Inughuit families were forcibly relocated to make way for American occupation of Thule Air Force Base in 1953. Around the same time the last Iñupiaq residents of Big Diomede Island were removed to the Soviet mainland to make way for a military base. In Alaska the Naval Arctic Research Laboratory existed alongside the Iñupiaq village of Barrow, while at Frobisher Bay (Iqaluit) in Canada, U.S. and Canadian military personnel were a primary source of alcohol. In 1957 the U.S. Atomic Energy Commission proposed Project Chariot—a test of a nuclear device to dredge a harbor near the Iñupiat village of Point Hope, Alaska. It is possible to trace Iñupiat activism in land claims negotiations a decade later to their organized opposition to Project Chariot. The plans for the atomic explosion were eventually scrapped, but Iñupiat lands in northwest Alaska were used for secret Atomic Energy Commission experiments to map the movement of radioactive wastes in groundwater. At the other side of the Inuit circumpolar North, Greenlanders continue to question whether the U.S. military recovered all of the nuclear material scattered on the ice and in the ocean by the 1968 crash of a B-52 bomber near Thule Air Force Base. There is no doubt, however, that the jet stream carried radioactive material from distant atmospheric nuclear tests north. The fallout fouled tundra throughout the North and continues to enter the human food chain.

Anyone who doubts that Inuit were personally engaged in the Superpowers' Cold War struggles would do well to keep in mind the claim of Masiiñ, the last shaman in the traditional Iñupiaq village of Tikigaq. Tom Lowenstein (1992: 196) recorded the following account of the monolingual Masiiñ's shamanic work from Iñupiaq elder Alec Millik: "It was 1953, wintertime. My wife invited Masiiñ to supper. And after we had eaten, the old man told stories. Then he called me by name, and told us he'd been traveling last night. He'd been to Russia. And when he'd flown round for a while, he saw the Russian boss. 'That's a bad man,' said Masiiñ, 'so I killed him.' Next day, at three o'clock—we had a battery radio—I listened at my coffee break. The news announcer said Stalin was dead."

The militarization of the North made it politically necessary for Canada to provide schools, medical care, and housing to Inuit (Graburn 2003). The movement of Canadian Inuit into centralized permanent villages must be counted as a key event in both the history of Inuit and Inuit studies. The Canadian government, under the auspices of the Northern Co-ordination and Research Centre of the Department of Northern Affairs and National Resources, supported an enormous number of studies, done mostly by anthropologists, aimed at understanding the social conditions (and social problems) in the newly created towns (Abrahamson 1964; Clairmont 1962, 1963; Ervin 1968; Graburn 1963; Honigmann and Honigmann 1965, 1970; Lubart 1969; Usher 1971a, 1971b; Vallee 1962; Willmott 1961). Community studies conducted in Alaska during the same period (Chance 1966; Hughes 1960; Oswalt 1963; Vanstone 1962), like those done in Canada, are full of unquestioned assumptions about modernization (but see Chance 1990 for an example of rethinking earlier assumptions). Nonetheless, while the quality of the postwar studies is variable, they do provide information about this transitional period in Inuit social life that would otherwise be lost.

If arctic ethnographers of the 1950s and 1960s were concerned with the presumed acculturation of Inuit societies, in the 1970s and 1980s the environment and especially cultural ecology dominated anthropological research in the North. Boas may have abandoned environmental determinism in favor of historical particularism, but physical environment, notably the arctic climate, remained a powerful force in the minds of those who studied arctic peoples (Balikci 1970; Briggs 1978; Brody 1987; Condon 1983; Dahl 2000; Hensel 1996; Nelson 1969; E. A. Smith 1991; Spencer 1976 [1959]; Wenzel 1981, 1991). As Inuit culture came to be equated with subsistence hunting, an emphasis on studying the traditional activities of Inuit men meant that other important issues including the lives of women, colonialism, political movements, land claims, urban migration, wage labor, and governmentality received little or no attention from arctic ethnographers. The few exceptions to this may prove the rule. Nancy Fogel-Chance (1993), John C. Kennedy (1982), and Robert Paine (1977) studied and wrote about Inuit living in Anchorage, maintaining ethnic and social boundaries, and Inuit as colonial subjects, respectively. Graburn's edited book *Ethnic and Tourist Arts* (1976) was unique on many accounts, not least of which was the inclusion of Inuit in cross-cultural theory building. These studies are notable in part for their failure to adopt many of the dominant metanarratives of Inuit area studies.

Inuit Studies as Cultural Studies

The field of cultural studies grew out of a Marxian tradition in British sociology and is concerned with the symbolic and ideological ways that material relations are configured and maintained. As such it has emphasized social class as the enduring and powerful institution that creates and is created by social difference. Among other things, cultural studies aims to document the ways in which difference is constructed and maintained through assertions about history, science, and knowledge. In North America, cultural studies is associated with feminist theory and with critical studies of race and ethnicity, and it is often connected to intellectual expressions of identity politics.

Cultural studies has more in common with contemporary academic anthropology than most anthropologists would like to admit. Like anthropology, cultural studies uses ethnography and observations of lived experience as a research methodology. But the similarities are epistemological as well as methodological. In both fields, the primary concern is with uncovering the hidden processes that structure culturally patterned beliefs and behaviors in order to debunk notions of "natural" difference among peoples (cf. Handler 1998).

For Inuit studies, the adoption of some of the paradigms of cultural studies originates in political efforts by Inuit to assert control not only over their lands and their communities but also over the sorts of research—including anthropological research—that informed colonial administration and produced authoritative knowledge about Inuit culture and communities (see Kral and Idlout, this volume). This is most apparent with Inuit control over the licensing of research and researchers in some areas but also occurs as Inuit participate in policy and research forums. Since the 1970s Inuit have been especially interested in documenting what is variously called indigenous knowledge, local knowledge, traditional ecological knowledge (TEK), and most recently Inuit qaujimatuqangnit (IQ). The purpose of this documentation is not simply to record Inuit traditions before they are lost but rather to use the documentation of Inuit indigenous knowledge for political action. Inuit knowledge about climate, wildlife, child rearing, and social relations has been crucial to Inuit efforts to assert control over wildlife management, education, and criminal justice, to name just a few things. In this way Inuit indigenous knowledge has become institutionalized, not as a tradition prone to erosion but as part of a repertoire of distinctly Inuit ways of knowing and being in the world.

Like Inuit area studies, Inuit cultural studies needs to be considered as having two distinct phases: a classic salvage phase and a problem-oriented phase. While the documentation of Inuit indigenous knowledge is not merely a salvage project, there is a definite salvage quality to the rush to record the memories of elders (see the chapters in this volume by Graburn and Nagy). Nonetheless the Inuit Land Use and Occupancy Project in Canada (Freeman 1976), along with the traditional land use inventory conducted on Alaska's North Slope, relied on the careful documentation of then current and historical Inuit land use patterns in order to support Inuit land claims. Inuit and others are busy recording Inuit indigenous knowledge about religion (Laugrand et al. 2001), wildlife management (Thorpe et al. 2003), and child rearing (Briggs 2000), among other topics. One of the few projects that goes beyond the documentation of elders' memories is John MacDonald's compilation of Inuit astronomy, presented in The Arctic Sky (1998). This work, because it integrates older written sources with elders' narratives and includes analysis and interpretation, stands out as one of the best recent instances of the documentation of indigenous knowledge.

Like Inuit area studies, Inuit cultural studies is also dominated by particular metanarratives. At present the most prominent of these concerns the understanding of Inuit culture as intimately connected to the land and to subsistence hunting (see the contributions of Searles, Stevenson, and Wachowich in this volume). These assertions take on a particular political expediency, and in this way Inuit identity politics has breathed new life into historic categories. For example Greenlander Finn Lynge, an eloquent spokesman for Inuit indigenous rights and a consultant to the government of Greenland on indigenous issues, was quoted in the press as saying: "Our [meaning Inuit] values are tied to small-scale living and it is important for all of us that a significant part of our people keep their ties to land, sea and ice" (Bourgeois 1998). Similarly Inuit Circumpolar Conference President Aqqaluk Lynge (no relation) reportedly said: "If a[n Inuit] man doesn't hunt, he isn't man enough to be husband to anyone" (quoted in Brooke 2000). One lesson we can take from Searles's contribution to this volume concerns the double bind this inviolable association between Inuit culture and subsistence hunting puts on individual Inuit. Why should Inuit (or other indigenous peoples, for that matter) have to pass some sort of a "tradition" test in order to assert a collective identity and collective social rights?

The research questions of Inuit cultural studies are different, but no broader, than those of earlier area studies. Where area studies understood Inuit as a hunting and gathering population, under cultural studies Inuit have become part of the global network of indigenous peoples emotionally tied to their historic lands. The language of acculturation that was so prominent in earlier studies of Inuit communities is no longer prominent. Yet, as national cultures are no longer assumed to be homogeneous, there remains a concern that as Inuit lives change materially, Inuit are in danger of losing the things that make them uniquely Inuit. Under area studies, culture was understood as the thing that allowed Inuit to adapt to and thrive in the extreme climate of the Arctic. Under Inuit cultural studies, culture is sometimes code for differences that are presumed to be natural. How else are we to explain the (academic celebration of) various efforts by Inuit to separate politically from the national and regional institutions of government? (See, e.g., Dahl et al. 2000.) The push for some form of indigenous self-governance—be it by Inughuit in Greenland, the Yupiit Nation in southwest Alaska, or the multiple self-government agreements under negotiation in Canada—is based on the presumption that Inuit cultural difference cannot be accommodated within a modern liberal democracy.

The insistence by Inuit and other minorities on cultural difference that is meant to empower can, however, marginalize and isolate. Sadly, an emphasis on "the inviolable distinctiveness of each culture" (Gal 1987: 641), in addition to giving voice to the previously unheard, also almost inevitably reinforces stereotypes and existing hierarchies and allows those in power (and the public in general) to treat disparities in health, social benefits, and economic status as the consequences of that cultural difference. As I write these words, Toronto police are looking for a kidnapped nine-year-old girl. The child, who is ethnic Chinese, appears to have been taken by other ethnic Chinese, possibly for ransom. Few details have been released to the media; nonetheless, a newspaper reporter, quoting several academics, related this current tragedy to increasingly common abductions of young women for brides in rural China and to kidnappings for ransom in late imperial China (Wong 2003). The only way these three things could be connected is if there is something innate to Chinese culture that encourages kidnapping. Similarly academics, politicians, and popular media have been all too willing to attribute warfare in Africa to the persistence of tribalism rather than to legacies of colonial and Cold War underdevelopment and exploitation.

Fortunately the stakes for Inuit in claims to cultural difference appear to be less a matter of life and death. Still, I am deeply troubled that in order to make any claims to self-determination, Inuit find it necessary to draw on tropes of Inuit culture that essentialize people as (former) hunters. The existence of a "land program" at the Baffin Correctional Centre (see Stevenson, this volume) suggests that learning their unique culture is the key to rehabilitating Inuit criminals. Perhaps this is true, but might they also benefit from vocational or literacy training (not to mention a major structural overhaul of northern economies)? And would the inmates of southern prisons find rehabilitation through culture?

During the last decade and a half Inuit studies has increasingly been concerned with issues of identity. Interest in identity is not limited to Inuit studies but rather, in the post–Cold War era, has become a major preoccupation of the social sciences generally. It is likely that identity has become more salient as we have come to recognize globalization as a potent social force (Castells 1997). With respect to Inuit studies, Dorais and Searles (2001) suggest that nearly every study conducted in the Inuit circumpolar North since 1960 was in some way concerned with the matter of identity. Thus according to Dorais and Searles, research addressing Inuit-qallunaat relations, religion, cosmology, hunting, language, parenting, schooling, mental health, politics, social organization, and gender are reducible to a single overriding concern with when and under what circumstances a person or a group of people can claim to be Inuit. Identity may be a tool for political mobilization of the socially excluded, but it is also a tool of segregation and exclusion, and it behooves us to be mindful of both facets of identity politics.

A Critical Inuit Studies

Academic research is, and always has been, in dialectical relationship with the social communities that create and sustain it. By social communities, I mean not only the modern nation-states whose institutions, bureaucracies, and citizenries come to depend upon social typologies and explanations of difference reified by academic research but increasingly the very peoples and communities we purport to describe. Several of the contributors to this volume directly address how it is not enough for anthropologists to act with good intentions. We must also be conscious of how our research contributes to or disrupts the status quo. Inuit are increasingly involved in decisions about the conduct of research about them and their communities. In some places frustration with academic researchers is high, and there is a backlash against non-indigenous research and researchers. In Inuit communities it is not uncommon to hear comments and complaints about outsiders (including anthropologists) who come north, do a series of interviews, appropriate the words of elders, and go back to their universities where they advance their careers (or possibly enrich themselves) on what has come to be understood as the intellectual property of Inuit (Flaherty 1995).

Inuit organizations and individuals are frequently concerned with the immediate relevance and usefulness of research. Therefore the telos of acceptable research is often (implicitly) some kind of community transformation. If Inuit allow themselves to be objectified, surveilled, their words and actions analyzed, how do they benefit?

This situation forces us to consider how to define the concept of "good" in research. Does "doing good" with respect to indigenous peoples necessarily involve direct action within communities, as the models of participatory action research would suggest? Should we, instead, be satisfied with influencing policy decisions at national and international levels? Even as we acknowledge that our research has impacts on the lives of real people, we are forced to come to terms with the realization that many of the individuals and communities who are the subjects of our research reject the premise that the pursuit of knowledge for the sake of knowledge is good in and of itself. Clearly we must be unambiguous about the politics of representation inherent in our work, but I believe that if we limit our research to issues defined as of immediate relevance to Inuit, we must also ask ourselves: what important questions are we neglecting to ask? Are we guilty of homogenizing Inuit culture? What new metanarratives about Inuit cultures and communities are we creating?

We are not alone in our efforts to rethink area studies; rather this is a project that has occurred generally throughout social sciences over the last decade (see Slocum and Thomas 2003). What I propose is a critical Inuit studies in which careful effort is made to expose the theoretical assumptions implicit in our research and to situate our research historically. More than that, however, in contemporary anthropology and other social sciences, the term *critical* refers to research paradigms informed by praxis and dedicated to exposing the ways in which the exercise of power is reflected in the social lives of people. This must include explications of new and evolving relations of power in the North. It must make connections between communities of Inuit across the North and in and outside of the North. As one example, there is a great deal of current interest in the political and social aspects of defining and implementing Inuit qaujimatuqangnit within the new Nunavut Territory. To my knowledge, however, no scholarly references to IQ recognize or acknowledge the similarities between the political projects of IQ and *Iñupiat ilitqusiat* in northwest Alaska (McNabb 1991). Nunavut leaders interested in institutionalizing IQ might find the experiences of northwest Alaskans instructive as well. A critical, engaged Inuit studies must also treat the experiences of Inuit as illustrative of larger social processes, capable of explaining events elsewhere in the world and informed by events occurring elsewhere. And it must not become the handmaiden of new regimes of power. The preceding chapters begin this engaged, critical Inuit studies.

Acknowledgments

In writing this chapter I benefited from lively conversations with Kristin Bright, Julie Cruikshank, Nelson Graburn, Peter V. Hall, Lisa Stevenson, and Stuart Tannock. The views expressed are my own.

Notes

1. The concern with relevance is not unique to those who study Inuit societies. Anthropologists who study European societies also fret about their supposed inability to make social theory (Roland Moore, pers. comm.), and I suspect that a poll of anthropologists working in other culture areas would elicit similar concerns. Anthropologists and their particular concerns have long dominated Inuit studies. This has meant not only that have we generally failed to study up (Nader 1972) but also that until recently we left matters such as urban migration, aboriginal rights movements, the politics of land claims and industrial development, and wage labor to a small group of sociologists and political scientists. The bracketing of these important topics from northern ethnography limited the scope of analysis available to anthropologists conducting research in the Inuit circumpolar North.

2. There are counterparts to this in the natural sciences and in international relations. Natural scientists concerned with the circumpolar North participate in the International Arctic Science Committee founded in August 1990. The Arctic Council, which was formally launched on September 19, 1996, is a government-to-government forum for the eight circumpolar nations. International indigenous organizations participate as observers. In October 1987 Mikhail Gorbachev, speaking in Murmansk, called for the remaking of the circumpolar North as a zone of peace and international cooperation. This speech is seen as the turning point in international cooperation in the circumpolar North. The establishment of the Arctic Council is the concrete manifestation of that cooperation and the associated geopolitics.

3. In the United States the more significant administrative difference is between Alaska Natives, including Inuit, and Native Americans from the lower forty-eight states.

4. The nineteen-volume *Arctic Bibliography* (1953) was funded by the U.S. Department of Defense, and Richard K. Nelson's research that resulted in *Hunters of the Northern Ice* (1969) was supported by the U.S. military, which was interested in learning about arctic survival.

BIBLIOGRAPHY

Abrahamson, G. 1964. *Copper Eskimos: Area Economic Survey 1963*. Ottawa: Industrial Division, Department of Northern Affairs and National Resources.

Abu-Lughod, L. 1991. "Writing against Culture," in *Recapturing Anthropology: Working in the Present*, ed. R. G. Fox, pp. 137–62. Santa Fe NM: School of American Research Advanced Seminar Series.

Adams, C. 1972. "Flexibility in Canadian Eskimo Social Forms and Behavior: A Situational and Transactional Appraisal," in *Alliance in Eskimo Society*, Proceedings of the American Ethnological Society 1971, supplement, ed. L. Guemple, pp. 9–16. Seattle: University of Washington Press.

Adelson, N. C. 2001. "Gathering Knowledge: Reflections on the Anthropology of Identity, Aboriginality, and the Annual Gatherings in Whapmagoostui, Quebec," in *Aboriginal Autonomy and Development in Northern Quebec and Labrador*, ed. C. Scott, pp. 289–303. Vancouver: University of British Columbia Press.

Agamben, G. 2000. *Means without End: Notes on Politics*. Minneapolis: University of Minnesota Press.

Allison, A. 1994. *Nightwork: Sexuality, Pleasure, and Corporate Masculinity in a Tokyo Hostess Club*. Chicago: University of Chicago Press.

Amagoalik, J. 2000. "A Wasteland of Nobodies," in *Nunavut: Inuit Regain Control of Their Lands and Their Lives*, ed. J. Dahl, J. Hicks, and P. Jull. Copenhagen: International Work Group for Indigenous Affairs.

Anawak, J. 1989. "Inuit Perceptions of the Past," in *Who Needs the Past? Indigenous Values and Archeology*, ed. R. Layton, pp. 45–50. London: Unwin Hyman.

———. 1998. *Report of the Nunavut Traditional Knowledge Conference, 20 to 24 March 1998, Nunavut Social Development Council*. Interim Commissioner of Nunavut.

Anderson, B. 1991. *Imagined Communities*. London: Verso.

Anilniliak, R. 2002. "One Small Voice." *News/North*, p. A10. Iqaluit.

Appadurai, A. 1986. "Introduction: Commodities and the Politics of Value," in *The Social Life of Things: Commodities in Cultural Perspective*, ed. A. Appadurai, pp. 3–63. Cambridge: Cambridge University Press.

Arnakak, J. 2000. "Commentary: What Is Inuit Qaujimajatuqangit?" *Nunatsiaq News*. Iqaluit (www.nunatsiaq.com), accessed August 22, 2005.

Arngna'naaq, R. 1978. Akkisuijimut [Letter to the Editor]. *Inuit Ullumi/Inuit Today* 7:8–10.

Baillargeon, D. 1993. "Histoire orale et histoire des femmes: Itinéraires et points de rencontre." *Recherches Féministes* 6:53–68.

Bakhtin, M. M., M. Holquist, and C. Emerson. 1992. *Speech Genres and Other Late Essays*. Austin: University of Texas Press.

Balikci, A. 1970. *The Netsilik Eskimo*. Garden City NJ: Natural History Press.

———. 1989. "Ethnography and Theory in the Canadian Arctic." *Études/Inuit/Studies* 13:103–11.

Barnard, A. 2002. "The Foraging Mode of Thought," in *Self- and Other-Images of Hunter-Gatherers*, ed. H. Stewart, A Barnard, and K. Omuri, pp. 5–24. *Senri Ethnological Studies* 60. Osaka: National Museum of Ethnology.

Barr, W. 1985. *The Expeditions of the First International Polar Year, 1882–83*. Arctic Institute of North America Technical Paper 29. Calgary: University of Calgary.

Berger, T. R. 1977a. *Northern Frontier, Northern Homeland: The Report of the Mackenzie Valley Pipeline Inquiry*, vol. 1. Ottawa: Minister of Supply and Services.

———. 1977b. *Northern Frontier, Northern Homeland: The Report of the Mackenzie Valley Pipeline Inquiry*, vol. 2. Ottawa: Minister of Supply and Services.

Berman, Judith 1996. "The Culture as It Appears to the Indian Himself: Boas, George Hunt, and the Methods of Ethnography," in *Volksgeist as Method and Ethic: Essays on Boasian Ethnography and the German Anthropological Tradition*, ed. G. W. Stocking, pp. 215–57. Madison: University of Wisconsin Press.

Berry, J. W. 1999. "Aboriginal Cultural Identity." *Canadian Journal of Native Studies* 19:1–36.

Bird-David, N. 1990. "The Giving Environment: Another Perspective on the Economic System of Gatherer-Hunters." *Current Anthropology* 31:183–96.

Birket-Smith, K. 1929. *The Caribou Eskimos: Material and Social Life and the Cultural Position, Report of the Fifth Thule Expedition 1921–24*, vol. 5, pt. 1. Copenhagen: Gyldendalske.

———. 1959. *The Eskimos*. London: Methuen.

Bissoondath, N. 1994. *Selling Illusions: The Cult of Multiculturalism in Canada*. Toronto: Penguin Books.

Boas, F. 1885. "Baffin-Land. Geographische Ergebnisse einer in den Jahren 1883 und 1884 ausgeführten Forschungsreise." *Petermanns Mittheilungen, Ergänzungsheft*, Ergänzungsband XVII: 80.

———. 1964 [1888]. *The Central Eskimo*. Lincoln: University of Nebraska Press.

———. 1974 [1888]. *The Central Eskimo*. Toronto: Coles.

Bodenhorn, B. 1997. "People Who Are Like Our Books: Reading and Teaching on the North Slope of Alaska." *Arctic Anthropology* 34:117–35.

Bogoras, W. 1975 [1913]. *Eskimo of Siberia*. New York: AMS Press.

Bordo, J. 2000. "Picture and Witness at the Site of the Wilderness." *Critical Inquiry* 26:224–47.

Bourdieu, P. 1977. *Outline of a Theory of Practice*. Cambridge: Cambridge University Press.

———. 1993. *The Field of Cultural Production: Essays on Art and Literature*. New York: Columbia University Press.

Bourgeois, A. 1998. "Who Records the Value of Country Food?" *Nunatsiaq News*, Nunavut edition. Iqaluit (*www.nunatsiaq.com*), accessed August 22, 2005.

Brettell, C. B., ed. 1993. *When They Read What We Write: The Politics of Ethnography*. Westport CT: Bergin and Garvey.

Brewer, J. D. 2000. *Ethnography*. Buckingham, U.K.: Open University Press.

Briggs, J. L. 1970. *Never in Anger*. Cambridge MA: Harvard University Press.

———. 1978. "The Origins of Nonviolence: Inuit Management of Aggression," in *Learning Non-Aggression*, ed. A. Montagu, pp. 54–93. New York: Oxford University Press.

———. 1991. "Expecting the Unexpected: Canadian Inuit Training for an Experimental Lifestyle." *Ethos* 19:259–87.

———. 1997. "From Trait to Emblem and Back: Living and Representing Culture in Everyday Life." *Arctic Anthropology* 34:227–35.

————. 1998. *Inuit Morality Play: The Emotional Education of a Three-Year-Old*. New Haven: Yale University Press.

Briggs, J. L., ed. 2000. *Interviewing Inuit Elders*, vol. 3: *Childrearing Practices—Nagi Ekho and Ugsuralik Ottokie*. Iqaluit: Nunavut Arctic College.

Brody, H. 1975. *The People's Land: Eskimos and Whites in the Eastern Arctic*. New York: Penguin Books.

————. 1977. "Alcohol, Change and the Industrial Frontier." *Études/Inuit/Studies* 1:31–46.

————. 1987. *Living Arctic: Hunters of the Canadian North*. Seattle: University of Washington Press.

————. 2001. *The Other Side of Eden: Hunters, Farmers, and the Shaping of the World*. New York: North Point Press.

Brooke, J. 2000. "As Greenland's Seal Population Surges Its Fishermen Look to Revive the Hunt." *New York Times*, October 17, 2000, p. F5.

Burch, E. S., Jr. 1975. *Eskimo Kinsmen: Changing Family Relationships in Northwest Alaska*. St. Paul: West Publishing Company.

————. 1980. "Traditional Eskimo Societies in Northwest Alaska," in *Alaska Native Culture and History*, pp. 253–304. Senri Ethnological Studies 4. Osaka: National Museum of Ethnology.

————. 1988. "Knud Rasmussen and the 'Original' Inland Eskimos of Southern Kewatin." *Études/Inuit/Studies* 12:81–100.

Cairns, A. 2000. *Citizens Plus: Aboriginal Peoples and the Canadian State*. Vancouver: University of British Columbia Press.

Calhoun, C., and J. Karaganis. 2001. "Critical Theory," in *Handbook of Social Theory*, ed. G. Ritzer and B. Smart, pp. 179–200. London: Sage.

Canada, Government of. 1984. *The Western Arctic Claim: The Inuvialuit Final Agreement*. Ottawa: Department of Indian and Northern Affairs.

————. 1993. *Agreement between the Inuit of the Nunavut Settlement Area and Her Majesty the Queen in Right of Canada*. Ottawa: Tungavik Federation of Nunavut and Department of Indian and Northern Affairs.

Canadian Broadcasting Corporation. 2000. "Native Leaders Support Billion Dollar Pipeline." Canadian Broadcasting Corporation, www.cbc.ca, (accessed November 14, 2001).

Caruth, C. 1996. *Unclaimed Experience: Trauma, Narrative, and History*. Baltimore: Johns Hopkins University Press.

Castells, M. 1997. *The Power of Identity*. Malden MA: Blackwell.

Castles, S., and A. Davidson. 2000. *Citizenship and Migration: Globalization and the Politics of Belonging*. New York: Routledge.

Centre for International Statistics at the Canadian Council on Social Development. 1996. *Demographic Profile of Aboriginal Peoples in Major Canadian Metropolitan Centres*. Ottawa: National Association of Friendship Centres.

Chance, N. A. 1966. *The Eskimo of North Alaska*. New York: Holt, Rinehart, and Winston.

————. 1990. *The Inupiat and Arctic Alaska: An Ethnography of Development*. Fort Worth: Holt, Rinehart and Winston.

Charles, G. P. K. 2000. *Yuuyaraq (The Way of the Human Being): Yupiaq Voices in the Transmission of Religious and Cultural Knowledge*. Ph.D. diss., University of California, Santa Barbara.

Clairmont, D. H. 1962. *Notes on the Drinking Behavior of the Eskimos and Indians in the Aklavik Area*. NCRC 62-4. Ottawa: Northern Co-ordination and Research Centre, Department of Northern Affairs and National Resources.

Clairmont, D. H. J. 1963. *Deviance among Indians and Eskimos in Aklavik*, NWT. NCRC 63-9. Ottawa: Northern Co-ordination and Research Centre, Department of Northern Affairs and National Resources.

Clifford, J. 1988. *The Predicament of Culture: Twentieth-Century Ethnography, Literature, and Art*. Cambridge MA: Harvard University Press.

———. 1997. *Routes: Travel and Translation in the Late Twentieth Century*. Cambridge MA: Harvard University Press.

Clifford, J., and G. E. Marcus, eds. 1986. *Writing Culture: The Poetics and Politics of Ethnography*. Berkeley: University of California Press.

Cole, D., and L. Müller-Wille. 1984. "Franz Boas' Expedition to Baffin Island, 1883–1884." *Études/Inuit/Studies* 8:37–64.

Collignon, B. 1993. "The Variations of a Land Use Pattern: Seasonal Movements and Cultural Change among the Copper Inuit." *Études/Inuit/Studies* 17:71–90.

———. 1996. *Les Inuit: Ce qu'ils savent du territoire*. Paris: L'Harmattan.

———. 2002. "Les toponymes Inuit, mémoire du territoire: Étude de l'histoire des Inuinnait." *Anthropologie et Sociétés* 26:45–69.

———. 2006. *Knowing Places: Inuinnait, Landscapes and Environment*. Calgary: CCI Press.

Collings, P., G. Wenzel, and R. G. Condon. 1998. "Modern Food Sharing Networks and Community Integration in the Central Canadian Arctic." *Arctic* 51:301–14.

Collins, H. B. 1964. "Introduction to the Bison Book Edition," in F. Boas, *The Central Eskimo*. Lincoln: University of Nebraska Press.

Condon, R. G. 1983. *Inuit Behavior and Seasonal Change in the Canadian Arctic*. Ann Arbor MI: UMI Research Press.

———. 1994. "East Meets West: Fort Collinson, the Fur Trade, and the Economic Acculturation of the Northern Copper Inuit, 1928–1939." *Études/Inuit/Studies* 18:109–35.

———. 1996. *The Northern Copper Inuit: A History*. Norman: University of Oklahoma Press.

Cousineau, M. H. 1998. *Limites or Alternatives: Dead End for First Nations Producers in the Canadian Film and Television Financing System*. Videazimut Virtual Conference: The Right to Communicate and the Communication of Rights, http://commposite.uqam.ca/videaz/docs/macoen.html (accessed August 1, 2005).

Cruikshank, J. 1990. *Life Lived Like a Story: Life Stories of Three Yukon Native Elders*. Lincoln: University of Nebraska Press.

———. 1993. "The Politics of Ethnography in the Canadian North," in *Anthropology, Public Policy and Native Peoples in Canada*, ed. N. Dyck and J. B. Waldram, pp. 133–43. Montreal: McGill-Queen's University Press.

———. 1998. *The Social Life of Stories: Narrative and Knowledge in the Yukon Territory*. Lincoln: University of Nebraska Press.

Dacks, G. 1981. *A Choice of Futures: Politics in the Canadian North*. Toronto: Methuen.

Dahl, J. 2000. *Saqqaq: An Inuit Hunting Community in the Modern World*. Toronto: University of Toronto Press.

Dahl, J., J. Hicks, and P. Jull, eds. 2000. *Nunavut: Inuit Regain Control of Their Lands and Their Lives*. Copenhagen: International Work Group for Indigenous Affairs.

Damas, D. 1963. *Igluligmiut Kinship and Local Groupings*. Mercury Series 64. Ottawa: National Museum of Canada.

———. 1968. "Igluigmiut Kinship Terminology and Behaviour: Consanguines," in *Eskimo* of the Canadian Arctic, ed. Victor F. Valentine and Frank G. Vallee, pp. 85–105. Toronto: McClelland and Stewart.

Damas, David, ed. 1984. Handbook of North American Indians, vol. 5: Arctic. Washington DC: Smithsonian Institution Press.

Darou, W. G., A. Hum, and J. Kurtness. 1993. "An Investigation of the Impact of Psychosocial Research on a Native Population." Professional Psychology: Research and Practice 24.

Das, V. 1995. Critical Events: An Anthropological Perspective on the Contemporary India. New York: Oxford University Press.

de Laguna, F. 1994. "Some Early Circumpolar Studies," in Circumpolar Religion and Ecology: An Anthropology of the North, ed. T. Irimoto and T. Yamada, pp. 7–44. Tokyo: University of Tokyo Press.

Deloria, V., Jr. 2001. "Higher Education and Self Determination," in Power and Place: Indian Education in America, ed. V. Deloria Jr. and D. R. Wildcat. Golden CO: American Indian Graduate Center and Fulcrum Publishers.

Deloria, V., Jr., and D. R. Wildcat, eds. 2001. Power and Place: Indian Education in America. Golden CO: American Indian Graduate Center and Fulcrum Resources.

Department of Northern Affairs and National Resources. 1960. Eskimo Mortality and Housing. Canada: Northern Administration Branch, Department of Northern Affairs and National Resources, Industrial Division.

Derrida, J. 1992. "Force of Law: The 'Mystical' Foundation of Authority," in Deconstruction and the Possibility of Justice, ed. D. Cornell, M. Rosenfeld, and D. G. Carlson. New York: Routledge.

Dorais, L. J. 1988. "Inuit Identity in Canada." Folk 30:23–31.

————. 1989. "Bilinguism and Diglossia in the Canadian Eastern Arctic." Arctic 42:199–207.

————. 1990. "The Canadian Inuit and Their Language," in Arctic Languages: An Awakening, ed. D. R. F. Collis, pp. 185–290. Paris: UNESCO.

————. 1997. Quaqtaq: Modernity and Identity in an Inuit Community. Toronto: University of Toronto Press.

————. 2002. "Notes sur l'Inuktitut parlé à Iqaluit (Nunavut)." Études/Inuit/Studies 26:193–201.

Dorais, L. J., and S. Sammons. 2002. Language in Nunavut: Discourse and Identity in the Baffin Region. Iqaluit: Nunavut Arctic College.

Dorais, L. J., and E. Searles. 2001. "Inuit Identities." Études/Inuit/Studies 25:19–35.

Drummond, S. G. 2001. "Writing Legal Histories on Nunavik," in Aboriginal Autonomy and Development in Northern Quebec and Labrador, ed. C. Scott, pp. 41–62. Vancouver: University of British Columbia Press.

Dunning, R. W. 1959. "Ethnic Relations and Marginal Man in Canada." Human Organization 18:117–22.

Dybbroe, S. 1996. "Questions of Identity and Issues of Self-Determination." Études/Inuit/Studies 20:39–54.

Eber, D. 1989. When the Whalers Were Up North: Inuit Memories from the Eastern Arctic. Boston: D. R. Godine.

Ebner, D., and P. Brethour. 2005. "Mackenzie Fight Is Déjà Vu All Over Again." Globe and Mail (Toronto), May 12, 2005, B5.

Edwardsen, C. 1974. "The New Harpoon: An Essay," in Etok: A Study in Eskimo Power, ed. H. P. Gallagher. New York: Putnam.

Ervin, A. M. 1968. *New Northern Townsmen in Inuvik*. Ottawa: Department of Indian Affairs and Northern Development.

Esteva, G. 1992. "Development," in *The Development Dictionary*, ed. W. Sachs. London: Zed Books.

Études/Inuit/Studies. 1984. *Dans les traces de Boas: 100 ans d'anthropologie des Inuit/In Boas' Footsteps: 100 Years of Inuit Anthropology*. Vol. 8, no 1.

Evers, L., and B. Toelken, eds. 2001. *Native American Oral Traditions: Collaboration and Interpretation*. Logan: Utah State University Press.

Fals Borda, O. 2001. "Participatory (Action) Research in Social Theory: Origins and Challenges," in *Handbook of Action Research: Participative Inquiry and Practice*, ed. P. Reason and H. Bradbury, pp. xlii, 468. Thousand Oaks CA: Sage.

Fardon, R., ed. 1990. *Localizing Strategies: Regional Traditions of Ethnographic Writing*. Edinburgh: Scottish Academic Press.

Ferguson, J. 1994. *The Anti-Politics Machine*. Minneapolis: University of Minnesota Press.

Fienup-Riordan, A. 1983. *The Nelson Island Eskimo: Social Structure and Ritual Distribution*. Anchorage: Alaska Pacific University Press.

————. 1994. *Boundaries and Passages: Rule and Ritual in Yup'ik Eskimo Oral Tradition*. Norman: University of Oklahoma Press.

————. 2000. *Hunting Tradition in a Changing World: Yup'ik Lives in Alaska Today*. New Brunswick NJ: Rutgers University Press.

Finnie, R. 1940. *Lure of the North*. Philadelphia: David McKay Company.

Fixico, D. 1998. "Ethics and Responsibilities in Writing American Indian History," in *Natives and Academics: Researching and Writing about American Indians*, ed. by D. A. Mihesuah. Lincoln: University of Nebraska Press.

Flaherty, M. 1995. "Freedom of Expression or Freedom of Exploitation?" *Northern Review* 14:178–85.

Flaherty, R. J. 1922. *Nanook of the North* (film). Canada: Revellon-Frères.

Fleming, A. 1956. *Archibald the Arctic*. New York: Appleton-Century-Crofts.

Fogel-Chance, N. 1993. "Living in Both Worlds: 'Modernity' and 'Tradition' among North Slope Inupiaq Women in Anchorage." *Arctic Anthropology* 30:94–108.

Fortescue, M., S. Jacobson, and L. Kaplan. 1994. *Comparative Eskimo Dictionary with Aleut Cognates*. Fairbanks: Alaska Native Language Center, University of Alaska.

Foucault, M. 1977. *Discipline and Punish: The Birth of the Prison*. New York: Pantheon.

————. 1997. *Ethics: Subjectivity and Truth*. New York: New Press.

Fox, R. G., ed. 1991. *Recapturing Anthropology: Working in the Present*. Santa Fe: School of American Research Press.

Franklin, J. 1971 [1828]. *Narrative of a Second Expedition to the Shores of the Polar Sea in the Years 1825, 1826 and 1827*. Edmonton: Hurtig Publishers.

Freed, S. A., R. S. Freed, and L. Williamson. 1988. "Capitalist Philanthropy and Russian Revolutionaries: The Jessup North Pacific Expedition (1897–1902)." *American Anthropologist* 90:7–24.

Freeman, M. A. 1978. *Life among the Qallunaat*. Edmonton: Hurtig Publishers.

Freeman, M. M. R. 1979. "Traditional Land Users as a Legitimate Source of Environmental Expertise," in *The Canadian National Parks: Today and Tomorrow, Conference II: Ten Years Later*, ed. J. G. Nelson, R. D. Needham, S. H. Nelson, and R. C. Scace, pp. 345–61. Waterloo, Ontario: University of Waterloo.

―――. 1998. *Inuit, Whaling and Sustainability.* Walnut Creek CA: AltaMira.

―――. 2000. *Endangered Peoples of the Arctic: Struggles to Survive and Thrive.* Westport CT: Greenwood Press.

Freeman, M. M. R., ed. 1976. *Inuit Land Use and Occupancy Project.* Ottawa: Department of Indian and Northern Affairs.

Freuchen, P. 1935. *Arctic Adventure.* New York: Farrar and Rinehart.

Gadamer, H. G. 1987. "The Problem of Historical Consciousness," in *Interpretive Social Science: A Second Look*, ed. P. Rabinow and W. Sullivan, pp. 82–140. Berkeley: University of California Press.

Gagnon, Mélanie, and Iqaluit Elders. 2002. *Memory and History in Nunavut*, vol. 2: *Inuit Recollections on the Military Presence in Iqaluit.* Iqaluit: Nunavut Arctic College.

Gal, S. 1987. "Codeswitching and Consciousness in the European Periphery." *American Ethnologist* 14:637–53.

Galley, M. 1990. "De l'oral à l'écrit, une difficile fidélité." *Cahiers de Littérature Orale* 28:13–28.

Geertz, C. 1988. *Works and Lives.* Stanford: Stanford University Press.

Gilligan, C. 1982. *In a Different Voice: Psychological Theory and Women's Development.* Cambridge MA: Harvard University Press.

Ginsburg, F. 1991. "Indigenous Media: Faustian Contract or Global Village." *Cultural Anthropology* 6:92–112.

―――. 1994. *Media Worlds: Anthropology on New Terrains.* Berkeley: University of California Press.

Ginsburg, F., L. Abu-Lughod, and B. Larkin, eds. 2002. *Media Worlds: Anthropology on New Terrains.* Berkeley: University of California Press.

Godlewska, A., and N. Smith, eds. 1994. *Geography and Empire: Critical Studies in the History of Geography.* Oxford: Blackwell.

Goehring, B. 1989. *Aboriginal Toponymies in Canada.* Unpublished M.A. thesis, University of British Columbia.

Graburn, N. 1963. *Lake Harbour, NWT. NCRC 63–2.* Ottawa: Northern Co-ordination and Research Centre, Department of Northern Affairs and National Resources.

―――. 1968. *Inuariat: A Play.* Written for the Annual Meetings of the American Anthropological Association.

―――. 1969a. *Eskimos without Igloos: Economic and Social Development in Sugluk.* Boston: Little, Brown and Company.

―――. 1969b. Eskimo Law in the Light of Self- and Group Interest. *Law and Society Review* 4:45–60.

―――. 1982. "Television and the Canadian Inuit." *Études/Inuit/Studies* 6(1):7–17.

―――. 1987. "Inuit Art and the Expression of Eskimo Inuit Identity." *American Review of Canadian Studies* 17:47–66.

―――. 1998a. "Weirs in the River of Time: The Development of Historical Consciousness among Canadian Inuit." *Museum Anthropology* 22:18–32.

―――. 1998b. "The Present as History: Photography and the Canadian Inuit, 1959–1996," in *Imaging the Arctic*, ed. J. H. C. King and H. Lidchi. London: British Museum.

―――. 2003. Canadian Anthropology and the Cold War. Paper presented at the conference

"Historicizing Canadian Sociocultural Anthropology," February 20–23, 2003, Trent University, Peterborough, Ontario.

Graburn, N., ed. 1976. *Ethnic and Tourist Arts*. Berkeley: University of California Press.

Graburn, N., and R. Iutzi-Mitchell, eds. 1992. *Language and Educational Policy in the North*. International and Area Studies. Berkeley: University of California.

Graburn, N., and S. B. Strong. 1973. *Circumpolar Peoples: An Anthropological Perspective*. Pacific Palisades: Goodyear Publishing Company.

Grace, S. E. 2001. *Canada and the Idea of North*. Montreal: McGill-Queen's University Press.

Grant, S. 2002. *Arctic Justice*. Montreal: McGill-Queens University Press.

Gray, E. 1979. *Super Pipe: The Arctic Pipeline, World's Greatest Fiasco?* Toronto: Griffin House.

Gubser, N. J. 1965. *The Nunamiut Eskimos, Hunters of Caribou*. New Haven: Yale University Press.

Guemple, Lee 1972. *Alliance in Eskimo Society*. Seattle: American Ethnological Society and University of Washington Press.

Gupta, A., and J. Ferguson. 1997. *Culture, Power, Place: Explorations in Critical Ethnography*. Durham: Duke University Press.

Hall, C. F. 1865. *Arctic Researches and Life among the Esquimaux: Being the Narrative of an Expedition in Search of Sir John Franklin, in the Years 1860, 1861, and 1862*. New York: Harper.

Hamilton, J. D. 1994. *Arctic Revolution: Social Change in the Northwest Territories, 1935–1994*. Toronto: Dundurn Press.

Handler, R. 1998. "Studying Mainstreams and Minorities in North America," in *Making Majorities: Constitution the Nation in Japan, Korea, China, Malaysia, Fiji, Turkey, and the United States*. Edited by D. Gladney, pp. 249–63. Stanford: Stanford University Press.

Hannoum, A. 2002. "Translation and the Imaginary." *Anthropology News* 43:7–8.

Harding, S., ed. 1987. *Feminism and Methodology*. Bloomington: Indiana University Press.

Hardt, M., and A. Negri. 2000. *Empire*. Cambridge: Harvard University Press.

Haraway, D. 1991. "Situated Knowledges: The Science Question in Feminism and the Privilege of Partial Perspective," in *Simians, Cyborgs and Women: The Reinvention of Nature*, ed. D. Harraway, pp. 183–201. London: Routledge.

Harritt, R. K., ed. 2001. *In Pursuit of Agviq: Some Results of the Western Whaling Societies Regional Integration Project*. Anchorage: Environmental and Natural Resources Institute, University of Alaska–Anchorage.

Health Canada. 2003. *Acting on What We Know: Preventing Youth Suicide in First Nations*. Report of the Advisory Group on Suicide Prevention. Ottawa: Minister of Supply and Services Canada.

Hensel, C. 1996. *Telling Our Selves: Ethnicity and Discourse in Southwestern Alaska*. New York: Oxford University Press.

Herzfeld, M. 1992. *The Social Production of Indifference: Exploring the Symbolic Roots of Western Bureaucracy*. New York: Berg.

Hicks, J., and G. White. 2000. "Nunavut: Inuit Self-Determination through a Land Claim and Public Government," in *Nunavut: Inuit Regain Control of Their Lands and Their Lives*, ed. J. Dahl, J. Hicks, and P. Jull. Copenhagen: International Work Group for Indigenous Affairs.

Holm, G. 1914 [1888]. *Ethnological Sketch of the Angmagsalik Eskimo*, ed. W. Thalbitzer. *Meddelelser om Grønland* 39. Copenhagen.

Holmer, N. M. 1967. "The Native Place Names of Arctic America," pt. 1. *Names* 15:182–96.

————. 1969. "The Native Place Names of Arctic America," pt. 2. *Names* 17:138–48.

Holston, J., and A. Appadurai. 1999. "Cities and Citizenship," in *Cities and Citizenship*, ed. J. Holston, pp. 1–18. Durham: Duke University Press.

Holtved, E. 1967. *Contributions to Polar Eskimo Ethnography*. Meddelelser Om Grønland. Copenhagen: C. A. Reitzels Forlag.

Honigmann, J. J., and I. Honigmann. 1965. *Eskimo Townsmen*. Ottawa: Saint Paul University, Canadian Research Centre for Anthropology.

————. 1970. *Arctic Townsmen: Ethnic Backgrounds and Modernization*. Ottawa: Saint Paul University, Canadian Research Centre for Anthropology.

Houston, J. A. 1972. *Songs of the Dream People: Chants and Images from the Indians and Eskimos of North America*, 1st edition. New York: Atheneum.

Hughes, C. C. 1960. *An Eskimo Village in the Modern World*. Ithaca NY: Cornell University Press.

————. 1965. "Under Four Flags: Recent Culture Change among the Eskimos." *Current Anthropology* 6:3–69.

Huntington, H. P. 1992. *Wildlife Management and Subsistence Hunting in Alaska*. Seattle: University of Washington Press.

Hurston, Z. N. 1995. *Dust Tracks on a Road*. New York: Literary Classics of the United States.

Hymes, D. H. 1981. *"In Vain I Tried to Tell You": Essays in Native American Ethnopoetics*. Philadelphia: University of Pennsylvania Press.

Igloolik Isuma Productions. 2000. *Atanarjuat*. Igloolik.

Inuit Circumpolar Conference. 2005. "ICC's Beginning." www.inuitcircumpolar.com (accessed August 23, 2005).

Inuit Tapiriit Kanatami. 2002. "Inuvialuit Region" http://www.itk.ca/english/inuit_canada/regions/inuvialuit.htm, (accessed October 2003).

Inuit Tapirisat of Canada. 2000. *Inuujugut: 1999–2000 Annual Report*. Ottawa: Inuit Taprisat of Canada.

Inutiq, S. K. 2001. "Inuit Knowledge Different than Western Knowledge." *Nunatsiaq News*, June 22, 2001. Iqaluit, www.nunatsiaq.com (accessed August 23, 2005).

Irwin, C. 1989. "Lords of the Arctic, Wards of the State" (abridged version). *Northern Perspectives* 17:2–12.

Jackson, J. 1989. "Is There a Way to Talk about Culture without Making Enemies?" *Dialectical Anthropology* 14:127–43.

Jacobson, S. 1984. *Yup'ik Eskimo Dictionary*. Fairbanks: Alaska Native Language Center, University of Alaska.

James, C. 2001. "Cultural Change in Mistissini: Implications for Self-Determination and Cultural Survival," in *Aboriginal Autonomy and Development in Northern Quebec and Labrador*, ed. C. Scott, pp. 316–31. Vancouver: University of British Columbia Press.

Jenness, D. 1924. *Report of the Canadian Arctic Expedition, 1913–18, Southern Party, 1913–16*, vol. 13A: *Eskimo Folk-lore: Myths and Traditions from Northern Alaska, the Mackenzie Delta and Coronation Gulf*. Ottawa: Kings Printer.

————. 1928. *Report of the Canadian Arctic Expedition 1913–18*, vol. 15A: *Comparative Vocabulary of the Western Eskimo Dialects*. Ottawa: Kings Printer.

————. 1962. *Eskimo Administration I: Alaska*. Technical Paper 10. Montreal: Arctic Institute of North America.

———. 1964. *Eskimo Administration II: Canada.* Technical Paper 14. Montreal: Arctic Institute of North America.

———. 1965. *Eskimo Administration III: Labrador.* Montreal: Arctic Institute of North America.

———. 1967. *Eskimo Administration IV: Greenland.* Montreal: Arctic Institute of North America.

———. 1968. *Eskimo Administration V: Analysis and Reflections.* Technical Paper 21. Montreal: Arctic Institute of North America.

———. 1970 [1922]. *Report of the Canadian Arctic Expedition, 1913–18,* vol. 12, pt. A: *The Life of the Copper Eskimos.* New York: Johnson Reprint Corporation.

Jolles, C. Z., and Kaningok. 1991. "Qayuutat and Angyapiget: Gender Relations and Subsistence Activities in Sivuqaq (Gambell, St. Lawrence Island, Alaska)." *Études/Inuit/Studies* 15:23–53.

Jolles, C. Z., and E. M. Oozeva. 2002. *Faith, Food and Family in a Yupik Whaling Community.* Seattle: University of Washington Press.

Katz, R. 1982. *Boiling Energy: Community Healing among the Kalahari !Kung.* Cambridge: Harvard University Press.

Kearney, M. 1986. "From Invisible Hand to Visible Feet: Anthropological Studies of Migration and Development." *Annual Review of Anthropology* 15:331–61.

Kelly, J. D., and M. Kaplan. 2001. "Nation and Decolonization: Toward a New Anthropology of Nationalism." *Anthropological Theory* 1 (4):419–37.

Kemp, W. B. 1971. "The Flow of Energy in a Hunting Society." *Scientific American* 225:105–15.

Kennedy, J. C. 1982. *Holding the Line: Ethnic Boundaries in a Northern Labrador Community.* St. Johns: Institute of Social and Economic Research, Memorial University of Newfoundland.

Kiepert, H. 1886. *Gutachten.* Acta betreffend Habilitation des Dr. Boas, H. 1.XVI, Bl 96–112, Universitätsarchiv der Humboldt-Universität zu Berlin.

King, J. C. H., and H. Lidchi, eds. 1998. *Imaging the Arctic.* Seattle: University of Washington Press.

Kirmayer, Laurence J., and Gail Valaskakis, eds. In press. *Healing Traditions: The Mental Health of Canadian Aboriginal Peoples.* Vancouver: University of British Columbia Press.

Kishigami, N. 1995. "Extended Family and Food Sharing Practices among the Contemporary Netsilik Inuit: A Case Study of Pelly Bay, NWT, Canada." *Journal of Hokkaido University of Education* 45:1–9.

———. 1997. "Personal Names, Name Souls, and Social Change among Canadian Inuit: A Case Study of the Akulivik Inuit," in *Circumpolar Animism and Shamanism,* ed. T. Irimoto and T. Yamada, pp. 151–66. Sapporo: Hokkaido University Press.

———. 1999. "Why Do Inuit Move to Montreal? A Research Note on Urban Inuit." *Études/Inuit/Studies* 23:221–27.

———. 2000. "Contemporary Inuit Food Sharing and Hunter Support Program of Nunavik, Canada," in *The Social Economy of Sharing: Resource Allocation and Modern Hunter Gatherers,* ed. G. W. Wenzel, G. Hovelsrud-Broda, and N. Kishigami, pp. 171–92. Senri Ethnological Studies 53. Osaka: National Museum of Ethnology.

———. 2002. "Inuit Identities in Montreal." *Études/Inuit/Studies* 26:183–91.

———. 2004. "A New Typology of Food-Sharing Practices among Hunter-Gatherers, with a Special Focus on Inuit Examples." *Journal of Anthropological Research* 60:341–58.

Klausner, S. Z., and E. F. Foulks. 1982. *Eskimo Capitalists: Oil, Politics, and Alcohol.* Towata NJ: Allanheld, Osmun and Company.

Korsmo, F., and A. Graham. 2002. "Research in the North American North: Action and Reaction." *Arctic* 55:319–28.

Kral, M. J. 1998. "Suicide and the Internalization of Culture: Three Questions." *Transcultural Psychiatry* 35:221–33.

———. 2003. *Unikkaartuit: Meanings of Well-Being, Sadness, Suicide, and Change in Two Inuit Communities.* Report submitted to Health Canada.

Kral, M. J., K. J. Burkhardt, and S. Kidd. 2002. "The New Research Agenda for a Cultural Psychology." *Canadian Psychology* 43:154–62.

Kroeber, A. 1938. *Cultural and Natural Areas of Native North America.* Berkeley: University of California Press.

Kroeber, A., and T. Parsons. 1958. "The Concepts of Culture and of Social System." *American Sociological Review* 23:582–90.

Krupnik, I. I. 1992. "One Nation—One Language: Ideology and Results of Soviet Minority Policies in Siberia," in *Language and Educational Policy in the North*, ed. N. Graburn and R. Iutzi-Mitchell, pp. 201–12. Berkeley: International and Area Studies, University of California at Berkeley.

Kymlicka, W. 1995. *Multicultural Citizenship.* Oxford: Clarendon Press.

LaCapra, D. 1985. *History and Criticism.* Ithaca: Cornell University Press.

Laugrand, F., J. Oosten, and F. Trudel. 2001. *Memory and History in Nunavut*, vol. 1: *Representing Tuurngait.* Iqaluit: Nunavut Arctic College.

Le Mouël, J. F. 1978. *"Ceux des Mouettes": Les Eskimo Naujâmiut, Groënland Ouest.* Paris: Muséum d'Histoire Naturelle, Mémoires de l'Institut d'Ethnologie.

Lee, M. 1998. *Baleen Basketry of the North Alaskan Eskimo*, 2nd edition. Seattle: University of Washington Press.

———. 1999. "Strands of Gold." *Anchorage Daily News*, October 17, 1999, pp. E8–13.

———. 2002. "The Cooler Ring: Urban Alaska Native Women and the Subsistence Debate." *Arctic Anthropology* 39:3–9.

Lee, R.B. 1979. *The !Kung San: Men, Women, and Work in a Foraging Society.* Cambridge: Cambridge University Press.

Leenhardt, M. 1979. *Do Kamo: Person and Myth in the Melanesian World.* Chicago: University of Chicago Press.

Lévi-Strauss, C. 1953. "Social Structure." *Anthropology Today:* 524–53.

Lister, R. 1997. *Citizenship: Feminist Perspectives.* New York: New York University Press.

Lock, M. M. 2002. *Twice Dead: Organ Transplants and the Reinvention of Death.* Berkeley: University of California Press.

Lowe, R. 1983. *Kangiryuarmiut Uqauhingita Numiktittitdjutingit/Basic Kangiryuarmiut Eskimo Dictionary.* Inuvik: Committee for Original Peoples Entitlement.

———. 1984a. *Uummarmiut Uqalungiha Mumikhitchirutingit/Basic Uummarmiut Eskimo Dictionary.* Inuvik: Committee for Original Peoples Entitlement.

———. 1984b. *Siglit Inuvialuit Uqausiita Kipuktirutait/Basic Siglit Inuvialuit Eskimo Dictionary.* Inuvik: Committee for Original Peoples Entitlement.

———. 1985a. *Siglit Inuvialuit Uqausiita Ilisarviksait/Basic Siglit Inuvialuit Eskimo Grammar.* Inuvik: Committee for Original People Entitlement.

———. 1985b. *Kangiryuarmiut Uqauhingita Ilihautdjutikhangit/Basic Kangiryuarmiut Eskimo Grammar.* Inuvik: Committee for Original Peoples Entitlement.

————. 1985c. *Uummarmiut Uqalungiha Ilihaurrutikrangit/Basic Uummarmiut Eskimo Grammar.* Inuvik: Committee for Original Peoples Entitlement.

————. 2001. *Siglit Inuvialuit Uqautchiita Nutaat Kipuktirutait Aglipkaqtat/Siglit Inuvialuit Eskimo Dictionary,* 2nd, revised and expanded edition. Quebec: Editions Nota Bene.

Lowenstein, T. 1992. *The Things That Were Said of Them: Shaman Stories and Oral Histories of the Tikigaq People.* Berkeley: University of California Press.

Lubart, J. M. 1969. *Psychodynamic Problems of Adaptation: MacKenzie Delta Eskimos.* Ottawa: Department of Indian Affairs and Northern Development.

Lunan, D. 2001. "Second Coming." *Oilweek* 52, p. 18.

Lyotard, J. F. 1984. *The Postmodern Condition: A Report on Knowledge.* Minneapolis: University of Minnesota Press.

MacDonald, J. 1998. *The Arctic Sky: Inuit Astronomy, Star Lore, and Legend.* Toronto and Iqaluit: Royal Ontario Museum and Nunavut Research Institute.

MacLean, E. A. 1980. *Iñupiallu Tannillu Uqalunisa Ilanich/Abridged Iñupiaq and English Dictionary.* Fairbanks and Barrow: Alaska Native Language Center, University of Alaska Fairbanks and Iñupiat Language Commission, North Slope Borough.

MacLuhan, M. 1967. *The Medium is the Message.* New York: Random House.

Makivik Corporation. 2000. *Capturing Spirit: The Inuit Journey,* Kuujjuaq: Makivik Corporation.

Malinowski, B. 1984 [1922]. *Argonauts of the Western Pacific: An Account of Native Enterprise and Adventure in the Archipelagoes of Melanesian New Guinea.* Prospect Heights IL: Waveland Press.

Mannik, H., ed. 1998. *Inuit Nunamiut: Inland Inuit.* Altona, Manitoba: Friesen Corporation.

Marcus, A. R. 1995. *Relocating Eden: The Image and Politics of Inuit Exile in the Canadian Arctic.* Hanover: University Press of New England.

Marcus, G. E. 1986. "Contemporary Problems of Ethnography in the Modern World System," in *Writing Culture: The Poetics and Politics of Ethnography,* ed. J. Clifford and G. E. Marcus. Berkeley: University of California Press.

Marcus, G. E., and M. M. J. Fischer. 1986. *Anthropology as Cultural Critique: An Experimental Moment in the Human Sciences.* Chicago: University of Chicago Press.

Martin, E. 1994. *Flexible Bodies: Tracking Immunity in American Culture from the Days of Polio to the Age of* AIDS. Boston: Beacon Press.

Mary-Rousselière, G. 1972. "The New Eskimo Names: A Real Mess." *Eskimo:* 18–19.

————. 1974. "Right to Liquor Questioned." *Eskimo:* 3–5.

————. 1976–77. "The Eskimo in a Squandering World." *Eskimo:* 1–4.

————. 1984. "Iglulik," in *Handbook of North American Indians: Arctic,* vol. 5, ed. D. Damas, pp. 431–47. Washington DC: Smithsonian Institution Press.

Mason, C. 1985. *A Study of Inuit Geographical Perception and Land Use through an Analysis of Place Names.* B.A. honors thesis, McGill University.

Mathiassen, T. 1928. *Material Culture of the Iglulik Eskimos, Report of the Fifth Thule Expedition, 1921–24,* vol. 6. Copenhagen: Gyldendalske.

Mauss, M. 1979. *Seasonal Variations of the Eskimo: A Study in Social Morphology.* London: Routledge and Kegan Paul.

Mauzé, M. 1997. *Present Is Past: Some Uses of Tradition in Native Societies.* Lanham MD: University Press of America.

McCartney, Allen P. 1984. "Daniel Weetaluktuk: Contributions to Canadian Arctic Anthropology." *Études/Inuit/Studies* 8:103–15.

McCormick, Rod M. 2003. *Identifying the Facilitation of Healing and Resiliency amongst Suicidal Aboriginal Youth in Canada*. Vancouver: Department of Educational and Counseling Psychology, and Special Education, University of British Columbia.

McFeely, T. 1999. "Move Them to Florida: Nunavut Communities Compete for a Share of the New Territory's Huge Federal Transfers." *Report Newsmagazine*, November 22, 1999, vol. 26, pp. 12–13.

McGhee, R. 1974. *Beluga Hunters: An Archeological Reconstruction of the History and Culture of the Mackenzie Delta Kittegaryumiut*. St John's: Memorial University of Newfoundland.

———. 1996. *Ancient People of the Arctic*. Vancouver: University of British Columbia Press.

McKibbon, S. 2000. "Igloolik Elders Win Northern Science Award." *Nunatsiaq News*, January 21, 2000. Iqaluit, www.nunatsiaq.com, (accessed August 23, 2005).

McNabb, S. 1991. "Elders, Inupiat Ilitqusiat, and Culture Goals in the Northwest Arctic." *Arctic Anthropology* 28:63–76.

Mead, M. 1961 [1928]. *Coming of Age in Samoa*. New York: Dell.

Mesher, V. J. 2000. "No Longer Alone: A Haven of Happiness with the Association of Montreal Inuit." *Makivik Magazine*, vol. 54, pp. 57–67.

Métayer, M. 1973. *Unipkat: tradition esquimaude de Coppermine, Territoires du Nord Ouest, Canada*. Collection Nordicana, vol. 42. Sainte-Foy, Quebec: Centre d'études nordiques, Université Laval.

Mill, J. S. 1955 [1859]. *On Liberty*. Chicago: Regnery.

Miller, D., ed. 1995. *Worlds Apart: Modernity through the Prism of the Local*. New York: Routledge.

Mitchell, M. 1996. *From Talking Chiefs to a Native Corporate Elite: The Birth of Class and Nationalism among Canadian Inuit*. Montreal: McGill-Queen's University Press.

Moller, N. 1992. "The Language Situation of the Youth in Greenland," in *Language and Educational Policy in the North*, ed. N. Graburn and R. Iutzi-Mitchell, pp. 179–89. International and Area Studies. Berkeley: University of California.

Morin, F. 2001. "La construction de nouveaux espaces politiques inuits à l'heure de la mondialisation." *Recherches Amerindiennes au Québec* 31 (3).

Morrison, D. A. 1988. *The Kugaluk Site and the Nuvorugmiut: The Archaeology and History of a Nineteenth-Century Mackenzie Inuit Society*. Mercury Series 137. Hull, Quebec: Canadian Museum of Civilization.

Moss, W. 1995. "Inuit Perspectives on Treaty Rights and Governance Issues," in *Aboriginal Self Government: Legal and Constitutional Issues. Papers Prepared as Part of the Research Program of the Royal Commission on Aboriginal Peoples*, pp. 55–141. Ottawa: Ministry of Supply and Services Canada.

Müller-Wille, L. 1984a. "The Legacy of Native Toponyms. Towards the Establishing of the Inuit Place Inventory of the Kativik Region (Québec)." *Onomastica Canadiana* 65:2–19.

———. 1984b. *Inuit Place Name Survey of the Pangnirtuuq Land Use Area, July 28–August 14, 1984*. St-Lambert, Québec: Indigenous Names Survey.

———. 1985. "Une méthodologie pour les enqêtes toponymiques autochtones: Le répertoire inuit de la région de Kativik et de sa zone côtière." *Études/Inuit/Studies* 9:61–66.

———. 1987. *Gazetteer of Inuit Place Names in Nunavik*. Inukjuak: Avataq Cultural Institute.

Müller-Wille, L., ed. 1998. *Franz Boas among the Inuit of Baffin Island, 1883–1884*. Toronto: University of Toronto Press.

Müller-Wille, L., and L. Weber. 1982–95. NUNA-TOP *Inuit Place Name Surveys of Nunavik (Québec)*,

Cumberland Sound (Baffin Island) and Kivalliq (Northwest Territories, Canada). St-Lambert, Québec: Indigenous Names Survey.

————. 1984. NUNA-TOP Inuit Place Name Surveys of Cumberland Sound (Baffin Island, Northwest Territories, Canada). St-Lambert, Québec: Indigenous Names Survey.

Murdoch, J. 1988 [1892]. Ethnological Results of the Point Barrow Expedition. Classics of Smithsonian Anthropology. Washington DC: Smithsonian Institution Press.

Myers, F. R., ed. 2001. The Empire of Things: Regimes of Value and Material Culture, 1st edition. Santa Fe NM: School of American Research Press.

Myers, H. 2001. "Changing Environment, Changing Times, Environmental Issues and Political Action in the Canadian North." Environment 43:32–44.

Nader, L. 1972. "Up the Anthropologist: Perspectives Gained from Studying Up," in Reinventing Anthropology, ed. D. Hymes pp. 284–311. New York: Random House.

Nagy, M. 1994. Yukon North Slope Inuvialuit Oral History, Hudç Hudän Series. Occasional Papers in Yukon History, vol. 1. Whitehorse: Government of the Yukon.

————. 1999. Aulavik Oral History Project on Banks Island, NWT, Final Report. Inuvik: Inuvialuit Social Development Program.

————. 2002. "Comment les Inuvialuit parlent de leur passé." Anthropologie et Sociétés 26:193–213.

Nagy, M., ed. 1999a. Aulavik Oral History Project: English Translations and Transcriptions of Interviews 3–72. Inuvik: Inuvialuit Social Development Program.

————. 1999b. Aulavik Oral History Project: English Translations and Transcriptions of Archival Tapes. Inuvik: Inuvialuit Social Development Program.

————. 1999c. Aulavik Oral History Project: Inuvialuktun Transcriptions of Interviews 4–72, 2 vols. Inuvik: Inuvialuit Social Development Program.

————. 1999d. Aulavik Oral History Project: Inuvialuktun Transcriptions of Archival Tapes. Inuvik: Inuvialuit Social Development Program.

Nash, J. 2001. "Globalization and the Cultivation of Peripheral Vision." Anthropology Today 17:15–22.

Nelson, E. W. 1983 [1899]. The Eskimo about Bering Strait. Washington DC: Smithsonian Institution Press.

Nelson, R. K. 1969. Hunters of the Northern Ice. New York: University of Chicago Press.

Nemeth, M. 1995. " 'A Great Country': A Veteran Northern Politician Takes Her Leave." Maclean's 108, October 16, 1995, p. 34.

Nora, P. 1989. "Between Memory and History: Les Lieux de Memoire." Representations 26:7–24.

Nunavut, Government of. 1999a. Policy on Toponymy, Geographical and Community Names. Iqaluit: Culture and Heritage Program, Department of Culture, Language, Elders and Youth.

————. 1999b. Report from the September Inuit Qaujimajatuqangit Workshop. Iqaluit: Department of Culture, Language, Elders and Youth, Government of Nunavut.

————. 2003. Report of the Workshop on Best Practices in Suicide Prevention and the Evaluation of Suicide Prevention Programs in the Arctic. Iqaluit: Government of Nunavut, Department of Executive and Intergovernmental Affairs.

Nunavut Social Development Council. 1998. Report of the Nunavut Traditional Knowledge Conference. Iqaluit: Nunavut Social Development Council.

———. 2000. *Ihumaliurhimajaptingnik / On Our Own Terms: the State of Inuit Culture and Society.* Iqaluit: Nunavut Social Development Council.

Nungak, Z., and E. Y. Arima. 1969. *Unikkaatuat Sanaugarngnik Atyingualiit Puvirngniturngmit/Eskimo Stories from Povungnituk, Quebec.* Ottawa: Queen's Printer.

Nuttall, M. 1992. *Arctic Homeland: Kinship, Community, and Development in Northwest Greenland.* Toronto: University of Toronto Press.

———. 1998a. "Critical Reflections on Knowledge Gathering in the Arctic," in *Aboriginal Environmental Knowledge in the North*, ed. L. J. Dorais, M. Nagy, and L. Müller-Wille, pp. 21–35. Québec: GETIC, Université Laval.

———. 1998b. *Protecting the Arctic: Indigenous Peoples and Cultural Survival.* Amsterdam: Harwood Academic Publishers.

———. 2001. "Locality, Identity, and Memory in South Greenland." *Études/Inuit/Studies* 25:53–72.

Oakes, J., and R. Riewe. 1996. "Communicating Inuit Perspectives on Research," in *Issues in the North*, vol. 1, ed. J. Oakes and R. Riewe. Edmonton: Canadian Circumpolar Institute.

Okely, J. 1996 [1975]. *Own and Other Culture.* London: Routledge.

O'Neil, J. D. 1986. "Colonial Stress in the Canadian Arctic: An Ethnography of Young Adults Changing," in *Anthropology and Epidemiology: Interdisciplinary Approaches to the Study of Health and Disease*, ed. C. R. Janes, R. Stall, and S. M. Gifford, pp. 249–74. Boston: D. Reidel Publishing Company.

O'Neil, J. D., and P. Gilbert, eds. 1990. *Childbirth in the Canadian North: Epidemiological, Clinical and Cultural Perspectives.* Winnipeg: Department of Community Health Services, University of Manitoba.

O'Neil, J. D., J. M. Kaufert, P. L. Kaufert, and W. W. Coolage. 1993. "Political Considerations in Health-Related Participatory Research in Northern Canada," in *Anthropology, Public Policy and Native Peoples in Canada*, ed. N. Dyck and J. B. Waldram, pp. 215–32. Montreal: McGill-Queen's University Press.

O'Neil, J. D., J. R. Reading, and A. Leader. 1998. "Changing Relations of Surveillance: The Development of Discourse of Resistance in Aboriginal Epidemiology." *Human Organization* 57:230–37.

Oosten, J., and F. Laugrand, eds. 1999. *Interviewing Inuit Elders*, vol. 1: *Introduction*—Pauloosie Angmalik, Saullu Nakasuk, Elisapee Otoova and Herve Paniaq. Iqaluit: Nunavut Arctic College.

———. 2000. *Inuit Perspectives on the 20th Century*, vol. 1: *The Transition to Christianity*—Victor Tungilik and Rachel Uyarasuk. Iqaluit: Nunavut Arctic College.

———. 2001. *Inuit Perspectives on the 20th Century*, vol. 2: *Travelling and Surviving on Our Land.* Iqaluit: Nunavut Arctic College.

Oosten, J., F. Laugrand, and W. Rasing, eds. 1999. *Interviewing Inuit Elders*, vol. 2: *Perspectives on Traditional Law*—Emile Immarittuq, Lucassie Nutaraaluk, Mariano and Tulumaaq Aupilaarjuk, Akeeshoo Joamee. Iqaluit: Nunavut Arctic College.

Orr, E. C., B. Orr, V. J. Kanrilak, and A. J. Charlie. 1997. *Ellangellemni . . . When I Became Aware.* Fairbanks: Lower Kuskokwim School District and Alaska Native Language Center.

Ortner, S. 1984. "Theory in Anthropology since the Sixties." *Comparative Studies in Society and History* 26:126–66.

Oswalt, W. 1963. *Napaskiak: An Alaskan Eskimo Community.* Tucson: University of Arizona Press.

Paine, R. 1977. *The White Arctic: Anthropological Essays on Tutelage and Ethnicity.* St. John's: Institute of Social and Economic Research, Memorial University of Newfoundland.

———. 1999. "Aboriginality, Multiculturalism, and Liberal Rights Philosphy." *Ethnos* 64:325–49.

Parkin, D., ed. 1982. *Semantic Anthropology.* New York: Academic Press.

Parry, W. E. 1826. *Journal of a Third Voyage for the Discovery of a Northwest Passage, From the Atlantic to the Pacific; Performed in the Years 1824–25, in His Majesty's Ships Hecla and Fury, Under the Orders of Captain William Edward Parry.* London: J. Murray.

Perner, J., and T. Ruffman. 1995. "Episodic Memory and Autonoetic Consciousness: Developmental Evidence and a Theory of Childhood Amnesia." *Journal of Experimental Child Psychology* 59:516–48.

Petitot, E. 1876. *Bibliothèque de Linguistique et d'Ethnographie Américaines,* vol. 3: *Vocabulaire Français-Esquimau: Dialecte des Tchiglit des bouches du Mackenzie et de l'Anderson.* Paris: Ernest Leroux.

———. 1887. *Les Grands Esquimaux.* Paris: Plon, Nourrit et Cie.

Petrone, P., ed. 1988. *Northern Voices: Inuit Writing in English.* Toronto: University of Toronto Press.

Phillips, R. B., and C. B. Steiner. 1999. *Unpacking Culture: Art and Commodity in Colonial and Postcolonial Worlds.* Berkeley: University of California Press.

Pitseolak, P., and D. Eber. 1975. *People from Our Side: An Inuit Record of Seekooseelak, the Land of the People of Cape Dorset, Baffin Island—A Life Story with Photographs.* Edmonton: Hurtig Publishers.

Proust, M., and P. Kolb. 1983. *Marcel Proust: Selected Letters,* vol. 3. London: Collins.

Pryor, F. L., and N. Graburn. 1977. "Exchange and Transfer: A Case Study," in *The Origins of the Economy,* ed. F. L. Pryor, pp. 69–101. New York: Academic Press.

Qumak, T. 1990. *Inuit Uqausillaringiit: Ulinaisigutit* (The genuine Inuit words: A dictionary of definitions in Nunavik [Arctic Quebec] Inuktitut). Quebec: Inuksiutiit/Avataq.

Rabinow, P. 1983. "Humanism as Nihilism: The Bracketing of Truth and Seriousness in American Cultural Anthropology," in *Social Science as Moral Inquiry,* ed. N. Haan, R. N. Bellah, P. Rabinow, and W. M. Sullivan, pp. 52–75. New York: Columbia University Press.

———. 1989. *French Modern: Norms and Forms of the Social Environment.* Cambridge: MIT Press.

Rasing, W. C. E. 1994. *"Too Many People": Order and Nonconformity in Iglulingmiut Social Process.* Nijmegen: Recht and Samenleving.

———. 1999. "Hunting for Identity: Thoughts on the Practice of Hunting and Its Significance for Iglulingmiut Identity," in *Arctic Identities: Continuity and Change in Inuit and Saami Societies,* ed. J. Oosten and C. Remie, pp. 79–108. Leiden: University of Leiden.

Rasmussen, K. 1927. *Across Arctic America: Narrative of the Fifth Thule Expedition.* New York: G. P. Putnam and Sons.

———. 1929. "Intellectual Culture of the Iglulik Eskimos," in *Report of the Fifth Thule Expedition, 1921–24,* vol. 7, pt. 1. Copenhagen: Gyldendalske.

———. 1930a. "Intellectual Culture of the Hudson Bay Eskimos," in *Report of the Fifth Thule Expedition, 1921–24,* vol. 7, pts. 1–3. Copenhagen: Gyldendalske.

———. 1930b. "Intellectual Culture of the Caribou Eskimos," in *Report of the Fifth Thule Expedition, 1921–24.* Copenhagen: Gyldendalske.

———. 1931. "The Netsilik Eskimos: Social Life and Spiritual Culture," in *Report of the Fifth Thule Expedition, 1921–24,* vol. 8, pts. 1–2. Copenhagen: Gyldendalske.

———. 1932. "Intellectual Culture of the Copper Eskimos," in *Report of the Fifth Thule Expedition, 1921–24*, vol. 9. Copenhagen: Gyldendalske.

Riches, D. 1990. "The Force of Tradition in Eskimology," in *Localizing Strategies: Regional Traditions of Ethnographic Writing*, ed. R. Fardon, pp. 71–89. Edinburgh: Scottish Academic Press.

Ridington, R. 2002. "When You Sing It Now, Just Like New: Re-Creation in Native American Narrative Tradition," in *Self and Other-Images of Hunter-Gatherers*, ed. H. Stewart, A. Barnard, and K. Omuri, pp. 113–31. *Senri Ethnological Studies* 60. Osaka: National Museum of Ethnology.

Riles, A. 2000. *The Network Inside Out*. Ann Arbor: University of Michigan Press.

Robic, M. C. 1991. "La Stratégie épistémologique du mixte: Le dossier vidalien." *Espaces Temps–Les Cahiers* 47–48:53–66.

Rosaldo, R. 1980. *Ilongot Headhunting, 1883–1974: A Study in Society and History*. Stanford: Stanford University Press.

———. 1989. "Imperialist Nostalgia." *Representations* 26:107–22.

Ross, W. G., ed. 1984. *An Arctic Whaling Diary: The Journal of Captain George Comer in Hudson Bay, 1903–1905*. Toronto: University of Toronto Press.

Royal Commission on Aboriginal Peoples. 1993. *Aboriginal Peoples in Urban Centres*. Ottawa: Supply and Services.

Sahlins, M. D. 1972. *Stone Age Economics*. Chicago: Aldine-Atherton.

———. 1976. *Culture and Practical Reason*. Chicago: University of Chicago Press.

———. 1999. "What Is Anthropological Enlightenment? Some Lessons of the Twentieth Century." *Annual Review of Anthropology* 28:i–xxiii.

———. 2000. *Culture in Practice*. New York: Zone Books.

Saku, J. C. 1999. "Aboriginal Census Data in Canada: A Research Note." *Canadian Journal of Native Studies* 19:365–79.

Saladin d'Anglure, B. 1978. *La parole changée en pierre: Vie et oeuvre de Davidialuk Alasuak, artiste Inuit du Québec artique*. Québec: Ministère des Affairs Culturelles.

———. 1984. "Les Masques de Boas: Franz Boas et l'ethnographie des Inuit." *Études/Inuit/Studies* 8:165–79.

———. 1988. "Kunut et les Angakkut Iglulik." *Études/Inuit/Studies* 12:57–80.

Saladin d'Anglure, B., ed, 2001. *Interviewing Inuit Elders*, vol. 4: *Cosmology and Shamanism—Mariano and Tulimaaq Aupilaarjuk, Lucassie Nutaraaluk, Rose Iqallijuq, Johanasi Ujarak, Isidore Ijituuq and Michel Kupaaq*. Iqaluit: Nunavut Arctic College.

Sartre, J. P. 1976. *Critique of Dialectical Reason*. London: NLB.

Sauer, C. 1925. *The Morphology of Landscape*, vol. 2. University of California Publications in Geography.

Schneider, L. 1985. *Ulirnaisigutiit: An Inuktitut-English Dictionary of Northern Quebec, Labrador and Eastern Arctic Dialects*. Québec: Presses de l'Université Laval.

Schweitzer, P. P., and M. Lee. 1997. "The Arctic Culture Area," in *Native North Americans: An Ethno Historic Approach*, ed. M. R. Mignon and D. L. Boxberger, pp. 29–83. Dubuque, Iowa: Kendall/Hunt Publishing Company.

Searles, E. 1998a. *From Town to Outpost Camp: Symbolism and Social Action in the Canadian Eastern Arctic*. Ph.D. diss., University of Washington, Seattle.

————. 1998b. "The Crisis of Youth and the Poetics of Place: Juvenile Justice, Outpost Camps, and Inuit Identity in the Canadian Arctic." Études/Inuit/Studies 22:137–55.

————. 2001a. "Fashioning Selves and Tradition: Case Studies on Personhood and Experience in Nunavut." American Review of Canadian Studies 31:121–36.

————. 2001b. "Interpersonal Politics, Social Science Research and the Construction of Inuit Identity." Études/Inuit/Studies 25:101–19.

Shostak, M. 1983. Nisa: The Life and Words of a !Kung Woman. New York: Vintage House.

Simmel, G. 1950. The Sociology of Georg Simmel. Glencoe IL: Free Press.

Simon, M. M. 1996. Inuit: One Future—One Arctic. Peterborough, Ontario: Cider Press.

Slocum, K., and D. A. Thomas. 2003. "Rethinking Global and Area Studies: Insights from Caribbeanist Anthropology." American Anthropologist 105:553–65.

Smith, D. G. 1984. "Mackenzie Delta Eskimo," in Handbook of North American Indians, vol. 5: Arctic, ed. D. Damas, pp. 347–58. Washington DC: Smithsonian Institution Press.

Smith, E. A. 1984. "Approaches to Inuit Socioecology." Études/Inuit/Studies 8:65–87.

————. 1991. Inujjuamuit Foraging Strategies: Evolutionary Ecology of an Arctic Hunting Economy. New York: Aldine de Gruyter.

Smith, E. A., and J. McCarter. 1997. Contested Arctic: Indigenous Peoples, Industrial States, and the Circumpolar Environment. Seattle: Russian East European and Central Asian Studies Center, Henry M. Jackson School of International Studies, in association with University of Washington Press.

Smith, L. T. 1999. Decolonizing Methodologies: Research and Indigenous Peoples. London: Zed Books.

Sonne, B. 1988. "In Love with Eskimo Imagination and Intelligence." Études/Inuit/Studies 12:21–44.

Spencer, R. F. 1976 [1959]. The North Alaskan Eskimo: A Study in Ecology and Society. Bureau of American Ethnology, Bulletin 171. New York: Dover Publications.

Spink, J., and D. W. Moodie. 1972. Eskimo Maps from the Canadian Eastern Arctic. Toronto: Department of Geography, York University.

Sprott, J. 1994. "Symbolic Ethnicity and Alaska Natives of Mixed Ancestry Living in Anchorage." Human Organization 53:311–22.

Stack, C. 1974. All Our Kin: Strategies for Survival in a Black Community. New York: Harper and Row.

Stack, C., and L. Burton. 1998. "Kinscripts: Reflections on Family, Generation, and Culture," in Families in the U.S.: Kinship and Domestic Politics, ed. K. V. Hansen and A. I. Garey, pp. 405–17. Philadelphia: Temple University Press.

Stairs, A. 1992. "Self-image, World-image: Speculations on Identity from Experiences with Inuit." Ethos 20:116–26.

Statistics Canada. 1994. Canada's Aboriginal Population by Census Subdivisions and Census Metropolitan Areas: Aborignal Data (1991 Census of Canada). Ottawa: Industry Science and Technology Canada.

————. 2003. "Aboriginal Identity Population, 2001 Counts, for Census Metropolitan Areas and Census Agglomerations—20% sample data." http://www12.statcan.ca/english/census01/home/index.cfm (accessed August 22, 2005).

Stern, P. 1999. "Learning to Be Smart: An Examination of the Culture of Intelligence in a Canadian Inuit Community." American Anthropologist 101:502–14.

————. 2001. Modernity at Work: Wage Labor, Unemployment, and the Moral Economy of Work in a Canadian Inuit Community. Ph.D. diss., University of California, Berkeley.

Stevenson, L., and Q. Ellsworth. 2003. *National Inuit Youth Suicide Prevention Framework.* Iqaluit: Qikiqtani Inuit Association with Health Canada, National Inuit Youth Council, and Inuit Tapiriit Kanatami.

Stevenson, M. G. 1997. *Inuit, Whalers, and Cultural Persistence: Structure in Cumberland Sound and Central Inuit Social Organization.* Toronto: Oxford University Press.

Stocking, G. W. 1968. "Franz Boas and the Culture Concept in Historical Perspective," in *Race, Culture, and Evolution: Essays on the History of Anthropology,* ed. G. W. Stocking, pp. 195–233. New York: Free Press.

Stocking, G. W., ed. 1992. *The Ethnographer's Magic and Other Essays in the History of Anthropology.* Madison: University of Wisconsin Press.

Strong, P. D., and B. Van Winkle. 1996. " 'Indian Blood': Reflections on the Reckoning and Refiguring of Native North American Identity." *Cultural Anthropology* 11:547–76.

Struzik, E. 2001. "River Journey Reveals How North Is Changing." Edmonton Journal, http://www.canada.com/edmonton/edmontonjournal/specials/features/mackenzie/mackenzie26.html (accessed 9/27/01).

Sturm, C. 2002. *Blood Politics: Race, Culture, and Identity in the Cherokee Nation of Oklahoma.* Berkeley: University of California Press.

Susman, G. I., and R. D. Evered. 1978. "An Assessment of the Scientific Merits of Action Research." *Administrative Science Quarterly* 24:582–603.

Swann, B. ed. 1992. *On the Translation of Native American Literatures.* Washington DC: Smithsonian Institution Press.

Swift, M. D. 2000. *The Development of Temporal Reference in Inuktitut Child Language.* Ph.D. diss., University of Texas, Austin.

Tagoona, E. 1979. Tagoona urqalimausirkavurq namagiyaungitunik Qamanirtuamiunu/ Tagoona discusses concerns with Baker Lake Residents (Transcript of phone-in-radio show). *Inuit Ullumi/Inuit Today* 8:12–22.

Tamarack Productions. 1991. *Starting Fire with Gunpowder.* Toronto: Tamarack Productions. Montreal: National Film Board of Canada.

Taussig, M. T. 1997. *The Magic of the State.* New York: Routledge.

Taylor, C. 1994. "The Politics of Recognition," in *Multiculturalism,* ed. A. Guttman. Princeton NJ: Princeton University Press.

Tester, F. 2001. "Review of Derek Rasmussen's Dissolving Inuit Society through Education and Money." *Études/Inuit/Studies* 25:351–52.

Tester, F., and P. Kulchyski. 1994. *Tammarniit (Mistakes): Inuit Relocation in the Eastern Arctic 1939–63.* Vancouver: University of British Columbia Press.

Therrien, M. 1987. *Le Corps Inuit.* Paris: SELAF.

Therrien, M., and F. Laugrand, eds. 2001. *Interviewing Inuit Elders,* vol. 5: *Health Practices—Tipula Attagutsiaq, Alasi and Akeeshoo Joamie, Jayko Pitseolak, Elisapee Ootoova and Therese Ijjangiaq.* Iqaluit: Nunavut Arctic College.

Thomas, D. K., and C. T. Thompson. 1972. *Eskimo Housing as Planned Culture Change.* Ottawa: Information Canada.

Thomas, N. 1994. *Colonialism's Culture: Anthropology, Travel and Government.* Princeton NJ: Princeton University Press.

———. 1999. *Possessions: Indigenous Art, Colonial Culture.* London: Thames and Hudson.

Thorpe, N., S. Eyegetok, N. Hakongak, and Kitikmeot Elders. 2003. *Thunder on the Tundra: Inuit Qaujimajatuqangit of the Bathurst Caribou*. Vancouver: Douglas and McIntyre.

Tihanyi, C. 2002. "Ethnographic and Translation Practices." *Anthropology News* 43:5–6.

Tilley, C. 1994. *A Phenomenology of Landscape: Places, Paths and Monuments*. Providence RI: Berg.

Tronto, J. 1993. *Moral Boundaries*. New York: Routledge.

Trouillot, M. R. 1991. "Anthropology and the Savage Slot: The Poetics and Politics of Otherness," in *Recapturing Anthropology: Working in the Present*, ed. R. G. Fox, pp. 17–44. Santa Fe NM: School of American Research Advanced Seminar Series.

Tulving, E. 1995. "Varieties of Consciousness and Levels of Awareness in Memory," in *Attention: Selection, Awareness and Control: A Tribute to Donald Broadbent*, ed. A. Baddeley and L. Weiskrantz, pp. 283–99. Oxford: Clarendon Press.

Turner, L. M. 1894. *Ethnology of the Ungava District, Hudson Bay Territory*. Annual Report, U.S. Bureau of American Ethnology, vol. 11, pt. 2. Washington DC: Smithsonian.

Turner, T. 1991. "Representing, Resisting, Rethinking: Historical Transformations of Kayapo Culture and Anthropological Consciousness," in *Colonial Situations: Essays on the Contextualization of Ethnographic Knowledge*, ed. G. Stocking, pp. 285–313. Madison: University of Wisconsin Press.

———. 1992. "Defiant Images: The Kayapo Appropriation of Video." *Anthropology Today* 8:5–16.

———. 2002. "Representation, Politics, and Cultural Imagination in Indigenous Video," in *Media Worlds: Anthropology on New Terrains*, ed. F. Ginsburg, L. Abu-Lughod, and B. Larkin, pp. 75–89. Berkeley: University of California Press.

Ungalaaq, M. A. 1985. *Inuit Life Fifty Years Ago*. Inuit Autobiography Series. Eskimo Point (Arviat): Inuit Cultural Institute.

Usher, P. J. 1971a. *The Bankslanders: Economy and Ecology of a Frontier Trapping Community*, NSRG 71-3. Ottawa: Department of Indian Affairs and Northern Development, Northern Science Research Group.

———. 1971b. *The Bankslanders: Economy and Ecology of a Frontier Trapping Community*, NSRG 71-1. Ottawa: Department of Indian Affairs and Northern Development, Northern Science Research Group.

———. 1993. "Northern Development, Impact Assessment, and Social Change," in *Anthropology, Public Policy, and Native Peoples in Canada*, ed. N. Dyck and J. B. Waldram, pp. 98–130. Montreal: McGill-Queen's University Press.

Vallee, F. G. 1962. *Kabloona and Eskimo in the Central Keewatin*. NCRC 62-2. Ottawa: Department of Northern Affairs and National Resources, Northern Co-ordination and Research Centre.

van Willigen, J. 1993. *Applied Anthropology: An Introduction*. Westport CT: Bergin and Garvey.

Vanstone, J. W. 1962. *Point Hope: An Eskimo Village in Transition*. Seattle: University of Washington Press.

Wachowich, N. 2001. *Making a Living, Making a Life: Subsistence and the Re-enactment of Iglulingmiut Cultural Processes*. Ph.D. diss., University of British Columbia, Vancouver.

Wachowich, N., A. A. Awa, R. K. Katsak, and S. P. Katsak. 1999. *Saqiyuq: Stories from the Lives of Three Inuit Women*. Montreal: McGill-Queen's University Press.

Walker, R. 2001. "Return of the Arctic Prospectors." *Christian Science Monitor* http://www.csmonitor.com/durable/2001/05/10/pls2.htm (accessed 9/26/01).

Weber, M. 1949. *The Methodology of the Social Sciences*. New York: Free Press.

Weiner, J. F. 1997. Televisualist Anthropology: Representation, Aesthetics, Politics. *Current Anthropology* 38:197–235.

Wenzel, G. W. 1981. *Clyde Inuit Adaptation and Ecology: The Organization of Subsistence*. Ottawa: National Museums of Canada.

———. 1991. *Animal Rights, Human Rights: Ecology, Economy and Ideology in the Canadian Arctic*. Toronto: University of Toronto Press.

———. 1997. "Using Harvest Research in Nunavut: An Example from Hall Beach." *Arctic Anthropology* 34:18–28.

Wenzel, George. 2000. "Inuit Subsistence and Hunter Support in Nunavut," in *Nunavut: Inuit Regain Control of Their Lands and Their Lives*, ed. J. Dahl, J. Hicks, and P. Jull, pp. 180–93. Copenhagen: International Work Group for Indigenous Affairs.

Weyer, E. M. 1932. *The Eskimos: Their Environment and Folkways*. New Haven: Yale University Press.

White, Jennifer, and Nadine Jodoin. 2003. *Aboriginal Youth: A Manual of Promising Suicide Prevention Strategies*. Calgary: Centre for Suicide Prevention and RCMP National Aboriginal Policing Services.

Whyte, W. F. 1991. *Participatory Action Research*. London: Sage.

Wildcat, D. R. 2001. "Indigenizing Education: Playing to Our Strengths," in *Power and Place: Indian Education in America*, ed. V. Deloria Jr. and D. R. Wildcat. Golden CO: American Indian Graduate Center and Fulcrum Resources.

Williams, R. 1977. *Marxism and Literature*. Oxford: Oxford University Press.

Willmott, W. E. 1961. *The Eskimo Community at Port Harrison, PQ*. NCRC 61-1. Ottawa: Department of Northern Affairs and National Resources, Northern Co-ordination and Research Centre.

Wilman, M. E. 2002. "Governance through Inuit Qaujimajatuqangit: Changing the Paradigm for the Future of Inuit Society," in *The Power of Traditions*, ed. M. Nagy, pp. 33–38. Quebec: International Arctic Social Sciences Association.

Wittgenstein, L. 1953. *Philosophical Investigations*. New York: Macmillan.

———. 1999. *Envisioning Power: Ideologies of Dominance and Crisis*. Berkeley: University of California Press.

Wong, J. 2003. "What They Know." *Globe and Mail* (Toronto), November 1, 2003, pp. M1, 8.

Workshop on Inuit Qaujimanituqangit. 2001. *Summary*. Québec and Iqaluit: GETIC Université Laval, Nunavut Arctic College and Pairijait Tigummivik (Iqaluit Elders Society).

Young, O. R. 1992. *Arctic Politics: Conflict and Cooperation in the Circumpolar North*. Hanover NH: University Press of New England.

CONTRIBUTORS

BÉATRICE COLLIGNON is associate professor in geography at the Université Panthéon-Sorbonne (Paris 1) of Paris and is a member of the Institut Universitaire de France. Her main research interests are the intersections of nonscientific (vernacular) geographic knowledges and academic geography. Her research in the Arctic concentrates on the Inuinnait people of the west-central Canadian Arctic, whom she first met at the age of fifteen. In addition to completing the first comprehensive Inuinnait place names survey, she has studied Inuinnait uses of domestic spaces, looking at the consequences of the shift from igloos to multibedroom houses. Beyond her scholarly writing she has produced two video documentaries in English, one on place names and one on housing. She is the author of *Knowing Places: Inuinnait, Landscapes and Environment* (CCI Press, 2006, edited translation from the French original, 1996).

NELSON GRABURN is professor of sociocultural anthropology, curator of North American ethnology for the Phoebe A. Hearst Museum of Anthropology, and the Thomas Garden Barnes chair of Canadian Studies at the University of California, Berkeley. He has carried out field research in the Canadian Arctic on Inuit kinship, social organization, art, and identity since 1959. He has also researched tourism and internationalization in Japan since 1974. Nelson's current research focuses on art, tourism, museums, and the expression and representation of identity. He is the author or editor of several books, including *Eskimos without Igloos* (Little Brown, 1969) and *Ethnic and Tourist Arts: Cultural Expressions from the Fourth World* (California, 1976), and is now preparing books on contemporary tourism in Asia and on multiculturalism in Japan. Nelson also works with Avatak, the Inuit cultural organization of Nunavik (northern Quebec), on aspects of cultural preservation and autonomy and is continuing his research on contemporary Inuit arts, including urban Inuit arts.

LORI IDLOUT is a young mother of four and the director for policy and planning in the Department Health and Social Services for the government of Nunavut. Lori began her public service career in 1997, as a trainee in the Department of Health and Social Services of the government of the Northwest Territories. The passion and commitment of her mentor grounded her career in the health and social services field. Once the government of Nunavut came into being on April 1, 1999, Lori maintained her position within the Department of Health and Social Services, now within the government of Nunavut. Later that year, she joined the team of highly skilled staff and board members of the Nunavut Social Development Council, a career move that also encouraged her confidence in Inuit self-reliance. She began

her term there as a policy analyst, later becoming the acting executive director until NSDC was reorganized by Nunavut Tunngavik Inc. This allowed her to rethink
her still early career, whereby she accepted a position back with the Department of
Health and Social Services as the director for policy and planning. Lori is now the
executive director of the Isaksimagit Inuusirmi Katujjigatiglit Embrace Life Council.
The council is a Nunavut-wide organization made up of eleven organizations set up
to address suicide in Nunavut.

CAROL ZANE JOLLES is an associate professor in the Anthropology Department
at the University of Washington in Seattle. She began work on identity and religious history in 1987 with the Yup'ik communities of Gambell and Savoonga on St.
Lawrence Island. More recently she and her colleague, Herbert Anungazuk, have
worked together with the Wales and Little Diomede Island Iñupiaq communities
to identify changes impacting community identity in the areas of subsistence and
related traditions, with special attention given to attachment to local landscapes.
Carol is the author of *Faith, Food, and Family in a Yupik Whaling Community* (University
of Washington Press, 2002).

NOBUHIRO KISHIGAMI is associate professor at the National Museum of Ethnology, Osaka, Japan. He has carried out research among Inuit in Nunavik and Montreal, Canada, since 1984. His research interests include marine resource management, food sharing systems, and hunter support programs among the Nunavik Inuit
as well as formation of the urban Inuit community in Montreal. He has published
extensively in Japanese and English on Inuit culture and social change.

MICHAEL J. KRAL taught at the universities of Manitoba (psychiatry), Windsor
(psychology), and Yale (anthropology), and is currently a doctoral student in medical
anthropology at McGill University and a fellow in the Department of Psychiatry,
University of Toronto. He co-edited the books *Suicide in Canada* and *About Psychology:
Essays at the Crossroads of History, Theory, and Philosophy*. For the past decade Michael
has worked with Inuit on suicide prevention and community wellness.

PETER KULCHYSKI is head of the Department of Native Studies at the University
of Manitoba. He has worked extensively in the western arctic and in Nunavut, spe-
cializing in community-level cultural politics. He is co-author, with Frank Tester, of
Tammarniit (Mistakes) (UBC Press, 1994) and the forthcoming *Kiumajuk (Talking Back)*
(UBC Press), among many other books and articles.

MOLLY LEE holds a joint appointment at the University of Alaska in Fairbanks
as professor of anthropology and curator of ethnology at the University of Alaska
Museum. She is the author of numerous articles on the anthropology of art, Es-
kimo/Inuit art, the history of museums, and the urbanization of Alaska Native wom-
en. Her most recent book (co-authored with Gregory A. Reinhardt) is *Eskimo Ar-
chitecture: Dwelling and Structure in the Early Historic Period* (University of Alaska Press,

2003). From January until June of 2004 she was visiting research professor at the National Museum of Ethnology (Minpaku) in Osaka, Japan, where she completed a manuscript on the cultural dimensions of Yup'ik Eskimo women's grass basketry, tentatively titled "Mingqaaq: The Life and Times of the Yup'ik Grass Basket."

LINNA WEBER MÜLLER-WILLE has been involved in projects revolving around mapping and collecting place names and indigenous geographical knowledge since the early 1970s. She is a scientific translator and editor and a computer consultant for researchers' special needs. As a translator and editor her concentration has been on scientific works in natural and social sciences and publications of a cultural or legal nature for indigenous organizations. She works from various languages (French, German, Finnish, Swedish, Norwegian) into English. She has lengthy experience as a researcher during extended stays living and working among Sámi, Dene, and Inuit. Her computer designs have included data management programs for the International Arctic Social Sciences Association (IASSA) and its congresses, for the NUNA-TOP map and place name projects, for legal documents, correspondence, museum collections, and analysis of research material, among many others internationally. She is executive director of *Indigenous Names Surveys*, founded with Ludger Müller-Wille in 1984. Significant editing and translations include *Saqqaq* by Jens Dahl (2000) and *The Sámi People* by Veli-Pekka Lehtola (2002).

LUDGER MÜLLER-WILLE is a cultural anthropologist in the Department of Geography at McGill University, where he has taught human geography and northern studies since the 1970s. He has conducted research with Sámi and Finns in northern Finland and with Inuit and Dene in arctic and subarctic Canada since the 1960s. His research foci have been on ethnic identity in cultural contact, local community development, socioeconomic change in reindeer herding and the use of the mountain birch forests in northern Fennoscandia, caribou and sea mammal hunting in northern Canada, documentation of geographical knowledge through large-scale place name surveys with Inuit elders and experts in Nunavik and Nunavut (with Linna Weber Müller-Wille), and the history of arctic social sciences. He has conducted his research through long-term stays and commitment to local northern communities engaging in partnerships with local researchers through the application of participatory research. He served as the director of the Arctic Centre in Rovaniemi (Finland) in the mid-1990s and was the founding president of IASSA (1990–95) and organizer of its first congresses. He published Franz Boas's Baffin Island field diaries of 1883–84 in German (Berlin, 1994) and in English (Toronto, 1998).

MURIELLE NAGY is the editor of the journal *Études/Inuit/Studies* and is a research associate with the Centre interuniversitaire d'études et de recherches autochtones (CIERA) of Université Laval. She has an MA in archaeology from Simon Fraser University (1988) and a Ph.D. in anthropology from the University of Alberta (1997). From 1990 to 2000, she coordinated three major oral history projects for the Inuvialuit of the western Canadian Arctic. She was awarded postdoctoral bursaries to work on the anthropological research of Oblate missionary Emile Petitot. She served as coordinator of IASSA from 1998 to 2001.

EDMUND (NED) SEARLES is assistant professor of anthropology at Bucknell University. His ethnographic research in Iqaluit, Nunavut, and in an outpost camp some two hundred miles away concerns how local ideas about sense of place, tradition, and hunting knowledge contribute to Inuit conceptions of self and other. He has published in *Food and Foodways*, *Anthropologie et Sociétés*, *Études/Inuit/Studies*, and the *Annual Review of Canadian Studies*. He has received grants and fellowships from the National Science Foundation, the Wenner-Gren Foundation for Anthropological Research, the Canada-U.S. Fulbright Program, and the International Council for Canadian Studies. His newest research addresses the intersection of Inuit religious identity, spirituality, and human-animal relationships in the Canadian Arctic.

PAMELA STERN is assistant professor of anthropology at the University of Waterloo. Her research among Inuit began in 1982 when she was a participant with Richard Condon in the Harvard Adolescence Project directed by John and Beatrice B. Whiting. Her current research concerns the relationship between economic development, citizenship, and alcohol control policies in the Canadian North. Pamela is beginning research on a citizen-initiated local economic development project in northern Ontario. She is the author of *Historical Dictionary of the Inuit* (Scarecrow, 2004).

LISA STEVENSON received her Ph.D. in medical anthropology at the University of California at Berkeley. After spending the summer of 1993 in Iqaluit doing community development work for the Canadian Mental Health Association, she returned in 2000 to do preliminary research on the vexed relationship between modernity and mental illness among the Inuit. Her theoretical work focuses on questions of subjectivity, social suffering, and the formation of community. Following sixteen months of fieldwork in Iqaluit and Pangnirtung in 2002–2003, she completed her dissertation entitled *Life in Question: Inuit Youth, Suicide, and the Canadian State*. She is currently a National Institute of Mental Health postdoctoral fellow at Harvard University.

FRANK JAMES TESTER is a professor of social work and an affiliate of the Institute for Resources and Environmental Studies, University of British Columbia. He has degrees in environmental studies, medical research, geography, and social work. His experience working in the eastern Arctic includes time spent in Arctic Bay and Resolute in the 1970s, shortly after Inuit had completed the move from camps to consolidated settlements. In the late 1970s, he chaired an inquiry into the Polar Gas Pipeline proposed for the region. He is co-author with Peter Kulchyski of *Tammarniit (Mistakes)* (UBC Press, 1994), a study of Inuit relocation, and of a forthcoming joint volume on community development in Nunavut; contributed to an edited volume on social impact assessment (Detselig, 1981); and has authored papers dealing with Canadian social and environmental issues. Frank has an abiding interest in Inuit social history and contemporary social issues, including housing and young Inuit suicide.

NANCY WACHOWICH is a lecturer in social anthropology at the University of Aberdeen, Scotland. Since 1991, Nancy has carried out ethnographic research with people in the Inuit communities of Pond Inlet and Igloolik in Canada's Eastern Arctic. Her theoretical work focuses primarily on social movements and the politics of identity construction, drawing on the fields of historical anthropology, oral traditions, visual anthropology, museum studies, and the anthropology of media. Her 1999 book *Saqiyuq: Stories from the Lives of Three Inuit Women*, written in collaboration with Apphia Agalakti Awa, Rhoda Kaukjak Katsak, and Sandra Pikujak Katsak, won the 1999 Canadian Historical Association's Clio Award for the North and the 2000 Oral History Association (U.S.A.) Award for Best Project.

INDEX